Tibetan Ritual

Tibetan Ritual

EDITED BY JOSÉ IGNACIO CABEZÓN

OXFORD
UNIVERSITY PRESS
2010

OXFORD
UNIVERSITY PRESS

Oxford University Press, Inc., publishes works that further
Oxford University's objective of excellence
in research, scholarship, and education.

Oxford New York
Auckland Cape Town Dar es Salaam Hong Kong Karachi
Kuala Lumpur Madrid Melbourne Mexico City Nairobi
New Delhi Shanghai Taipei Toronto

With offices in
Argentina Austria Brazil Chile Czech Republic France Greece
Guatemala Hungary Italy Japan Poland Portugal Singapore
South Korea Switzerland Thailand Turkey Ukraine Vietnam

Published by Oxford University Press, Inc.
198 Madison Avenue, New York, New York 10016

www.oup.com

Library of Congress Cataloging-in-Publication Data
Tibetan ritual / edited by José Ignacio Cabezón.
p. cm.
Includes bibliographical references and index.
ISBN 978-0-19-539281-4; 978-0-19-539282-1 (pbk.)
1. Tibet (China)—Religious life and customs. 2. Rites
and ceremonies—China—Tibet.
I. Cabezón, José Ignacio, 1956–
BL1945.T5T54 2010
294.3'438—dc22 2009012773

Contents

Contributors

Yael Bentor is a Senior Lecturer in the Department of Indian Studies at the Hebrew University of Jerusalem. She is the author of a number of books and articles on the theory and practice of Tantra, most recently "Do 'The Tantras Embody What The Practitioners Actually Do'?" (in *Contributions to the Study of Tibetan Literature*, 2008), and "Can Women Attain Enlightenment Through Vajrayāna Practices" (in *Karmic Passages: Israeli Scholarship on India*, 2009). Currently, she is working on a book on the creation stage of the *Guhyasamāja*.

Cathy Cantwell and **Robert Mayer** are Research Officers and Members of the Buddhist Studies Unit of the Oriental Institute, University of Oxford, and Senior Researchers at the University of Cardiff. They have coauthored two books: *The Kīlaya Nirvāna Tantra and the Vajra Wrath Tantra: Two Texts from the Ancient Tantra Collection* (2007) and *Early Tibetan Documents on Phur pa from Dunhuang* (2009). Their current research focuses on the *Tabzhag* (*Thabs zhags*) or *Noose of Methods Tantra*, on the early Bön and Buddhist traditions of the deity Purpa (Dagger), and (together with Professor Geoffrey Samuel) on a twentieth-century ritual cycle of the Dujom tradition.

Bryan J. Cuevas is Associate Professor of Buddhist and Tibetan Studies in the Department of Religion at Florida State University. He is the author of *The Hidden History of the Tibetan Book of the Dead* (2003) and *Travels in the Netherworld: Buddhist Popular Narratives* *of Death and the Afterlife in Tibet* (2008), and is the editor, with Jacqueline I. Stone, of *The Buddhist Dead: Practices, Discourses, Representations* (2007). He is currently working on a study of Tibetan sorcery and the politics of war magic from the sixteenth to eighteenth centuries.

J. F. Marc des Jardins is Assistant Professor of the Religions of China and Tibet in the Department of Religion of Concordia University in Montréal. He specializes on the Tibetan Bön religion and the practice of religion along the Sino-Tibetan frontiers. He has been engaged in field-based research in Tibetan territories within the PRC since 1991. He not only studies Bön textual material, but also rituals and other religious practices in contemporary settings.

James Gentry is a doctoral candidate in the Committee on the Study of Religion at Harvard University. He is working on a dissertation on the life and times of Sogdogpa Lodrö Gyaltsen (Sog bzlog pa Blo gros rgyal mtshan), focusing on his memoir, the *History of How the Mongols Were Turned Back* (*Sog bzlog bgyis tshul gyi lo rgyus*). He is the author of "Historical Skepticism in 'Pre-modern' Tibet: the Contested Historicity of Traditional Padmasambhava Narratives," in *New Perspectives on Tibetan Traditionality*, Columbia University Press (2009).

Jared Lindahl has completed his MA in Religious Studies from the University of California Santa Barbara and is presently a doctoral candidate at that same institution. He did field research on sacred geography in Mongolia in 2004. Lindahl is currently working on a doctoral dissertation focusing on the doctrine of light and use of light imagery in Tibetan Buddhism and early Christianity.

Irmgard Mengele is a research scholar in the Religious Studies Department at the University of California Santa Barbara. She is the author of *dGe-'dun-chos-'phel: A Biography of the 20th-Century Tibetan Scholar* (1999) and *The Life and Art of the Tenth Karma-pa Chos-dbyings-rdo-rje (1604–1674): A Biography of a Great Tibetan Lama and Artist of the Turbulent Seventeenth Century* (forthcoming). Currently she is working on a project on the theory and practice of healing, medicine, and longevity in Indo-Tibetan Buddhism.

Françoise Pommaret is Directeur de recherche at the Centre National de la Recherche Scientifique, Paris, and advisor to the Institute of Language and Cultural Studies, Royal University of Bhutan. She has authored *Tibet, A Wounded Civilization* (2005) and has contributed to as well as edited *Bhutan: Mountain Fortress of the Gods* (2005), *Lhasa in the 17th century: The Capital of the*

Dalai-Lamas (2005), and *Bhutan: Tradition and Change* (2007 with J. Ardussi). She works on the sociopolitical significance of rituals and their evolution.

Samten Karmay is Directeur de recherche emeriate at the Centre National de la Recherche Scientifique, Paris. He is the author of *The Great Perfection, A Meditative and Philosophical Teaching of Tibetan Buddhism* (1988, reprint 2007); *Secret Visions of the Fifth Dalai Lama* (1988, reprint 1998); and the two-volume *The Arrow and the Spindle, Studies in History, Myths, Rituals and Beliefs in Tibet* (1998 and 2005). Currently he is working on the *Dukula*, the autobiography of the Fifth Dalai Lama.

Nicolas Sihlé is Assistant Professor in the Department of Anthropology at the University of Virginia and Associated Member of the Laboratory "Milieux, Sociétés et Cultures en Himalaya" of the CNRS (France). His work focuses, from an anthropological perspective, on Tibet and the Himalayas, on Tibetan religion in particular, and more generally on the comparative study of Buddhist societies, as well as on theories of ritual and religion. He is completing a book entitled *Rituals of Power and Violence: Tantric Buddhism in the Tibetan Himalayas*.

Vesna Wallace is Professor in the Department of Religious Studies at the University of California, Santa Barbara. She is author of *The Inner Kālacakratantra: A Buddhist Tantric View of the Individual*, and has published several books of translation from Sanskrit, Tibetan, and Mongolian. She has also authored a series of articles on esoteric Buddhism and produced four documentary films on Mongolia. Vesna Wallace has been conducting annual field research in Mongolia on the revival of Mongolian Buddhism since 2000, research that will result in her new volume on contemporary Buddhism in Mongolia.

Tibetan Ritual

Introduction

JOSÉ IGNACIO CABEZÓN

Look around almost anywhere you find yourself in the greater Tibetan cultural world—in Tibet, certainly, but also in Bhutan, Mongolia, and the Nepalese Himalayas—and you see ritual. If you live near a monastery, chances are that you will awaken to the sound of a gong calling monks to their morning prayer-assembly or *tsog* (*tshogs*). Even if you live far from a monastery, you may well be roused from sleep by the high-pitched clanging of someone ringing a ritual bell, or by the soft murmur of neighbors reciting *khandön* (*kha 'don*), their daily ritual commitments. When you walk out of your door into the courtyard of your home, you see a family member burning *sang* (*bsang*), juniper incense, for the daily purification of the household or as a ritual offering to the gods. Before you begin eating your breakfast, you will recite a prayer offering the food to the Three Jewels. If you live in an urban area like Lhasa, when you walk out into the streets, you will not have to wander very far before you see young men dressed in monks' garb sitting on a sidewalk intoning rituals as a way of procuring a little money. And when you pass the local temple, you hear the fast, rhythmic chanting and drum-beating of a protector deity *kangso* (*bskang gso*) ritual. At the next intersection, in the middle of a busy street, you come across a discarded "thread-cross" or *namkha* (*nam mkha'*), the remnants of an exorcism ritual from the night before. Walking past an old woman, you hear her softly reciting a prayer for the long life of His Holiness the Dalai Lama. At the Khyichu river's edge, you stumble upon a lone *torma* (*gtor ma*), a ritual cake that failed to make its way into the rushing stream, the vestige of a tantric ritual from the night before. And everywhere, literally everywhere, you see people carrying rosaries and softly chanting the mantra of Avalokiteśvara, *om maṇi padme hūṃ*. To a far greater extent than either abstract philosophy or silent meditation, it is ritual that pervades the Tibetan religious landscape.

Not only does ritual fill Tibetan space, but it also pervades Tibetan time. While prayers and rituals of various types are the daily practices of many Tibetans, ritual activity increases significantly on *düzang* (*dus bzang*), days considered holy or auspicious. For example, it has become a custom in contemporary Tibetan society to make burnt juniper offerings in public spaces—in Lhasa, Drapchi (Grwa bzhi) Temple is especially popular—on Wednesdays, the day of the week when the present Dalai Lama was born. New or full moon days, to which is sometimes added the eighth day of the Tibetan lunar month, are said to be times when both virtuous and nonvirtuous actions are "magnified." Hence, merit-making rituals, especially of the exoteric or *sūtra* variety, are popular on these days. New and full moon days are also the days when monks and nuns do their bimonthly "confession" or *sojong* (*gso sbyong*) rituals. Lay Buddhists often ritually vow to uphold the eight "Mahāyāna precepts" (*theg chen gso sbyong*) on these same two days. Other days of the month are just as ritually charged. The eighth day, for instance, is considered auspicious for performing the Medicine Buddha rituals (*Sman bla'i mdo chog*). Rituals to Padmasambhava and ritual offerings to deities, called *tsogchö* (*tshogs mchod*), are often done on the tenth of the lunar calendar. The twenty-fifth day is considered especially appropriate for engaging in offering rituals to a specific group of tantric deities that includes Vajrayoginī and Cakrasaṃvara. Finally, the twenty-ninth day of the month is the most favorable for carrying out ritual propitiations of *sungma* (*srung ma*), protector deities. More than a week out of every month is therefore ritually auspicious.

Ritual activities also dramatically increase at certain points in the *yearly* calendar.[1] For example, multiple-day ritual cycles are enacted in the first two weeks of the first Tibetan month as part of the New Year festivities, culminating, on the fifteenth of the month, with the Festival of the Buddha's Great Miracles (Cho 'phrul chen po'i dus chen). That day is also the birth celebration of Tönpa Shenrab (Ston pa Gshen rab), the founder of Tibet's Bön religion.[2] The fourth Tibetan month, called Sagadawa (*sa ga zla ba*), is arguably the holiest month of the Buddhist liturgical year, the month in which Tibetans celebrate the Buddha's birth, and according to some sources also his enlightenment and death. Sagadawa is a particularly popular time for engaging in communal fasting rites known as *nyungné* (*smyung gnas*). On the fourth day of the sixth month, Tibetans Buddhists celebrate the Festival of the Turning of the Wheel of the Doctrine (Chos 'khor dus chen) that marks the day the Buddha delivered his first sermon. And in the second fortnight of the ninth month, they celebrate the Buddha's return from his visit to the god realm, the Lhabab Düchen (Lha babs dus chen). Finally, a giant *torma* offering called *gutor* (*dgu gtor*) is performed in many places on the last day of the old year to drive out evil influences. A similar ritual is enacted in Bön, just one of many overlaps between the rituals of Buddhism and Tibet's indigenous religion. Monks spend most of the day performing elaborate rituals in their monasteries during these festival days, and the laity will visit monasteries, make offerings, and engage in a variety of rituals of their own.

There are also specific days throughout the year commemorating the birth, death, or special events in the lives of different Tibetan saints. These too are times of intense ritual activity. The fourteenth day of the first Tibetan month, for example, commemorates the great Tibetan yogi Milarepa (Rje btsun Mi la ras pa, 1052–1135), and Jé Tsongkhapa (Rje Tsong kha pa, 1357–1419) is memorialized in the "Ganden Feast of the Twenty-Fifth," Ganden Ngamchö (Dga' ldan lnga mchod), so-called because it takes place on the twenty-fifth day of the tenth month. Finally, given the centrality of agriculture and animal husbandry to Tibetan society, planting and harvest rituals[3] are often an important part of the yearly ritual calendar, as are rituals for the protection and well-being of farm animals, and for the control of weather.

All this is just the proverbial tip of the iceberg, for in addition to these largely pan-Tibetan ceremonial traditions, there are many local festivals with their own specific rites that may include everything from ritual dances, called *cham* (*'cham/s*), to oracular displays.[4]

Anti-ritual rhetoric is not unknown in Tibetan religions. For example, some texts see ritual as a mere precursor to the more profound practice of meditation (*sgom*), implying a kind of hierarchy of religious practices in which meditation in some way supercedes liturgical ritual. In other texts, ritual, and even meditation itself, are portrayed as contrived (*bcos ma*), and therefore as practices that must eventually be transcended.[5] But, significantly, the figures in whose works we find such views expressed never, in point of fact, completely abandon rituals in their own lives, nor do their latter-day heirs.

Ritual and Cosmology

It is difficult to understand the Tibetan passion for ritual without understanding something of the Tibetan cosmological worldview. Tibetans see themselves as living in a universe populated by Buddhas and deities who transcend space and time, by powerful gods and demigods who live in various heavenly realms, and by spirits who have diverse relationships to specific sites in the natural landscape. The Tibetan pantheon is one of the most extensive among the world's religions.[6] Some of these gods and spirits are of Indian origin. Others are variants of Indic deities who appeared in new forms to Tibetan saints. Still others are non-Buddhist in origin, gods who were incorporated into the Tibetan Buddhist pantheon from the indigenous religious systems of Tibet and surrounding cultures. Mythic narratives often explain the origin of different deities and spirits—how they were born, how they made first contact with humanity, and how they became a part of religious (usually ritual) practices. Like the gods themselves, some of these myths are of Indian origin. Others are part of Tibetan pre-Buddhist lore. Samten Karmay's chapter in this volume (chapter 2) explores a myth related to a class of Tibetan spirits known as *nyen* (*gnyan*), a myth that charts the evolution of the relationship between humans and *nyen* culminating in the advent of ritual, *to* (*gto*). Individual rituals and ritual cycles often make reference to these mythic narratives, and sometimes recapitulate parts of the myths in a stylized fashion within liturgies.

In the Tibetan worldview, the boundary between the human and nonhuman worlds is permeable. Enlightened beings sometimes incarnate in the world, taking on human form. At other times they appear to human beings in visions and dreams. Highly accomplished adepts sometimes travel to celestial realms, where they procure doctrines and practices that they then bring back to earth. Lesser spirits, of course, are also active agents in the world, acting at times to help, and at other times to hinder human beings in their pursuit of both worldly and spiritual goals. Men and women endowed with the gift of the "divine eye" (*lha'i mig*), a kind of supernormal power, can make contact with, receive information from, and request the intervention of various nonhuman agents. Some rare individuals even have the capacity to act as the "vessels" for spirits who descend (*bab*) into their bodies and speak through them—the phenomenon of the oracle.[7] Tantric specialists, even those who lack such supernormal abilities, engage in practices to request the "enlightened activity," or *trinlé* (*'phrin las*), of deities, or to force lesser spirits to intervene on their behalf. Ritual is most often the medium through which such communications and interventions take place.

Various schemes have been used in both the Buddhist and Bönpo traditions to organize their complex pantheons. Some of these classificiations are indigenous to the Tibetan world. Others are "imported"—for example, from India. Other schemes combine indigenous and foreign categories. Indigenous Tibetan schemes include a bipartite classification into gods and demons (*lha 'dre*), and a tripartite one into (1) "site spirits," or *sadag* (*sa bdag*), (2) *lu* (*klu*, after the introduction of Buddhism in Tibet made to correspond to the Indian *nāgas*), and (3) *nyen*. There are also more complex eightfold and ninefold classifications that divide the nonhuman world according to the colors of the spirits, and according to their habitat.[8] Some of these eight or nine types of spirits—for example, the *si* (*sri*)—can be further subclassified according to whom they afflict (adults or children), and according to the harm they bring (disease, death, loss, etc.).

In broader schemes, gods can be classified according to whether they are "peaceful" (*zhi ba*) or "wrathful" (*khro bo*); according to whether they are tutelary deities (*yi dam*) or protectors (*srung ma, bka' skyong*). They are also classified according to their "specialty"—for example, whether their main function is to bring about wisdom, long life, etc. Tutelary deities, the "high" tantric gods, are further subdivided according to their degree of accessibility—whether, for instance, they are an exemplification of the most ethereal body, the *dharmakāya* (*chos sku*; Bon: *bon sku*), of the slightly more accessible enjoyment or perfect body, the *sambhogakāya* (*longs sku*; Bon: *rdzogs sku*), or of the most accessible emanation body (*sprul sku*).

One of the most important classification schemes, found in many elite texts, divides the pantheon into two categories: (1) supramundane gods,[9] enlightened deities who have achieved perfection, and (2) mundane gods[10] who, though powerful, are far from perfect, being easily offended and at times fickle and moody. Both mundane gods and supramundane deities, as just mentioned, are seen as acting within the human world. Whereas worldly spirits intervene in human affairs in both positive *and negative* ways, enlightened beings, by definition, can only work for the welfare of others. The actions of enlightened beings, however, can take a variety of forms. For example, supramundane deities can sometimes act violently when this is for the greater good of beings, as when a deity kills an evildoer (*sdig can*), or an "enemy of the Dharma" (*bstan dgra*). The elite tradition maintains that because enlightened beings are beyond the forces of the natural world (including the human world), they can, in principle, never be forced to act in a way that contradicts their compassionate nature. These gods, whose goal is to help sentient beings, can therefore never act in a way that brings long-term harm to others. Mundane spirits, on the other hand—spirits who are still under the influence of anger, self-cherishing, and other mental "afflictions"—*can* be manipulated so as to bring about worldly aims, even when these run counter to the long-term spiritual welfare of beings. For example, worldly spirits can be propitiated for wealth, even when such riches serve as an impediment to the practitioner's own spiritual progress. Often motivated by negative emotions, spirits can also become annoyed with, and act aggressively toward, human beings, quite apart from any ritual enticements (e.g., by sorcerers). Such "interferences" or *barché* (*bar chad*) can, however, be ritually counteracted. For example, a spirit's anger can be assuaged through material offerings. A spirit can also be coerced into cooperation through the sheer power of the tantric specialist, who, through ritual means, assumes the mighty form of a tantric deity so as to make the spirit bow to his or her will.

The mundane–supramundane distinction is an attempt to bring order to the vast and complex pantheon. Aside from simply allowing Tibetans to organize the types of gods with whom they interact, this and the other ways of categorizing the gods also provide ritual specialists with a set of rules that defines these interactions: which gods might be approached under what circumstances, and what ritual methods should be employed for achieving specific aims. For example, an adept does not expect to achieve enlightenment through the ritual propitiation of a mundane protector. Neither would it make sense to engage in the profound deity-yoga practice or *sādhana* of a supramundane deity with the sole goal of fulfilling a "mundane," temporary purpose—for example, gaining power over an enemy.

Like all attempts at creating order out of a historically heterogeneous set of data, however, the mundane–supramundane distinction is not without fissures, ambiguities, or inconsistencies. For one thing, the dividing line between the mundane and supramundane is not always clear. Some gods are considered "half-wisdom and half mundane."[11] Moreover, gods that start out historically as worldly spirits are sometimes "promoted," and later come to be considered emanations of fully enlightened beings. Conversely, gods that are originally considered highly realized beings sometimes get "demoted" and come to be considered unstable worldly spirits. As in the human realm, there is both upward and downward mobility. Such promotions and demotions, moreover, often become sites of contestation and a source of factionalism within the Tibetan world.[12] In addition, the rules that govern the ritual "use" of different gods are not always clear. For example, while Tibetans consider the wrathful deities Vajrakīla and Hayagrīva to be supramundane, many of their rites are pragmatic—that is, they are methods of protecting individuals or communities, or subjugating worldly or spiritual enemies. As Cuevas's chapter in this volume (chapter 7) makes clear, the elite tradition couches such practices within a religious rubric that stresses the importance of a proper motivation (compassion) as the basis for these wrathful rites, called *dragpö lé* (*drag po'i las*). But the fact remains that many of these rituals contain elements that are procedurally indistinguishable from magic or sorcery.

The mundane–supramundane distinction is an "emic" one—that is, a distinction made by tradition itself. Another such division, the local–translocal one, is "etic": a distinction made by Western scholars in their attempt to bring some semblance of order to the pantheon. In this latter scheme, one typically finds Buddhas and tantric deities characterized as "translocal," while mundane spirits, whom Tibetans often associate with specific mountains, lakes, springs, rocks, and trees are characterized as "local." Many local spirits—like Adamantine Turquoise Mist, Great Mother of the Snows (Gangs kyi yum chen rdo rje g.yu bun ma), and the five Long-Life Goddesses (Tshe ring ma)—are pre-Buddhist in origin. Buddhist sources tells us that, although originally opposed to the foreign Buddhist doctrine, they were subdued, bound under oath, and sworn to protect the Buddhist teachings by great tantric masters like Padmasambhava.[13] Like the mundane–supramundane distinction, the local–translocal one can be helpful when it comes to understanding the Tibetan pantheon. But like the former, the latter is not without its ambiguities. So-called "local spirits," for example, at times become popular over a vast area, as has happened with the goddess Dorje Yüdrönma (Rdo rje g.yu sgron ma), Adamantine Lamp of Turquoise. What is more, purportedly place-bound spirits at times travel and change their place of residence. Case in point is the god Tawog (Tha 'og). Originally a "resident" of the area around Samyé (Bsam yas) Monastery, he is said to have left his original home to become the protector of Sera Monastery's Mé (Smad) College.[14] Likewise, the goddess who makes Lhasa's famous Drapchi Temple her home is said to be of Chinese origin, having left China to accompany a Tibetan monk to the capital (Figures 1 and 2). Nor does the ritual propitiation of a "local" deity necessarily have to take place at the site where the deity lives. For example, exiled Tibetans from far eastern Tibet continue to propitiate their protector deity Machen Pomra (Rma chen spom ra) even in India. During that ritual, the deity is believed to be present at a place thousands of miles away from its mountain abode. I have even heard Tibetans claim that this protector has permanently relocated to Dharamsala to be close to the A mdo region's most famous native son, His Holiness the Dalai Lama. The so-called local spirits, therefore, are frequently on the move.

Conversely, purportedly translocal deities—tantric deities of Indian origin like Yamāntaka and Cakrasaṃvara—often come to be associated with specific places in the Tibetan landscape. The images of these deities can emerge out of rocks on the sides of mountains, the phenomenon of the "self-arisen image" or *rangjön* (*rang byon*), indicating their "real presence" on Tibetan soil. Other examples of the "localization" of translocal gods abound. For instance, the cemeteries on the outskirts of Lhasa are said to be the charnel grounds of Cakrasaṃvara—a tantric deity of Indian origin; and one of the peaks overlooking Garu (Ga ru) Nunnery near Lhasa, called Demchog Lari (Bde mchog bla ri), is said to be the "Soul Mountain" of this same god.[15] In this case, a pre-Buddhist notion of sacred geography (that of "soul mountain" or *lari*)

FIGURE 1 The Drabchi Goddess, from a mural in her temple in Lhasa. Photo: J. Cabezón (2006).

comes to be associated with an Indian tantric deity precisely to localize the deity within the Tibetan landscape.[16] The topic of "soul force" or *la* (*bla*) is treated in both Karmay's and Cuevas's chapters (chapters 2 and 7) in this volume. Lindahl's chapter (chapter 10) argues that the association of sacred mountains in Mongolia with Buddhist tantric deities was a strategy for displacing the cult of indigenous spirits, and therefore constituted a Buddhist enculturation strategy—making Buddhism "local" by providing a Mongolian home to its foreign (translocal) gods.

Like all complex cosmologies that are cobbled together out of different bits and pieces from different traditions over long stretches of history, the Tibetan cosmological worldview is not always coherent or consistent. We should not take this as implying, however, that generalizations are impossible or that

FIGURE 2 The Goddess Drabchi in her altar at Drabchi Temple, Lhasa. Photo: P. Hackett (2006).

these categories should simply be dismissed. Emic and etic attempts at organizing the Tibetan pantheon—the ones just mentioned, but also other dichotomies like Indian–Tibetan, Bönpo–Buddhist, and historical–ahistorical—can be heuristically useful. Of course, we should always be attentive to the gaps and inconsistencies inherent in such generalizing schemes. As an example of such ambiguities, consider the fact that the protector goddess of the Dalai Lamas, Palden Lhamo (Dpal ldan lha mo), appears to be of Tibetan origin, but has been given an Indian pedigree by amalgamating her to Indian deities like Rematī and Ekajaṭā/ī.[17] Other deities of non-Buddhist origin, like Begtse Chamsing (Beg tse lcam sring), have found their way into the entourage of Indian deities (in Begtse's case, into the entourage of Hayagrīva), thereby achieving a kind of honorary Indian citizenship. Nor is the Bönpo–Buddhist dichotomy hard and fast. As Marc Des Jardin's chapter in this book (chapter 8) shows, Hayagrīva is worshipped both by Bönpos and by Buddhists. And while one might think that there is a clear distinction between historical human beings like Tsongkhapa and Sakya Paṇḍita (Sa skya Paṇḍita, 1182–1251) on the one hand, and ahistorical deities like Mañjuśrī on the other, the Tibetan tradition eventually came to believe that both of the former historical figures were actually emanations (*sprul pa*) of the latter deity. To reiterate the earlier point: it is not that organizing schemes or dichotomies, like human–nonhuman, are useless, but that they should be approached with a critical eye.

Tensions of a more general nature arise in the attempt to reconcile Tibetan cosmological notions to Buddhist philosophical ones. For example, is the Tibetan belief in a "life force" (*srog*), or in a "soul" (*bla*) consistent with the Buddhist notion that there is no self (*bdag med*)?[18] Other similar tensions predate the importation of Buddhism to Tibet, being endemic to Mahāyāna and tantric Buddhism even in India. Hence, is reliance on mundane protector deities consistent with the claim that the Buddha is the highest source of refuge—the only protection that one really needs? How is it possible, on the one hand, that everything experienced in life is the result of one's own previous actions (karma), while, on the other, that good and evil can be the result of spirits freely intervening in human affairs? Is beseeching a deity for blessings or requesting a spirit to cure one's illness consistent with a belief in karma? How can rituals that are enacted by grieving relatives help a deceased person? Such theological questions point to fundamental problems within the Tibetan and Indian worldviews. These issues are not, of course, unknown either to the elite texts or to less literate traditions, both of which attempt to resolve them in a variety of ways. Such ideological problems, however, seem to have little effect on Tibetans' attitudes or daily behaviors vis-à-vis the nonhuman world, or on their belief in the efficacy of ritual.

What Is a Ritual?

A great deal of literature in the field of Religious Studies has been generated in an attempt to define, categorize, and explain ritual, or ritual's more current iterations—categories like "ritualization" and "ritual performance." Much of this literature constructs and unpacks ritual as a theoretical category useful across cultures and religious traditions.[19] Some of these works emphasize the role of "space" in the understanding of ritual; others favor the variable of "time." Some are more synchronic and structuralist, reducing a given ritual or ritual corpus to fundamental units, and analyzing the relationship of these elements to one another, and to other phenomena (like the body), so as to uncover fundamental patterns. Other theories are more diachronic and/or functionalist: "How do rituals change over time?" and "What social purpose do rituals serve?" Often in conversation with other disciplines like psychoanalysis, performance studies, literary criticism, and communication studies, this mammoth body of work can be valuable in helping us to think about Tibetan rituals. Several of the chapters in this volume, in fact, make reference to this literature.

Used strategically as conversation partners, the Western theoretical literature on ritual can give us fresh insights into particular aspects of Tibetan ritual texts and practices. But problems arise when one or another of these theories is used as the single, univocal key to interpret *an entire body* of religious practices, especially one as rich and diverse as the Tibetan ritual corpus. For example, some theorists of ritual have stressed the importance of "emplacement": that rituals are enacted in physical spaces that in the process come to be constructed as "sacred," setting them apart from other sites that, by contrast, come to be considered "profane."[20] This observation is useful in helping us to think about the so-called site-rituals (*sa chog*) that take place prior to many Tibetan tantric ceremonies. (See later.) But in the Tibetan context, the site rituals are seen as preambles to the "real" (*dngos gzhi*) part of the ritual, where spatial considerations are arguably less important.

Likewise, although many Tibetan rituals are done communally—and therefore can plausibly be said (functionally) to reinforce social bonds and to strenghthen communal relationships—many rituals are done in isolation. Some ritualists even lead permanent eremetical lives, having minimal contact with others. Some even end up repudiating social norms altogether. Whether enacted communally or in isolation, Tibetan rituals often have as their professed purpose (at least from an elite perspective) the obliteration of the world of "ordinary appearances" (*tha mal gyi snang zhen*), which is often seen to include the transcendence of ordinary social bonds. How does one reconcile this emic view of ritual with the etic functionalist one that sees ritual as necessarily reinforcing the social order? The point here is *not* that ritual theories that stress social integration are irrelevant to the Tibetan case, but that they must be used with care, and with an eye to Tibetans' own theories of what ritual is and how it functions.

As with function, so too with structure. Structuralist analysis can be quite helpful in understanding ritual symbolism. It allows us to understand the constituent elements of a given ritual, to clarify how those elements combine in different instances, and to differentiate between those elements that are essential to a given ritual type and those that are, as it were, "optional." There is a good case to be made for the fact that Tibetan rituals, generally speaking, are combinations of a finite set of fundamental "subrituals" pieces that can be combined in different ways for different purposes. (See later.) Some of these elements—like prayers requesting inspiration and blessings from the lineage masters (*bla brgyud*), a genre mentioned by both Sihlé and Des Jardins in this volume—are found in many different kinds of rituals. Other elements, like the use of effigies (*ngar mi, 'dra gzugs, ling ga,* etc.), as chapters 5 and 7 show, are much more specific, being found in a smaller subset of rituals. Some elements, like the "burning stones" procedure described by Des Jardins, may even be unique. A structuralist approach to Tibetan ritual might, in theory, identify these various pieces, and in a kind of combinatorix, show how subritual elements come together to create larger rituals of different genres and levels of complexity. Given the sheer number of possibilities, however, one can only imagine how complex such a "matrix" of possible combinations would have to be to do justice to the phenomenon of Tibetan ritual as a whole.

For all these reasons, it seems unlikely that there will ever be (to borrow a term from theoretical physics) a "Grand Unified Theory" of Tibetan ritual, a theory that will explain all rituals everywhere in the Tibetan world once and for all. Historical, structualist, functionalist, aesthetic, psychological, historical, literary, and other considerations will always be useful to the analysis of Tibetan rituals, but none of these theoretical perspectives will ever be the last word on a given ritual event, much less on the Tibetan ritual canon as a whole. But to restate the earlier point, this does not mean that the Western scholarly literature cannot be used strategically. There are many areas within the academic study of ritual—from the economics of patronage to the aesthetics of liturgies to their political functions—that can shed light on individual Tibetan case studies. Scholars of Tibetan ritual have generally taken a very pragmatic approach to the Western theoretical literature, turning to it as needed to elucidate a specific issue or problem. But Tibetologists have also eschewed totalizing approaches—a "one size fits all" model—the "Grand Unified Theories" mentioned earlier that attempt to explain everything ritual everywhere and "everywhen." The authors of those grand theories—the great luminaries like Freud, Durkheim, Lévi-Strauss, Turner, and so on—have offered us "top-down" models. They began with intuitions about what ritual is, and they (or their heirs) have then attempted to apply this to real-world examples. Most Tibetologists, by contrast, have traditionally worked from the bottom up, slowly and cautiously arriving at broader conclusions from the textual and ethnographic data "up." Such an approach is in part due to the historical evolution of the field (more on which later). But in part, it is a principled reluctance to allow the grand etic theories, as fascinating as these may be, to set the agenda, or to completely displace or silence the emic voice of the text or informant. While there is no theoretical perspective that pervades Tibetan ritual studies, there may therefore be a *meta*theoretical one: the refusal to simply dismiss indigenous accounts of the meaning of ritual in favor of the grand theoretical narratives. This more "bottom-up," strategic and pragmatic approach to theory—an approach that is in constant conversation with the first-order data, and with Tibetans' own self-understanding of the rituals they enact—will be evident throughout this book.

The sheer diversity of ritual practices in the Tibetan world makes a simple definition of Tibetan ritual impossible. But no student of Tibetan religions would seriously doubt the existence of things called "rituals." What precisely, then, *is* a ritual? At this point there is always the temptation to throw up one's hands and to eschew any attempt at generalization or definition: "I can't tell you what they are, but I know'em when I see'em." That no single definition of Tibetan ritual will be able to do justice to the complex phenomena that fall under this rubric does not mean that we cannot speak of the phenomenon of Tibetan ritual. Tibetans, after all, *do* speak about "rituals." Let us examine some of the nomenclature they use.

Several Tibetan words are typically translated by the word "ritual,"[21] but probably none is semantically closer to the English word than the Tibetan *choga* (*cho ga*).[22] *Choga* is used to translate the Sanskrit *vidhi*,[23] a word that can mean "the manner or way of acting" or "a rule." In the Indian religious context, the word *vidhi* refers to the rules governing the performance of worship and sacrifice, or simply to the rule-governed rite itself. The Tibetan word *choga* does not map perfectly onto the term "ritual," however. Take, for example, simple mantra recitation, *ngag dawa* (*sngags bzla ba*). The intoning of mantras is often a public and performative act; it involves the verbalization of a defined "text"; it is formulaic, ruled-governed, and repeatable. For all these reasons, it might be considered a paradigmatic ritual. But in Tibetan usage, one would not call mantra recitation itself a *choga*, even though it is *a part of* many *chogas*. Other examples of "ritual" that do not fall under the rubric of *cho ga* could be cited, including *kora* (*skor ba*)[24] or circumambulation, and *chölog* (*chos klog*) or scripture reading. Taken together, these examples suggest that our category "ritual" is broader than the Tibetan notion of *choga*.

What then is a *choga?* Indigenous lexicographical definitions are not very helpful. One contemporary Tibetan dictionary tells us that a *choga* is "a method for accomplishing a goal, a way of performing an action, a procedure."[25] Aside from informing us that *chogas* are goal-directed and that they have a certain systematic or procedural quality to them, the definition sheds little light on what *chogas* actually are. It is perhaps more useful to examine the way in which the term is used in common parlance. In this context a *choga* is usually understood as a formal (usually tantric) rite focused on one or more deities, and usually performed by one or more specialists. In their most elaborate form, *chogas* have chanted melodies (*dbyangs*); they involve the use of costumes (*chas*), of ritual implements—like vajras (*rdo rje*), bells (*dril bu*), and ritual vases (*bum pa*)—and of hand gestures (*phyag rgya*); they may involve the construction of *maṇḍalas* made out of colored sands (*rdul tshon*); and they can include dances (*gar, 'chams*). A prime example of such a complex *choga* is the Kālacakra empowerment (*'Dus 'khor dbang chen*).[26] While a *choga* is, more often than not, a tantric ritual (at least in common parlance), there are *chogas* that do not focus on tantric deities[27] and that, rather than belonging to the esoteric or tantric corpus, instead belong to the exoteric or *sūtra* genre. The Vinaya rituals enacted by monastic communities are examples of this latter type.[28] Other *sūtra*-based rituals, like the practices associated with the Sixteen Arhats (*Gnas brtan bcu drug gi cho ga*), do focus on superhuman agents, but are not considered tantric. Like all such distinction, the exoteric–esoteric one has its fissures; some rites that one would expect to be exoteric—for example, the Heart Sūtra-based liturgy for repelling demons (*Sher snying bdud bzlog*), and the Medicine Buddha "*sūtra* ritual" (*Sman bla'i mdo chog*)—end up having a very tantric flavor to them. The same type of ambiguity is also found among the Mongolian rituals for the veneration of exoteric scriptures described by Vesna Wallace in this volume.

The dividing line between sūtric and tantric *chogas*, therefore, is not always clear. What *is* clear is that it would be incorrect to assert that all *chogas* are tantric in character. That being said, the vast majority of *cho gas* in the pan-Tibetan repertoire are indeed tantric, so it behooves us to say a few words about this important category of ritual.

Tantric Ritual

Tantric rituals, the quintessential type of *chogas*, typically focus on a specific deity. They involve the recitation of fixed liturgies whose words, in theory at least, are meant to elicit mental images or visualizations (*dmigs pa* or *dmigs rnam*): for example, the visualization of deities external to the ritual performer (*mdun bskyed*), the visualization of the performer *as* the deity (*bdag bskyed*), etc. Tantric rituals are also modular. As mentioned earlier, they are composed of distinct subritual pieces. Mengele's chapter in this volume (chapter 5) describes the specific pieces that together constitute "death-deceiving" rituals, Des Jardins does the same with an exorcism, and Pommaret argues that the typical aspects of Bhutanese pilgrimage to Tibet also function ritualistically.

Some of these modular elements are essential to a given ritual type, others are optional. These different elements also exist in variously abbreviated or expanded forms. Integrating different elements of different length allows the ritualist to draw out or to truncate a specific rite as desired.[29] Although the vast majority of rituals in use today have been written by Tibetans, the actual words of such liturgies often derive from the Tibetan translations of Indian canonical works or their Bönpo equivalents, or else they derive from the *terma* (*gter ma*) or revealed "treasures" that, especially in the Nyingma (Rnying ma) school, often have the same canonical status as the Indian Tantras. In her chapter in this book (chapter 4), Yael Bentor examines the various interpretations given to a single verse of the *Guhyasamāja Tantra*, a verse that has an important ritual function in Tibetan liturgies. Chapter 2 examines how the rites related to the *nyen* spirits may have their origin in a work found in the Bönpo canon. The point is that tantric rituals make constant allusion to canonical works—sometimes by explicitly incorporating canonical passages, sometimes by indirectly referencing the myths, symbols, and doctrines found in the canons.

No two tantric rituals are ever identical. Even when we focus on a single genre of ritual—empowerment, say—different deities belonging to different tantric classes require different subrites. Nor is the order of these elements always precisely the same. There is variation from one class of deities to another; and even in regard to a single deity, there are variations depending on lineage and sect. Still, patterns are discernible. Let us work through one example, an ideal-typical empowerment (or initiation, *dbang*) ritual of the "highest yoga" tantra class, to get a sense of these modular elements.

- Preliminary rituals (*sta gon*) or preparations (*lhag gnas, sbyor ba*). When the empowerment is offered over two days, the preliminary rituals often take place on the first day.
  - Preliminaries related to the site spirit (*sa yi lha mo sta gon*). Since the site of the empowerment is seen as belonging to a spirit, it is first necessary to ritually take possession of the site (*sa chog*).
  - Related to deity's universe or *maṇḍala* (*dkyil 'khor gyi lha sta gon*).

        - The creation of a physical *maṇḍala* (e.g., drawn on cloth or made from colored powders).
        - Using the physical *maṇḍala* as a basis, the "generation" of the deity, the deity's palace, and its surrounding areas as a visualized form (*dam tshig pa bskyed pa*).
        - The invitation and melding of the actual deities of the *maṇḍala* into the visualized image (*ye shes pa spyan drangs nas thim pa*).
        - Offerings (*mchod pa*), praises (*bstod pa*), etc.
    - Related to the vase(s) (*bum pa sta gon*). Generating the deities inside the ritual vase(s) that will be used to grant empowerment, making offerings to the deities and reciting praises.
    - Related to the disciple (*slob ma sta gon*). Certain procedures and rituals to prepare the disciple for the empowerment, which include imparting bodhisattva and tantric vows, blessings, instructions on dream analysis, etc.
- The actual ritual (*dngos gzhi*), the bestowal of the empowerment (*dbang bskur ba*).
    - Vase empowerment (*bum dbang*).
    - Secret empowerment (*gsang dbang*).
    - Wisdom-gnosis empowerment (*shes rab ye shes kyi dbang*).
    - Word empowerment (*tshig dbang*), also known as the fourth empowerment (*dbang bzhi pa*).
- The post-ritual (*rjes chog*) or concluding actions (*mjug gi bya ba*), which may include:
    - A burnt offering ritual, so as to expiate faults of omission and commission in the enactment of the rite, and so as to "satisfy the deity" (*lhag chad kyi nyes pa zhi ba dang lha tshim pa'i phyir zhi rgyas kyi sbyin sreg bya ba*).
    - Additional offerings and praises to the deities, and *torma* offerings to the protectors (*dkyil 'khor mchod bstod dang phyogs skyong la gtor ma dbul ba*).
    - Prostrating and requesting the deity's tolerance in the face of errors committed during the ritual (*dkyil 'khor la phyag byas te bzod gsol bya ba*).
    - Requesting that the deities to return to their abodes (*ye shes pa gshegs su gsol ba*).
    - Dissolution of the visualized palace into one's self and destruction of the sand *maṇḍala* (*dam tshig pa rang la bsdus te rdul tshon chur gshegs pa*)
    - Dedication of merit (*bsngo ba*).
    - Prayers for good fortune (*bkra shis pa'i tshigs bcad*).

These are just the bare-bones outline of an empowerment ritual. Some of these pieces are themselves internally complex and contain subrituals of their own. For example, the "vase empowerment"—the first of the four-part "acutal rite"—typically contains eleven parts.[30] "Offering," in turn, is often classified into:

- Outer offerings (*phyi'i mchod pa*)—water, perfume, light, food, music, etc.—that please the five senses.
- Inner offering (*nang mchod*): impure substances—the so-called five meats and five nectars (*sha lnga bdud rtsi lnga*)—transformed into pure ambrosia that generates bliss.
- Offering of ritual cakes (*gtor ma*).
- Offering of the entire universe (*maṇḍal*).

What is more, the inner and *torma* offerings often are further subdivided into distinct subrituals, such as cleansing, purification, generation as nectar, multiplication in quantity, and the actual offering to the god(s).

As regards the empowerment as a whole, other modules may be added at different points throughout the ceremony, including praises (*bstod pa*), supplications (*gsol ba 'debs pa*), requests for blessings (*byin 'bebs*), and so forth.

It is, of course, beyond the scope of this introduction to discuss even a single rite like empowerment in any detail, but this very brief overview at least conveys something of the complexity of a Tibetan tantric ritual. It also gives one a sense of its modular character. The relationship between the elements, the relative positions of the parts vis-à-vis one another, and the relationship between parts and whole give rituals, I would contend, a *narrative quality*. Understanding this aspect of tantric ritual—its logic, or, perhaps more appropriately, its "storyline"—is an important part of understanding such rites. Take the case of empowerment. Before one can be granted a favor (empowerment), one must first invite the individual (the god) who is going to grant such a kindness. Before that can take place, however, one must ready the home (the palace). But to have a home in the first place, one must first acquire the land from its owner (the site-procurement rite). The favor comes at a price (the commitments that must be taken), and both before and after the favor is granted, gifts (offerings) are appropriate. Of course, this is an oversimplification of what is actually a very complex "plot." But this embedded narrative quality is an important part of many tantric rituals. In the life-prolongation ritual described by Mengele in this book, for example, the narrative is one of getting malevolent spirits to accept a substitute for the life of the person being threatened. Sometimes narrative elements are not explicit in the ritual itself, but are rather presumed as part of the background lore that undergirds a liturgy: the "charter myths" that explain how certain spirits and deities came to have the powers that they do.

In other instances, narratives have to be elaborated in the *aftermath* of rituals to explain why a certain ritual functioned, or why it did not. Not all *chogas* have very complex plots,[31] but most seem to have at least some narrative quality to them, even if at times these are only implicit.

Some of the modular elements found in an empowerment ritual—for example, the act of generating oneself as the deity, making offerings,[32] and the concluding expiatory rites—are ubiquitous to tantric ritual generally. They are found in deity-yoga practices (*sādhana, sgrub thabs*), in burnt-offerings (*sbyin sreg*), in consecration rites (*rab gnas*), and in many other types of tantric liturgies. Modular elements like self-generation, offering, and expiation can *also* serve as the central theme of stand-alone rites, of *sādhana*, offering rituals (*mchod pa'i cho ga*), and confessional rites (*bskang bshags*), respectively. Some ritual texts provide only a bare-bones outline and expect ritual experts to know how to "accessorize" them, changing elements as needed for different purposes.[33] Expertise as a writer of tantric liturgies or as a director of tantric rituals—for example, as an *umdzé* (*dbu mdzad*) or chant leader—is in large part determined by one's knowledge of how to modify liturgical elements, and by one's ability to manipulate these modular pieces in a way that makes sense, a point made by Cantwell and Mayer in this volume. Put another way, an expert is someone who has knowledge of "the grammar" of the elements of these various subrituals, someone who can combine them into meaningful wholes.

The Organization of the Tibetan Ritual Corpus

Tibetan scholars and ritual experts have tried to bring order to this unwieldy mass of ritual materials in a variety of ways. In some instances, all of the material related to a single deity was brought together into compendia called "cycles" (*skor*), or "collected actions" (*las tshogs*).[34] Nicolas Sihlé's chapter in this volume (chapter 1) discusses one such compendium used by Buddhist tantric priests in Chongkor village, as does Des Jardins chapter (chapter 8), which focuses on the cycle of rituals used in the Bönpo monastery of Yeshé. In their most extensive forms, such collections, which can be several volumes in length, might contain the Tantra (*rgyud*) of a given deity, the history (*lo rgyus*) of its transmission, empowerment liturgies, *sādhanas*, instructions (*gdams ngag*), important commentaries on the practice (*khrid*), retreat manuals, *torma* offering rituals, burnt-offering rites, consecration liturgies, protector-deity practices, prayers, and other practices of a more practical or magical nature (e.g., rituals to procure long life and protection, rites to defeat enemies, to create magical pills, etc.).[35] In their organization, these collections often evince an internal logic, and perhaps even a "narrative," of their own. For example, beginning from the end of the collection just mentioned and working forward: in order to be able to elicit the intercession (*phrin las*) of the deity—for instance, the boon of long life—one must first achieve a closeness (*bsnyen sgrub*) to the deity through the prolonged practice of *sādhana* and retreat, and through the periodic offering of things like *tormas*. But in order to practice *sādhanas* and *torma* offerings in the first place, one must first receive empowerment. Moreover, for an empowerment to be valid, there must exist an unbroken lineage that goes back to the human being(s) who received the Tantra. So, even in the organization of the collected rites of a deity—root Tantra, lineage history, empowerment, *sādhana, torma,* and minor rites—we see an implicit logical or narrative structure.[36] There are dozens if not hundreds of such collections in the Tibetan literary corpus.

So much for collections based on a single deity. Other collections assemble together the rites of *different* deities. Examples include the *Bari Hundred* (*Ba ri brgya rtsa*)[37] of the translator Bari Rinchen Drag (Ba ri Rin chen grags, 1040–1112), and the *Jewel Source: The Sādhanas of an Ocean of Deities*[38] of Tāranātha (1575–1634), works that are compilations of the *sādhanas* and/or permission-rituals (*rjes gnang*) of hundreds of different deities. And then there is, pretty much in a league of its own, *The Great Storehouse of Precious Treasures*[39] of Jamgön Kongtrül ('Jam mgon kong sprul, 1813–99), a mammoth work in 111 volumes that assembles under a single rubric a variety of (mostly) ritual practices discovered by various (mostly) Nyingma *tertön* (*gter ston*) or "treasure revealers." Neither the single-deity "collected actions" collections, nor these larger multiple-deity compendia are mere anthologies. They are attempts to organize vast portions of the elite ritual corpus. As such, they are not only bibliographical undertakings, but also theoretical musings on the nature and function of ritual. Investigating the logic of these works and drawing out their implicit theoretical underpinnings remains one of the great challenges ahead of us in the field of Tibetan ritual studies.

Most of the examples examined up to this point have been drawn from the elite, textual tradition of tantric ritual practice. Scholars have often used the term "elite" to refer to soteriologically focused practices whose ostensible goal is the attainment of enlightenment. The elite tradition is often seen as exemplified by large, scholastic, male-monastic institutions. The opposite of "elite" is "popular." Like the other dichotomies mentioned earlier in this Introduction, the elite–popular one is not without its problems.[40] As just mentioned, while the single-deity compendia often begin on a soteriological note (empowerments, *sādhanas*, etc.), they often end with rites that are more pragmatic (magical pill and amulet creation, etc.). But the elite–popular (or soteriological–pragmatic) distinction is problematic for other reasons as well. On the one hand, it is not uncommon to find nonmonastic, institutionally unaffiliated, and illiterate individuals, including women, engaged in highly specialized, complex enlightenment-directed practices. On the other hand, monks of the elite scholastic institutions, like the Gelug monastic universities or *densas* (*gdan sa*), often engage in practices that would typically be characterized as "popular." For example, it is not uncommon for the monks of these institutions to engage in wealth-rituals (*g.yang 'gugs*) or to go to a local lay diviner or healer. There are even instances of illiterate village women acting as the official oracles of the regional houses or *khangtsen* (*khang tshan*) of these elite institutions. So the boundaries between elite and nonelite have always been porous. To dismiss the distinction altogether, however, seems a bit like throwing the baby out with the bath water. Nonetheless, it is wise to treat such a distinction with a certain amount of caution. With these caveats, we now turn from the practices of "elite" salvation-centered rites to the more pragmatic rituals of ordinary life.

Magic and Pragmatic Rituals

In traditional Tibetan societies, when a family member becomes seriously ill, or when bad luck befalls a household, a monastery or a community, diviners[41] are usually consulted to determine the cause of the misfortune. Whatever a diviner's diagnosis may be—whether it is past negative karma, the exhaustion of merit, malevolent spirits (*'dre srin*), psychic pollution (*s/grib*), impurity (*mi gtshang ba*), others' "badmouthing"[42] or black magic (*ngan sngags*)—ritual is almost always part of what will set things aright. If it is black magic or an evil spirit that is the cause of the problem, then ritual is one of the most effective means of solving it. In such cases, a wrathful ritual is usually called for: a rite to catch and exorcise (*sel ba, skrod pa, bzlog pa*) the demonic influence or to overturn the power of the curse (*byad kha*). Or else one might resort to a "ransom ritual" (*glud*), in which an effigy is offered to a spirit as a substitute for the afflicted individual or group. When the cause of misfortune is the more ethereal "pollution," then rituals for its purification (*s/grib dag byed kyi cho ga*) might be performed—using *tormas*, ablutions (*s/grib khrus*), or complex thread-cross structures called *drib-dö* (*grib mdos*). But even when the diagnosis is "karmic"—when the tragedy is seen as being the result of a person's past actions or as the effect of unresolved karmic debt (*lan chags*)[43]—rituals can be enacted to restore a person's merit, their store of "good karma," and to avert calamity by repaying the debt owed to karmic "creditors." In this case, merit-making or offering rituals are usually called for. The family might then sponsor the reading of the canon in the local monastery, or they may request the recitation of 100,000 repetitions of the famous prayer to the goddess Tārā.

Even when individuals suffering from an illness have already decided to follow the path of medical treatment, they will often go to diviners to determine what rituals might increase the efficacy of the healing process. In this case, ritual is seen as a complement to a more materialistic, nonreligious course of action. While rituals may not be able to counteract every mishap that befalls human beings (see Mengele's discussion of death-prevention rituals in this volume), rituals are not only considered useful, but they are also often seen as indispensable to success in a variety of human affairs. They are enacted not only once calamity strikes, but also to avert mishap in the first place. Rituals are performed, or more often sponsored, not only to cure physical and mental illness and bad luck, but also for protection, so that such calamities never befall one. Rituals also insure a positive outcome to a variety of worldly endeavors that include travel, business ventures, harvests, love, and warfare. (The last of these is the subject of chapter 6 in this book, and the list compiled by Cuevas alludes to all of these as possible goals.) There are even rituals to insure the efficacy of rituals, and as we have seen, rituals to make up for mistakes or shortcomings that might occur during the performance of other rituals. And when, despite all attempts at ritual intervention, death strikes, there are rituals for purifying and disposing of the bodily remains of the deceased, to help the departed in their journey through the intermediate state, and to insure that the dead will not return as ghosts. There are also, of course, rituals like *powa* (*'pho ba*), the "transference of consciousness," that assure rebirth in pure lands, heavenly states where enlightenment is guaranteed.

As mentioned earlier, the soteriological–pragmatic dichotomy is not without its aporias. Hence, there are a variety of rituals that have *both* pragmatic and soteriological uses. For example, amulets and pills protect one from harm in the here and now, but these are often also touted as being capable of granting liberation through merely wearing and ingesting them, respectively. And while village ritualists frequently often do "transference of consciousness" rites for the deceased as part of their clerical duties, this practice is also part of elite, soteriologically focused cycles of practices. The dividing line between soteriological and pragmatic is therefore fuzzy. At one end of the spectrum there are clearly soteriological rites, like the *sādhanas* or "proximity retreats" when done by the highly literate elite—rites that Jamgön Kongtrül calls "the essence of the path" (*lam gyi ngo bo*). At the other end, there are magical acts, like the ones described in chapter 7, some of which aim at such mundane goals as winning at archery and dice, arousing the love of a woman, or catching thieves.[44] These "minor rites," as well as the more complex and scripted "army repelling" (*dmag bzlog*) rituals mentioned by Gentry in chapter 6, are not directly concerned with enlightenment, having more immediate and pragmatic goals. At the same time, success in these more magical practices is sometimes said to depend on the metaphysical ties that a ritualist has to his or her previous incarnations, ties whose validation require extensive literary elaboration, something that chapter 6 explores. According to the elite tradition at least, success in magic is also said to depend on soteriologically grounded practice—for example, on the achievement of *sādhana*-based "proximity" to the deity.[45] What is more, what distinguishes Buddhist magic from black magic is said to be prior training in Mahāyāna ethics. This is reinforced in most of these pragmatic rituals through liturgical elements such as "the correction of the motivation" that is found at the beginning of almost every Tibetan rite. So, while some rituals can clearly be said to be more directly soteriological and others more pragmatic or magical, the elite tradition goes to great lengths to couch (and therefore to legitimize) the latter by relating them to the former, as Cathy Cantwell and Robert Mayer's discussion of killing rites in this volume shows. All of that being said, just as one person's tutelary deity is sometimes another person's demon, it has also been the case that one person's compassionate magic will be seen by someone else as sorcery. The point, of course, is that what constitutes soteriological rituals and sorcery is (sometimes at least) in the eye of the beholder.

The Place of Ritual Studies in the Changing Fields of Buddhology and Tibetology

The field of Buddhist Studies has changed significantly in the past four decades, and these changes have created the conditions for the flourishing of fields like ritual studies. Outlining these shifts will help us to understand why Tibetologists have become more interested in rituals—more interested than they were just a few years ago.

Earlier generations of Buddhologists were concerned almost exclusively with texts, and not with "texts" in the broad way that we understand the term today, but with written documents. These texts were studied not so much because of what they told us about the people or the societies in which they were written, but because of the ideas—the doctrines and philosophy—contained within them. Early Buddhology was therefore chiefly the study of ideas found in doctrinal texts. This concern with the classical and literary was the result, on the one hand, of the (largely unspoken) presupposition, inherited from the European Renaissance, that ancient and classical culture was more pure and worthy of study: that it represented a highpoint in civilization, the pinnacle of human achievement from which there had been a steady decline. On the other hand, it was the result of a privileging of the textual over the material and oral, the legacy of Protestantism. To the extent that there was a concern with "culture" at all, it was a concern with elite institutions, with the culture of the writers of texts, who were almost exclusively monks.

Because of the preoccupation with origins, early Buddhology also tended to privilege Indian and Chinese Buddhism. The study of Buddhism in other societies—societies in which Buddhism entered at a later date, as was the case with Tibet—tended to be neglected or else was seen as a handmaiden of Buddhist Indology or Sinology. Hence, Tibetan Buddhist Studies was not initially seen as an autonomous subarea of Buddhology, but rather as a kind supplement to Indian Buddhist Studies. As late as the 1970s, we find scholars like David Seyfort Ruegg having to argue for the autonomy of Tibetan Buddhist Studies, indicating the persistence of this mindset up to recent times. Moreover, being concerned principally with the ideas found in written texts, few earlier scholars wrote on the social, political, and economic contexts of the societies in which Buddhism flourished even in classical times, much less in the modern period.

The earliest Buddhologists were also usually armchair scholars who worked with texts that had been brought to Europe and North America by missionaries and colonial officers. Rarely, if ever, did they go into the field, and rarely did they speak the languages that they read. A few even admitted their reticence to travel to a Buddhist society for fear that this might taint their ideal picture of "pure" Buddhism, a bubble that they realized would, of necessity, burst when they entered the real and messy world of a lived Buddhist tradition. This portrait of early Buddhology is painted in broad strokes. There were always, among the early scholars, exceptions to the rule, a few Buddhologists who were concerned with more than written texts, and a few who actually lived for periods of time in Buddhist societies. That being said, the overall picture is not inaccurate.

The most important changes in the discipline have arguably transpired in the past three or four decades. These changes have been profound. They are transformations in what we study, in how we study it, in the tools at our disposal, and most recently in the media we use to disseminate our research. The notion of "text," for example, is much broader than it once was. While we still study written, doctrinal, and philosophical texts, we also study Buddhist biographies, fiction, plays, and a variety of other narrative texts. We still study the written works of the elite male clergy, but increasingly we study the writings and oral traditions of nuns and of the Buddhist laity. We not only study what Buddhists have written or what they think, but also what they *do* in both elite rituals and in popular practices. (Chapter 11 by Françoise Pommaret on Bhutanese pilgrimage to Tibet in this volume is a good example of this.) We also focus on nonverbal "texts," reading Buddhism through the lens of material culture—from high art to kitschy plastic Buddhas; and from archaeology to epigraphy, or as one scholar has put it, "from bones to stones." In short, having realized that our work had yielded only a partial picture of Buddhism, one that excluded a good part of Buddhists' lived experience, and what most Buddhists actually *did*, we have increasingly turned our attention, as a corrective, precisely to those areas that had previously been neglected, including the study of ritual.

While the textual and elite focus of classical Buddhology is still very much alive, Buddhist Studies today is *also* concerned with nonelite institutions and practices, and with traditions that are in many instances hybrids of Buddhist and non-Buddhist religious elements. (Chapter 8 by Marc Des Jardin in this volume is a fine example of this.) While we continue to be interested in classical Buddhist institutions, we are also now concerned with new religious movements that are often considered (by elite Buddhists at least) to transgress the bounds of orthodoxy. Indeed, the very notion of a single thing called "Buddhism" has itself been problematized, if not quite abandoned.

As the object of our study has changed, so too have our methods. Eschewing broad generalizations, our studies now deal with more specific periods, places, individuals, and institutions. The ahistoricism of earlier scholarship has been replaced by a keen historical consciousness. And scholars, for the most part, no longer sit in armchairs. They go into the field. Indeed, it is often a requirement for doctoral students to spend at least a year in a Buddhist culture, whatever their area of specialty. Increasingly, Buddhologists find themselves asking questions about power, material culture, the production of goods, and forms of exchange, thereby bringing the methods of political science and economics to bear on their studies. Finally, information technology is revolutionizing the field in ways that we never could have imagined. All these changes amount to a paradigm shift within the discipline of Buddhist studies.

The field of Tibetology has seen similar changes, becoming institutionally autonomous, more diverse in terms of what it studies, and much more interdisciplinary and comparative. Institutionally, what began as a meeting of a handful of "young Tibetologists" just three decades ago is today the International Association of Tibetan Studies, a professional organization that hosts a meeting with hundreds of paper presentations by scholars from all over the world.[46] These scholars continue to work on classical, doctrinal texts, but increasingly they also devote themselves to other genres of literature—to biography, classical narrative literature, history (both classical and modern), and fiction. Scholars increasingly turn to China and Central Asia to find historical antecedents for the texts and practices they investigate, and so India is no longer the only or most relevant comparative reference point for Tibetologists. Tibetan studies scholars still work on philosophical texts—indeed, after a "dry spell" in this area, Tibetan philosophy is enjoying something of a comeback—but in the past decades more attention has been paid to the practical dimensions of religion, and not only to Buddhist practices, but also to those of Bön. While the field has yet to turn its attention to Tibetan Islam in any significant way, it is just a matter of time before it moves in that direction as well. Tibetology has also expanded methodologically. An increasing number of scholars work in archaeology, economics, sociology, geography, literary studies, medicine, and Tibetan art, to name just a few of the directions that the discipline has taken. The cultural turn and the increased interdisciplinarity of Tibetan studies have opened up an unprecedented space for the study of ritual.

The Present Volume

A miniscule subfield just a few decades ago, Tibetan ritual studies has grown in leaps and bounds. Since the 1960s, the number of scholarly articles on Tibetan ritual in Western languages has more or less doubled annually. Today, there are over a hundred articles per year in this area. The subfield has not only changed quantitatively, but also qualitatively. A few decades ago Tibetan rituals were, more often than not, the concern of anthropologists who mostly studied the ritual lives of Himalayan peoples in remote village settings. Detailed studies of elite ritual traditions were rare. Most anthropologists could not read classical Tibetan, and therefore had to rely on informants' accounts for their interpretations of these rites. Many of the anthropologists who work on Tibetan ritual today, by contrast, have been trained in the classical texts. Some are even interested, as Nicolas Sihlé is, in how even moderately literate traditions (that of Chongkor village on the Nepal–Tibet frontier) understand, appropriate, and transmit written ritual texts—not only as physical objects, as verbal and somatic liturgies, as emblems of status and lineage, but also as doctrinally and philosophically laden works.

Although the first and last chapters in this volume are written by anthropologists, it is noteworthy that the rest of the chapters are not. Ritual is clearly no longer the sole purview of the Tibetan anthropologist. As the study of Tibet has become more interdisciplinary, so too has the subfield of Tibetan ritual studies. Scholars who work on rituals can be found in fields as disparate as philology, literary studies, history, religious studies, and ethnomusicology. While the present volume does not purport to represent anything like the full gamut of contemporary research on Tibetan rituals—among other things, our focus here is only on *religious* rituals[47]—this collection does give one a sense of the broad range of questions that interest scholars, and of the lenses they use to make sense of these practices.

Just as anthropologists who study Tibetan ritual have become more interested in literary texts, Tibetologists who study classical texts have become increasingly interested in ritual practices. How does a specific ritual or corpus of rituals draw on the doctrines and narratives found in classical texts? Samten Karmay, a pioneer in elaborating the connection between myths and rituals, continues his work on this topic in his chapter in this book (chapter 2), this time with a focus on the mythic foundations of the *nyen* spirit cult. Karmay shows how texts preserved in the Bönpo canon (Bon po bka' 'gyur) provide us with some of the narrative background against which to understand rituals related to the *nyen*.

Because so much more is known today about the Indian and Tibetan tantric textual corpus, and because we have access to a much wider range of texts—including the very early works discovered in the Dunhuang caves—textual scholars today have the tools for more focused and detailed studies of specific ritual traditions. Chapter 3 by Cathy Cantwell and Robert Mayer focuses on a body of ritual works that belong to the Mahāyoga Tantra, including rituals related to the little studied cycle of the Tantra *Lasso of Methods* (*Thabs kyi zhags pa*). Cantwell and Mayer are interested in the similarities and differences between the Dunhuang Mahāyoga texts and Indian Buddhist tantra, but in this volume they are especially concerned with the continuities and discontinuities between the texts found at Dunhuang and the Mahāyoga rituals practiced throughout Tibetan history up to the present day. The similarities between the Dunhuang ritual traditions and those enacted today, a thousand years later, are indeed quite remarkable. Like Cantwell and Mayer's work, Yael Bentor's chapter (chapter 4) is also concerned with issues of continuity and change, although of a different kind. Bentor shows how a single, pivotal verse in the *Guhyasamāja Tantra*, a verse with important ritual uses, becomes the object of divergent interpretations. As Bentor's shows, it is the malleability of this verse—a verse used in various Guhyasamāja rituals—that allows for different philosophical positions to be read into it. Hundreds of years of exegetical precedent, as the reader will see, does not stop Tibetans from offering their own, unique doctrinal interpretations of pivotal passages from the Tantras—passages with important ritual uses.

The next four chapters in this book deal with specific types of ritual. Irmgard Mengele focuses on an Indo-Tibetan genre of ritual known as *chilu* (*'chi bslu*) or "death-deception," a rite for averting premature death. Mengele traces the genealogy of such practices and not only describes several of them in detail, but also treats some of doctrinal problems that the notion of "cheating death" raises. Does cheating death mean cheating karma? Mengele is also interested in what the tradition has to say about the efficacy of such rites—about when they work and when they do not. The issue of efficacy (and its rhetoric) is also a central concern of chapter 6. There, James Gentry is interested in exorcism or *dogpa* (*zlog pa*) rites, and more specifically in rituals used to repel or vanquish armies, *magdog* (*dmag zlog*). His chapter focuses on one figure, the great "expeller of the Mongols" Sogdogpa Lodrö Gyaltsen (Sog bzlog pa Blo gros rgyal mtshan, 1552–1624). Gentry is especially interested in Sogdogpa's self-portrayal as a ritual destroyer of Mongolian armies and in the arguments Sogdogpa uses to show that his rituals work—arguments based on prophecies, signs, and dreams. Reading the sociopolitical function of these rituals through the interstices of Sogdogpa's mostly supernaturalistic account, Gentry concludes that these rites (also) had a variety of this-worldly outcomes—for example, allowing Sogdogpa to create for himself a niche in the turbulent political world in which he lived. Bryan Cuevas's chapter (chapter 7) also deals with the topic of ritual magic, and like Gentry's, his chapter focuses on the work of a single author—in Cuevas's case, the famous Nyingmapa polymath Ju Mipam ('Ju Mi pham, 1846–1912). Mipam's compilation of a wide range of magical rites in a work called *The Calf's Nipple*, or *Beu Bum* (*be'u 'bum*), is one of the most important extant collections of this type. Cuevas explains the organizing principles at work in the collection. He also provides us with a fascinating and nuanced discussion of the term "magic," exploring the extent to which such a category—a category with a long history in the study of religion—can shed light on the practices found in Mipam's compendium. Chapter 7 concludes with a table of contents to *The Calf's Nipple*, providing readers with a glimpse of the actual rites found in this genre of text. Of the four chapters that deal with specific ritual cycles, Marc Des Jardin's (chapter 8) is concerned with a particular Bönpo healing and exorcistic ritual based on the deity Hayagrīva. The rite is the specialty of monks at the Yeshé Monastery (Ye shes dgon) in Nyagrong (Nyag rong), eastern Tibet. Aside from describing the very dramatic rite of "the burning stones," Des Jardins considers a variety of broader issues: What makes rituals popular? How useful is the Buddhist–Bön dichotomy in categorizing or explaining rituals? The ritual of the burning stones is a particularly useful site for exploring this latter question, given that it involves a deity that is propitiated by both Buddhists and Bönpos.

Scholarly work on Tibetan ritual to date has tended to focus on Tibet and on the Tibetan-speaking portions of Nepal. The present volume expands the discussion to Mongolia, a region that has been influenced by Tibet for more than 700 years. Chapter 9 by Vesna Wallace deals with Mongolian rituals used in the veneration of Mahāyāna scriptures. The worship of these texts has both private and public dimensions; it also has a wide array of goals, including healing, merit-making, and protection (of individuals and the state). These rites, however, also have more mundane objectives, like finding a wealthy husband, and even the preservation of dead bodies. Among other things, Wallace's study raises the question of the boundary between ritual and nonritual religious practices. While all of these different techniques for venerating scriptures seem to involve some level of ritualism, a few appear to be quite formal and even tantric in character, resembling elite tantric *chogas*. Others are much more informal. The diversity of *sūtra* veneration rituals serves for Wallace, therefore, as an entrée into theoretical reflection concerning the nature of ritual itself. If Wallace's chapter problematizes the boundaries between what is and is not ritual, Jared Lindahl's chapter complexifies the boundary between Buddhist and non-Buddhist religions at an important site for the performance of rituals: Mongolia's sacred mountains. Through an examination of incense offering rites, called *sangchö* (*bsang mchod*), Lindahl shows how Buddhist rites "reinforce and even reenact" the conversion of the Mongols to Buddhism. Rather than seeing the mountain veneration cult in Mongolia as a syncretic or hybrid form incorporating Buddhist and "shamanistic" elements, Lindahl sees them as a conscious strategy on the part of Buddhists to map Buddhism and its pantheon onto the Mongolian landscape.

Mongolia is at the far northeastern periphery of the region influenced by Tibetan culture; at the other extreme, in the far south, is Bhutan. The last chapter of this book (chapter 11) is Françoise Pommaret's narrative of what it was like to accompany a group of Bhutanese pilgrims to Tibet. Although a great deal has been written about Tibetan pilgrimage in recent years, nothing has been written about Bhutanese pilgrimage practices. Chapter 11 gives us a glimpse into Bhutanese pilgrims' encounter with Tibet, Tibetans, and Tibetan Buddhism. Pommaret also uses this particular pilgrimage as a way of engaging the broader question of the relationship of pilgrimage to ritual. She argues that much of what takes place in a pilgrimage belongs to the ritual corpus, in the sense that we have here religious action performed with a religious guide for defined aims with a special attitude and in a well-defined spatio-temporal dimension.

While the chapters in this book are certainly not exhaustive of the field of Tibetan ritual studies, they do give one a glimpse of the very exciting directions the field is taking. Given what I have mentioned about the changes in the field of Tibetan studies in the past decades, it should not be surprising that anthropologists, historians, philologists, and specialists in religious studies—scholars of Buddhism and Bön, and of Tibet, Nepal, Mongolia, and Bhutan—should be able to have such a successful conversation about this thing called "ritual." The editor, in some ways an interloper to this field, would like to express his gratitude to all of the contributors for having been allowed to be the instigator of this fascinating dialogue.

NOTES

Most of the chapters in this volume were originally presented at an international conference, "The Practice and Theory of Tibetan Ritual," held in May of 2007 under the auspices of the Dalai Lama Endowment at the University of California Santa Barbara. The conference, which brought participants from as far away as Israel and Bhutan, was made possible by a generous gift from Robert and Marlene Veloz. The editor wishes to express his gratitude to the Velozes for their support. For their help with conference organization, the editor would like to thank Ms. Joy Davis, Dr. Gregory Hillis, Ms. Venus Nasri, and especially the Buddhist Studies graduate students at UCSB. Finally, thanks to Joel Gruber and Nathan McGovern for their help with the compilation of the bibliography and with proofreading, respectively; and thanks to Zoran Lazovic for compiling the index.

1. Tibetan calendrical specialists also identify certain days in the yearly cycle when specific rituals—for example, the hanging of prayer flags (*rlung rta*) and funerary practices—should *not* be performed, but these are rare compared to the number of auspicious days in the calendar. In contrast to this, certain days are identified as auspicious for doing specific rituals—like *homa* or burnt offerings (*byin sreg*).

2. Indeed, so much ritual is enacted in the first Tibetan month that it is also known as the "ritual month" (*cho ga zla ba*).

3. Relatively few such rituals are found in the literary corpus, but this is probably because many of these rites were transmitted orally by village priests, constituting informal traditions and practices that were never recorded in written texts. Examples of formal rituals and prayers for abundant harvests (*lo tog la phan pa'i cho ga, lo tog rgyas pa'i smon lam*); rituals for ransoming harvests from malevolent spirits (*lo glud*); and rituals of praise, supplication, and/or offering to "the god(s) of the field" (often Brahmā) can be found in written form, but many agricultural ritual traditions—like the tradition of taking the scriptures in a procession of the fields in the springtime (*'ong bskor*), or that of offering the first fruits of the harvest (*thog phud*)—constitute folk practices that, to my knowledge, never found their way into formal written liturgies. Likewise, we find in the literary canon rituals for the bathing and purification of livestock (*rkang bzhi khrus chog*), for ransoming their lives when they are attacked by evil spirits (*phyugs glud*), and for healing animal diseases (*phyugs nad sel thabs*). But one surmises that there were probably dozens of other types of rituals related to livestock—rituals that, being local, orally transmitted traditions, were never written down. Only more extensive ethnographic work will give us a complete picture of the agricultural and livestock rituals practiced among Tibetan farmers and nomads.

4. See, for example, Hugh Richardson, *Ceremonies of the Lhasa Year*, ed. Michael Aris (London: Serindia Publications, 1993), where about fifty days per year are identified as being set aside for one or another (usually religious) purpose.

5. See, for example, the claim of the *Heaped Jewel Sūtra*, cited in Longchen Rabjam, *A Treasure Trove of Scriptural Transmission: A Commentary on The Precious Treasury of the Basic Space of Phenomena*, tr. and ed. Richard Barron et al. (Junction City, CA: Padma Publishing, 2001), 93. The *sūtra* passage reads:

> There are no mantras or mudras in this.
> There is no specific need at all in this,
> Even for mandalas, deities and offerings.
> There is no need to prepare ritual articles or perform formal ceremonies.

6. For an accessible introduction to the Tibetan pantheon from an art historical perspective, see Christian Luczanits, "Infinite Variety: Form and Appearance in Tibetan Buddhist Art, Part I," *Lotus Leaves* 7/4 (2005): 1–9; "Part II," *Lotus Leaves* 8/1 (2005): 7–14.

7. Oracles are known under a variety of names like *lhapa* (*lha pa*), literally "god person," as well as "body receptacle" (*sku rten*), "dharma lord" (*chos rje*), and "hero" (*dpa' bo*).

8. See the special issue of *Revue d'Etudes Tibétains* 2 (April 2003) on the *lha srin sde brgyad;* also Stephan Beyer, *The Cult of Tārā: Magic and Ritual in Tibet* (Berkeley, CA: University of California Press, 1978), 292–301; and also Mengele's chapter in this volume.

9. *'jig rten las 'das pa'i lha*, literally, "gods who are beyond the world."

10. *'jig rten pa'i lha*, "gods of the world."

11. See Erik Pema Kunsang and Marcia Binder Schmidt, *Blazing Splendor: The Memoirs of the Dzogchen Yogi Tulku Urgyen Rinpoche* (Boudnath: Rangjung Yeshe Publications, 2005), 19, 375n22, and 377n41.

12. One is reminded here of the recent controversies surrounding the "protector" Dorje Shugden (Rdo rje shugs ldan); see Georges Dreyfus, "The Shukden Affair: History and Nature of a Quarrel," *Journal of the International Association of Buddhist Studies* 21/2 (1999): 227–70. But this is only one of a number of such controversies that has existed throughout Tibetan history. Sle lung rje drung Bzhad pa'i rdo rje (b. 1679), for example, cites such controversies as the motivation for his composition of the important *Lives of an Ocean of Oath-Bound Protectors of the Teachings; Dam can bstan srung rgya mtsho rnam par thar pa cha shas tsam brjod pa sngon med legs bshad*, 2 vols. (Leh, Ladakh: T. S. Tashigang, 1979), 1: 3–4.

13. An example of this is found in the *Zangs gling ma* biography of Padmasambhava attributed to Ye shes mstho rgyal and revealed by Nyang ral Nyi ma 'od zer (1136–1204); Eril Pema Kunsang, tr., *The Lotus-Born: The Life Story of Padmasambhava* (Boudhnath: Rangjung Yeshe Publications, 2004), chap. 9.

14. For the fascinating story of this deity's move, see the account in the video tour of his chapel at Sera by the monk Tshul khrims, "The Chapel of the Protector Deity Taok at the Mé College of Sera Monastery." [Online] Rev. July 4, 2008. Available: http://www.thdl.org/avarch/mediaflowcat/titles_browse.php?searchTerms=1044&searchType=id. [January 1, 2009].

15. See José Ignacio Cabezón, *The Hermitages of Sera* (Charlottesville, VA: THDL Publications, 2006), 37. [Online monograph] Rev. July 4, 2006. Available http://www.thdl.org/collections/cultgeo/mons/sera/hermitages/pdfs/sera_hermitages.pdf. [January 1, 2009].

16. Other, even more dramatic examples are known. For instance, concerning the way in which "the threefold *maṇḍala* of Yamāntaka" is mapped onto the rectangular plan of city of Beijing, see Ferdinand Lessing's brief note, "The Topographical Identification of Peking with Yamāntaka," in Ferdinand Lessing, *Ritual and Symbol: Collected Essays on Lamaism and Chinese Symbolism* (Taipei: Orient Cultural Service, 1976), 89–90.

17. I have Dr. Amy Heller to thank for confirming this for me.

18. See Georges Dreyfus's discussion of this issue in *The Sound of Two Hands Clapping: The Education of a Tibetan Buddhist Monk* (Berkeley, CA: University of California Press, 2003), 297.

19. For a broad overview of this litetrature, see Jens Kreinath, Jan Snoek, and Michael Stausberg, *Theorizing Ritual: Annotated Bibliography of Ritual Theory, 1966–2005* (Leiden: Brill, 2007). Books that have been especially influential in the field of religious studies include Catherine Bell, *Ritual: Perspectives and Dimensions* (Oxford: Oxford University Press, 1997); Jonathan Z. Smith, *To Take Place: Toward Theory in Ritual* (Chicago, IL: University of Chicago Press, 1987); Ronald L. Grimes, *Rite out of Place: Ritual, Media, and the Arts* (Oxford: Oxford University Press, 2006). Perhaps the best anthology of the modern Western theorization of ritual is Ronald L. Grimes, *Readings in Ritual Studies* (Upper Saddle River, NJ: Prentice Hall, 1996). More Buddhist-specific, though nonetheless broad treatments, of ritual include Robert H. Sharf, "Ritual," in *Critical Terms for the Study of Buddhism*, ed. Donald L. Lopez, Jr. (Chicago, IL: University of Chicago Press, 2005), 245–69; and Richard K. Payne, "Ritual," in *Encyclopedia of Buddhism*, ed. Robert E. Buswell, 2 vols (New York: Macmillan Reference, 2004) 2: 723–26.

20. Smith, *To Take Place*, 104.

21. Among the terms that might be translated "ritual" are words with Sanskrit equivalents, like *rim gro* (Sanskrit *paricaryā* = service/worship, *upacāra* = service/ceremony, *satkāra* = religious observance, *upasthā* = worship, etc.) and *las* (Sanskrit *karma/kriyā* = ritual action). There are also a variety of words with no Sanskrit equivalents: *zhabs brtan, phyag len* (and the compound *cho ga phyag len*), *las thabs*, and *'phyong*. See also Karmay's chapter in this volume for references to the indigenous category *gto*.

22. The word *cho ga* is old, being found in a variety of Dunhuang texts. For example, it is found in PT 1051, a treatise on dice divination. We also find it in IOL Tib J 401, a work containing a variety of healing and divination rituals, and in PT 221 and IOL Tib J 337, that contain different *dhāraṇī* rituals. These are just a few examples. The etymology of the word *cho ga* is obscure. The noun *cho* has the connotation of "meaning" or "worth"; and its opposite, *cho med* ("without *cho*") means "silly" or "meaningless." The word *cho* is also part of the compound *cho 'phrul*, meaning "miracle" or "magical display." The verb *cho ba* means "to set on," "to incite to attack," "to sic," as in "to sic a dog on somone." Although one might derive etymologies of *cho ga* based on any of these nouns or verbs, to do so would be conjectural at best, and whether or not any of these meanings of *cho* are implicit

in the word *cho ga* remains to be seen. Nor can we rule out that the fact that the word *cho ga* is etymologically primitive.

23. The Tibetan word *cho ga* is also used to translate Sanskrit *kalpa* (fitness or rule, but also simply rite or ceremony), *ācāraḥ* (conduct or rule of conduct) and a variety of words associated with the latter including *caritra* (conduct, observance, or ceremony), and *upacāra* (a practice, a service, a ceremony). *Cho ga* is also used to translate *prayoga* (a practice, an utterance, a formula to be recited, a ceremonial form).

24. For an example of the characterization of circumambulation as a form of ritual in the Western literature, see Ronald D. Schwarz, *Circle of Protest: Political Ritual in the Tibetan Uprising* (London: Hurst and Company, 1994); and Robert B. Ekvall, *Religious Observances in Tibet: Patterns and Functions* (Chicago, IL: University of Chicago Press, 1964).

25. Dbyangs can lha mo and Ko'o po'i kung, *Bod rgya nang don rig pa'i tshig mdzod*, 2 vols. (Chengdu: Si khron mi rigs dpe skrun khang, 1993), 1: 433–34: *las don sgrub thabs dang/ bya ba byed stangs sam/ go rim*. See also Krang dbyi sun et al., *Bod rgya tshig mdzod chen mo* (Beijing: Mi rigs dpe skrun khang, 1998), 821–22: *sgrub thabs dang/ bya ba'i rnam bzhag/ dmigs bsal gyi mdzad sgo/* ("A method of accomplishing [something]; an arrangement of actions; a special procedure"). A medical dictionary, Dbang 'dus, *Gso ba rig pa'i tshig mdzod g.yu thog dgongs rgyan* (Beijing: Mi rigs dpe skrun khang, 1983), 169–70, which may be the source of the two entries just cited, quotes two old sources—Zhang Gzi brjid 'bar (11th century) and De'u dmar dge bshes (b. 1672)—on the subject: *sgrub byed thabs kyi ming ste/ Zhang Gzi brjid 'bar gyis mdzad pa'i* Gdams pa sum cu pa *las/ cho ga zhes rang gi 'dod don bsgrub par byed pa'i skabs grub par byed pa'i thabs kyi ming ngo/ zhes dang/ De'u dmar dge bshes Bstan 'dzin phun tshogs kyis mdzad pa'i* Gso rig skor gyi ming tshig nyer mkho'i don gsal *las/ cho ga sgrub byed thabs kyi ming/ zhes gsung pa ltar ro/*. "[A *cho ga*] is the name given to a method of accomplishing [something]. According to Zhang Gzi brjid 'bar's *Thirty Pieces of Advice*, 'in the context of acting so as to accomplish one's own desired goal, a *cho ga* is the method followed to bring about [that aim].' And according to De'u dmar dge bshes's *A Clarification of the Meaning of Essential Medicinal Nomenclature*, 'a *cho ga* is the name given to the method for accomplishing something.' "

26. For an overview of this ritual, see His Holiness the Dalai Lama and Jeffrey Hopkins, *Kalachakra Tantra: Rite of Initiation* (Boston, MA: Wisdom Publications, 1999, 3rd edition).

27. See Beyer's discussion of simple magical rites that do not involve any deity; *The Cult of Tārā*, 303.

28. Vinaya rituals include ordination (*sdom pa 'bogs chog*), the three basic monastic rites (*gzhi gsum cho ga*)—the rite of confession (*gso sbyong*), the rite for entering into the rainy season retreat (*dbyar gnas*), and the rite for exiting from the rainy season retreat (*dgag dbye*)—as well as rituals for blessing various monastic accoutrements, such as robes (*chos gos byin rlabs kyi cho ga*).

29. For examples of this, see Beyer, *The Cult of Tārā*, 290.

30. The five related to the disciple (*slob ma'i dbang*) are water (*chu*), diadem or crown (*cod pan*), vajra (*rdo rje*), bell (*dril bu*), and name (*ming*). The five related to the vajra master (*rdo rje slob dpon*) are mantra (*sngags*), prophecy (*lung bstan*), relief (*dbugs

dbyung), vajra conduct (*rdo rje brtul zhugs*), and practical conduct (*spyod pa'i brtul zhugs*). Finally, the last portion of the vase initiation is called "permission" (*rjes gnang*). In the Kālacakra, seven rather than eleven parts of the vase empowerment are mentioned; see Hopkins, *Kalachakra Tantra*, 69, 73.

31. One thinks here of the so-called symbolic empowerment (*brda dbang*) or other "unelaborated" (*spros med*) rituals. There are also a host of simple ritual procedures, like the magical acts described in Cuevas's chapter, where the storyline, if present at all, is minimal.

32. On the ubiquity of offering to a variety of ritual genres, see John Makransky, "Offering (mChod pa) in Tibetan Ritual Literature," in *Tibetan Literature: Studies in Genre*, ed. José Ignaio Cabezón and Roger R. Jackson (Ithaca, NY: Snow Lion, 1996), 312–30.

33. See Beyer, *The Cult of Tārā*, 278, for a description of the way in which mantras (by appending different syllables, or rearranging those syllables or their directionality), and visualizations (using different colors of light etc.) can be modified "for the different functions."

34. Many Indian Tantras already contain the seeds of compendia. Such collections are also found in late Indian Buddhist works like the *Kriyāsaṃgraha;* see Tadeusz Skorupski, *Kriyāsaṃgraha: Compendium of Buddhist Rituals, An Abridged Version*, Bibliotheca Britannica, Series Continua X (Tring, UK: The Institute of Buddhist Studies, 2002). In Tibet, while the nomenclature *las tshogs* is found in the title of Tibetan works as early as the twelfth century—for example, in Sa chen Kun dga' snying po's *Sengge sgra'i sgrub thabs las tshogs dang bcas pa*—the genre as we know it probably does not really begin to flourish until two centuries later, reaching its most developed form only in the seventeenth century.

35. These topics are culled from my reading of two *las tshogs* of the deity Hayagrīva in his "Extremely Secret" form: (1) Khal kha dam tshig rdo rje, *Rta mgrin yang gsang khros pa'i chos skor* (Bylakuppe, India: Sera Byes College, 1997), 3 vols.; and a two volume collection of unknown authorship called *Rta mgrin padma yang gsang khros pa'i chos skor* (photoreproduction of a blockprint, no bibliographical information).

36. Such a structure is made explicit in 'Jam mgon kong sprul's catalogue (*dkar chag*) to the Rin chen gter mdzod. Kong sprul organizes his mammoth collection in sections: (1) empowerment, the root of the path (*lam gyi rtsa ba*); (2) proximity to and achievement of [the deity], the essence of the path (*lam gyi ngo bo*); (3) *gtor ma* rituals, which are to be done in between sessions of *sādhana* practice (*thun mtshams su bya ba*); and so forth. I have Gene Smith to thank for making his transcription of this catalogue available to me.

37. *Lha pa'i lha rnams kyi sgrub thabs kun las btus pa ba ri brgya rtsa'i rgya gzhung rnams* (Dehradun, India: G. T. K. Jodoy, N. Gyaltsen and N. Lungtok, 1970), 14 vols. See also Loden Sherab Dagyab, *Die Sadhanas der Sammlung Ba-ri Brgya-rtsa (Ikonographie und Symbolik des tibetischen Buddhismus)* (Wiesbaden: Otto Harrassowitz, 1983).

38. *Yi dam rgya mtsho'i sgrub thabs rin chen 'byung gnas* (New Delhi: Chophel Legdan, 1974–75), 2 vols. See also Martin Wilson and Martin Brauen, *Deities of Tibetan Buddhism: The Zürich Paintings of the Icons Worthwhile to See* (Bris sku mthoṅ ba don ldan) (Boston, MA: Wisdom Publications, 2000), where a collection of miniature paint-

ings related to this cycle are reproduced together with sections of the *Rin 'byung brgya rtsa.*

39. *Rin chen gter mdzod chen mo* (Paro, Bhutan: Ngrodrup and Sherab Drimay, 1976–80), 111 vols.

40. A similar point has been made by Bryan J. Cuevas, *Travels in the Nether World: Buddhist Popular Narratives of Death and the Afterlife in Tibet* (Oxford: Oxford University Press, 2008), 6–11.

41. "Diviners" is a broad category that includes a variety of individuals who utilize different means for communicating with superhuman agents: from throwing dice (*mo*) to counting the beads on a rosary (*phreng mo*), to "reading mirrors" (*phra phab pa*), to channeling spirits (*lha phab pa*). For a concise and accessible introduction to Tibetan systems of divination see Dorjee Tseten, "Tibetan Art of Divination." [Online] Available: http://www.tibet.com/Buddhism/divination.html. [December 20, 2008] See also Mengele's discussion of the interpretation of death signs in this volume.

42. In Tibetan culture generally, others' "bad-mouthing" or "gossip" (*mi kha*) was seen as a cause of misfortune, and there were rituals to counteract this.

43. Karmic debt, according to Dung dkar Blo bzang 'phrin las, being of three types—related to body (*lus*), life (*srog*), and possessions/wealth (*longs spyod*)—refers to "debts that must be repaid" (*bu lon 'jal dgos pa*); *Dung dkar tshig mdzod chen mo* (Beijing: Krung go'i bod rig pa dpe skrung khang, 2002), 1949. That repayment of debt can be ritually accomplished through the offering of ritual cakes (*lan gtor*), for example.

44. It is noteworthy that even the handbook of magic described by Cuevas was written by one of the most famous *scholars* of the Nyingma tradition, 'Ju Mi pham, an "elite" monk if there ever was one. This once again goes to show that the elite/popular or soteriological/pragmatic boundary is always porous.

45. See Beyer, *The Cult of Tārā*, 249.

46. For a list of the various *Proceedings of the International Association of Tibetan Studies* (PIATS), with the number of articles published in each volume, see "The International Association of Tibetan Studies." [Online] Available at: http://www.thdl.org/collections/journal/jiats/index.php?m=iats [December 20, 2008]. The last IATS meeting proceedings, from 2000, had 155 articles in ten volumes.

47. As this volume is going to press, another volume dealing with Tibetan ritual in a broader sense is being edited by Katia Buffetrille.

I

Written Texts at the Juncture of the Local and the Global

Some Anthropological Considerations on a Local Corpus of Tantric Ritual Manuals (Lower Mustang, Nepal)

NICOLAS SIHLÉ

[A]nthropology has signally neglected the analysis of liturgical ritual...

—*Caroline Humphrey and James Laidlaw*[1]

Anthropologists of complex, literate religious traditions have rarely succeeded at properly integrating local corpora of written religious texts (canonical scriptures, ritual manuals, etc.) into their ethnographically based analyses. The reasons for this are probably multiple. Messick has suggested that the exclusion of written texts is "virtually an organizing principle" in the disciplinary history of the social sciences.[2] In the particular case of Islam, Bowen has noted that Islamic rituals have been shaped to "local cultural concerns and... universalistic scriptural imperatives"; as such, they "fit comfortably neither in an ethnographic discourse of bounded cultural wholes nor in an Islamicist discourse of a scripture-based normative Islam."[3] There would thus seem to be some inherent lack of fit between written religious texts as objects of study and (at least traditional) understandings of anthropological practices and concerns. Actually, the assumption that "cultures" are distinct, bounded wholes has been by now thoroughly critiqued.[4] But even armed with such insights—and assuming training in the locally relevant literary languages—one is forced to admit that written texts are particularly difficult, hybrid, and complex objects. Very often, religious texts have been created at points in time and space far removed from their ethnographic contexts; they have thus in a sense a (partially) "alien" or "exogenous" character—although they can be at the same time crucial elements of distinctly local constructions of meanings. Leaving aside questions of interpreting authorial meaning, one may want to argue, with Lambek, that for the anthropologist religious "texts by themselves are silent; they become socially relevant through their enunciation, through citation, through acts of reading, reference, and interpretation."[5] Yet, teasing out their relevance in acts of reading—as when ritual manuals are read during the performances of rituals—can be extremely challenging.

Compared, for instance, to the localized variants of the Islamic Feast of Sacrifice studied by Bowen,[6] Tibetan Buddhist rituals are often characterized by a strongly dominant textual, liturgical component, a component which can be of grueling length to the dedicated but often imperfectly literate anthropologist, who may be struggling to read cursive scripts of varying quality over the shoulders of the officiants, while remaining attentive to possible nontextual or peri-ritual dimensions of the event, as well as trying to fight off the penetrating cold! However, the greatest challenge, by far, is of a theoretical and methodological nature: What is the local, ethnographic relevance of the ritual manuals and other texts that religious specialists intone, sometimes for hours at a stretch? Anthropologists have looked more often at the social or political economy of texts as value-laden objects, or at the magical uses of such texts' inherent power, be it through contact, through the mere intonation of the words, or otherwise.[7] But in the present case, these texts are not just circulated, or manipulated, but definitely *read* (or recited)—sometimes for hours or even days at a time—as core components of exorcisms or other rituals. Are these (most often exogenous) ritual manuals, in their very textuality, anthropologically relevant objects that lend themselves to thinking about a local sociocultural order, or possibly about the complex juncture between a local order and the larger tradition that encompasses it?[8] Tambiah, in a rural Thai-Lao Buddhist context, repeatedly expressed his sense of the "paradox" that the often radical disjunction between exogenous textual meanings and local practices appeared to constitute.[9]

This study focuses on the case of a small Tibetan society (approximately 3,500 inhabitants), known as Baragaon, or Lower Mustang, in northern Nepal, where a southwestern Tibetan dialect is spoken. In particular, this essay is about Chongkor (Chos 'khor), a small village and temple community of moderately literate tantrists or *ngagpa* (*sngags pa*), nonmonastic, householder tantric priests. I conducted eighteen months of fieldwork there in the late 1990s. Chongkor consisted at that time of some twenty households, with altogether eight tantrists, all patrilineal descendents of the founder, a tantric master from Central Tibet who settled there in the seventeenth century.

In Chongkor, as elsewhere in the Tibetan world, most of the local religious texts are exogenous, in the sense that they were composed outside of the local community or prior to its founding. Some of the Chongkor texts are commonly used throughout large parts of the Tibetan world; many others belong to more obscure traditions. This largely exogenous, written corpus with historical genealogies that branch out to the larger world of Tibetan Buddhism is a fundamental component of the local religious tradition, and has strongly contributed to shaping it. At the same time, there is in no way a simple correspondence between these texts' "content" (a notion that needs to be problematized) and local religious understandings and practices. It simply will not do to treat these texts as vessels of some unproblematic "meaning" just waiting to be translated (or, for the locals, to be internalized). Here, I approach the local corpus of religious written texts, and especially tantric ritual manuals, with their local appendices and variants, and their specific social economy, as key (albeit all too often neglected) elements situated at the juncture between a local sociocultural universe and the larger world of Tibetan Buddhism.

A number of influential, or formerly influential, mainly dualist models of the structure of the religious field may seem to possess some relevance for our study; after further examination, however, the present case seems to resist their application. Thus, in the study of such a community of moderately literate tantrists, drawing relations and contrasts with the elite of Tibetan Buddhism is useful and important. However, a simple scheme opposing elite and popular religion would be inappropriate. Two-tiered elite versus popular models, however they are articulated,[10] do not sufficiently recognize the variety and relativity of positions. How do we account for the local religious elite, which are perceived by the elite of the great religious centers as ignorant, and as belonging to the uncouth world of the village? The dualism of these models does not leave any space for people like the Chongkor tantrists—for religious specialists other than those who belong to the more learned and prestigious Tibetan religious elites. Instead, at Chongkor, we have specialists who are strongly inscribed within a local universe with its own coherence, but who at the same time are part of a greater, diverse, pan-Tibetan tradition, which partially impregnates the local socioreligious universe.

Similarly, I would argue that the important duality of "universal Church" versus "local religion," as we find in William Christian's study of Catholicism in sixteenth-century Spain, is not very useful in this particular case. Christian distinguishes between two "levels": that of the sacraments, liturgies, and calendar of the universal Church, and a "local religion" based on saints, sanctuaries, and festivals with a properly local character, a domain in which the clergy had only limited authority.[11] In Chongkor, however, the main deities that are worshipped are in no real sense "local." Thus, as opposed to the Virgin or the saint who is worshipped in a given place under a specific name, or to Avalokiteśvara in his identity of Bungadyah in the Kathmandu valley,[12] here the main tutelary deity, Mañjuśrī Yamāntaka, is a universal tantric Buddhist deity, devoid of particular associations with the temple in which his cult takes place.

A model that has been influential particularly in studies of the Hindu as well as of the Buddhist world is Redfield and Marriott's model of the literate, urban "great tradition" and the village, oral "little traditions."[13] I do not wish to dwell on the critiques that have been formulated here. Suffice it to say that this model's association of two social groups with two assumedly very different cultural constructions is problematic.[14] In the anthropology of Theravada Buddhism, Redfield's model was reformulated as an opposition between the "great tradition" of scriptural Buddhism and the "little traditions" of Thai, Burmese, or Sri Lankan Buddhism, in particular in their more popular or common manifestations.[15] Some of these formulations, like a number of other dualist schemes that oppose learned and popular levels, doctrinal precepts and practice, or normative text and lived traditions, are marked by a somewhat asociological and ahistorical view of the first term of the duality.

More important, however, Redfield's model did address an essential question: that of the relations between a local order and a great translocal tradition. In particular, Redfield stressed the importance of studying the role of religious specialists and of diverse media in the communication between the two.[16] My work joins this conversation, the recent attention given to institutions, media, and processes (of communication, conversion, or integration and differentiation, etc.) that operate at the juncture between great religious traditions, local sociocultural universes, and regional, national, or more global contexts.[17]

In my work on Chongkor, I have emphasized that this local tradition of specialists cannot be understood outside of an entire context of relative geographical isolation, of socially constructed relative closure (with descent, especially, functioning as a primary determinant of social and religious recruitment), and also of interactions with the great tradition of Tibetan Buddhism, with the broader Tibetan world, with the Nepalese state, etc.[18] For this community, which lacks institutionalized links to Tibetan religious centers, one may note that religious contacts have been only sporadic, and often fortuitous. Finally, larger, global, structural changes have also impacted the local tradition. For instance, the Tibetan exile has led to a reconfiguration of the transnational order of Tibetan Buddhism, with special consequences for its monastic component. Thus an increasing number of young monks from small Himalayan societies are now receiving training in Tibetan exile monasteries, institutions that have been able to garner considerable transnational patronage. (Equivalent institutions for the training of tantrists do not exist.) In an indirect way, this is now also impacting the power relations and prestige differentials between monks and tantrists in these small Himalayan societies.

An important medium in the interaction between the local order of Chongkor tantrists and the world of Tibetan Buddhism is the written word, and in particular religious texts. In a context where literacy is modest at best, and limited to a minority, the nature of this medium needs to be carefully examined. I summarize just a few points here. Thus, one should emphasize the strong interpenetration of writing and orality.[19] The assumed fixity of the written word should also be nuanced.[20] Generally speaking, a ritual text is held to be invariable, and this is constitutive of its authority; however, the local tantrists live in a world where the different manuscript exemplars of a text show a number of alterations, and sometimes diverge. Here, the authority of the written word is never absolute.

Finally, one should beware of overly logocentric approaches to writing and religious transmission. Religious transmission here is essentially a matter of training in the performance of ritual, a training which is based largely on students' observation and repetition of their elders' bodily practices (ritual gestures, chanting, etc.). A large part of the texts is devoid of meaning for the tantrists: Sanskrit mantras, or abstruse technical terms, and tantric symbolism. There is also a certain degree of incoherence or obscurity in many tantric texts, not to mention the physical degradation of many of the ritual manuals. To quite an extent, ritual texts and words, over and above their semantic content, are here primarily instruments for the mobilization of ritual power.

I would now like to look at the Chongkor written texts from three different angles, which together allow us a glimpse of the historical process of structuring that this tradition went through, of the particular social economy of the local texts, and of how elements of a (partially) written large, encompassing tradition have been "domesticated" in, or adapted to, this local sociocultural universe.[21]

The Emergent Structure of the Chongkor Ritual Corpus

At the risk of oversimplifying things, and of disregarding the nuanced textual scholarship of several of the contributions found in this volume, if one leaves out a number of minor components, one may say that most Tantric rituals performed in the present village context are composed of two main sections. The first is composed primarily of what we can call the *shung* (*gzhung*), or "main texts," addressed to one or more tutelary deities, and consisting of invitations, offerings, and requests of a general nature. The second section is focused on a particular aim (exorcism, the calling hither of prosperity, etc.), which is pursued through specific appendices. (Simpler tantric rituals may often do without the first section.)

Tantric rituals often belong to a larger cycle, or *kor* (*skor*): a collection of rituals all centered on a single tutelary deity or set of tutelary deities, and on their associated protectors. In a large Tibetan monastic center, for any given purpose, one will typically choose a complete ritual, including the appropriate appendices, within one of the several ritual cycles in use. In Chongkor, however, the boundaries of the ritual cycles appear to have been highly porous: the ritual texts of different cycles have been combined in various ways. Thus, ritual appendices derived from a cycle different than that of the first section of the ritual may be enacted, and these secondary actions may be entrusted to different tutelary deities than those actually invoked in the first part. The first section in itself may comprise the main texts (*shung*) of tutelary deities from several different cycles. On the altar, the ritual cakes or *torma*, which serve as offerings to and sometimes as the "support" of the different deities, are simply juxtaposed, and during the ritual, the texts of these deities are read following a technique called *pel* (*spel*), or "grouping": all the invitations are read together, then all the offerings, etc. In that process, the officiants go back and forth between texts belonging to different ritual cycles. Sometimes they manage to switch from one to the next *without* breaking the flow of the chanting; in those moments, these texts from different cycles truly merge into one continuous chant. In some rituals, the merging is stronger still, the ritual cakes for two tutelary deities of different cycles being merged, *dü* (*bsdus*), into one single cake.

Finally, all the important (and many minor) deities invoked in the Chongkor rituals are addressed in one short ritual sequence that closes off all Chongkor rituals, called *Shagsöl* (*gshegs gsol*), the *Invitation to Depart*. Here, the boundaries between tantric cycles break down completely, and the term *bricolage* comes to mind as appropriate; but this text, importantly, is also a relatively *synthetic*, locally constructed discourse on the Chongkor tradition.[22] This concluding rite in effect performs a certain ordering of the local tradition, through the linear sequence of deities' names, through the particular importance it gives to one central deity, Mañjuśrī Yamāntaka (the wrathful "Slayer of Yama"), and through its emphasis on exorcism and the domain of violent, *dragpo* (*drag po*, Skt. *raudra*), ritual activity. This structural analysis, when conjoined with written and oral sources that provide us with some indications of the historical sequence in which new cycles were successively added to the local, evolving tradition, gives us an idea of the processes through which a local tantric tradition was created. Everything discussed here seems to contradict the tantric logic of separate transmission of sacred ritual cycles (*kor*), the basic units of ritual revelation, but the principles that we see at play in this Himalayan community are probably far more general than we would guess from the perspective of ritual practice in, say, elite Tibetan monastic contexts.

The Particular Social Economy of the Local Texts

Religious specialization may ultimately depend on individuals agreeing to engage in a given path of religious training, but in the Chongkor community such specialization is also strongly determined by sociological factors. The particular social economy of the ritual manuals is just one example of this. Although tantrists tend to place special emphasis on descent, the basic social and juridical unit of the local society is the house, with "main houses," or *drongba* (*grong pa*), having permanency and the full privileges of citizenship, and a variety of types of "secondary houses," *khaldura* (*kha 'thor ba*), that have less permanence and fewer civic rights. Religious texts like ritual manuals belong typically to the owner of the house. After his marriage, the eldest son becomes the new master of the house. His father, who might be an elderly tantrist, might decide to leave the main house to his son, and to live in a secondary house. He can still use the texts, but they do not belong to him any more; he only retains a limited usufruct. The texts the father does not commonly use need to be deposited in the main house, even if the son is not a tantrist. Thus, the proximity and access to the religious texts are sociologically determined.

The importance of texts extends far beyond their immediate religious use. In the Chongkor community of tantrists, although no one would put it this way, a crucial material and sociological factor of recruitment is the possession of a complete set of ritual manuals. Typically, and very strongly, in local ideology, tantrists are recruited from among the eldest sons of tantrists; and these, with a few exceptions, are typically masters of main houses. During my stay, a boy from a secondary house, whose father was not a tantrist, requested repeatedly of an elder tantrist that he teach him the alphabet. His requests were always ignored. I was all the more surprised, given that the community had a real dearth of young men engaged in the learning of the local religious tradition, and I asked the elder tantrist in private the reasons for his refusal. He answered simply that there were no tantrists in the boy's house. On the surface, this answer simply seemed to reflect the tendency toward patrilineal succession that is so widespread among tantrists. In recent generations, only in a few, very exceptional cases has a young Chongkor man started religious training when neither his father nor his paternal grandfather were themselves tantrists. However, after further inquiry, it emerged that my informant's answer also implied a more material form of determinism: Someone who would not inherit texts could not become a tantrist. I realized that none of the current Chongkor tantrists had ever copied more than just a few folios of text. Most of the manuals in use had been copied in the nineteenth century. In a community, where writing in Tibetan was hardly taught and learnt any longer (and where the ability to write in Nepali had definitely become more appealing in terms of potential economic benefits), the individual reproduction of several hundred folios in the Tibetan script had become an insurmountable task.

All this is a potent reminder of the inadequacy of the modern Western assumption that "religious practice" is a matter of individual choice. It shows the powerful impact that material and sociological conditions can have on literacy and religious activity or identity. A Bourdieu-inspired perspective might suggest that the elderly tantrist's refusal was a case of protecting the socioreligious monopoly of a priestly group. I agree that we can talk here of a socially constructed, relative closure of the group, but in a less strategic sense; I would suggest that for the elderly tantrist, starting to teach the boy how to read the complicated Tibetan script was simply not worth the effort. For him, the boy, lacking a set of texts, could never become a tantrist.

The Domestication of a Particular Genre of Religious Literature

In one sequence of their rituals, called *Lorgyü* (*bla rgyud*, literally "Lineage of Masters"), the Chongkor tantrists invoke a certain sequence of names. In appearance, this text belongs to the genre of the "prayer to the masters," *lamé söldeb* (*bla ma'i gsol 'debs*). These texts, in Beyer's terms, address "the entire lineage of the gurus," who "are asked to empower the practitioners to the effective performance of the ritual."[23] Learned members of the Tibetan clergy, and many a textual scholar, would consider the lineage of the Chongkor *Lorgyü* "incomplete": rather than starting from the deity or master who initially revealed the teaching, it starts from the seventeenth-century founder of Chongkor; it also does not reach down to the recent generations of the community's masters.

Although this text is a local composition, it poses problems of interpretation for the Chongkor tantrists. Does the sequence of names it contains refer to a master-to-disciple lineage, as is typically the case in the "prayer to the masters" genre, or is it the sequence of the tantrists who occupied the position of lama, or religious head, of the Chongkor community and village temple, a position granted by seniority to one of the qualified tantrists? The Chongkor descendants of the founder constitute a clan, subdivided into four segments, which I will call A, B, C, and D. The Chongkor tantrists' *Lorgyü* manuscripts are of variable length. Some have only fifteen names; the longest one, belonging to an elderly tantrist of segment B, has twenty-three names. The last name in this version, Panjor Gyamtso (Dpal 'byor rgya mtsho), possibly refers to the master of this tantrist's grandfather, who may have added this last name to the sequence after his master's demise. The manuscript was later inherited by his grandson, the current owner. The large number of names, covering a period spanning less than three hundred years, suggests that the text actually lists tantrists who served as lama of the community—although not all of them, since some of Panjor Gyamtso's predecessors, still remembered in local memory, seem to be missing. So this may not be exactly the same thing as a typical Tibetan "prayer to the masters." But this genre has definitely provided the form and the vocabulary for the present text: its very name is characteristic of the "prayer to the masters" genre, and the tantrists invoked by the text are called in one instance "Fathers and Sons," *yabsé* (*yab sras*), a typical designation for masters and disciples.

It is noteworthy that the first names of the sequence have the title "lama," or "master," whereas the following ones all have the title *ngagchang* (*sngags 'chang*), "mantra-holder" or "mantra adept"—a rather literary synonym of *ngagpa*, "tantrist," rarely used in colloquial speech, and definitely with elite connotations. However, "mantra-holder" does not quite carry the same connotation or religious status as the word "lama." It may not be irrelevant to mention that for a number of generations the Chongkor community has been transmitting its religious tradition without any formal initiation or empowerment, *wang* (*dbang*, Skt. *abhiśeka*). (See the Introduction to this volume.) One may want to speculate whether the switch in titles from "lama" to the somewhat less elevated *ngagchang*, in the text, reflects a historical accident. Did this possibly occur at the moment when the Chongkor lama stopped conferring initiations (a practice integral to the notion of lama as religious master in many Tibetan understandings)? However, here one can only speculate; more historical evidence would be needed in order to reconstruct the twin trajectories, in Chongkor, of the lama institution and of the *Lorgyü* text.

In the local discourses on this text, beyond the master-to-disciple lineage and the sequence of those who held the position of lama in the local community, yet another type of lineage appears: the agnatic, hereditary lineage. One tantrist of segment C, maybe slightly emboldened by the generous amount of beer he had drunk on one cold, wintry day, claimed to me that the term *ngagchang* was specific to his own clan segment. According to a layman of segment D, his father, Lama Tsering (Bla ma Tshe ring), who was the son of the aforementioned Panjor Gyamtso, claimed to belong to a lineage of twenty-five lamas.[24] Lama Tsering's count might have been based on the fact that he himself and his grandfather, also a former lama of the community, were not a part of the sequence of twenty-three names. Proud of this illustrious line, Lama Tsering's son would sometimes argue over this with his neighbor, a member of segment B, at that time the lama of the community, stating that there had not been a single other lama before him in his line (and that there would be no other). Finally, a tantrist of segment A, who descends from the founder in the senior line of descent, claims that most of the Chongkor lamas ("maybe forty or fifty") originated from his house.

These contradictory and unverifiable claims show the temptation to think of this text as a genealogy, and to see the sequence of Chongkor lamas in terms of the residential descent groups that are at the heart of the social life and identity of the Chongkor people. We may note that a text bearing the imprint of the local social order may constitute a strategic resource even for illiterate actors like Lama Tsering's son. Fundamentally, the "Lineage of Masters" text shows how an important genre of the Indo-Tibetan Buddhist ritual literature was adapted to Chongkor religious institutions. It further shows how the hybrid product, with its crucial implications in terms of status or symbolic capital—what is at stake here is nothing less than the social affiliation of the lamas, the highest religious officeholders of the community—is finally reinterpreted locally in accordance with a worldview centered on descent. This worldview is largely shared throughout the local society, and there are numerous other Tibetan examples in which teachings, religious qualities, or qualifications for religious offices are transmitted in biological lineages—although ultimately, these phenomena largely lack scriptural authority in the normative Buddhist treatises. Thus, this text gives us an insight into some of the complex relations between local and larger norms, practices and interpretations—between the local production of a religious text, its contested interpretation, and the norms of the larger genre that was its inspiration.

As a last example, let me briefly suggest some of the limits of this enterprise of examining the relations between a local socioreligious order and a larger, complex, literate religious tradition from the angle of religious texts. We have seen instances of adaptations of ritual traditions, textual materials, and genres to a particular sociocultural context. We should not lose sight of the fact that the written word has a pronounced tendency to be transmitted unchanged. What about the relations between largely invariant liturgical rituals and their social contexts?

Scripted, Liturgical Rituals, and Their Contexts

As I have argued elsewhere, the ritual that best lends itself to thinking about the Chongkor tantrists (both for the anthropologist and, to some extent, for these tantrists themselves) is the *hrinen* (*sri gnon, sri mnan*), the "pressing down of the *hri* (*sri*) demons," which are responsible especially for recurrent deaths in the community, be it in a household or among the livestock. For lack of space, I provide here only a brief description of this ritual, and the reader is asked, in effect, to bear with a primarily methodological discussion in which the ethnographic detail is in large part substituted by footnote references.[25]

The *hrinen* is the most violent (*drag po*) domestic exorcism of the Chongkor tantrists. Until the 1950s, they were asked to carry out this exorcism in conjunction with the annual cult, *lhachö* (*lha mchod*), of the household protector deities in almost all households of the northern side of their valley: the *hrinen* would be performed in the evening and into the night, and then the *lhachö* on the next morning. As a result of a conflict, however, the patronage enjoyed by the Chongkor tantrists declined, and the critiques of a reformist Tibetan monk regarding the excessive recourse to this "extreme" kind of ritual have led to a further reduction of its practice. It remains, however, one of the most commonly performed exorcisms of the Chongkor repertoire.

The ritual is striking in the degree of power and violence that it manifests. Throughout the many hours of reading the ritual texts, beating the drum, and clashing the cymbals, one sees displayed a redundancy of modes of slaying the demons or enemies. Effigies of *hri* demons are upset, showered with "toxic substances," and stuffed into a skull.[26] The effigy of an "enemy," or *drao* (*dgra bo*), is threatened with various weapons, bound, stabbed, cut up (at this point, the idea of killing is very present in the tantrists' comments), then offered to the deities and ingested partially by the officiant himself. The skull is wrapped, bound, sealed, and pressed down under the feet of all those in attendance. The trapped *hri* is submitted to a form of *powa* (*'pho ba*), a rite which ideally dispatches the slain demon to some Buddha's pure land, and which is then followed by a *dogpa* (*zlog pa*), or "repelling" rite. The package is finally buried, pounded under the earth, and imprisoned under heavy stones and fire.

The ritual's redundancy is both a highly convincing manifestation of violent power and a sign of just how hard it is to get rid of *hri* demons—by definition, agents of recurrent misfortune. It is quite telling that the demons are both "killed" (actually, several times) *and* repelled, or prevented from returning.[27]

As we are concerned here primarily with issues surrounding the texts and their meanings, it should be mentioned that the tantrist officiates throughout most of the ritual essentially alone, most often in the altar room of the house. He is provided with all the necessary material ingredients for the ritual, his cup of beer is maintained full throughout, and, during the final phases of the ritual, which involve more manipulation of the effigies, knives, and other implements, an assistant is delegated on behalf of the householder. It would be very uncommon, however, for anyone from the patron's household to remain with him throughout the long hours of reading and reciting, the texts being written, it should be repeated, in a complex and sometimes obscure literary language that nonliterate laypeople cannot possibly follow in any substantial way. Only in the final phases, and especially when the skull is to be pressed under the feet of all members of the household, does the room fill up.

Compared to the séance of a medium, for instance, the *hrinen*, like all textual rituals of the Chongkor tantrists, leaves very little room for personal initiative; the quality of the officiant's "performance" is therefore hardly an issue. We have here a "liturgy-centered" (as opposed to performance-centered) form of ritual.[28] One officiant may master the crescendo and intensity of the climax a little better than another, or he may be more skilled in creating a sense of seamless flow as the ritual moves from one section to the next, but on the whole, the ritual is scripted: it follows a text and a precise choreography which are independent of the circumstances of the performance. Whether the *hri* demons are exorcised for a prosperous hotel owner who, over the preceding months, has lost several mules, or in a house that has experienced a series of deaths, or in the officiant's own home after he dreamt of *hri* demons "rising," the ritual is basically the same. In Rappaport's terms, the "canonical," invariant component or dimension of the ritual appears to predominate almost to the exclusion of its "indexical," context-specific dimension.[29] Of course, the "indexical" is not totally absent: consider, for instance, the *social organization* of the ritual, or the integration of the *ritual experience* within domestic trajectories of success, misfortune, concerns, and so forth. Nonetheless, the contrast, as stated earlier, does ring quite true if we focus on the textual, liturgical component of the ritual—which is precisely what we are concerned with here. The importance of the "canonical," invariant component is here largely related to the written basis of the ritual, albeit in complex ways.[30] The (relative) transportability and permanence of the written word have contributed to a highly particular fact: the spread of thousands of folios of virtually identical textual materials throughout the Tibetan cultural area and throughout the centuries. Some of the texts, or themes, are even the translation of Indic antecedents. How can rituals based in a substantial way on this kind of written texts be analyzed with reference to particular contexts of transmission and performance?

The most widely read analysis of a Tibetan exorcism is a chapter of Ortner's *Sherpas Through Their Rituals*.[31] Unfortunately, it is based on a mode of symbolic interpretation which plays ingeniously with the semantic categories, but displays a recurring arbitrary character.[32] Justifications internal to the Sherpa culture are often tenuous or absent, as in a passage where the effigies violently destroyed in a common exorcism are interpreted to represent a god, itself presented as a symbol of the rich and the clergy.[33] The general aim of the book, which guides the entire analysis, is itself debatable: the claim, following Geertz's scheme, is that rituals, as both models *of* Sherpa society and models *for* action, reflect the tensions of the Sherpa socioeconomic order, and provide solutions to those tensions through a transformation of the experience of the participants, in Lienhardt's sense.[34] The study, however, fails to show that the Buddhist exorcisms studied there play this double role.[35]

However, some of the criticisms directed at the book have themselves been somewhat inadequate. Some critics have argued that a textual, historically invariant, and geographically very widespread ritual form cannot exhibit any (strong) correlation with a given, local social order.[36] This critique omits, however, symbols' fundamental potential for multivocality. The ritual also should not be conflated with its text. Ortner's analysis actually ignores the texts, and is based on other elements: the manipulation of effigies, the social identity of the different actors (officiants, subaltern assistants, etc.), and elements of local discourse. There is assuredly a place here for an analysis that integrates patterns of ritual practice with a local context of social relations and unfinished systems of essentially multivocal symbols.

But how far can the texts, as artifacts that (for their readers) simultaneously carry local, external, and sometimes obscure meanings, be drawn into this analysis? For lack of space, I will just briefly suggest some of the relatively little-trodden and ill-charted paths of inquiry that open up here at the juncture of largely exogenous written texts and local worlds of meaning. I have attempted to pursue these directions elsewhere, notably in the description and analysis of the *hrinen* exorcism.[37] One important factor is obviously the degree of literacy of those who interact with the texts. In their exegeses, more literate and learned informants typically tend to fall back on normative, text-based theological constructions—interpretive systems characterized by a high degree of internal coherence, which are very often articulated independently from local, lived experiences. On the other hand, in the case of Chongkor's semiliterate tantrists, faced with texts that are full of corrupted spellings, attempts to obtain exegeses of textual passages are often unproductive, and can induce a strong sense of awkwardness. Choosing the right informants, setting up situations where an informant would feel inclined to provide some degree of spontaneous comments, and sensing how far one can probe into the frontier of what does and does not makes sense for informants is methodologically challenging, but crucial. Informants may here be somewhat less loquacious than their more learned counterparts; but on the whole, their interpretations probably tend to be grounded in locally more relevant schemes of understanding and practice. In cases of lesser degrees of literacy, the aim of such soundings can be to try to suggest some of the local contours of the aforementioned frontier between the familiar and the unknown or alien; in my experience, starting with something that the priests are familiar with, such as the details of the structure of the ritual, provides a useful point of departure. In this way, we can gradually recognize how (in Rappaport's terms) a primarily "canonical," liturgical, textual ritual like the *hrinen* actually is (in part) integrated within the local cultural fabric, as well as the substantial element of incoherence and obscurity which the ritual manuals do retain for the officiating tantrists. As in all ethnographic explorations, one must here probe in the dark, but most importantly, let oneself be guided by the informants' more spontaneous comments, and follow their hints as to what passages of the texts speak more to them. Crucially, in this approach, it will not do to simply substitute a translation of the text for the local understandings, as is all too often still done in ethnographic writing. Rather, in the analysis of the *hrinen*, I have shown, for instance, how the ritual as practiced (in the reading, in the other actions, and in the symbolism of the ritual implements) both follows and, occasionally, departs from the text, revealing places where an oral tradition separate from the text takes over in prescribing the course of action. I suggest that, through this kind of careful ethnography of the written word and of its place in local meanings and practices, one can try to bring liturgical (or other) texts into the analysis of the larger themes of a local sociocultural world. For instance, I have shown that in the interplay between texts, effigies, oral commentaries, and legends, there is an ambiguity that is maintained concerning the identity of the agents against whom the exorcism is directed: the fine line between "demons" and personal enemies—that is, between exorcism and sorcery—is often blurred.

Conclusions

Especially when one is dealing with complex, partially obscure texts like tantric ritual manuals and with semiliterate officiants, much of what is found in the texts may ultimately mean little to their readers, and may largely evade the ethnographer's net. However, provided the ethnographer listens attentively, informants' comments will suggest a local (in Rappaport's terms, "indexical") flavor to the seemingly "canonical" and presumably rather stable, if not invariant, liturgies of the rituals. Through the selection of elements discussed earlier, I hope to have suggested the importance and some of the possibilities of a fuller ethnographical engagement with liturgical rituals, and of a more fully anthropological appreciation of the role of religious texts, as well as the limits of such an undertaking. I also hope to have shown how texts are rich, complex objects situated at a crucial juncture for the anthropologist interested in the transactions that take place between local orders and larger flows of culture, as occurs here between the local socioreligious order of a Himalayan tantric priestly community and the larger, complex religious tradition of Tibetan tantric Buddhism.

NOTES

I would like to gratefully acknowledge the stimulating comments of Fernand Meyer, Eve Danziger, Fred Damon, and José Cabezón at various stages of the elaboration of this work.

1. Caroline Humphrey and James Laidlaw, *The Archetypal Actions of Ritual: A Theory of Ritual Illustrated by the Jain Rite of Worship* (New York: Oxford University Press, 1994), 80.

2. Brinkley M. Messick, *Written Culture* (CSST Working Paper #96, 1993), 2 (permission for citing received from author). A number of prominent scholars actually have emphasized the need to integrate a familiarity with indigenous literatures and textual scholarship into the anthropology of complex, literary cultures: Louis Dumont and David F. Pocock, "For a Sociology of India," *Contributions to Indian Sociology*, no. 1 (1957): 7; David L. Snellgrove, "For a Sociology of Tibetan Speaking Regions," *Central Asiatic Journal* 11/3 (1966): 199–219; Stanley J. Tambiah, *Buddhism and the Spirit Cults in North-East Thailand* (Cambridge: Cambridge University Press, 1970), chap. 21; and Michel Strickmann, "History, Anthropology, and Chinese Religion," *Harvard Journal of Asiatic Studies* 40/1 (1980): 203–48. These discussions, however, have not gone into the complex methodological issues raised by an *ethnography* of local textual corpora.

3. John R. Bowen, "On Scriptural Essentialism and Ritual Variation: Muslim Sacrifice in Sumatra and Morocco," *American Ethnologist* 19/4 (1992): 656.

4. See for instance Eric R. Wolf, *Europe and the People without History* (Berkeley: University of California Press, 1982), 3–7; Lila Abu-Lughod, "Writing Against Culture," in *Recapturing Anthropology: Working in the Present*, ed. Richard G. Fox (Santa Fe: School of American Research Press, 1991), 137–62; or, in Tibetan studies, Stan R. Mumford, *Himalayan Dialogue: Tibetan Lamas and Gurung Shamans in Nepal* (Madison: University of Wisconsin Press, 1989).

5. Michael Lambek, "Certain Knowledge, Contestable Authority: Power and Practice on the Islamic Periphery," *American Ethnologist* 17/1 (1990): 23. One may want,

however, to slightly temper the first statement by noting that written texts are endowed with a degree of semantic autonomy from their various sociocultural contexts of production, reproduction, and use. On the concept of "semantic autonomy" in Ricœur's theory of hermeneutics, see Paul Ricœur, "Speaking and Writing," in *Interpretation Theory: Discourse and the Surplus of Meaning* (Fort Worth: Texas Christian University Press, 1976), *passim*.

6. Bowen, "On Scriptural Essentialism and Ritual Variation."

7. See, for instance, Stan R. Mumford, *Himalayan Dialogue*, 80–92; Geoff H. Childs, "How to Fund a Ritual: Notes on the Social Usage of the Kanjur (bKa' 'gyur) in a Tibetan Village," *Tibet Journal* 30/2 (2005): 41–48; or, for other Buddhist traditions, Tambiah, *Buddhism and the Spirit Cults in North-East Thailand*, and "The Magical Power of Words," *Man* N.S. 3/2 (1968): 175–208; David N. Gellner, "'The Perfection of Wisdom': A Text and Its Uses in Kwā Bāhāh, Lalitpur," in *Change and Continuity: Studies in the Nepalese Culture of the Kathmandu Valley*, ed. S. Lienhard (Alessandrio: Edizioni dell'Orso, 1996), 223–40.

8. For an elegant attempt to relate certain popular Newar religious texts to some of the features of their past sociocultural contexts, see Todd Lewis, *Popular Buddhist Texts from Nepal: Narratives and Rituals of Newar Buddhism* (Albany: State University of New York Press, 2000).

9. Tambiah, *Buddhism and the Spirit Cults in North-East Thailand*, 166–67 and chap. 12, *passim*.

10. In one common use of these terms they refer to the opposition between institutionalized religions and a set of nonsystematized beliefs and practices, devoid of specific institutional contexts. For China, see Meir Shahar and Robert P. Weller, "Introduction: Gods and Society in China," in *Unruly Gods: Divinity and Society in China*, ed. Meir Shahar and Robert P. Weller (Honolulu: University of Hawai'i Press, 1996), 1. For Tibet, see Geoffrey Samuel, *Civilized Shamans: Buddhism in Tibetan Societies* (Washington DC: Smithsonian Institution Press, 1993), chap. 10; but also Nicolas Sihlé, "Buddhism in Tibet and Nepal: Vicissitudes of Traditions of Power and Merit," in *Buddhism in World Cultures: Comparative Perspectives*, ed. Stephen C. Berkwitz (Santa Barbara: ABC-CLIO, 2006), 250–51. This framework has little relevance for our present purposes. Possibly the most useful way of conceptualizing the elite versus popular duality here would be in terms of the opposition between religious elites (whether hierocracy or virtuosi) and the others, typically the popular masses, without any prior assumption with regard to their respective forms of religiosity, and without excluding the possible sharing of numerous religious traits. See Stephen Sharot, *A Comparative Sociology of World Religions: Virtuosos, Priests, and Popular Religion* (New York: New York University Press, 2001), 10–19.

11. William A. Christian, Jr., *Local Religion in Sixteenth-Century Spain* (Princeton: Princeton University, 1981), 3, 20, 158–66.

12. On the complex layers of identity of Bungadyah, see Bruce M. Owens, "The Politics of Divinity in the Kathmandu Valley: The Festival of Bungadya/Rato Matsyendranath" (Ph.D. diss., Columbia University, 1989), chap. 5.

13. See Robert Redfield, "The Social Organization of Tradition," *Far Eastern Quarterly* 15/1 (1955): 13–21, and McKim Marriott, "Little Communities in an Indigenous

Civilization," in *Village India: Studies in the Little Community*, ed. McKim Marriott (Chicago: University of Chicago Press, 1955), 171–222.

14. See Christopher J. Fuller, *The Camphor Flame: Popular Hinduism and Society in India* (Princeton: Princeton University Press, 1992), 25–26, and Stephen Sharot, *A Comparative Sociology of World Religions*, 14, 265n33.

15. See especially Gananath Obeyesekere, "The Great Tradition and the Little in the Perspective of Sinhalese Buddhism," *Journal of Asian Studies* 22/2 (1963): 142.

16. Redfield, "The Social Organization of Tradition," 19–21.

17. See P. Steven Sangren, "Great Tradition and Little Traditions Reconsidered: The Question of Cultural Integration in China," *Journal of Chinese Studies* 1(1984): 1–24; Shahar and Weller, "Introduction"; John R. Bowen, "The Forms Culture Takes: A State-of-the-Field Essay on the Anthropology of Southeast Asia," *The Journal of Asian Studies* 54/4 (1995): 1053–57. Regarding similar issues in the Tibetan case, see Charles Ramble, "The Founding of a Tibetan Village: the Popular Transformation of History," *Kailash, a Journal of Himalayan Studies* 10/ 3–4 (1983): 267–90.

18. Nicolas Sihlé, "Les tantristes tibétains (ngakpa), religieux dans le monde, religieux du rituel terrible: Étude de Ch'ongkor, communauté villageoise de tantristes du Baragaon (nord du Népal)" (Ph.D. diss., Université de Paris-X Nanterre, 2001), chap. 1–3, and 5; and Nicolas Sihlé, *Rituels de pouvoir et de violence: Bouddhisme tantrique dans l'Himalaya tibétain* (forthcoming).

19. See for instance William A. Graham's concluding comments in *Beyond the Written Word: Oral Aspects of Scripture in the History of Religion* (Cambridge: Cambridge University Press, 1987), 156.

20. Compare Jack Goody, *The Logic of Writing and the Organization of Society* (Cambridge: Cambridge University Press, 1986), 9–10, and Jonathan P. Parry, "The Brahmanical Tradition and the Technology of the Intellect," in *Reason and Morality*, ed. Joanna Overing (London: Tavistock Press, 1985), 211–13.

21. Of course, much more could be said about the texts: their types, their different ritual (or other) uses (involving or not the reading of the words), their manipulation and storage, the reading techniques, and so forth. All this would be part of a properly anthropological approach to texts.

22. I especially have in mind Gellner's suggestion of a typology of composite traditions—from "*bricolage*" to "syncretism" to "synthetic traditions"—differentiated according to their degree of coherence and systematicity. See David N. Gellner, "For Syncretism: The Position of Buddhism in Nepal and Japan Compared," *Social Anthropology: The Journal of the European Association of Social Anthropology* 5/3 (1997): 288–89.

23. Beyer, *The Cult of Tārā*, 38.

24. In his words, "*bla rgyud nyi shu rtsa lnga yod.*"

25. A description and analysis of this ritual has been offered, and progressively refined, in the following works: Nicolas Sihlé, "Lhachö [Lha mchod] and Hrinän [Sri gnon]: The Structure and Diachrony of a Pair of Rituals (Baragaon, Northern Nepal)," in *Religion and Secular Culture in Tibet: Tibetan Studies II*, ed. Henk Blezer (Leiden: Brill, 2002), 189–96; Sihlé, *Les tantristes tibétains*, 428–44; and Sihlé, *Rituels de pouvoir et de violence.*

26. On effigies, see also the chapters by Mengele and Cuevas in this volume.

27. A similar observation is made by Mumford, *Himalayan Dialogue*, 143.

28. See Jane M. Atkinson, *The Art and Politics of Wana Shamanship* (Berkeley: University of California Press, 1989), 14–15; and Humphrey and Laidlaw, *The Archetypal Actions of Ritual*, 8–12.

29. I am drawing here selectively from Rappaport's ideas on ritual. Rappaport emphasizes the "transmission" of canonical and indexical "messages" in rituals, but I do not share his view of ritual as primarily "a mode of communication." See Roy A. Rappaport, "The Obvious Aspects of Ritual," in *Ecology, Meaning and Religion* (Richmond, CA: North Atlantic Books, 1979), 178–83.

30. Written texts constitute neither a sufficient nor a necessary condition of invariance, as Parry's critique of some of Goody's more deterministic claims reminds us, to take one example. See Parry, "The Brahmanical Tradition and the Technology of the Intellect," 210–13.

31. Sherry B. Ortner, *Sherpas through their Rituals* (Cambridge: Cambridge University Press, 1978), 91–127.

32. See the following critiques: Charles Ramble, "Recent Books on Tibet and the Buddhist Himalaya II," *Journal of the Anthropological Society of Oxford* 1/2 (1980): 113; Cathy M. Cantwell, "An Ethnographic Account of the Religious Practice in a Tibetan Buddhist Refugee Monastery in Northern India" (Ph.D. diss., University of Kent, 1989), 19–20; or even Donald A. Messerschmidt, "New Heights and New Insights in Himalayan Research," *Reviews in Anthropology* 6/2 (1979): 200.

33. See Ortner, *Sherpas Through Their Rituals*, 93–94, 101–103, 122; and, for a critique, Cantwell, *An Ethnographic Account*, 44n43.

34. Ortner, *Sherpas Through Their Rituals*, 5–9; Godfrey Lienhardt, *Divinity and Experience: The Religion of the Dinka* (Oxford: Clarendon Press, 1961), 233–97; Clifford Geertz, "Religion as a Cultural System," in *Anthropological Approaches to the Study of Religion*, ed. M. Banton (London: Tavistock publications, 1966), 1–46.

35. David Jacobson, *Reading Ethnography* (Albany: State University of New York Press, 1991), 54–66.

36. See Cantwell, *An Ethnographic Account*, 20, or, more implicitly, Ramble, "Recent Books," 117. For critical comments on Cantwell's own alternative mode of analysis, which emphasizes the continuity of practice across Tibetan regions, see Martin A. Mills, *Identity, Ritual and State in Tibetan Buddhism: The Foundations of Authority in Gelukpa Monasticism* (Richmond: Curzon Press, 2003), 106–107.

37. Sihlé, *Les tantristes tibétains*, 428–44; and Sihlé, *Rituels de pouvoir et de violence*.

2

Tibetan Indigenous Myths and Rituals with Reference to the Ancient Bön Text

The Nyenbum (Gnyan'bum)

SAMTEN G. KARMAY

It was in Kyoto University, in 2006, while working on the sources of a fourteenth-century Bön text,[1] that I stumbled upon a collection of Bön canonical works. There are four texts in this collection:

1. *Lubum* (*Klu'bum*)
2. *Nyenbum* (*Gnyan'bum*)
3. *Sadag-bum* (*Sa bdag'bum*)
4. *Töbum* (*Gtod'bum*)[2]

They are concerned with four types of spirits believed to dwell in the natural environment, such as water, mountain, ground, and rocks.

The *Lubum*, the first of the four texts, is in three volumes. It is about the *lu* or water spirits (*nāga* in Buddhist texts). This text is known to scholars from the studies of A. Schiefner[3] and R. A. Stein,[4] but the remaining three of the four have hardly been investigated by any scholars until now.

It is the second, the *Nyenbum*, The Nyen Collection, that is the subject of this chapter.[5] The word *bum* (*'bum*) literally means "one hundred thousands," but it also stands more broadly for "a collection," as in the expression *sungbum* (*gsung 'bum*), "collected works." Before analyzing the contents of the text, a few words on the importance of this work in relation to studies of Tibetan rituals, particularly the indigenous rituals, are in order.

Tibetan religious rituals, particularly Buddhist ones, are in general of Indian inspiration. They mostly present themselves in the framework of *sādhana*, a term translated by the Tibetan *drubtab* (*sgrub thabs*), literally "method of realization." There exists a *sādhana* for almost every member of the Buddhist pantheon. The texts of *sādhana* are either translated from Sanskrit, or composed by Tibetan Buddhists based on the Indian model or variants of it. A good example of this type of ritual are the ones instituted by the Fifth Dalai Lama as state ceremonies.[6] The Buddhist deities involved in these ceremonies are mostly Avalokiteśvara, Amitāyus, Hayagrīva, or Buddhist *siddhas* such as Padmasambhava. Even in the Bön religion there are of course *drubtab* types of rituals which are mainly of Buddhist inspiration.

In my research into indigenous rituals covered by the term *to* (*gto*), I noticed that the *to* rituals generally begin with a reference to a preceding action or a sort of event that is supposed to have taken place in the distant past. It appears that without this precedent, the ritual itself does not seem to have much significance regarding the effect that it is intended to have. This preceding act is usually referred to in the briefest possible way, always leaving us wondering what it was. This antecedent is often a myth shrouded in either a holy action or a heroic deed. From this point of view, the ritual itself therefore consists in the reenacting of the myth, thereby legitimizing the ritual performer, as well as sanctifying his action in the process of performance.

The term *to* does not have a lexical meaning, but what it designates is very clear. In Dunhuang manuscripts it is sometimes used as a verb: "ritual is performed and diagnosis applied again and again" (*gto zhing dpyad dpyad na*).[7] The terms "ritual" or *to* and "diagnosis," or *ché* (*dpyad*), are given as two of the four types of Bön practices—(1) divination (*mo*), (2) astrological calculation or *tsi* (*rtsis*), (3) *to*, and (4) *ché*.[8]

Since the term *to* has no lexical meaning, in Buddhist ritual texts it is often pejoratively spelled *lto* "food" instead of *gto*. This meaning is derived from the term's first meaning: "stomach" or "belly." By spelling the term *lto*, the Buddhists wanted to mock the Bön practitioners who make a living by performing the "*lto*" rituals. Later the word *tochog* (*gto chog*) came into use in order to make the distinction between the *to* and other types of rituals.

The *drubtab* type of ritual has a specific goal. It is generally the realization of the divinity by the *sādhaka* or *drubpapo* (*sgrub pa po*), the performer of the ritual, although the ritual is often performed for other various purposes, including mundane gains. The Tibetan autochthonous ritual, on the other hand, was often concerned with the everyday life of the people. It functions to create social cohesion and moral obligation among the members of the village community. It encourages communal organization centering upon the cult of the local spirits connected with water, soil, rocks, and mountains.

The performer of rituals, the local priest, is called *shen* (*gshen*) or simply *bön* (*bon*). The word *lhabön* (*lha bon*) is also used to designate the local priest who performs rituals,[9] and has the connotation of a person who invokes deities.

There are two terms for the mythical antecedent: *mang* (*smrang*) and *rab* (*rabs*). Both words often occur in the early ritual texts such as those discovered in Dunhaung at the beginning of the twentieth century. It is the mythical archetype that precedes the ritual proper. In other words, the indigenous rituals always begin with myths of this type.

The *lhabön* priest, who performs rituals, is traditionally considered to be someone versed in mythical archetypes, but in fact this is not the case. Ritual texts containing the verses for chanting, and the written manual texts that contain instructions on how to perform the rituals rarely give a full account of the myth. They are simply alluded to by mentioning the names of the chief characters in the myth.

Among the Dunhuang manuscripts, there are a number of ritual texts affiliated to the Bön belief system.[10] In these ancient manuscripts, the situation is the same as in later ritual texts. The myths are not recounted in full, as we might have wished. It appears that there was no real standard story for all types of ritual.

The main theme of the myth is often built on the same stereotyped structure, and the chief characters of the same name that occur again and again in different contexts. The stereotyped structure found in the myths may be summarized as follows. At the beginning of the world nothing exists. The world is created by itself. A human couple appears and has children. The family is happy, and their lives seemingly harmonious in relation to the environment in which they live. It is a good age. The next stage begins with problems often characterized by disharmony with the natural environment and its suprahuman inhabitants: with the spirits such as the *nyen* that reside in the high atmospheric realm such as the summit of mountains, with the *lu* that reside in springs, lakes, rivers, the nether land, with the *tö* that live in rocks, and with the *sadag* that dwell on the ground.

The disharmony is brought about by Man's activities, like hunting wildlife, polluting the waters, digging the ground, and cutting down trees. The pollution is called *nöl* (*mnol*). Other types of action that cause social disharmony are given—for example, murder or *mé* (*dme*), particularly within the family.[11] The disharmony engenders the stage of the decline of the good age. Man is at a loss when things go wrong, particularly when he becomes ill and finds that the society in which he lives is also affected. It is the decline of the good age that provides the occasion for the *lhabön* to intervene. Only the *lhabön* has the knowledge of how to communicate with the spirits that share the natural surroundings with Man and his environment. The *lhabön* reestablishes the harmony of the good age that existed before. He does this by reenacting the state depicted in the origin myth. The means of reenactment is the performance of the ritual itself.

In Tibetan folklore, the *nyen* spirits of the heavenly atmosphere dwell upon mountain summits. These spirits play a very important role in the narrative of the original myths of the first Tibetan king. This king is believed to have descended from heaven and alighted on the summit of Mount Gyangto (Gyang tho ri) in Kongpo (Kong po). There is a long account of his having a family relationship with the spirits of other high mountains in Tibet.[12] When the *nyen* spirits are associated with a particular mountain, such as normally dominating a given region, they are then often called *yul lha*, "local deity" or *zhidag* (*gzhi bdag*), "owner of the site." The local deities are the object of periodic propitiation and are often regarded as the "ancestor" of the local population (see Figure 2.1). This is the reason why kinship terms are applied to these deities when the local people call their names. Their names are often preceded by terms such as *amnyé* (*a myes*), "grandfather," and *achi* (*a phyi*), "grandmother," particularly in A mdo (eastern Tibet)—as is the case, for example, with the deity Amnyé Machen (A myes Rma chen) (see Figure 2.2).

In the early classification of the nine mountains in Tibet, neither Mount Tisé (Ti se) nor Mount Amnyé Machen, also called Manyen Pomra (Rma gnyan Pom ra), were included since they were outside of what constituted the territories of the Yarlung (Yar glung) Kingdom.[13] Mount Tisé is located in what was known as Zhang-zhung, a country in western Tibet annexed by the Tibetans around 640 CE. Tsongkha (Tsong kha), later called Amdo (A mdo), where Mount Amnyé Machen is situated, became a military and commercially strategic region when the empire of the Yarlung kings expanded toward the northeast, also around the middle of the seventh century CE. It was from Tsongkha that the Tibetans invaded the Dunhuang region in 787 CE. They held it for three-quarters of a century. Dunhuang, called Gya Shachu (Rgya Sha cu) in Tibetan, was a place where Buddhism flourished from about the fifth century CE. It became an extremely important center of Buddhism in China before the Tibetan invasion. As mentioned earlier, among the manuscripts discovered in Dunhuang, there are also a number of manuscripts that contain Bön myths and rituals. Scholars such as Marcelle Lalou and Frederic W. Thomas already studied some of these rituals.[14] They were later joined by R. A. Stein, who published a very detailed comparative analysis of several Dunhuang manuscripts that treat myths and rituals affiliated to the Bön belief.[15] In the words

FIGURE 2.1. Amnyé Chakhyung. Photo S. Karmay, Rebkong (1997).

of Marcelle Lalou, these manuscripts contain "astonishing passages of texts of the Bön mythology where a prodigious lyricism in both the form and substance is unleashed."[16] F. W. Thomas describes the content of the same type of ritual texts from Dunhuang in the following terms: "It may be said to exhibit the rather wild eloquence of a Bon-po priesthood, superimposed upon a more primitive, religious, stratum." He further remarks: "the subject is poetical, and the sentiment and language natural."[17]

As we have noted, these remarks are made with regard to the ancient manuscripts from Dunhuang. Does this mean that only the ritual texts from Dunhuang are of this quality and antiquity? The answer to this question would be affirmative for the scholars just mentioned. They must be forgiven if they

FIGURE 2.2. Amnyé Machen. Photo S. Karmay, Yungdrungling Monastery (1997).

really had thought that no such texts would have been found among the Bön canonical texts, because until 1986 the whole collection of the Kangyur (Bka' 'gyur) had not been available to them. The situation has now changed radically since the publication of the Bön canon.[18]

The *Nyenbum* Text

The subject of this study is a text entitled *The Precious Collection of the Nyen* (*Rin po che gnyan gyi 'bum*).[19] It has twenty-six chapters of varying length. It has no colophon. That leaves us wanting to know who the real author is, but unfortunately just as in the manuscripts from Dunhuang mentioned earlier, no indication is made concerning its authorship. According to the Bön tradition, three hunters, led by one Marpa Penzang (Mar pa 'Phen bzang) went in search of wood fuel. When they began to dig up the root of a dead bush on the bank of the lake Mu-lé-hé (Mu le had), three wooden boxes emerged containing manuscripts. Being illiterate, they could not understand what the manuscripts were about. They eventually gave them to Shubön Genyen Tsugpü (Shu bon dGe bsnyen gtsug phud).[20] The identity of this man remains unknown. He is obviously a Bön practitioner, judging from his name. It would seem that it was he who had assembled the myths and arranged them in a single text in twenty-six chapters. Apart from the main theme, which is the *nyen* spirits, there is no thread in the subject matter woven to join one chapter to another, but most of the chapters have a common character or name of a character. Tradition seems to suggest that its having been found by the hunters took place prior to the revelation of Shenchen Luga (Gshen chen Klu dga,' 996–1035). If this is the case, it would date back to the early tenth century CE.

The hunters are said to have recovered the manuscripts on the bank of the lake Mu-lé-hé. Mu-lé-hé is another name of the lake Lag-ngar Tso (Lag ngar mtsho, Rakṣas Tal). It is situated to the west of the lake Mapang Yutso (Ma pang g.yu mtsho, Manasarovar). This therefore suggests that the manuscripts originated in the vicinity of Mount Tisé (Kailash).

While most of the chapters of the *Nyenbum* each focus on one single myth, a few of them treat several myths in the same chapter. The names of the characters in these myths are sometimes given in what is known as the language (*skad*) of Nampadong (Nam pa ldong), as well as in the language of Menyag (Me nyag). It is hard to verify whether these correspond to real languages or not. However, F. W. Thomas has already noted that the Nam people played an important role in rituals found among the Dunhuang manuscripts. According to him, the Nam people lived in the vicinity of Mount Amnyé Machen.[21] In this regard, it is interesting to note that in myths contained in the *Nyenbum*, the local deity Amnyé Machen, mentioned earlier, is one of the prominent characters. This also reminds us of the fact that Amnyé Pomra was considered to be the ancestral deity of the Dong (Ldong) clan, one of the six original clans of Tibet known as the *miu dung drug* (*mi'u gdung drug*).[22]

Regarding the content of the *Nyenbum*, the main theme is usually a conflict between the spirits *lha* and *nyen* on the one hand, and Man on the other. It is Man who for the most part provokes the conflict through his actions against nature. This consists of cutting down trees; digging up stones from the ground; polluting lakes, springs, and rivers; and hunting wild animals. Man's actions disturb the aforementioned spirits that dwell in water, stone, ground, and mountains. Men incur the wrath of the spirits, and as retribution, invariably become ill. Their livestock suffer as well. The soul, symbolized by turquoise or *layu* (*bla g.yu*),[23] which men wear around their necks, wanders away or is captured by the spirits. The *yang* (*g.yang*), quintessence of yaks, *dri* (*'bri*), horses, and sheep vanishes. Man seeks to remedy this situation through the services of the local priest, the *lhabön*. The latter tries to restore the harmonious state which formerly existed, by performing a ritual. However, he often fails. In this case, he recommends that the matter be taken to another *lhabön* who is depicted as being more effective. Through the performance of ritual, the harmony is reestablished and Man is then made to propitiate the local spirits and is restrained from his actions against nature.

The Language of the Text

Just as in many of the Dunhuang manuscripts, the language of the text is extremely difficult to understand. This is partly because of its archaic vocabulary and also partly because of its composition in verses. A large part of the text remains incoherent and obscure. It is the sequence of the story that gets lost. The manuscript copy of the text in the Bön Kangyur is a unique copy and therefore very important, but it is also riddled with faults, embedded with misspellings, inconsistencies, and contradictions. The stories are often unduly condensed and their thread lost. It is also full of unusual and difficult terminology—for example, *pung tseng* (*phung 'tsheng*) for "defeat and victory."

Birds, and to a lesser extent wild animals, play a predominant role in the mythical accounts. The language is poetic, written in verse mostly with five or six syllables, but not constant. Now and then the lines continue into many more syllables. However, the antiquity of the text is self-evident. Its ancient writing is similar both in form and content to the Bön ritual texts found among Dunhuang manuscripts. A number of passages are exactly identical word for word to those in Dunhuang documents.

In order to give the reader an idea of the text and its contents, I conclude here with a summary translation of a myth from the *Nyenbum*'s chapter sixteen entitled "The Medium Length of the Opening of the Padlock of the Nyen."[24]

Summary Translation of the Nyenbum Chapter Sixteen

(141–220) "Salutation! Here is the opening of the padlock of the Nyen.
Formerly, the Si (Srid) pitched the sky.
The Kö (Skos) spread the earth.
The Cha (Phywa) constructed forts.[25]
The Nyen reigned.
Man took possession of the locality.
The first god was Lha Tsenpa-teng (Lha btsan pa steng).
The first Man was Tsenpa Nga-nga (Btsan pa nga snga).
The first Nyen was Nyenjé Kharwa (Gnyan rje mkhar ba).
The first Lu was Lutsen Ngardrag Dingwa (Klu btsan ngar drag ding ba).
The first Men (Sman)[26] was Mentsun Tangpo (Sman btsun thang po).

The first Zé (Gzed)[27] was Zé Gyaltangpo (Gzed rgyal thang po).
The first Sin (Srin) was Sitsen Guwa (Sri btsan rgu ba).
There were the Gods, the Lu, the Nyen, the Ze, the Men, Man, and the Sin, seven (kinds of beings) in all.
The country was small.
The earth was narrow.
The sky was not extensive, only just about all.
Man had no room to roam about.
His cattle were unable to find food.
So Man called loudly up to the sky.
The Si, the Kö and the Cha all heard him. (141–221)
They said: "the land must be divided."
They sent down stakes to be played for.
At Gungtang (Gung thang), land of the Gods,
The Gods won Zedrang (Ze 'brang), fort of the gods (as their stakes).
At Poma Yagteng (Pho ma yags steng), land of the Nyen,
The Nyen won Tsegu (rTse dgu), fort of the Nyen.
In Natog (Na tog), land of the Lu,
The Lu won Gyangdang (Rgyang dang), fort of the Lu.
The Men won Dungpang (Dung 'phang), land of the Men.
The Zé won Pangtra (Spang bkra), land of the Zé.
The Sin won Nagpo Gusel (Nag po dgu sral), land of the Sin.
Man won Kyiting (Skyi mthing),[28] land of Man.
Thus the land sphere was designated and earth was divided.
The Gods were victorious.
The fort Zédrang need not be restored even if it is damaged.
The clothes of the Gods need not be sewn even if they are torn.
Their wealth need not be looked after.
Their food was made from nine kinds of grains, and no fields need to be dug and ploughed for it. (141–222)
The Men and the Zé also won.
(The same for the Lu and Sin).
Sakhar Kyawo (Sa mkhar skya bo), fort of Man, however, needs to be restored if it is damaged.
The domestic animals of Man need to be looked after.
The clothes of Man need to be sewn if they are torn.
The (fields of) food grains of Man need to be dug and ploughed.
So Man felt: "Oh! We lost (our stakes)!"
Re'u Mig Nön (Re'u mig non) and Lo Sonön (Glo so rnon) [of the Nyen],
Went to report to the Gods, the Lu and the Nyen about Man's (situation).

They said: "Will extra be given? Who lost? We, the Nyen, lost.
The land is small, it cannot be extended.
The fort Zédrang of the Gods (141–223) need not be restored even if it is damaged.
The white clothes of the Gods need not be sewn even if they are torn.
But the white horned deer of the Gods have no hair on their back.
If one milks them, no milk would come....
The forts of the Lu and the Nyen
Need not be restored if they are damaged.
The clothes of the Lu and those of the Nyen
Need not be sewn if they are torn.
But the cattle of the Lu and the Nyen have no hair on their back.
No milk would come if they were milked.
The forts of the Men and the Zé need not be restored
If they are damaged.
The clothes of the Men and the Zé need not be sewn if they are torn.
The fort of the Sin need not be restored if it is damaged.
But the cattle of the Sin have no hair on their back.
If milked, no milk would come.
The Sin need not wear hats.
Who lost? It is us, the Nyen, who lost!
Who won? It is Man who won!
Even though the land of Man is small, it can be extended.
Even though the fort Sakhar Kyawo is low,
It can be built higher.
If the clothes of Man are torn,
They can be sewn up.
If they get old, they can be changed.
Man has much food.
He eats food in the morning and in the evening.
His older generation is not yet dead (141–224).
His future generations will be increased.
His cattle and sheep have hair on their backs.
Their breasts produce milk.
But for the Nyen, us, nothing can be added to our loss."
Having said that, Re'u Mig Nön and Lo Sonön left.
Then they went to the land of Man.
They sowed calumny between Man and the Nyen.
They misinterpreted their conversation (with the Gods, Lu and Nyen).

Re'u said: "The Gods, Lu and Nyen said: 'It is true. Man lost. For the loss, (we give them): hundreds of thousands of snow leopards and wildcats of snow; hundreds of thousands of dear and reindeer of the meadows; hundreds of thousands of bears and the *dré* (*dred*) bears of the forests; hundreds of thousands of vultures and eagles of the rocks; hundreds of thousands of beavers and otters of the water.

Man cuts the trees of the Nyen with an axe.

He digs the stones of the Nyen (from the ground) with a hook, and stirs water of the Nyen with a ladle.

Man cries out from the high mountain pass.

Here is the compensation to Man for the loss.' "

Mitsen Ngapa (Mi btsan nga pa) thought:

"I will kill hundreds of thousands of the beasts of the white snow mountain.

I will kill hundreds of thousands of snow cocks and grouse of the blue slate mountain. (141–225)

I will kill hundreds of thousands of beavers and otters of the rivers.

I will cut the trees of the Nyen.

Dig up the stones of the Nyen.

I will plough the land of the Nyen as my field.

I will irrigate my home land with the water of the Nyen.

If I need to set up a cemetery,

I will do that on the slope of the brown mountain."

Then Re'u Mig Nön said to the Nyen:

"Man is angry.

The Nyen should send bad omens to Man:

A hundred deer that eat frogs.

A hundred snakes that eat men."

Nyibu Kangring (Nyi bu rkang ring) and Dabu Lagring (Zla bu lag ring),

The messengers of the Nyen,

Went to steal the (turquoise) of soul of Mitsen Ngapa and the soul of his animals.

They hid the turquoise of souls.

They killed the snakes and deer that came as bad omens. The Nyen therefore summoned their army.

The Nyen of the snow rose from snow.

The Nyen of the rock rolled off like boulders.

The Nyen of the slate mountain blazed like fire.

The Nyen of the meadow agitated like a gush of water.

The soul of Mitsen Ngapa and that of his animals
Were locked in the interior of a fort that had nine walls around it. (141–226)
The padlocks were locked on the eastern side.
(The sense of the line here is unclear).
Other padlocks are locked on the northern side.
The doors of the fort made the noise "trag-se-trag" (*khrags se khrags*) [when they are open or shut].
They are sealed, *war re war*.
The Nyen and Man began to dispute.
Mitsen Ngapa had now no locality where he could live. If he herds his cattle up-stream, wolves attack them.
If he ploughs his fields downstream, they are harmed by drought and hail.
His descendants risk having no offspring.
The *yang* (*g.yang*, "quintessential core") of his cattle is seized.
In summer, lightning comes down from the sky.
Mitsen Ngapa therefore asked male and female *shen* [priests]
To perform divination and prognostication.
But they could not identify the malignant spirits.
So Shenrab Miwo (Gshen rab Mi bo) was requested to do the same.
Shenrab Miwo said: "What went wrong was the dispute between Man and the Nyen.
The soul of Man is locked up in the padlocks of the Nyen."
Mitsen said: "I request you to perform the *to* ritual and diagnosis."
Shenrab said: "Go and find the priest Nyenbön Tangtang Drölwa (Gnyan bon Thang thang grol ba)." (141–227)
The Nyenbön said: "We need to look for ritual items to offer to the Nyen.
Look for snow leopards and wildcats for the Nyen of snow mountain.
Look for snow cocks and grouse for the Nyen of slate mountain.
Look for deer and reindeer for the Nyen of meadow.
Look for eagles for the red Nyen of the rocks.
Look for tigers and leopards for the Nyen of forests.
Look for beavers and otters for the Nyen of water.
Look for gold and silver for Nyibu Kangring (Nyi bu rkang ring) and Dabu Lagring (Zla bu lag ring).
They are the messengers of the Nyen.
To open the padlock of the Nyen, we also need gold, turquoise, silver and conch.

We must have silk curtains and wool dyed in five colors. Look for goats, sheep, horses, and yaks of the Nyen.
Mitsen had a hard time finding them.
He put forward all that he had by way of wealth.
That which he did not have, he obtained from the plain (i.e., elsewhere).
He offered them all to the Nyenbön.
The Nyenbön opened the first padlock with (the key in the form of) a white bird of the Nyen.
He opened (141–228) the second padlock with (the key in the form of) a sheep of the Nyen.
He opened the third padlock with (the key in the form of) a yak of the Nyen.
He opened the fourth padlock (with key in the form of) an ox.
He opened the fifth padlock with a white horse.
The rooster of Mitsen,
Is it the wealth of his ancestors?
Its father was the warmth of the sky.
Its mother was the essence of the earth.
It was hatched out of a brown egg.
It was then given to Mitsen,
By the nine brothers of the gods.
Its crest is red like copper, *zangs-se-zang*.
Its ear is white like a conch and hears clearly.
Its sound overpowers the Nyen.
Its feathers are adorned with silk.
A gold key is attached to an iron axe that hung around its neck.
The rooster opened the nine padlocks without hindrance.
The turquoises of the soul of Man and cattle were recovered."

The Tibetan text follows (Figure 2.3).

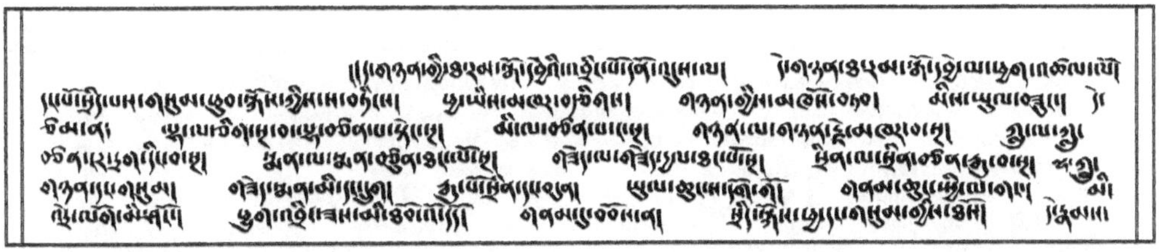

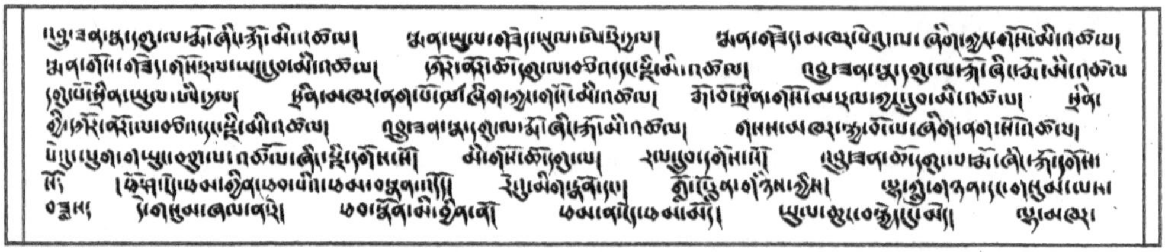

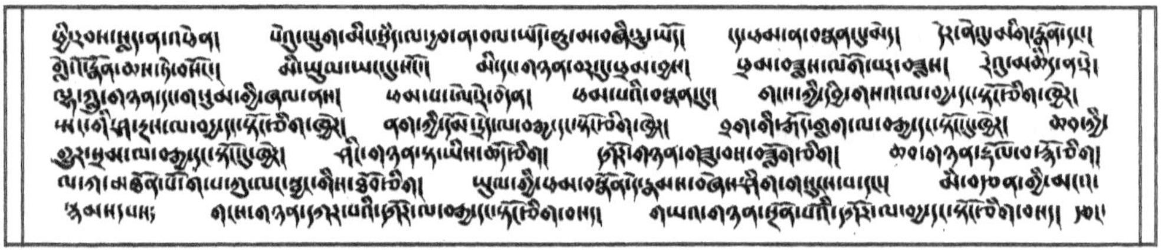

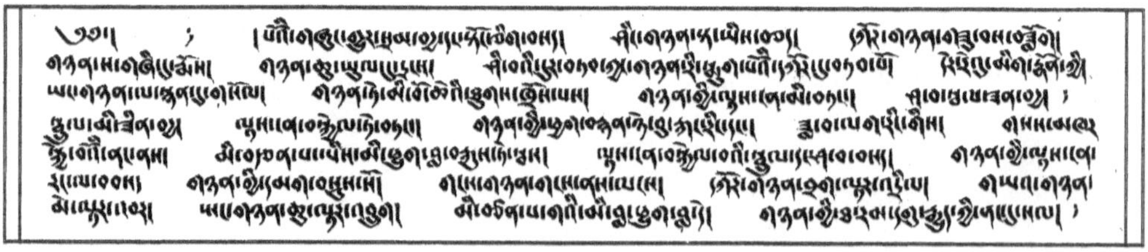

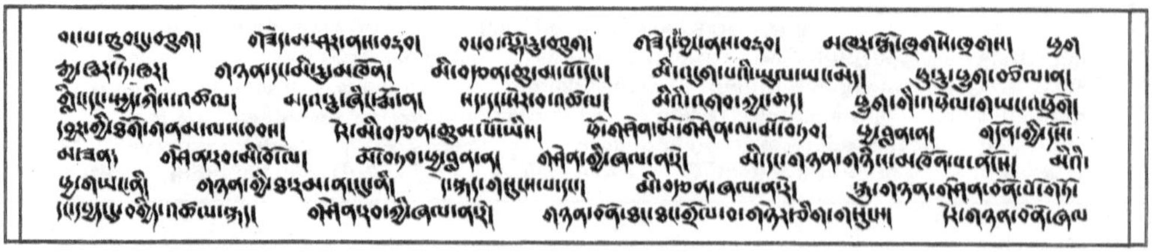

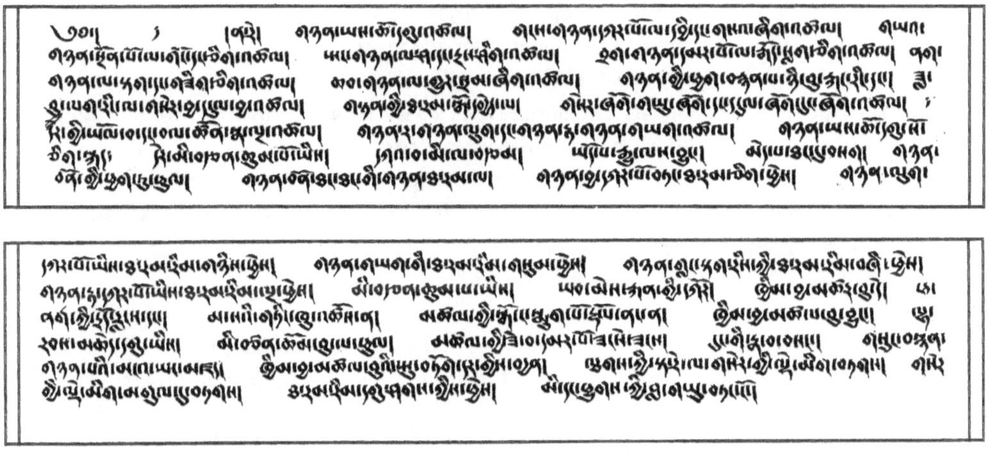

FIGURE 2.3. The Tibetan text of the Gnyan 'bum chapter sixteen.

NOTES

1. A critical edition of this text is now published. Katsumi Mimaki and Samten Karmay, *Bon sgo gsal byed (Clarification of the Gates of Bon), A Fourteenth Century Bon po Doxographical Treatise* (Kyoto: Graduate School of Letters, Kyoto University, 2007).

2. Dan Martin, Per Kvaerne, and Yasuhiko Nagano, *A Catalogue of the Bon Kanjur* (Osaka: National Museum of Ethnology, 2003), numbers 8, 76, 77,2, 78, 79.

3. "Über das Bonpo-Sutra: 'Das weisse Nâga-Hunderttausen,'" *Mémoires de l'Académie impériale des Sciences de St. Pétersbourg (MAIS)*, VIIe Sér., XXVIII/1 (1880): 1–86.

4. *L'annuaire de Collège de France*, Résumé des Cours de 1966–70.

5. *Theg chen g.yung drung bon gyi bka' 'gyur* (Lhasa: Kun grol lha sras mi pham rnam rgyal, 1996), vol. 141.

6. Samten G. Karmay, *The Arrow and the Spindle, Studies in History, Myths, Rituals and Beliefs in Tibet* (Kathmandu: Mandala Publications, 2005), vol. 2: 80–87.

7. Marcelle Lalou, "Fiefs, Poisons et Guérisseurs," *Journal Asiatique* 246/2 (1958): Plate III, line 69, and Plate V, line 153.

8. David L. Snellgrove, *The Nine Ways of Bon* (London: Oxford University Press, 1967), 24–25.

9. The word also designates a certain type of ritual, see Shar rdza Bkra shis rgyal mtshan, *Legs bshad mdzod*, translated in Samten G. Karmay, *The Treasury of Good Sayings: A Tibetan History of Bon* (London: Oxford University Press, 1972), 62–63, 238. In Bhutan, certain communal rituals of local deities are still called *lhabön*; see Françoise Pommaret, "Bon and Chos. Local Community Rituals in Bhutan," in *Buddhism Beyond Monasticism*, ed. Antonio Terrone (Leiden: Brill, forthcoming).

10. For example, Pelliot tibétain 126 and 239 in Ariane Macdonald and Yoshiro Imaeda, *Choix de Documents tibétains conservé à la Bibliothèque nationale* (Paris: Bibliothèque national, 1978), vol. I; Pelliot tibétain 1040, 1042, 1134, 1136, 1194, 1285 in Macdonald and Imaeda, *Choix de Documents*, vol. II.

11. Karmay, *The Arrow and the Spindle* (1998) vol. 1, 382–83.

12. Karmay, *The Arrow and the Spindle*, vol. 1, 432–50.

13. Karmay, *The Arrow and the Spindle* (1998), vol. 1, 435–41.

14. Lalou, "Fiefs, Poisons et Guérisseurs"; F. W. Thomas, *Ancient Folk Literature from North-Eastern Tibet* (Berlin: Akademie-Verlag, 1957), 52–102.

15. Rolf A. Stein, "Du récit au rituel dans les manuscrits tibétains de Touen-houang," in *Études tibétaines dédiées à la mémoire de Marcelle Lalou*, ed. Ariane Macdonald, (Paris: A. Maisonneuve, 1971), 479–547.

16. Lalou, "Fiefs, Poisons et Guérisseurs," 2.

17. Thomas, *Ancient Folk Literature*, 14.

18. See Martin, Kvaerne and Nagano, *A Catalogue of the Bon Kanjur.*

19. Martin, Kvaerne and Nagano, *A Catalogue of the Bon Kanjur*, numbers 8, 76, 77,2, 78, 79.

20. Shar rdza Bkra shis rgyal mtshan, *Legs bshad mdzod*, translated in Karmay, *The Treasury*, 124.

21. Thomas, *Ancient Folk Literature*, 2–5.

22. See Karmay, *The Arrow and the Spindle* (1998), vol. 1, 249.

23. See Karmay, *The Arrow and the Spindle* (1998), *vol.* 1, 318–20.

24. It begins from folio 220, line 2 of vol. 141. My summary stops at folio 228, line 6, though the story still continues.

25. Srid refers to Srid rje 'Brang dkar, Skos to Skor rje Drang dkar, and Phywa to Phywa rje Ring dkar, three deities in Bon cosmogony often known as Phywa srid skos gsum; see Karmay, *The Arrow and the Spindle* (1998) vol. 1, 128.

26. A type of celestial spirit, see Drang rje btsun pa Gser mig, *Gzer mig* (Beijing: Krung go'i bod kyi shes rig dpe skrun khang, 1991), 36. The reader is cautioned that in this translation Man refers to human beings and Men to the Sman spirits.

27. A type of celestial spirit, see Gser mig, *Gzer mig*, 36.

28. In Dunhuang manuscripts, it is known as Mi yul skyi mthing, and it is in fact a name of a place in Kong po. See Karmay, *The Arrow*, vol. 1, 219–18.

3

Continuity and Change in Tibetan Mahāyoga Ritual

Some Evidence from the Tabzhag (Thabs zhags) *Manuscript and Other Dunhuang Texts*

CATHY CANTWELL AND ROB MAYER

As with so many other archaeological sources from around the world, it is always tempting to try to use the Dunhuang manuscripts as a basis for significant historical generalizations far beyond their direct remit. However, we must accept that this will always remain a potentially perilous undertaking, because these manuscripts, dating to the early eleventh century or before, wonderful though they are, in fact comprise only a partial and possibly unrepresentative sample of the total manuscript corpus of their time, since all are taken from a single multiethnic location situated at a geographical and political extremity of the Tibetan cultural world. Nevertheless, it is quite proper that we do try to derive some broader meaning from such an extraordinary historical treasure as the Dunhuang Tibetan texts: there is little doubt they can shed a brilliant if partial light on the wider Tibetan world before the "New [Translation]" (Gsar ma pa) period.

In the last few years, there has been a very welcome upsurge of interest in the Dunhuang Tibetan Mahāyoga texts, which, like most tantric texts, are either predominantly concerned with ritual, or at least contain significant quantities of ritual materials. The study of Dunhuang Tibetan Mahāyoga texts inevitably raises fundamental questions of ritual continuity and change: To what extent is

Dunhuang Tibetan Mahāyoga ritual the same as that imported from India, and to what extent is it different? To what extent is it the same as that practiced today, and to what extent different? The answers of course are that both changes and continuities are in evidence. Social contexts and horizons of interpretation have surely changed beyond recognition—for example, between India and Tibet, or between the tenth and the twenty-first centuries. Nevertheless, continuity with the past is one of the most important ways in which Tibetan Mahāyoga has sought to remain plausible and effective, and for this purpose it has retained intact from the tenth century and earlier, both textual items and grammars of ritual in significant quantities. In addition, it is a textual tradition, so that innovation is rarely radical, and there is always continuity. Clearly then, it is important in the analysis of Dunhuang Tibetan Mahāyoga ritual that one strikes an appropriate balance between continuity and change.

More than that, one naturally also seeks to understand the precise manner in which continuity and change have occurred. How exactly did Tibetan Mahāyoga differ from its Indian counterparts, and why? Were there coherent indigenizing strategies, or was change less self-conscious? Can one describe Tibetan Dunhuang Mahāyoga texts as hybrid—or are they wholly Buddhist? What elements remained the same into the later tradition, and why were those particular elements preserved? What changes occurred, and why those particular changes? The pages that follow represent a preliminary approach to addressing such questions, based on the evidence from a selected sample of Dunhuang Tibetan Mahāyoga ritual texts we have been reading over the last few years. Most of these were either ritual texts related to the "dagger" (*phur pa*) ritual implement and precursors of the deity Dorje Purba (Rdo rje phur pa), or a manuscript comprising a complete Mahāyoga tantra embedded as lemmata within a long commentary (Dunhuang text IOL Tib J 321). The Tantra is called the *Tabki Zhagpa* (*Thabs kyi zhags pa*), or *Lasso of Methods*, and its commentary is simply described as its *drelpa* (*'grel pa*). Current thinking places these documents in the last half of the tenth century,[1] while the text they contain may well be older; but views on dating such manuscripts are still in flux, and different theories might emerge in due course. Our findings so far, based on the aforementioned sample of texts, can be summarized as follows:

1. As much previous discussion of ritual might predict,[2] we find that the Tibetan tradition has been typically conservative over time. Rather than unearthing a trove of ritual archaisms that are for the most part

now lost, so far we have read rather little among the Dunhuang Mahāyoga texts in our sample that is not still clearly evidenced in the later tradition in some form or another. Thus, we have located much of what we have read so far within living extant Nyingma traditions, either canonized within the Collected Tantras of the Nyingma (Rnying ma rgyud 'bum = NGB), or codified within rituals, or preserved in historical texts.

2. Some of this Dunhuang material is already broadly comparable to the later tradition in its form, complexity, and sophistication.
3. Nevertheless, there is evidence that other Mahāyoga traditions which appear at Dunhuang were further expanded and doctrinally codified with time.
4. In addition, items that appear to be strongly emphasized at Dunhuang can become comparatively less emphatic in the later tradition.
5. Some Dunhuang Tibetan Mahāyoga material contains a small proportion of indigenous developments, many of which have continued into the later tradition. Within the sample so far analyzed, these indigenous developments do not appear to reflect any simple hybridization with indigenous pre-Buddhist religion (although evidence for that might appear elsewhere), nor do they appear random and haphazard. Instead, we perceive an adaptation of Buddhism to the Tibetan cultural environment carried out very much on Buddhist terms, although involving the integration of a few distinctively Tibetan tropes. Some of these adaptations enable the location of aspects of Buddhist ritual within the frame of Tibetan geography and history, by providing specifically Tibetan Buddhist charter myths for Buddhist rites. (See also Samten Karmay's chapter in this volume for similar usages of myth in a Bönpo context.) This process might indicate an interest in providing Buddhist ritual calques on pre-Buddhist ritual structures, where such charter myths with Tibetan characteristics (typically connected with the sacral emperor and mountains) were of central importance. In other instances, indigenous ritual categories are more simply homologized with Indian Buddhist ritual categories. The extent to which these adaptations collectively might represent a conscious policy for Buddhist localization worked out by the dynastic Buddhist hierarchy or its post-dynastic successors, or the extent to which they represent processes that arose somewhat less self-consciously, is not yet clear.

Evidence from Dunhuang Purba Materials

Unfortunately, we do not have a full length Purba Tantra from Dunhuang, although we know that they already existed by that time because at least one is cited in the *Tabzhag* manuscript.[3] However, the Dunhuang Purba materials do include a substantial twenty-two page text, with many interlinear notes, identified in the British Library as part III of IOL Tib J 331. This is the closest we get to a full length Purba work from Dunhuang.

From a codicological point of view, Tib J 331 is a book (*po ti*) containing three separate texts that appears to have been made to professional specifications. The page numberings and markings also appear to indicate that it represents three remaining parts of what was originally a larger collection. As we have it now, the twenty-two page Purba text is the third of the three texts. The first and second are instructions for meditating on the deity Vajrasattva, including one text attributed to a famous name within the Nyingmapa tradition, Mañjuśrīmitra of Ceylon. These Vajrasattva texts teach the development phase of Mahāyoga in terms quite familiar to the modern tradition: First come the three *samādhis* (*ting 'dzin gsum*),[4] then the building up of the foundation of the elements (fire, wind, water, and earth), one above the other, arising from the appropriate seed syllables, and the Immeasurable Palace above that, with oneself as the deity; then enjoining (*bskul ba*); making offerings; the descent (of blessings); mantra recitation of the hundred-syllable Vajrasattva mantra; and so on. There is not much here that is unfamiliar to ritualists of the contemporary Nyingma Mahāyoga tradition.

Our main focus, however, was the following Purba text, which has the title, *The Supreme Pacification, the Concise Enlightened Activity of Transference* (*Zhi ba'i mchog 'pho ba'i 'phrin las bsdus pa*).

We found two things particularly striking about this work. First, almost every single phrase and word of the text still carries through verbatim into the modern scriptural and commentarial traditions. Second, it seems to represent a well-developed and complex Mahāyoga tradition that does not appear particularly primitive or only partially developed, when compared with the modern Purba tradition.

The highly structured text seeks to organize Purba ritual within the categories of Seven Perfections (*phun sum tshogs pa bdun*). They are the perfections of (1) form (*gzugs*), (2) consecrations (*byIn rlabs*), (3) recitation (*bzlas brjod*), (4) activities (*'phrIn las*), (5) time (*dus*), (6) place (*gnas*), and (7) oneself (i.e., the practitioner) (*bdag nyid*). These are not to be confused with the better-known Five Perfections of Mahāyoga, of (1) the place, (2) the principal practitioner,

(3) the retinue, (4) the requisite substances, and (5) the time—a list widely referred to in ritual manuals and commentaries in a general Mahāyoga Generation Stage context. In fact, the Seven Perfections found in our Dunhuang text are slightly rare. Yet, they are not by any means forgotten. The entire twenty-two page description of the Seven Perfections found in the Dunhuang text nowadays exists more or less verbatim as chapters 8–11 of a NGB Purba tantra, appropriately called the *Tantra of the Perfections of Enlightened Activity* (*'Phrin las phun sum tshogs pa'i rgyud*).[5] The only real difference between the Dunhuang text and the NGB text is that the latter inserts chapter endings and beginnings, and also applies a different logic to the structure of the Seven Perfections by ordering them to progress from the general to the particular, rather than vice versa.[6] From its inviolably preserved sanctuary within the canonical NGB, we can easily see how this passage continues to inform the living commentarial tradition. In 2006, at the International Association of Tibetan Studies conference in Bonn, Matthew Kapstein kindly introduced us to the Tibetan scholar, Hūṃchen Chenagtshang, who made us a gift of his recently published edition of the famous Purba commentary by the Reb-kong master, Magsar Paṇḍita (Mag gsar Paṇḍita Kun bzang stobs ldan dbang po), who lived from 1781 to 1828.[7] We were delighted to find that Magsar Paṇḍita had decided to use the *Tantra of the Perfections of Enlightened Activity* system of Seven Perfections as the basis for organizing his entire work. In that way, no doubt unknowingly, Magsar was also propagating the teachings of Tib J 331.III, as was Hūṃchen, in reproducing and popularizing Magsar's work.

The long and complex rituals of the perfection of consecrations section of Tib J 331.III—the second of its Seven Perfections—are also reproduced in at least two other NGB tantras, the *Purba Chunyi* (*Phur pa bcu gnyis*), and the *Purbu Nyangdé* (*Phur bu Myang 'das*). No doubt, we will find them elsewhere as well, in due course. As one might expect from their ongoing canonical status, these passages are in no way a simple or less sophisticated version of the Purba consecration ceremony when compared to modern ritual: on the contrary, they are very much the same thing, highly complex and intricate in their performance.

Not everything about Tib J 331.III has remained exactly the same within the modern tradition, however. For example, the three syllables for body speech and mind, *oṃ aṃ hūṃ*, are standard in Tib J 331, as in many other Dunhuang Mahāyoga texts, but have become rarer in the modern tradition, which has moved to variants of *oṃ āḥ hūṃ* as standard, while still retaining *oṃ aṃ hūṃ* as a less frequently used alternative.[8] More substantially, the nineteenth century Magsar's use of the "Seven Perfections" is rather selective in retaining its structure along with the entire content of the minor sections, but departing from and elaborating significantly on the content of the major two sections on consecrations and activity, as well as for the shorter section on recitation.

The particular sample of Purba literature that has happened to survive intact for us in the twenty-two pages of Tib J 331.III includes a full-fledged version of what is nowadays described in Nyingma Mahāyoga literature as subsidiary rites, or *mé-lé* (*smad las*). *Mé-lé* makes use of destructive rites, but turns them toward Buddhist soteriological goals embodying the highest Mahāyoga view. *Drölwa* (*sgrol ba*), or "liberation"—a euphemism for ritual sacrifice—is nowadays the most famous Purba *mé-lé* rite. It is a complex ritual procedure that draws a good deal from Indian sacrificial categories, at the apex of which an effigy representing spiritual negativities, primarily ego-clinging, but also secondarily obstructing spirits, is stabbed with a ritual dagger (*phur pa*).[9] It is with this famous rite of *drölwa* that Tib J 331.III culminates.

A classic feature of Mahāyoga is that rites like *drölwa* have complex doctrinal exegeses without which the ritual might be in Buddhist terms meaningless. These too are represented at Dunhuang in terms similar to those found in contemporary texts. Tib J 436[10] gives a definition of Mahāyoga *drölwa* as liberation of onself (*bdag bsgral ba*) and liberation of others (*gzhan bsgral ba*). A thousand years later, in a standard work representing mainstream understandings of Purba ritual, Jamgön Kongtrül ('Jam mgon Kong sprul, 1813–99) likewise describes *drölwa* as twofold using exactly the same words: liberating oneself through wisdom (*bdag bsgral*), and liberating others through compassion (*gzhan bsgral*).[11] Tib J 436 goes on to describe self-liberation as achieving the "approach" practice to the deity; Kongtrül goes on to explain self-liberation as practicing visualization of oneself in the form of the deity—which amounts to precisely the same thing. Tib J 436 (line 6) describes liberation of others in terms of the ten fields for liberation (*zhing bcu*); Kongtrül does exactly the same.[12]

More obscure survivals into modern times can be witnessed by examining another Dunhuang Purba text, Pelliot tibétain (PT) 349, where we find evidence for rites that, while still preserved within the modern tradition, have perhaps become less prominent than they were in ancient times. PT 349 contains some conceptually quite problematic verses which unequivocally identify the male offspring *heruka* by the name Dīptacakra, which nowadays is usually associated with the ritually important female consort only. We have shown these verses to a learned contemporary Nyingma master, and they caused him some consternation and disbelief, presumably because of the key importance of gender and sexual symbolism in these Purba rites. Since they cause such problems for a representative of the modern tradition, one might have expected them gradually to have been overlooked since Dunhuang times. Not at all. Even these verses manage to find a niche in several NGB scriptures; and also in a corner of the most extensive of the present day Sakyapa (Sa skya pa) Purba rites, known as the Purchen (Phur chen), which consequently uses the same name for both the ritual *purba* visualized as a male offspring deity and for the female consort deity.[13] These verses also exist much more comfortably in Guhyasamāja commentaries, which we speculate were perhaps closer to their earlier environment.

Lang Pelgi Sengé (Rlang Dpal gyi seng ge) in PT 307

PT 307 offers a further example of ritual survivals from Dunhuang times. Here, however, we also find evidence of development and codification over time that, moreover, seemingly incorporates extremely interesting indigenization processes. The indigenizing and codifying strategy discernable in this material is typical of a pattern repeated elsewhere in Dunhuang and Nyingma literature, so it is worth analyzing.

The ritual or liturgical text PT 307 narrates Padmasambhava and his disciple, Lang Pelgi Sengé, together subduing and converting the seven goddesses of Tibet, homologizing the well-known Indic *saptamātṛkā* with these indigenous female deities.[14] But more than this, the ritual has been codified, developed, and preserved in the transmitted liturgical tradition. In countless Nyingma rituals still regularly perfomed—one might even say as a part of the standard basic template of all Mahāyoga (and often Anuyoga) ritual—the same team of Padmasambhava and Lang Pelgi Sengé continues to be celebrated as subduing the powerful female protectresses of Tibet. We find this, to give just four examples out of the hundreds available, in the early twentieth century Chimé Sogtig Terma (*'Chi med srog thig gter ma*) of Zilnön Namkhé Dorje (Zil gnon nam mkha'i rdo rje),[15] in the mid-twentieth century *Dujom Namchag Putri Lejang* (*Bdud 'joms Gnam lcags spu gri las byang*),[16] in the late Dilgo Khyentsé's (Dil mgo Mkhyen brtse) notes to the composite treasure text (*gter ma*), *Lamrim Yeshe Nyingpo* (*Lam rim ye shes snying po*),[17] and in Terdag Lingpa (Gter bdag gling pa) and Dharma Śrī's seventeenth-century Anuyoga sādhana, *Tsogchen düpa* (*Tshogs chen 'dus pa*).[18]

Just as important as the survival of Lang Pelgi Sengé in the narrative, or the simple substitution of the *saptamātṛkā* for indigenous goddesses, is the very particular manner in which the narrative has been embedded in and employed within Mahāyoga ritual. We suggest that the narrative with its ritual reenactments might represent an ingenious and symbolically potent Buddhist calque on the indigenous Tibetan pattern in which each ritual system was inextricably associated with its specific charter myth. Samten Karmay has eloquently argued in a series of famous articles published over the last twenty years that such a usage of charter myths was absolutely fundamental to pre-Buddhist Tibetan culture. To summarize this topic, it is useful to cite one of Samten Karmay's several discussions:

> [I]n Tibetan tradition myth is an integral part of rite. Together with the ritual it forms a "model" (*dpe srol*). The ritual cannot function without the myth and is therefore dependent upon it. In Tibetan popular rituals, particularly those belonging to the Bonpo tradition, the mythical part is called *rabs* (account). In this account, the officiant often identifies himself with the main deity or another character of the myth. In some cases, in order to justify his ritual action or to ensure its efficacy, he recalls that he is a follower (*brgyud 'dzin*) of the master who initially founded the ritual. The latter is therefore situated in a mythical spatio-temporal context. Knowledge of the preceding myth is therefore indispensable in order to perform the ritual action which is seen as the reenactment of the mythical past.[19]

The word *mang* (*smrang*) is also used elsewhere for this kind of origin and archetype myth as employed in ritual. In the narrative found within PT 307, we see that the Nyingma ritual tradition has, from as early as Dunhuang times until today, consistently taken up this very old and indigenously Tibetan (but Buddhist) narrative to use as its equivalent to an indigenous charter myth, or *rab* (*rabs*), to be reenacted in every subsequent ritual performance as *mang*, or ritual reenactment of the original charter myth—together constituting a Buddhist equivalent to the *pesöl* (*dpe srol*) complex. We have proposed elsewhere that the accentuation of Buddhist equivalents of such pre-Buddhist charter myth structures became an important feature of Nyingmapa adaptation or indigenization of Indian Buddhist ritual.[20] Here we must emphasize that we are definitely not claiming that charter myths were unknown to Indian Buddhism, but rather that the Nyingma employed them in a distinctively indigenized fashion.[21] Thus the developed Nyingma tradition now presents a category of female deity known as the Ancient Established Protectresses, or Tenma (*brtan ma*), often enumerated as twelve-fold (*brtan ma bcu gnyis*), whose names, as Dalton already has remarked, although typically fluid, nevertheless closely coincide with the list of names given in PT 307. To the modern tradition, these Tenma are mundane or semi-mundane leaders of hosts of further female deities whose initial taming and binding under oath by Padma and Lang Pelgi Sengé must be recalled at the end of all Nyingmapa ritual feast (*tshogs*) practices. The Tenma offering rites are so integral that they are very much the rule, rather than the exception.

Hence, we can see that in the mythologies of Guru Padma, it is important that the focus on the main Guru figure himself should not cause us to underestimate the symbolic value expressed in the accounts of the "team" efforts of the archetypal students and patrons in promoting and continuing the tantric tradition in Tibet. This aspect is not only stressed in the mythological stories, but is built into tantric ritual liturgies and practice. It is symbolically crucial, since Mahāyoga teachings are designed for subsequent practitioners to identify themselves with the deity's full enlightened expression. In the context of the regular tantric ritual assembly feasts (*tshogs*), the group of practitioners seeks to reenact and re-embody the archetypal creation of the tantric *maṇḍala* in the Tibetan environment, in which the local spirits are integrated into the tantric assembly. Idealized Tibetan predecessors of the subsequent practitioners thus have a vital symbolic place. This is why Lang Pelgi Sengé—and, in other contexts, other early Tibetan figures as well—are explicitly referred to in such rites as the Tenma and *chetor* (*chad gtor*) offering sections of the *tsog* rite. Another example of "team work" in subduing local deities beyond the Tenma example can be found in the *Dujom Namchag Putri Lejang*,[22] where one finds a longer list of Tibetan disciples (but still including Lang) who here help the Guru to subdue the female Purba protectresses within Tibet.

Textual Continuities and Transformations

One begins to get the impression that rather little in the Dunhuang Tantric Buddhist ritual repertoire, however obscure it might at first appear, was ever subsequently thrown away. The ethos seems to have been that all rituals will somehow, somewhere have a use, and so must be preserved intact for posterity in the communal ritual treasury. At the same time, there is, of course, abundant evidence that ritual texts could be broken down into component parts, and recombined with other component parts to create new ritual wholes. The central skill in authoring new ritual texts is to achieve a recombination of existing ritual parts into a new ritual whole, in a manner which nevertheless reasserts with great precision the particular ethos and symbolism of the tantric genre being attempted. In pursuit of this goal, one can also find overlapping passages between texts of ostensibly quite different Tantric genres. PT 349, a Purba text, has exact parallels to canonical Guhyasamāja passages,[23] which in turn incorporate materials from *dhāraṇī* texts for the deity Dorje Dermo

(Rdo rje sder mo),[24] which in turn share passages with canonical *dhāraṇī* texts of the White Umbrella (Gdugs dkar)[25]—and so on and on. Thus, genetic connections are sometimes discernible within the ritual details shared between tantric texts of differing genres and periods. Textual recycling can be at the larger structural level as well: as mentioned earlier, the nineteenth-century scholar Magsar retained the structure of the Seven Perfections, citing the *Tantra of the Perfections of Enlightened Activity* as his source, but somewhat reconstrued the uses of its principal categories. There are few, if any, rules governing the type or nature or size of recyclable ritual items—only that they must work in their new ritual context and genre. Of course, there is no doubt that this process happened constantly in India, as in Tibet. Beyond that, it is not only tantric ritual that develops this way, but much of the world's ritual and mythic systems. A classic anthropological description of the process is found in Lévi-Strauss's exposition of what he dubbed "bricolage," which he describes as the subtle and ingenious "bending" of inherited items to new uses.[26]

The *Tabzhag* Manuscript

One of the most impressive Dunhuang tantric manuscripts is Tib J 321, complete in 167 pages. As we have mentioned earlier, this text consists of a NGB Mahāyoga scripture (also found in a few Kangyur editions), the *Lotus Garland of "Lasso of Method"* (*Thabs kyi zhags pa padma 'phreng ba*), embedded as lemmata within its commentary. There is no colophon. Copious interlinear notes, however, add clarifications to the main texts, and these claim the commentary to represent the teachings of Padmasambhava. A severely mutilated and corrupted version of the text, including the embedded Tantra, survives in some Tengyur (Bstan 'gyur) editions, in all cases resembling the Dunhuang text in lacking any colophon.[27] Yet, this commentary does not occur in most major Nyingma collections. Our study of this text is still in its infancy, but is already yielding valuable data.[28]

Codicologically, the manuscript is produced to a high professional standard with pretty much consistently excellent calligraphy. It gives every sign of institutional origin, quite different from some Dunhuang manuscripts such as PT 349 (discussed earlier), which give the impression that they might have represented an individual's set of notes.

Doctrinally, it is a highly sophisticated exposition of Mahāyoga theory and practice, with strong resemblances to the chief Mahāyoga Tantra of the Nyingmapa, the *Guhyagarbha*, in its advocacy of the doctrine of the sameness of all dharmas (*mnyam pa'i chos*). Vajrasattva is the interlocutor, and Vairocana the expounder of the *Tabzhag Tantra.* Right from the start, it presents complex technical terms that remain to this day part of Nyingma tantric exegesis. For example, in chapter 1, there is reference to the Three Characteristics (*mtshan nyid gsum*) (of the Continuum of the Path) of Mahāyoga. These categories remain very much a part of contemporary Mahāyoga exegesis: the late Dujom Rinpoché, for example, analyzed them in his *Exposition of the Teachings* (*Bstan pa'i rnam gzhag*), taking Padmasambhava's *Garland of Essential Instructions* (*Man ngag lta 'phreng*) as his source.[29] Dujom Rinpoché's and the *Garland's* language and understanding both seem much the same as that of the *Tabzhag* commentator. On the other hand, a complex teaching on the Three Maṇḍalas (*dkyil 'khor gsum*), developed over the first few chapters, seems quite distinctive, although as yet, we are far from a considered assessment of how this may fit with other transmitted interpretations.[30]

The commentary contains some pure theory and doctrine: for example, on the relative merits of the Śrāvakayāna, the ordinary Mahāyāna, and the Vajrayāna, on the ultimate and relative truths, and so on. Most of it, however, comprises dense ritual instruction, but very much in the Mahāyoga idiom of creatively integrating personal experience with Mahāyana view through the medium of Mahāyoga ritual, taking the understanding of the sameness of all dharmas or the *dharmadhātu* as the foundation. Hence, we find instructions for transforming the everyday act of eating into a burnt offering (*sbyin sreg,* Skt. *homa*) and for transforming all sensual enjoyments into offerings to the Buddhas; special Vajrayāna interpretations of the ten perfections (*pha rol tu phyin pa,* Skt. *pāramitās*); mention of transforming the five senses into the five Buddha families, and the five sense objects into their consorts; very complex instruction on transforming sexual intercourse into a practice of yoga; realization of emotional defilements as having the commitments, or *samayas,* of the five Buddhas as their ultimate nature; *homa* rites and *purba* rites organized according to the different classes of enlightened activities, and so on and so forth. A striking feature of the *Tabzhag* and its commentary is their emphasis on the use of ritual for transcendental rather than mundane goals. We will be publishing a more detailed study of this text later, including a more considered appraisal of its possible origin from the same author as the *Garland of Essential Instructions.*

So far as we have read, and we must emphasize that we still have some way to go, we cannot see anything in the *Tabzhag* root text that might betray a non-Indic origin. This probably helped justify its placement in some editions of the Bka' 'gyur, where it finds its way into their "Ancient Tantras" (Rnying rgyud) sections. Such acceptance was presumably further facilitated through the *Tantra's* endorsement by the early Sakya patriarchs, as we have discussed earlier. It seems that no Sanskrit original could be found by Butön (Bu ston), since the title is not listed in his *History* (*Chos 'byung*) of 1322–23, nor in his *Catalogue of the Collection of Tantras* (*Rgyud 'bum gyi dkar chag*) of 1339. But looking at the page layout of the original manuscript, and the way the text is embedded in its commentary, some possible reasons to question the reliability of the root text's redaction (even if not its ultimate Indic provenance) do emerge. Unlike the root tantra, the commentary might show signs of being taught to or composed for Tibetans—for example, it etymologizes Tibetan translational terms like *kyil-khor* (*dkyil 'khor*). Now, the *Tabzhag* manuscript has some root-tantra chapters so completely embedded in the commentary (and without any distinguishing indications) that in many cases it is not at all easy to distinguish between the root text and the commentary. In fact, unless the reader is very highly educated and patient, it can sometimes be well nigh impossible to discern the exact boundaries of the root text. Faced with such a circumstance, a scribe seeking to extract the root text only is likely to copy more rather than less, to make sure that none of the precious *Tantra* is left out of his copy; thus perhaps incorporating partially local materials into the Indian text. We have only just begun work on our detailed critical edition, but it is interesting that we have already found significant variants between the different versions of the root text, whose specific characteristics might well be accounted for by scribes having picked up on different parts of the root text as contained in the commentary.[31]

There might be a possible example of exactly this process of incorporating commentarial material in the Tibetan transmissions of the *Guhyasamāja Root Tantra*.[32] The two NGB versions we have consulted agree on one additional line (*tshig rkang*), which they give in the second verse of the third chapter, and this corresponds to an interlinear note in the Dunhuang version, IOL Tib J 438, but it is not found in four Bka' 'gyur editions (three consulted by Eastman and one we additionally considered), nor, in one case at least, in the extant Sanskrit root verses.[33] More broadly, it seems safe to say that faulty mechanisms of scribal transmission may inadvertently introduce variation and elaboration into a scriptural text, and may also suggest a striking way in which a textually based ritual tradition may develop without any deliberate rationale.[34]

Concluding Reflections

The *Tabzhag* commentary opens an amazing window onto the ritual and doctrinal world of Tibetan tantra before the New (Gsar ma) Translation period. It shows a thoroughly sophisticated and scholarly understanding of Mahāyāna

Buddhism and of Mahāyoga Tantrism that is in many ways the equal of the present-day tradition. Reading it alongside learned contemporary Nyingmapa lamas in 2006/07, it was striking how familiar much of it was to them. While it certainly has its own particular slant and ritual details, as one expects of a famous Tantra, the *Tabzhag* is not in any way surprising or alien to the contemporary tradition.

It also quotes from a number of other famous Mahāyoga titles, mainly from the Eighteen Tantras, including some exclusively NGB titles excluded from the Bka' 'gyur, such as the *Langchen Rab-bog* (*Glang chen rab 'bog*), the *Karmamāla*, and a *Kīlaya Chunyi* (*Kīlaya bcu gnyis*), and *Purba Chunyi-ki Gyü Chima* (*Phur pa bcu gnyis kyi rgyud phyi ma*; see note 4). Yet, it is interesting that several of these quoted passages do not seem to exist in the surviving NGB versions of those texts.

The Mahāyoga manuscripts we have studied probably date from the late tenth to early eleventh century, although it is hard to be very clear in many cases. They seem to represent a Tibetan Buddhism immediately prior to the Sarma period. Since these are the earliest extant Mahāyoga texts, we must conclude that when Tibetan Mahāyoga first enters our historical vision, it is a tradition already well developed—as with the first appearances of Mahāyāna in India. Are these signs of traditions that were once peripheral in Tibet, subsequently taking center stage? Or of traditions that were originally oral, or partially oral?

Seen as a whole, the Dunhuang collection signals an active Tantric Buddhism in that region by the late tenth century. Significant parts of Nyingma tantric practice as we currently know it had already emerged in developed form, while numerous *dhāraṇī* texts were also in use, as were some Kriyā, Carya, and Yogatantra materials. Moreover, PT 849 shows that a handful of early precursors of the Yoginī or Yoganiruttara tantras later associated with the Sarma period were already being signaled, including, as Kapstein has recently shown,[35] an earlier variant of verses later to be associated with the Sarmapa (Gsar ma pa) siddha tradition of Cintā, consort of Dārikapāda. One of the two *Catuṣpīṭhatantras*, nowadays part of the Sarma tradition, is also cited in PT 849, confirming the veracity of its Kangyur colophon, which mentions a first translation prior even to Smṛti's of the tenth century.[36]

Unfortunately, the inadequacies and ambiguities in the surviving historical sources from the post-Imperial period means that we are not yet confidently able to contextualize the evidence that the Dunhuang tantric texts offer us. Paul Smith and Bianca Horlemann have demonstrated that the Tibetan federations in the northeast in the early eleventh century were powerful in both military and economic terms, acting as middlemen in trade between China and Inner Asia, especially dealing in horses, and we even know the Chinese rendering of the name of a famous Tibetan leader from that time: Jiaosiluo.[37] Oblique insights into the social and institutional base of Tibetan life at that time come from Iwasaki,[38] whose old Chinese sources describe a vibrant and populous Tibetan Buddhist culture in nearby Tsongkha at the turn of the eleventh century, with active monasteries. Political leaders with whom the Chinese had to deal at that time were frequently monks, with the title Rinpoché (Rin po che). The old imperial usage of *tsenpo* (*btsan po*) was also current among lay rulers. This fits well with other evidence. In 1990, using Dunhuang texts, Helga Uebach was the first to demonstrate that a lineage of successors to Śāntarakṣita still bearing the imperial eclesiastical title of *chomdendé-ki ringlug* (*bcom ldan 'das kyi ring lugs*) had persisted at Samyé (Bsam yas),[39] a finding further supported in Kapstein's work on PT 849. More significant still, Uebach also showed that monastic activity, including both ordination lineages and colleges of higher studies, had persisted after Lang Darma's (Glang Dar ma) time. This was particularly so in the northeast, where several of Tri Relpachen's (Khri Ral pa can) original religious foundations had been situated, and where they continued unbroken after 842. Ronald Davidson[40] has since sought to expand on Uebach's findings, describing a vigorous tradition of Eastern Vinaya monks at that time. Not for the last time in history, the sudden demise of a Tibetan state in 842 clearly did not signify the sudden demise of Tibetan civilization, nor the instant deaths of all learned Tibetans. The capacity of commerce, civilization, and culture to continue without a functioning state is amply demonstrated in numerous historical examples, including modern Nepal.

What we can deduce from a careful examination of the Dunhuang Mahāyoga texts is a fascinating picture of a rich resource of well-made institutional text productions along with more informal writings, evidencing both ritual continuities and changes. We find definite persistence of many ritual and textual elements into later periods, but these may be accompanied by some changes in their framing, and a concern to achieve viable indigenous adaptations, for example, with the apparently quite early generation of charter myths with strongly Tibetan or national characteristics that are still in use in Nyingma Mahāyoga ritual today. We also sense the possibility of textual change occasionally being stimulated by more spontaneous factors such as scribally generated variants, perhaps involving the incorporation of annotations into root text.

NOTES

Our grateful thanks to the Arts and Humanities Research Council of the United Kingdom, who funded this research at the University of Oxford, and to Professor José Cabezón at the University of California Santa Barbara for generously inviting us to attend the conference, during which an earlier version of this chapter was presented.

Our thanks also to Professor Geoffrey Samuel for his insightful comments on the nature of ritual.

1. Takeuchi, personal communication, February 2008; and also as repeated in Dalton and van Schaik *Tibetan Tantric Manuscripts from Dunhuang. A Descriptive Catalogue of the Stein Collection at the British Library* (Leiden: Brill, 2006), xxi.

2. Gavin Flood, *An Introduction to Hinduism* (Cambridge: Cambridge University Press, 1996), 41–42; Maurice Bloch, *From Blessing to Violence: History and Ideology in the Circumcision Ritual of the Merina of Madagascar* (Cambridge: Cambridge University Press, 1986), especially 184–85, 194.

3. The *Kīlaya bcu gnyis* is cited, as is the *Phur pa bcu gnyis kyi rgyud phyi ma*. None of the three extant *Phur pa bcu gnyis* texts in the NGB seem to contain the lines cited in the *Thabs zhags* (we have made a full search in one case, and have browsed the other two without finding the lines), nor does any of the three extant NGB texts have a *phyi ma*, so it is a little unlikely that the *Thabs zhags* is referring to a Phur pa tantra that still survives.

4. These are the *samādhi* of suchness (*de bzhin nyid kyi ting nge 'dzin*); the *samādhi* of universal illumination (*kun tu snang ba'i ting nge 'dzin*); the causal *samādhi* (*rgyu'i ting nge 'dzin*).

5. We have consulted three editions of the Rnying ma rgyud 'bum (NGB) in considering this long parallel: the Mtshams brag manuscript edition, beginning volume *chi*, 1023.4; the Sde dge xylograph edition, beginning volume *wa*, 348v.7; and the Gting skyes manuscript edition, beginning volume *sha*, 523.6. These three can be taken as representing each of the three lines of textual descent (Bhutanese, Eastern Tibetan, and Southern Central Tibetan) which we discovered in our previous stemmatic analyses of Phur pa texts from the Rnying ma rgyud 'bum; see Cathy Cantwell and Robert Mayer, *The Kīlaya Nirvāṇa Tantra and the Vajra Wrath Tantra: Two texts from the Ancient Tantra Collection* (Vienna: Verlag der Osterreischischen Akademie der Wissenschaften, 2007), 16–18, 65–74.

6. The order of the Seven Perfections given in the NGB's *'Phrin las phun sum tshogs pa'i rgyud* is the perfection of: 1. oneself (*bdag nyid*); 2. time (*dus*); 3. place (*gnas*); 4. form (*gzugs*); 5. consecrations (*byin rlabs*); 6. recitation (*bzlas brjod*); 7. activity (*'phrin las*). These correspond respectively to numbers 7, 5, 6, 1, 2, 3, 4 in Tib J 331.III. In the *'Phrin las phun sum tshogs pa'i rgyud*, perfection of oneself, the practitioner, is completed in Chapter Eight; Chapter Nine includes the perfections of time, place and form, and begins consecrations; the remainder of the section on the perfection of consecrations takes up Chapter Ten, and Chapter Eleven consists of the sections on the perfection of recitation and activities.

7. Mag gsar Kun bzang stobs ldan dbang pa, *Phur pa'i rnam bshad he ru ka dpal bzhad pa'i zhal lung* (*Bcom ldan 'das dpal chen rdo rje gzhon nu'i 'phrin las kyi rnam par bshad pa he ru ka dpal bzhad pa'i zhal lung*), sNgags mang zhib 'jug khang (Ngak Mang Institute) (Beijing: Mi rigs dpe skrun khang, 2003).

8. In Tib J 331, the syllable *āṃ* or *aṃ* occurs both in the context of the body, speech, and mind trio and in the case of the syllables associated with the five places of the body (red *āṃ* at the tongue). Other Dunhuang manuscripts which also give *āṃ/aṃ* include Tib J 332 (f. 7a2–3), Tib J 754, Section 8, Pelliot tibétain 42 (f. 46.1–2 and 50.2–3), Pelliot

tibétain 626 and 634; see Sam van Schaik and Jacob Dalton, "Where Chan and Tantra Meet: Tibetan Syncretism in Dunhuang," in Susan Whitfield and Ursula Sims-Williams, eds., *The Silk Road: Trade, Travel, War and Faith* (London: The British Library, 2004), 66. The usage is also found in some NGB texts, such as the *Myang 'das*, Chapter Eighteen; NGB, Sde dge ed., vol. *zha*, f. 68a; and Mtshams brag ed., vol. *chi*, f. 149b, (298). It is also found in the root *Guhyagarbha Tantra; Gsang ba'i snying po de kho na nyid nges pa*, NGB, Mtshams brag ed., vol. *wa*, 176–77.

9. On the use of effigies in rituals, see also the chapters by Mengele and Cuevas in this volume.

10. Jacob S. Dalton and Sam van Schaik, *Catalogue of the Tibetan Tantric Manuscripts from Dunhuang in the Stein Collection*, International Dunhuang Project, 2005, [Online] available at http://idp.bl.uk/database/oo_scroll_h.a4d?uid=85029293610;bst=1;recnum=5288;index=1, image 4, top.

11. 'Jam mgon Kong sprul Blo gros mtha' yas, *Dpal rdo rje phur pa rtsa ba'i rgyud kyi dum bu'i 'grel pa snying po bsdud pa dpal chen dgyes pa'i zhal lung*, in his *Rgya chen bka' mdzod* (n.d, n.p.), vol. X, 94.6. TBRC Resource Code W24173; www.tbrc.org gives publication details as Paro: Ngodup, 1975–76.

12. 'Jam mgon Kong sprul, *Phur pa rtsa rgyud kyi 'grel pa*, 97.3.

13. There is a major *Phur chen* commentary by the great seventeenth century Sa skya pa scholar A myes zhabs ('Jam mgon A myes zhabs Ngag dbang kun dga' bsod nams, 1597–1659), *Bcom ldan das rdo rje gzhon nu'i gdams pa nyams len gyi chu bo chen po sgrub pa'i thabs kyi rnam par bshad pa 'phrin las kyi pad mo rab tu rgyas pa'i nyin byed*, reproduced from manuscript copies of the ancient Sa-skya xylographic prints (New Delhi: Ngawang Sopa, 1973); microfiche, The Institute for Advanced Studies of World Religions, *'Khon lugs Phur pa'i rnam bśad, 'Chams yig brjed byaṅ*, LMpj 012,223. The *Phur chen* was compiled over generations by the Sa skya hierarchs. For its citation of Dīptacakra, see *Sa skya Phur chen: Dpal rdo rje gzhon nu sgrub pa'i thabs bklags pas don grub* (Rajpur, India: Dpal sa skya'i chos tshogs, nd, Tibetan date given as 992), f. 24r.6.

14. Jacob Dalton, "The Early Development of the Padmasambhava Legend in Tibet: A Study of IOL Tib J 644 and Pelliot tibétain 307," *Journal of the American Oriental Society* 124/4 (2004), 759–72.

15. Although this *gter ma* was originally revealed by Zil gnon nam mkha'i rdo rje (19th century), the textual cycle has contributions from the Fifteenth Karma pa, Mkha' khyab rdo rje (1871–1922), and the late Bdud 'joms rin po che; hence, it is contained in Bdud 'joms Rin po che, 'Jigs bral ye shes rdo rje, *The Collected Writings and Revelations of H. H. bDud-'joms Rin-po-che 'Jigs bral ye shes rdo rje* (Kalimpong: Dupjung Lama, 1979–85), vol. *pha*, 134–35. This specific section is within the root practice text by the *gter ston* himself.

16. Bdud 'joms rin po che, *The Collected Writings*, vol. *tha*, 139, 143, in the *brtan ma* rite.

17. This *gter ma* was jointly revealed by Mchog gyur gling pa (1829–79) and Mkhyen brtse dbang po (1820–92), and its commentary written by Kong sprul; see Erik Pema Kunsang (trans.), The *Light of Wisdom, vol. II* (Boudhanath: Rangjung Yeshe Publications, 1998), 204–05.

18. In *Tshogs chen 'dus pa'i sgrub thabs dngogs grub char 'bebs* of the Smin grol gling tradition of Gter bdag gling pa (1646–1714) and Dharma Śrī (1654–1718), Rlangs chen Dpal gyi seng ge, together with the Slob dpon padma 'byung gnas, is similarly identified in the *brtan ma bskyang ba* section as the one responsible for binding the protectresses under oath; Bdud-'Joms 'Jigs-bral-ye-śes-rdo-rje, *Bdud 'joms Bka' ma: Rñin ma Bka' ma rgyas* pa (Kalimpong: Dupjung Lama, 1982–87), vol. *pha*, 436.1.

19. Karmay, *The Arrow and the Spindle* (1998), vol. 1: 245, 288–89, and elsewhere.

20. Although more analysis is still required, we believe we have also found that several such old indigenizing passages in later Buddhist Mahāyoga which integrate myth with ritual tend to reproduce an Old Tibetan tripartite narrative structure or literary form. This form typically renders the material into three distinct sections: myth, meditational or doctrinal explanation, and ritual instruction.

21. In Cantwell and Mayer, "Why did the Phur pa Tradition become so Prominent in Tibet?," we point out that a prime example of this embedding of charter myth structures within Buddhist Mahāyoga ritual is the taming of Rudra myth as used within the Phur pa tradition. The originally Indic taming of Rudra myth becomes just as inextricably entwined and essential to Tibetan Rnying ma Mahāyoga Phur pa rituals, as any of the Bön or pre-Buddhist *dpe srol* examples researched by Karmay. The taming of Rudra narratives in the canonical Phur pa scriptures relate such fundamental *rabs* (mythic narratives) as the origins of the entire Vajrayāna, and the origins of the Phur pa *yi dam* deity; so that in rituals it can provide the archetype for such major rites as deity yoga, nondual offerings, the visualization of the cemetery wrathful palace, *sgrol ba*, as well as other more minor aspects of ritual practice, such as the leftovers or excess offerings in *tshogs* rituals. Perhaps, even more important in overall terms are the mythic complexes surrounding Padmasambhava, which provide the charter for so much Rnying ma ritual life of every kind, from the revelation of *gter ma*, to the taming of local deities. It is well worth testing the hypothesis that the Padmasambhava mythic complex (likewise Shenrab and Gesar) could be considered in part to have gained some of its initial impetus as a Buddhist analogue (functionally and structurally speaking) to the pre-Buddhist mythic complex of the descent of the sacral emperor from the heavens, which, as Karmay has argued, provided a fundamental central matrix upon which so much of the autochthonous religion was based; Karmay, *Arrow and Spindle* (1998) vol. 1: 289. We will be looking more deeply into this question elsewhere.

22. Bdud 'joms rin po che, *The Collected Writings*, vol. *tha*, 139.

23. For example, from the *Piṇḍikramasādhana* of Nāgārjuna, Katsumi Mimaki and Toru Tomabechi, eds., *Pañcakrama: Sanskrit and Tibetan Texts Critically Edited with Verse Index and Facsimile Edition of the Sanskrit Manuscripts*, Bibliotheca Codicum Asiaticorum 8 (Tokyo: The Centre for East Asian Cultural Studies for Unesco, 1994), ff. 2a4–b3; and the *Piṇḍikṛta-sādhanopāyikā-vṛtti-ratnāvalī* or *Mdor bsdus pa'i sgrub thabs kyi 'grel pa rin chen phreng ba* attributed to Ratnākaraśānti, Peking no. 2690, vol. 62, ff. 297b.7–298b.2.

24. For example, the mantra *oṃ gha gha ghātaya ghātaya sarvaduṣṭān phaṭ kīlaya kīlaya sarvapāpān phaṭ hūṃ hūṃ vajrakīla vajradhara ājñāpayati sarvavighnānāṃ kāyavākcittaṃ kīlaya hūṃ phaṭ*—which is identified as Rdo rje sder mo's mantra and

which occurs in both Rdo rje sder mo's own texts and in *Guhyasamājatantra* literature, especially verse 58 of Chapter Fourteen of the *Guhyasamājatantra*.

25. For instance, the phrase, "The *phur bu* strikes, severing the vidyā mantra ..." (*rig* [or *rigs*] *sngags gcad do/ phur bus gdab bo/*) is repeated in rDo rje sder mo texts, such as that found in Dil mgo mkhyen brtse rin po che, *Skyabs rje dil mgo mkhyen brtse rin po che'i bka' 'bum* (Delhi: Shechen Publications, 1994), vol. *ta*, 265. It is also found in White Umbrella texts such as the, *'Phags pa de bzhin gshegs pa'i gtsug tor nas byung ba'i gdugs dkar po can gzhan gyis mi thub pa zhes bya ba'i gzungs;* the text is given in two versions in the *Sde dge Bka' 'gyur*, Toh. nos. 592 and 593, Rgyud 'bum *pha*, ff. 219a7–224b2; 224a2–229b7. Moreover, it is clear from the English version of a rDo rje sder mo *dhāraṇī* text in our possession—Joan Nicell, with the help of Ven. Geshe Jampa Gyatso, *The Dharani of Glorious Vajra Claws* (1996; reprint Pomaia, Italy: Istituto Lama Tzong Khapa, 2000)—that a long list of evils derives from the same ultimate source as those given in the White Umbrella texts. The items are shared, but slightly rearranged in order.

26. Claude Lévi-Strauss, *The Savage Mind* (London: Wiedenfield and Nicholson, 1976), 16 ff.

27. Dalton and van Schaik have reported that the Peking Bstan 'gyur version cites Vimalamitra in its colophon; in fact, the Peking Bstan 'gyur version has no colophon at all. See Dalton and van Schaik, *Tibetan Tantric Manuscripts from Dunhuang*, 51.

28. The root tantra (*'Phags pa thabs kyi zhags pa pad mo'i phreng don bsdus pa zhes bya ba*) is included in the "Old Tantras" (Rnying rgyud) section of Grags pa rgyal mtshan's *Kye'i rdo rje'i rgyud 'bum gyi dkar chags*, which was a source for the first Snar thang Bka' 'gyur, and it is also in 'Phags pa's slightly later Tantra catalogue; on the latter, see Helmut Eimer, "A Source for the First Narthang Kanjur: Two Early Sa skya pa Catalogues of the Tantras," in *Transmission of the Tibetan Canon: Papers Presented at a Panel of the 7th Seminar of the IATS, Graz 1995*, ed. Helmut eimer (Vienna: Verlag der Österreichischen Akademie der Wissenschaften, 1997), 52. So, although it never gained acceptance into the main bodies of all Bka' 'gyur editions, it was accepted within the separate Rnying rgyud sections of such Bka' 'gyurs as the Co ne, Sde dge, Lhasa, Li thang, Snar thang, Peking, and Urga. Among the Rnying ma pa, the root tantra was from the start prominently placed within the NGB as one of the 18 key Tantras of Mahāyoga. Conversely, despite the root tantra being such a central Rnying ma text, its commentary (*'Phags pa thabs kyi zhags padma 'phreng gi don bsdus pa'i 'grel pa*) seems lost to the Rnying ma tradition, and survives only in a somewhat mutilated form in the Peking, Snar thang, and Golden Bstan 'gyur editions (but not in Sde dge or Co ne). Many of the Tibetan canonical versions offer no Sanskrit title, although the Bhutanese NGB editions venture *ārya ka la pa sha padma mā le sang kra ha*, which might intend something along the lines of **Ārya upāya-pāśa padma-mālā saṃgraha*, although the *ka la* element is unclear—the best we can guess is that it might once have been related to *kalparāja*, since *rtog pa'i rgyal po* occurs in the Dunhuang text's colophonic title. Note that Alaka Chattopadhyaya suggests for the Bstan 'gyur commentary the reconstruction of **Upāya-pāśa-padma-mālā-piṇḍārtha-vṛtti; Catalogue of Kanjur and Tanjur: Vol. 1: Texts (Indian Titles) in Tanjur* (Calcutta: Indo–Tibetan Studies, 1972), 49. Adelheid Herrmann-Pfandt suggests for the Dunhuang commentary front title the reconstruction of

**Ārya-arthasaṃgraha-nāma-upāyapāśa-padmāvali-vṛtti*, and for the colophonic title, **Upāyapāśa-padmamālā-kalparāja-arthasaṃgraha-nāma-vṛtti;* see Adelheid Herrmann-Pfandt, "Eine Quellenkunde des esoterischen (tantrischen) Buddhismus in Indien von den Anfängen bis zum 9. Jahrhundert," unpublished Habilitationsschrift, Philipps-Universität Marburg/Lahn, 2000, 270–71. A much earlier and more contemporaneous reference to the Sanskrit title comes from the Dunhuang text that Hackin has referred to as the *Formulaire Sanscrit-Tibétain du X^E Siècle* (PT 849). In Joseph Hackin, ed., *Formulaire Sanscrit-Tibétain du X^E Siècle*, 2 vols., Mission Pelliot en Asie Centrale, Série Petit in Octavo (Paris: Librarie orientaliste Paul Geuthner, 1924), 2: 6, we see that *rgyud thabs kyi zhags pa* is rendered *a mo ga pa sa tan tra*. This is obviously wrong—a fundamental confusion between the popular *Amoghapāśa* literature and the somewhat rarer **Upayapāśa;* hence it serves not as evidence for the Sanskrit title of the *Thabs zhags*, but rather as evidence (were any more needed) that PT 849 is not necessarily a reliable source for Sanskrit title reconstructions, and this *pace* Ronald M. Davidson, *Tibetan Renaissance: Tantric Buddhism in the Rebirth of Tibetan Culture* (New York: Columbia University Press, 2005), 404, who uncritically accepts PT 849 as a reliable source for Sanskrit title reconstructions.

29. The annotations in the *Thabs zhags* Chapter One (f. 1b5) present them as: "When [one] understands through the Characteristic of Knowledge, by the inherent power of becoming familiarized with the Characteristic of the Entrance, the Characteristic of the Result is accomplished as Buddha body, speech and mind": *shes pa'i mtshan nyid gyis rtogs na 'jug pa'i mtshan nyid gyis goms pa'i mthus 'bras bu 'i mtshan nyid sku gsung thugs su 'grub bo*. In Bdud 'joms rin po che, following the *Man ngag lta 'phreng*; see Samten G. Karmay, *The Great Perfection: A Philosophical and Meditative Teaching of Tibetan Buddhism* (Leiden: E. J. Brill, 1988), 167. These are given (in Dorje and Kapstein's translation) as (1) *rtogs pa rnam pa bzhi'i tshul rig pa ni shes pa'i mtshan nyid* (awareness in the manner of the four kinds of realization is characteristic of knowledge), (2) *yang nas yang du goms par byed pa ni 'jug pa'i mtshan nyid* (repeated experience of it is characteristic of the entrance", and (3) *goms pa'i mthus mngon du gyur ba ni 'bras bu'i mtshan nyid* (actualization of it by the power of experience is the characteristic of the result). See Dudjom Rinpoche, *The Nyingma School of Tibetan Buddhism: Its Fundamentals and History*, trans. and ed. Gyurme Dorje and Matthew Kapstein, 2 vols (Boston: Wisdom Publications, 1991), 1: 265, and 2: 111.

30. The annotator (ff. 1b2, and 13b5) summarizes the list as consisting of: the *maṇḍala* of natural qualities, the *maṇḍala* of the mind and the *maṇḍala* of (its) reflections (*rang bzhin, yid,* and *gzugs brnyan*). However, the discussion in the main text does not seem quite so straightforward in its categorization of the three.

31. This in turn might indicate that the archetype of the *Thabs zhags* in Tibet was the version embedded in the commentary—or else that the commentary was later used to emend a separately transmitted root text, thus complicating the textual transmission.

32. See Eastman's preliminary 1980 study of the virtually complete Dunhuang manuscript, IOL Tib J 438; Kenneth W. Eastman, "The Dun-huang Tibetan Manuscript of the Guhyasamājatantra," *Report of the Japanese Association for Tibetan Studies*, 26 (March 1980): 8–12, English language appended version of "Chibetto-go Guhyasamājatantra no tonkō

shutsudo shahon". Eastman collates the verses of Chapter Three of the *Tantra*, together with three Bka' 'gyur witnesses (Sde dge, Snar thang and Peking) and one Southern Central Rnying ma rgyud 'bum edition. We have also consulted the Stog Palace Bka' 'gyur and another Rnying ma rgyud 'bum edition representing the Bhutanese line of descent.

33. Philological analysis of such transmissional variants remains only partially resolved at present; we hope to contribute more in forthcoming publications. In particular, we wish to problematize the widespread conception, repeated by Eastman, of distinctively NGB transmissions that differ from Bka' 'gyur transmissions, at least in the case of texts like the *Thabs zhags* and the *Guhyasamāja* that are shared between the Bka' 'gyur and the NGB. Might not regional factors of economy and convenience on some occasions outweigh sectarian factors in choice of exemplar? In the case of the *Thabs zhags*, the sDe dge bKa' 'gyur and the sDe dge NGB texts seem to have been made from the same blocks.

34. In the Phur pa tradition, two apparently minor scribal variants of a phrase within a key root verse (*srog gi go ru*, or *srog gi sgo ru*) have led to two rather different commentarial elaborations; see Robert Mayer, *A Scripture of the Ancient Tantra Collection: The Phur-pa bcu-gnyis* (Oxford: Kiscadale, 1996), 213–16.

35. Matthew Kapstein, "New Light on an Old Friend: PT 849 Reconsidered," in *Tibetan Buddhist Literature and Praxis: Studies in its Formative Period, 900–1400*, ed. Ronald M. Davidson and Christian K. Wedemeyer (Leiden: Brill, 2006), 23–29.

36. The Stog Bka' 'gyur catalogue includes the following words in the colophon to one of its two *Catuṣpīṭha* scriptures: "translated anew by Smṛtijñānakīrti" (*smṛtijñānakīrtis gsar du bsgyur te*); Tadeusz Skorupski *A Catalogue of the Stog Palace Kanjur* (Tokyo: The International Institute for Buddhist Studies, 1985), 206. This Indian paṇḍit's visit to Tibet in the late tenth or early eleventh century is often said in traditional sources to mark the watershed between Rnying ma and Gsar ma periods (Dudjom Rinpoche, *The Nyingma School*, 11), and Rongzom Mahāpaṇḍita was believed to be his reincarnation (Dudjom Rinpoche, *The Nyingma School*, 703). If Smṛtijñānakīrti had indeed retranslated this *Catuṣpīṭha*, or translated it anew, as the colophon suggests, this supports the evidence in PT 849 that a previous translation had been current in Tibet before the Gsar ma period.

37. Paul J Smith, *Taxing Heaven's Storehouse: Horses, Bureacrats, and the Destruction of the Sichuan Tea Industry 1074–1224*, Harvard-Yenching Institute Monograph Series no. 32 (Cambridge, MA: Harvard University, 1991), 27; and Bianca Horlemann, "On the Origin of Jiaosiluo, the first ruler of the Tsong kha tribal confederation in the eleventh century A mdo, in *Zentralasiatische Studien* 34 (2005): 127–54; also "The Relations of the Eleventh-Century Tsong kha Tribal Confederation to its Neighbour States on the Silk Road," in *Contributions to the Cultural History of Early Tibet*, ed. Matthew Kapstein and Brian Dotson (Leiden: Brill, 2007), 79–101.

38. Tsutomu Iwasaki, "The Tibetan Tribes of Ho-hsi and Buddhism During the Northern Sung Period," *Acta Asiatica* 64 (1993): 17–37.

39. Helga Uebach, "On Dharma Colleges and Their Teachers in the Ninth Century Tibetan Empire," in *Indo-sino-tibetica: studi in onore di Luciano Petech*, ed. Paolo Daffinà (Rome: Universita di Roma, 1990), 393–417.

40. Davidson, *Tibetan Renaissance*, chap. 3, 84–116.

4

The Convergence of Theoretical and Practical Concerns in a Single Verse of the *Guhyasamāja Tantra*

YAEL BENTOR

One of the most well-known verses of the *Guhyasamāja Tantra*—a verse incorporated into many practices of the *Guhyasamāja*—is found in its second chapter, the chapter on the "mind directed at enlightenment" (*bodhi-citta, byang chub sems*). Here the Tathāgata, whose name is "Vajra-Body, Vajra-Speech and Vajra-Mind of All Tathāgatas," dwelt in absorption,[1] and uttered the following verse.[2]

> *abhāve bhāvanābhāvo bhāvanā naiva bhāvanā |*
> *iti bhāvo na bhāvaḥ syād bhāvanā nopalabhyate ||*[3]

This chapter first examines the role of this verse in the practice of the *Guhyasamāja*, and then explores how it was understood. We then follow the shifts in philosophical affiliation this verse underwent over time.

The Role of Our Verse in the Practice of the *Guhyasamāja*

In the most important *sādhana* manual for the practice of the *Guhyasamāja* according to the Ārya tradition, the *Piṇḍī-krama-sādhana* (*Mdor byas sgrub thabs*), by Nāgārjuna,[4] our verse appears, with small variations, at the very beginning of the generation of the *maṇḍala* and the deities dwelling in it. In introducing it, Nāgārjuna explains:[5] "[The yogis] meditate that in the ultimate truth the three realms are devoid of intrinsic nature (*niḥsvabhāva*)." He then concludes:[6] "With this verse, [the yogis] meditate that the nature of the animate and inanimate [world] is empty (*śūnya, stong pa*), and with this ritual method, the animate and inanimate are blessed as the ground of pristine wisdom (*jñāna-bhūmi, ye shes kyi sa*)."

In another central manual on the practice of the *Guhyasamāja* of the Ārya tradition, the *Samāja-sādhana-vyavasthāli* (*Rnam gzhag rim pa*),[7] Nāgabuddhi instructs the practitioners to meditate, while reciting this verse, on everything as having the nature of the space that remains after the destruction of the three realms at the end of the eon.

Hence, the meditation here is a meditation on emptiness. In a type of ritual death, practitioners dissolve themselves and their entire world into emptiness. The new pure rebirth of the practitioners as deities in the celestial mansion of the *maṇḍala* then arises from emptiness. Emptiness here corresponds to the empty eon in between the previous and the later worlds in a cosmological cycle, which is understood not as nothingness, but as something that has the potential for the recreation of the new world. And for this reason, emptiness here is called the ground of pristine wisdom—it is the ground for all phenomena. During the practice of the creation stage, the *kyerim* (*bskyed rim*), the elimination of all appearances of the world and all its inhabitants within the practitioner's own mind is the ground for all the visualizations during the meditation that follows. And this initial meditation on emptiness is practiced while our verse is recited.

This verse is obviously mantra-like, alliterating (*anuprāsa*) the sounds *bha*, *va*, and *na*. Moreover, it puns on the meanings derived from the root √*bhū*. *Bhāva* is being, existing, that which exists, an entity, an existing thing, and all earthly objects. Thus, *bhāva* indicates both a thing and a state of existence. In the first sense it can be translated as an entity or a thing; and as a state of existence, *bhāva* can mean existing, and *abhāva* not existing. As for *bhāvanā*, it is usually translated as meditation. This noun is in the causative form, and carries the meanings of causing to be, bringing into existence, creating, and producing.

This meaning of meditation is indeed the foundation of the creation stage. Our verse is recited immediately after practitioners visualize away ordinary appearances, and right before they begin to visualize themselves as enlightened beings at the center of the celestial mansion of the *maṇḍala*. The pun on the meaning of the nature of existence (*bhū, bhāva*) and of meditation (*bhāvanā*)—in the sense of "causing to be"—is very germane at this point of the practice. The practitioners may reflect here: "Into what would the ordinary world disappear?" "How would the enlightened realm be created?" "Does the ordinary world exist?" "Is the ordinary world a meditation, that is to say, 'caused to be,' by the mind?" "Does the realm of the *maṇḍala* exist? Is it more real or less real than the ordinary world?" "Since it is obvious that this enlightened realm is created by the mind, isn't the ordinary world similarly a result of visualization or mental construction?" "On the other hand, the deities and the celestial mansion where they reside have arisen from emptiness, the true nature of all things, so they must be real." And so on.

The pun on *bhū* and *bhāvanā* is lost when the Sanskrit verse is translated into other languages. The etymology of the Tibetan verb for "to meditate," *gompa* (*sgom pa*), is not "to cause to be," but rather "to habituate." Still, in certain contexts the meaning of the Sanskrit word does carry through. The final verb *upa-√labh* also bears a variety of meanings. The difficulty in understanding the meaning of the Sanskrit verse itself, as well as the problem of translating it into Tibetan contributed to the great variety of interpretations the verse received. This is how this verse appears in the Tibetan translation of the *Guhyasamāja Tantra*:[8]

> *dngos po med pas sgom pa med/bsgom par bya ba bsgom pa min /*
> *de ltar dngos po dngos med pas/sgom pa dmigs su med pa'o //*

The differences between this Tibetan translation and the Sanskrit go beyond those that are the result of the grammar of these two languages. In the Tibetan translation, we have in the first line (*pāda*), *dngos po med pas* (because things do not exist) for *abhāve*, which is the usual translation of *abhāve*, but as noted already, does not have exactly the same meaning; in the second *pāda* we have *bsgom par bya ba* (one ought to meditate) for *bhāvanā*,[9] and in the third line again the verbal noun *med pas* (because they do not exist), while the Sanskrit has a negation of an optative of a verb of existence, *na bhāvaḥ syād*.

The Interpretation of Our Verse in the *Pradīpoddyotana* in Sanskrit

As we observed earlier, this verse may be rendered into English in more than one way. Let us now examine how this "mantra" was understood and interpreted. In the most famous commentary on the *Guhyasamāja Tantra* according to the Ārya tradition, the *Pradīpoddyotana*, Candrakīrti interprets our verse by means of the tantric hermeneutical method called the *tsulshi* (*tshul bzhi*) or "the four ways," which consists of the literal, common, hidden, and ultimate levels of interpretation.[10]

Even though Candrakīrti does not explicitly say so, the literal level of interpretation here is clearly based on Nāgārjuna's tetralemma. The four lines are explained in correspondence with the four possibilities: existing, not existing, both existing and not existing, and neither existing nor not existing. Still, we should not rush to the conclusion that since this work is written by a Candrakīrti, a Mādhyamika explanation is what we must expect here. Candrakīrti explains [I summarize and interpret]:[11]

1. [If there are no things], there can be no meditation (*bhāvanā* = causing to be) because if there are no things, there cannot be causing to be.
2. [If there are things], then meditation [causing to be] is not a meditation, because even without meditation [causing to be], there are existing things.
3. [If there are both things and no things]: that which is both a thing and a no thing would not exist, therefore, that thing [which is both] would not be a thing.
4. [If there are neither things nor no things], then, there cannot be meditation [causing to be]. Therefore, no meditation is to be perceived.

So far, this is the literal level of interpretation. If we look at all four levels of interpretation, then what we find here is not the usual tantric hermeneutic by means of the *tsulshi*.[12] Instead, it is the fourfold meditation common in Yogācāra writings that is applied here to explain our verse.

The stages of the fourfold meditation that are found in some of the Five Works of Maitreya (Byams chos sde lnga) and in Vasubandhu's commentaries on them are:[13]

1. Apprehending things to the extent they exist.
2. Apprehending mind-only or mental-events-only (*cittamātra, sems tsam*).
3. Apprehending that there is also no mind-only.
4. Realizing suchness.

How is this fourfold meditation applied in the *Pradīpoddyotana* in explaining our verse?[14]

1. The first level is "apprehending things to the extent they exist"—here, according to the four possibilities of Nāgārjuna.
2. The second stage is "apprehending mind-only" or "mental-events-only" (*cittamātra, sems tsam*) by realizing that external things are creations of the mind (*cittamaya*).
3. In the third stage, Candrakīrti maintains that given the absence of things, neither is there mind-only, and the two truths are indivisible.
4. On the ultimate level, for those who realize the stage of union[15]—and here Candrakīrti does use tantric terminology—there is no more clinging to meditator, meditation, and object of meditation.

The *sādhanas* use the recitation and meditation on our verse as a part of meditation on emptiness, and according to Candrakīrti's *Pradīpoddyotana*, this meditation is the fourfold meditation typical of treatises of the Yogācāra School. As often pointed out,[16] Yogācāra works offer more dynamic processes, especially meditative processes of transformation, and such processes are also the foundation of tantric practices, such as the creation stage. The fourfold meditation is a process that matches the creation stage well.

During the practice of the creation stage, at first the practitioners visualize away their ordinary world and reflect on the extent it exists. In the second stage, they create, in their minds, their enlightened realm—with themselves as deities and with their environment as the celestial mansion of the *maṇḍala*—and they meditate on mind-only. In the third stage, they realize that this creation, much like their ordinary world, is not real; and by understanding that the true nature of all phenomena is not mental-event only, they understand that neither is there mind-only. Finally, after dissolving their visualization into emptiness, they realize the suchness of all things, and the nonduality of emptiness and appearances.

Two Different Interpretations of Our Verse in Tibetan Translation

There are two different explanations of our verse in works translated into Tibetan: one in the Tibetan translation of the *Pradīpoddyotana*,[17] and the other in Śāntipa's commentary on the *Piṇḍī-krama-sādhana*, the *Ratnāvalī*,[18] which, as we saw, contains this verse as well. Here is Śāntipa's commentary on the first part of the verse (*abhāve bhāvanābhāvo, dngos po med pas sgom pa med*) in the literal level of interpretation, which seems to have survived only in its Tibetan translation.[19]

> *brtan pa dang g.yo ba'i dngos po thams cad med na sgom*[20] *pa ni med de/*
> *bsgom par bya ba med pa'i phyir ro /*

This seems to be a good translation of the Sanskrit of Candrakīrti's *Pradīpoddyotana*:[21]

> *sthira-cala-sarva-padārthānām abhāve sati bhāvanāyā abhāvaḥ bhāvyābhāvāt.*

Śāntipa's explanation can be rendered into English as: "When there are not any animate and inanimate things, there is no meditation [causing to be], because there is nothing to meditate upon [to cause to be]."

The Tibetan translation of the *Pradīpoddyotana* itself is somewhat different:[22]

> *brtan pa dang g.yo ba'i dngos po thams cad kyi ngo bo nyid ni med pa yin na ni sgom pa med ste bsgom par bya ba med pa'i phyir ro* /

This may be translated as: "When 'there is no' essence to all the animate and inanimate 'things,' 'there is no meditation,' because there is nothing to meditate upon."

In the Sanskrit there is no equivalent to the word "essence" (*ngo bo nyid*) found in the Tibetan. In terms of the "view," the difference between these two Tibetan translations is considerable. We can conclude then that the Tibetan translation of the *Pradīpoddyotana* is also a transition toward a more standard Mādhyamika view. Still, it is not clear when this philosophical shift took place. According to its colophon in the Bstan, 'gyur, the *Pradīpoddyotana* was translated and revised in the eleventh century.

Tibetan Commentaries

There was a short commentary on the *Guhyasāmaja Tantra* written by Chag Lotsāwa Chöjé Pel (Chag lo tsā ba Chos rje dpal), who lived in the thirteenth century,[23] but at present it is unavailable to me. The version that Butön Rinchen Drub (Bu ston Rin chen grub, 1290–1364) comments upon is very similar to that of the *Drönsel* (*Sgron gsal*), the Tibetan translation of the *Pradīpoddyotana*.[24] Butön more or less reproduces the fourfold meditation of the *Pradīpoddyotana* without commenting on it. Apparently for Butön, the question as to which school (Yogācāra or Mādhyamika) this meditation belongs was not an issue. Furthermore, in his explanation of another step in the creation stage of the *Guhyasamāja*,[25] Butön explicitly advocates Mind Only: "this is so that you will understand all [phenomena] as Mind Only (*sems tsam*)."

Butön was one of the last commentators on the Guhyasamāja Tantra who actually knew Sanskrit, and who could see that the meaning of our verse in its Tibetan rendering was different from the meaning of the Sanskrit. He could also see that, in its most important commentary, the *Praīpoddyotana* in its Tibetan translation, the meaning of our verse was further altered, at least since the fourteenth century, if not before. But Butön does not comment on this.

Among the Gelugpas, the Ārya School of the *Guhyasamāja* is considered to hold the philosophical positions of the Mādhyamika School, and the emptiness meditated upon in practices of the "Path of Mantra" (i.e., in the Tantra) is considered no different from the emptiness of the Mādhyamika School. As we would expect, the portion of the commentary of Tsongkhapa (1357–1419) that explains our verse[26] accords with his views on Mādhyamika and emptiness. In Tsongkhapa's interpretation, "a thing" must be glossed as "an inherently existing thing"; "no thing" therefore refers to "absence of own essence," and "meditation" (*sgom pa*) is meditation on suchness.

Furthermore, Tsongkhapa does not enter into the subject of the fourfold meditation. For him, the explanation of the *Pradīpoddyotana* here is, as Candrakīrti names it, an explanation by means of the tantric hermeneutical method called "the four ways" (*tshul bzhi*). In the section on the creation stage in his commentary on the *Namzhag Rimpa* (*Rnam gzhag rim pa*),[27] Tsongkhapa says that from among the "four ways" in which the *Pradīpoddyotana* explains our verse, it is the literal and common levels of interpretations which are relevant to the creation stage. The common level of interpretation is common to both the creation and completion stages. But the hidden and ultimate levels pertain to practices with the consort, to the subtle body, and to the completing stage alone. Hence, in his discussion of the creation stage, Tsongkhapa discusses only the first two levels of interpretations. Thus, in the context of the creation stage, his explanations do not go into the fourfold meditation and the problems that this poses for Mādhyamika.

Though Tsongkhapa did not concern himself with the fourfold meditation, he did address the question of the nature of the external world. Tsongkhapa[28] explains the meaning of "external appearance" or "external aspect" (*bāhyākāra, phyi rol gyi rnam pa*) in the *Pradīpoddyotana*[29] by specifying that this refers to external objects which "exist by their own essence (*rang gi ngo bo nyid kyis grub pa*)," and by adding that things have no existence "apart from being merely imputed by the mind (*sems kyis btags pa tsam las*)." Similarly, Tsongkhapa[30] glosses the phrase "created by the mind" (*cittamaya*) or "of the nature of the mind" (*sems kyi rang bzhin*) in the *Pradīpoddyotana*[31] with "of the nature of being merely imputed by the mind (*sems kyis btags pa tsam gyi rang bzhin*)."[32] Thus, rather than taking the explanation of the *Pradīpoddyotana* at its (Yogācāra) face value, Tsongkhapa gives it a Prāsaṇgika Mādhyamika spin.

In his commentary on difficult points in the *Pradīpoddyotana*, entitled the *Tachö Rinchen Nyugu* (*Mtha' gcod rin chen myu gu*),[33] Tsongkhapa elaborates on the subject of external objects and Mind Only:

> When [the *Pradīpoddyotana*] explains [the verse that] begins with *dngos po med pa* on the common level of interpretation, there appears something like a refutation of external objects and an establishment

> [of them] as mind-only; and there are similar occurrences also in other cases. It seems that [some people], unable to examine this very thoroughly, did not understand that the position of the Noble Father [Ārya Nāgārjuna] and his Spiritual Sons [Candrakīrti and so on] in general, and the position of the commentator [Candrakīrti] in particular, which accept external objects as conventional designations. Therefore, they say that the system of the *Pradīpoddyotana* does not accept external objects. However, since I already extensively explained elsewhere why this is unacceptable and how to eradicate the extreme views of eternalism and nihilism, I do not elaborate here.

It seems that the purpose of this passage is to explain how "some people" might come to the conclusion that the *Pradīpoddyotana* refutes external objects and maintains that they are "mind-only." Butön was an important teacher in the lineage that came down to Tsongkhapa, and it seems that Tsongkhapa had much reverence for Butön, although he did not always agree with him.[34] For Tsongkhapa, there is a crucial difference between holding that external objects exist as conventional designations, and holding that external objects do not exist *at all*. Tsongkhapa does not agree that the author of the *Pradīpoddyotana* rejects external objects. According to Tsongkhapa, the Ārya school of the *Guhyasamāja* maintains that external objects exist as conventional designations, and this causes him to offer an alternative gloss to the line of the *Drönsel* that refers to external objects—namely that while existing externally, inherently they do not exist, but are mere mental imputations.

In commenting on our verse, Tsongkhapa's disciple Khedrubjé (Mkhas grub rje, 1385–1438) follows his teacher. In the context in which Butön explains:[35] "This is so that you will understand all [phenomena] as Mind Only, and realize the two truths as indivisible," Khedrubjé refers to this very passage, without naming names, by saying:[36]

> Some lamas (*bla ma kha cig*) say that this is so that you will understand all [phenomena] as mind-only, and realize the two truths as indivisible. They do not understand that the author of the *Pradīpoddyotana* accepts external things as conventional designations, and that this is also the intention of Ārya Nāgārjuna. The world and its inhabitants... are only conventional truth.... Hence this [statement] is just pointless.

For Tsongkhapa and Khedrubjé then, there is no doubt that Candrakīrti, the author of the *Pradīpoddyotana*, as well as Nāgārjuna, the author of the *Piṇḍīkrama-sādhana*, do not accept the Mind-Only School, but hold the view of the Prāsaṇgika Mādhyamika School.

Conclusions

We have analyzed the recitation of a verse, or rather "mantra," as an important ritual event during the creation stage of the *Guhyasamāja*. As we saw, in his *Piṇḍī-krama-sādhana* Nāgārjuna calls this recitation of the mantra a "ritual" or "ritual method" (*vidhi, cho ga*). While rituals may remain almost unchanged, their interpretations are often adjusted in accordance with current theories. Indeed, the meaning of the Sanskrit mantra is fluid and enigmatic—the more one reflects on it, the more implications one finds—and it is precisely this fluidity that serves as the basis for reflections during the meditation and allows for different interpretations throughout history. Still, this mantra is somewhat different from other mantras recited during this tantric practice, insofar as it has overt philosophical content—that is, since it resembles verses from Buddhist philosophical treatises.

Our focus was the import given to this liminal point of the practice, just after the practitioners visualize away (*mi dmigs*) their ordinary identity and the ordinary appearances of themselves and their world, and just before they create in their mind the *maṇḍala* with the deities of their enlightened realm. On one level, this ritual may simply be taken as the erasure of one's own ordinary existence by transforming it into utter nothingness so that a new reality can arise. However, in a Buddhist philosophical context, this stage is understood as dissolution into emptiness. While in the *Mūla-madhyamaka-kārikā* (chapter 24) and in the *Vigrahavyāvartanī-kārikā* (v. 70),[37] Nāgārjuna does emphasize that emptiness is that which makes change possible, in Buddhist Tantric literature on the creation stage, such as the *Piṇḍī-krama-sādhana*, emptiness is more explicitly understood as the ground or potential for all phenomena.

The commentators saw it as their task to explain the mantra, and since it lends itself to a number of interpretations, various commentators stepped up to the challenge, and most of them explained it by employing the theoretical frameworks they most favored.[38] The *Pradīpoddyotana* applies first Nāgārjuna's tetralemma, but then it applies the fourfold meditation common in Yogācāra treatises. The meaning Candrakīrti, the author of the *Pradīpoddyotana*, saw in our verse was modified twice. The first philosophical reorientation toward a so-called authentic Mādhyamika or so-called authentic Prāsaṇgika Mādhyamika was written into the Tibetan translation of the *Pradīpoddyotana*. Unlike its Sanskrit version (and unlike the Tibetan translation of Śāntipa's *Ratnāvalī*, the *Rin chen phreng ba*), the Tibetan translation does not speak about the absence of things, but rather about the absence *of their essence*. Perhaps, when earlier versions of the translations of the Tengyur texts and some of the former commentaries on the *Pradīpoddyotana* become available, we will be able to determine with more precision when this modification occurred. The second transformation of the meaning of our verse took place in Tibetan compositions, when especially among the Gelugpa, typical Yogācāra practices and what came to be called Mādhyamika-Yogācāra fell from favor. Then, together with all the other authors of the Ārya School of the Guhyasamāja, Candrakīrti, the author of the *Pradīpoddyotana*, came to be identified with "orthodox" Prāsaṇgika Madhyamaka.

NOTES

This research was supported by *The Israel Science Foundation* (grant no. 874/02–1).

1. In the concentration called "the *vajra*-mode of awakening into manifestation of all Tathāgatas" (*sarva-tathāgatābhisaṃbodhi-naya-vajra, de bzhin gshegs pa thams cad kyi mngon par rdzogs par byang chub pa'i tshul rdo rje*); for references, see note 2.

2. This reading is found in the editions of Francesca Fremantle, "A Critical Study of the Guhyasamāja-tantra: (Ph.D. diss., London: School of Oriental and African Studies, 1971), 190; Yukei Matsunaga, ed., *The Guhyasamāja Tantra: A New Critical Edition* (Osaka: Toho Shuppan, 1978), 9; Benoytosh Bhattacharyya, ed., *Guhyasamāja Tantra or Tathāgataguhyaka* (Baroda: Oriental Institute, 1931), 11; S. Bagchi, ed., *Guhyasamāja Tantra or Tathāgataguhyaka* (Darbhanga: The Mithila Institute, 1965), 8. Fremantle notes a variant reading of *abhāvi* for *abhāve* in her manuscripts C and P and comments that a substitution of 'i' for 'e' occurs several times; Matsunaga notes the same variant reading in his manuscripts A and T5. The *Pradīpoddyotana* [Chintaharan Chakravarti, ed., *Guhya-samāja-tantra-Pradīpoddyotana-ṭīkā-ṣaṭ-koṭī-vyākhyā* (Patna: Kashi Prasad Jayaswal Research Institute, 1984), 31] explains the literal meaning with a locative absolute: *abhāve sati*, and most commentaries take the *abhāve* in the beginning of our verse to mean *abhāve sati*. In his edition of the *Piṇḍī-krama-sādhana*, which cites our verse, Louis de La Vallée Poussin [*Études et textes tantriques: Pañcakrama* (Gand: H. Engelcke, 1896), 2] has *abhāvabhāvanā bhāvo* for *abhāve bhāvanābhāvo*. According to David L. Snellgove, [*Hevajra Tantra: A Critical Study* (London: Oxford University Press, 1959), 77] the *Sekoddeśaṭīkā* also has this reading. Giuseppe Tucci ["Some Glosses upon the Guhyasamāja," *Mélanges Chinois et Bouddhiques*, no. 3 (1934–1935): 352] "corrects" the Sanskrit text in light of its Tibetan translation, by changing *abhāve* to *abhāvena*, although he admits that this makes the first line hypermetric.

3. As we shall see, the meaning of this verse is purposely enigmatic, and indeed it was interpreted in various ways. For some translations of this verse, see Benoytosh Bhattacharyya, *Guhyasamāja Tantra*, xx; Tucci, "Some Glosses," 353–53; Snellgrove, *Hevajra Tantra*, part 1, 77; Fremantle, "A Critical Study," 34 and 143–4, n.1; Pio Filippani-Ronconi, "La formulazione liturgica della dottrina del Bodhicitta nel 2 Capitolo de *Guhyasamājatantra*," *Annali* (Istituto Universitario Orientale di Napoli) vol. 32, no. 2, n.s. XXII (1972): 190; Kenneth Eastman, "Mahāyoga Texts at Tun-huang" (Master's thesis, Stanford University, 1983),

18–19; Raniero Gnoli, "Guhyasamājatantra (chapters 1, 2, & 5)," *Testi Buddhisti* (Turin: Unione Tipografico-editrice Torinese, 1983), 628; Peter Gäng, *Das Tantra der Verborgenen Vereinigung: Guhyasamāja-Tantra* (München: Eugen Diederichs Verlag, 1988), 123. I would like to thank Jake Dalton for providing me with a copy of Eastman's Thesis. Here is just one possible translation: "When there are no [existing] things, there is no meditation [causing to be]. Meditation indeed is no meditation. Thus, a thing would be no thing. No meditation is to be perceived [or, there is no object to the meditation]." As we shall see, there are various other alternative translations.

4. *Piṇḍīkrama-sādhana* (*Piṇḍīkṛta-sādhana*); the Sanskrit was edited by La Vallée Poussin, *Pañcakrama*, 1–14; also, Ram Shankar Tripathi, *Piṇḍīkrama and Pañcakrama of Ācārya Nāgārjuna* (Sarnath: Central Institute of Higher Tibetan Studies, 2001), 1–32. For the Tibetan translation, see *Sgrub pa'i thabs mdor byas pa*, Sde dge Bstan 'gyur, Toh. no. 1796, Rgyud *ngi*, folios 1b–11a; Peking Bstan 'gyur, Ōtani 2661, vol. 61, 268.1.1–273.1.6.

5. La Vallée Poussin, *Pañcakrama*, v. 16cd; Tripathi, *Piṇḍīkrama and Pañcakrama*, v. 15cd; Sde dge, *Sgrub pa'i thabs*, folio 2b3–4; Peking, *Sgrub pa'i thabs*, 269.3.2. While La Vallée Poussin (v. 16d) and Tripathi (v. 15d) have *bhavatrayam*, all versions of the Bstan 'gyur available to me have *dngos po rnams/ srid gsum*. For *niḥsvabhāva*, the Bstan 'gyur has *dngos po med pa*.

6. La Vallée Poussin, *Pañcakrama*, v. 18; Tripathi, *Piṇḍīkrama and Pañcakrama*, v. 17; Sde dge, *Sgrub pa'i thabs*, folio 2b4–5; Peking, *Sgrub pa'i thabs*, 269.3.3–4.

7. Nāgabuddhi (Klu'i blo), *Samāja-sādhana-vyavasthālī* (*'Dus pa'i sgrub pa'i thabs rnam par gzhag pa'i rim pa*), Sde dge Bstan 'gyur, Toh. no. 1809, Rgyud *ngi*, folio 121b4–5; Peking Bstan 'gyur, Ōtani 2674, vol. 62, 7.4.4–6.

8. *De bzhin gshegs pa thams cad kyi sku gsung thugs kyi gsang chen gsang ba 'dus pa zhes bya ba brtag pa'i rgyal po chen po*. The Tantra is found in a number of recensions: Dunhuang, IOL (India Office Library) Tib J 481 and IOL Tib. J 438; *The Rnying ma rgyud 'bum* (Thimbu: Dingo Khyentse Rimpoche, 1973), vol. 17, folios 1b1–314a4; Sde dge Bka' 'gyur, Toh. no. 442, Rgyud 'bum *ca*, folios 90a–148a (vol. 81, 181–295); Peking Bka' 'gyur, Ōtani 81, vol. 65, 174.3.5–203.2.1; Stog Palace, vol. 96, 2–190; also in *Dpal gsang ba 'dus pa'i rtsa rgyud 'grel pa bzhi sbrags dang bcas pa* (Lhasa: Zhol Printing House, made from block-prints carved in 1890). The reading of the verse given here is found in both the Stog Palace edition (vol. 96, 17.5–6) and the Zhol edition of the *'Grel pa bzhi sgrags* (folio 6a2). The most significant variant reading is found in the Sde dge edition (vol. 81, 187.7–188.1) and the Peking (vol. 65: 176.3.2–3) which have *bsgom pa bsgom pa ma yin nyid* for *bsgom par bya ba bsgom pa min* in the second line (*pāda*); and in the Dunhuang (IOL Tib. J 438, folio 8b4) which has *bsgom pa'i dngos* for *sgom pa med*, at the end of the first *pāda*. In the *Hevajra Tantra* (I.viii.44; Snellgrove, 30–31): *bhāvanā naiva bhāvanā* is similarly translated as *sgom pa nyid ni sgom pa min*. As for other variant readings in the first *pāda*, the Sde dge and the Peking have *la* and the Dunhuang has *par* for *pas;* the *Rnying ma rgyud 'bum* edition (vol. 17, 15.3) has *bsgom pa med* for *sgom pa med*. In the second *pāda*, the *Rnying ma rgyud 'bum* has *sgom pa min* for *bsgom pa min*. In the third *pāda*, the Sde dge and the Peking have *de* for *pas*. And in the fourth *pāda*, Dunhuang and the Peking have *bsgom* for *sgom* and the Dunhuang has *do zhes* for *pa'o*. The *Sgron gsal* (Sde dge Bstan 'gyur, Toh. no. 1785, Rgyud *ha*, vol. 30, 47.2; Peking Bstan 'gyur,

Ōtani 2650, vol. 60, 35.3.4; The Golden Bstan 'byur, vol. 30, 32a5–6) has similar readings to those of the Stog Palace and the Zhol editions; the variants are: *sgom pa med* at the end of the first *pāda*, and *bsgom par bya ba bsgom pa min* in the second *pāda*. The *Mdor byas sgrub thabs* (Sde dge, folio 2b4 and Peking, 269.3.3) has in the first *pāda: dngos po med la bsgom pa'i dngos*. In his commentary on the *Mdor byas sgrub thabs*, the *Rin chen phreng ba* (Sde dge Bstan 'gyur, Toh. no. 1826, Rgyud *ci*, vol. 36, 50.1), Śāntipa has *dngos po med pas sgom pa med*, as do the Zhol and the Stog Palace in the *Root Tantra*, and not *bsgom pa'i dngos*. Bu ston Rin chen grub [*Dpal gsang ba 'dus pa'i sgrub thabs mdor byas kyi rgya cher bshad pa bskyed rim gsal byed* (*Mdor byas 'grel chen*), *The Collected Works of Bu-Ston* (New Delhi: International Academy of Indian Culture, 1967), 708.6–710.3] rejects the reading *bsgom pa'i dngos*, because it lacks a negative particle, while Śāntipa's commentary explains it with a negation.

9. As Fremantle, "A Critical Study," 143 points out, the Tibetan here is a translation of *bhāvya* and not *bhāvanā*.

10. The literal (*akṣarārtha, tshig gi don* or *yi ge'i don*), the common (*samastāṅga, spyi'i don*), the hidden (*garbhin, sbas pa*) and the ultimate (*kolika, mthar thug pa*) levels of interpretations. This passage was also translated from Tibetan into Italian in Filippani-Ronconi. "La formulazione," 194–95. Unfortunately, until I can see the Sanskrit manuscript itself, everything I can say is rather tentative, since I must rely on Chakravarti's edition, *Guhya-samāja-tantra-ṭīkā*, 31–32.

11. Chakravarti, *Guhya-samāja-tantra-ṭīkā*, 31; the *Sgron gsal* (Sde dge, 47.2–3; Peking, 35.3.3–5; The Golden Bstan 'gyur, 32a5–32b1).

12. In the usual *tshul bzhi*, the common level of interpretation is common to both creation or generation stage (*bskyed rim*) and completion stage (*rdzogs rim*), both Sūtra and Tantra, and so on; the hidden level often refers to practices with the consort, the subtle body, and so on; and the ultimate level of interpretation applies to the *rdzogs rim* alone.

13. See Vasubandhu's *Triṃśikā* (vv. 28–29) and *Trisvabhāvanirdeśa* (vv. 36–37); also *Madhyāntavibhāga* (ch. 1, v. 6), *Mahāyāna-sūtrālaṃkāra* (ch. 6, v. 8 and ch. 14, vv. 23–28), and *Dharmadharmatāvibhāga*; see Klaus-Dieter Mathes, *Unterscheidung der Gegebenheiten von ihrem wahren Wesen [Dharmadharmatāvibhāga]* (Swisttal-Odendorf: Indica et Tibetica, 1996), 102–103, 64, 110, 139. Ronald Davidson ["Buddhist Systems of Transformation: Āśraya-parivṛtti / -parāvṛtti among the Yogācāra" (Ph.D. diss., University of California, Berkeley), 1985, 295–97], David Jackson [*The Entrance Gate for the Wise [section III]* (Vienna: Arbeitskreis für Tibetische und Buddhistische Studien, Universität Wien, 1987), 348–51 and notes thereon] and Christian Lindtner ["*Cittamātra* in Indian Mahāyāna until Kamalaśīla," *Wiener Zeitschrift für die Kunde Südasiens*, 41 (1997): 159–206] have pointed to still other parallels. This fourfold meditation appears also in the works of Śāntarakṣita and Kamalaśīla as well as Śāntipa (Ratnākaraśānti) and therefore came to be associated with what was later called the Yogācāra-Mādhyamika. Chizuko Yoshimizu ["The Theoretical Basis of the *bskyed rim* as Reflected in the *bskyed rim* Practice of the Ārya School," *Report of the Japanese Association for Tibetan Studies*, 33 (1987): 25–28] who edited and translated Bu ston's commentary on our verse as it appears in Nāgārjuna's *Piṇḍīkrama-sādhana* (Bu ston's *Mdor byas 'grel chen*; see below), also consulted the texts of the *Pradīpoddyotana* and the *Ratnāvalī*, and commented (27):

"[T]he Ārya school employed Yogācāra-Mādhyamika theory virtually from its starting point." Her conclusion on this point is (28): "Most Tantric authors including Nāgārjuna seem to lack any concrete understanding of Mahāyāna philosophies." Since Katsumi Mimaki ["The *Blo gsal grub mtha'* and the Mādhyamika Classification in Tibetan *Grub mtha'* Literature," in *Contributions on Tibetan and Buddhist Religion and Philosophy*, ed. Ernst Steinkellner, 2 vols. (Vienna: Arbeitskreis für Tibetische und Buddhistische Studien Universität Wien, 1982), 2: 163] maintains: "We know today that the terms indicating the sub-schools of the Mādhyamika, such as the... Yogācāra-Mādhyamika,... have been invented by Tibetan authors, and do not appear in Indian texts," I use here the term Yogācāra and not Yogācāra-Mādhyamika. My conclusion are different from those of yoshimizu on this point.

14. Chakravarti, *Guhya-samāja-tantra-ṭīkā*, 31–32.

15. The stage of union (*yuganaddha-krama, zung 'jug gi rim pa*) of the completion stage (*rdzogs rim*) is the fifth of the five stages in Nāgārjuna's text, the *Five Stages* (*Pañca-krama*).

16. See, for example, Gadjin M. Nagao, "What Remains in Śūnyatā: A Yogācāra Interpretation of Emptiness," in *Mahāyāna Buddhist Meditation*, ed. M. Kiyota (Honolulu, HI: University of Hawaii Press, 1978), 66–82, and David Malcolm Eckel, *To See the Buddha* (San Francisco: HarperSanFrancisco, 1992), 69–71.

17. The *Sgron gsal*, Sde dge Bstan 'gyur, Toh. no. 1785, Rgyud *ha*, vol. 30, 47.2–48.4; Peking Bstan 'gyur, Ōtani 2650, vol. 60, 35.3.3–4.7; The Golden Bstan 'gyur, vol. 30, 32a5–33a5; translated by Śraddhākaravarman, Rin chen bzang po, Śrījñānākara and 'Gos Lhas btsas and revised by Nag po and 'Gos Lhas btsas.

18. *Piṇḍī-kṛta-sādhana-vṛtti-ratnāvalī* (*Mdor bsdus pa'i sgrub thabs kyi 'grel pa rin chen phreng ba = Rin chen phreng ba*), Sde dge Bstan 'gyur, Toh. no. 1826, Rgyud *ci*, vol. 36: 50.1–51.3; translated into Tibetan by Karmavajra. In his commentary on the *Guhyasamāja Tantra* entitled *Kusumāñjali* (Sde dge Bstan 'gyur, Toh. no. 1851, Rgyud *ti*, 463.5–465.4) Śāntipa has quite a different discussion of this verse.

19. Śāntipa, *Rin chen phreng ba* (*Ratnāvalī*), Sde dge ed., 50.1–2.

20. Reading *sgom pa* for *som pa* in the Sde dge edition.

21. Chakravarti, *Guhya-samāja-tantra-ṭīkā*, 31.

22. Candrakīrti, *Sgron gsal* (*Pradīpoddyotana*), Sde dge ed., 47.2; Peking ed., 35.3.3–4; The Golden Bstan 'gyur ed., 32a5–6.

23. It is entitled *Gsang 'dus sgron gsal gyi bsdus don* [Tibetan Buddhist Resource Center, source code W11238].

24. Bu ston wrote commentaries on both the *Pradīpoddyotana* [the *Dpal gsang ba 'dus pa'i ṭīkkā sgron ma rab tu gsal ba = Sgron gsal bshad sbyar, The Collected Works of Bu-ston* (New Delhi: International Academy of Indian Culture, 1967), vol. 9, 141–682] and on the *Piṇḍī-krama-sādhana* [the *Mdor byas 'grel chen, The Collected Works of Bu-ston* (New Delhi: International Academy of Indian Culture, 1967), vol. 9, 683–979], but he comments on our verse only in the latter work (708.6–710.3). In this latter commentary, Bu ston often consults Śāntipa's commentary on the *Piṇḍī-krama-sādhana*, the *Ratnāvalī*. However, in writing about our verse, Bu ston's text corresponds to the Tibetan version, not of the *Ratnāvalī*, but of the *Pradīpoddyotana* (*Sgron gsal*). Like the *Sgron gsal* (Sde dge ed., 47.2), Bu ston (708.6–7) says, "there is *no essence* to all the animate and inanimate

things," and not "there *are no* animate and inanimate things," as in the Sanskrit edition (Chakravarti, *Guhya-samāja-tantra-ṭīkā*, 31) and in Śāntipa's *Rin chen phreng ba* (Sde dge ed., 50.1–2). And also parallel to the *Sgron gsal* (Sde dge ed., 47.7), in the hidden level of interpretation, Bu ston (709.5) has *dngos po med pa* and not just *med pa*, as in the *Rin chen phreng ba* (Sde dge ed., 50.6). There are only minor differences between his explanation and the explanation of the *Sgron gsal*. For an English translation of Bu ston commentary here, see Yoshimizu, "The Theoretical Basis of the bskyed rim," 25–27.

25. The dissolution into the moon in *Mdor byas 'grel chen*, 749.5–6.

26. *Rgyud thams cad kyi rgyal po dpal gsang ba 'dus pa'i rgya cher bshad pa sgron me gsal ba'i tshig don ji bzhin 'byed pa'i mchan gyi yang 'grel*, in *The Collected Works (Gsung 'bum) of Rje Tsong-kha-pa Blo-bzang-grags-pa* (New Delhi: Ngawang Gelek Demo, 1977), vol. 6: 180.2–186.6. Also in *Dpal gsang ba 'dus pa'i rtsa rgyud 'grel pa bzhi sbrags dang bcas pa* (Lhasa: Zhol Printing House, made from block-prints carved in 1890), 55b6–57b6.

27. *Rnam gzhag rim pa'i rnam bshad dpal gsang ba 'dus pa'i gnad kyi don gsal ba, The Collected Works (Gsung 'bum) of Rje Tsong-kha-pa Blo-bzang-grags-pa*, 27 vols. (New Delhi: Ngawang Gelek Demo, 1975–79) vol. 9: 296.2.

28. Tsong kha pa, *Sgron gsal mchan*, New Delhi edition, 182.3–4; Zhol edition, 56b2.

29. Chakravarti, *Guhya-samāja-tantra-ṭīkā*, 31; Sde dge ed., 47.5.

30. Tsong kha pa, *Sgron gsal mchan*, New Delhi edition, 182.6; Zhol edition, 56b3.

31. Chakravarti, *Guhya-samāja-tantra-ṭīkā*, 31; Sde dge ed., 47.6.

32. The term "mind-only" (*cittamātra, sems tsam*) itself appears only in the hidden level of interpretation, which Tsong kha pa explains in terms of the subtle body, and not of the fourfold meditation (New Delhi, 183.4; Zhol, 56b6).

33. *Rgyud kyi rgyal po dpal gsang ba 'dus pa'i rgya cher bshad pa sgron ma gsal ba'i dka' gnas kyi mtha' gcod rin chen myu gu, The Collected Works (Gsung 'bum) of Rje Tsong-kha-pa Blo-bzang-grags-pa* (New Delhi: Ngawang Gelek Demo, 1977), vol. 8, 207.6–208.2.

34. See Yael Bentor, "Identifying the Unnamed Opponents of Tsong-kha-pa and Mkhas-grub-rje Concerning the Transformation of Ordinary Birth, Death and the Intermediate State into the Three Bodies," in *Tibetan Buddhist Literature and Praxis: Studies in Its Formative Period 900–1400*, ed. Ronald M. Davidson and Christian K. Wedemeyer (Leiden: Brill, 2006), 185–200.

35. Bu ston, *Mdor byas 'grel chen*, 749.5–6.

36. Mkhas grub rje Dge legs dpal bzang po, *Rgyud thams cad kyi rgyal po dpal gsang ba 'dus pa'i bskyed rim dngos grub rgya mtsho, The Collected Works (Gsung 'bum) of the Lord Mkhas-grub Rje Dge-legs-dpal-bzang-po* (New Delhi: Gurudeva, 1982), vol. 7, 209.2–4.

37. I would like to thank José Cabezón for pointing this out to me.

38. While in Nāgārjuna's *sādhana*, the *Piṇḍī-krama-sādhana*, our verse is recited during meditation on emptiness, in the *Guhyasamāja Tantra*, this verse is spoken as an explanation of the arising of the mind for enlightenment (*bodhicitta*). The commentaries discuss both of these contexts.

5

Chilu (*'Chi bslu*)

Rituals for "Deceiving Death"

IRMGARD MENGELE

To counteract the "degeneration" of their life-force, and to remove adverse conditions (*rkyen sel*) that befall them, Tibetans seek the help of a variety of religious virtuosos. These specialists have at their disposal a wide array of sophisticated rituals serving one or more of the following purposes: (1) protection, (2) purification of negative deeds, (3) increase of merit, (4) elimination of obstacles, (5) fulfillment of wishes, (6) long life or prolonging of the life span, (7) health and (8) enhancement of the healing power of medicine. Astrological calculations to determine propitious stellar configurations also play a role in the elimination of obstacles, allowing one to carefully choose the day and time to set out on a journey, to marry, to start a new business, and so forth. Tibetans believe that every twelfth year in one's life, when the animal sign of one's birth year reoccurs, is an obstacle-year (*lo keg*). One is advised to avoid any risky undertakings during that year, and before the beginning of the year one visits a lama who may advise one to go on a pilgrimage, or to have certain rituals—like the *tsetar* (*tshe thar*) or "liberation of the lives of animals"[1]—performed.

But what if, in spite of all precautions, a person faces the threat of untimely death? Are there any measures that can be taken to counteract such a danger? Are there factors, over and above the obvious physical ones, that lead to an untimely death? Among the religious responses to these questions, the ones we find in the Tibetan Buddhist tradition are complex and sophisticated. The Tibetan texts differentiate between a wide range of causes and immediate conditions (*'phral rkyen*) leading to death, and offer corresponding rituals as a way of responding to these adverse conditions. These rituals include a wide array of methods for averting death—methods that involve meditation, visualization, recitation of mantras, and offerings. In this chapter I focus on *chilu* (*'chi bslu*) or "death-deceiving" rites, a unique type of ritual performed for a person facing untimely death. The aim of the ritual is to reverse impending death, and to eventually restore health.

Terminology and History

Tibetan–English dictionaries render the Tibetan term *chiwa luwa* (*'chi ba bslu ba*) either as "deceiving/cheating death" or, alternatively, as "ransoming from death."[2] These same Tibetan words are used to translate the Sanskrit *mṛtyu vañcana*. The Sanskrit word *vañcana*, however, only has the "deceiving/cheating" connotation and not the "ransoming" one.[3] The oldest *chilu* texts are found in the Tengyur, indicating their Indian origin.[4] It is possible to date two of the ten available Tengyur texts.[5] The first, a ritual text called simply *Deceiving Death* (*'Chi ba bslu ba*), was authored by Tathāgatarakṣita.[6] He worked on the translation of this text with the Tibetan Rinchen Drakpa (Rin chen grags pa), whose dates are known; he lived from 1040–1112. Consequently, Tathāgatarakṣita authored the *'Chi ba bslu ba* at the end of the eleventh, or at the beginning of the twelfth century. In the case of the second text, the *Instructions on Deceiving Death* (*'Chi ba blu ba'i man ngag*), only the dating of the translation from Sanskrit into Tibetan is possible. In the colophon to his later revision of this translation, Situ Penchen (Si tu Paṇ chen) mentions Atiśa (b. 972/982) and Rinchen Zangpo (Rin chen bzang po, 958–1055) as the earlier translators.[7] Given their dates, we know that the translation of the second text dates to the tenth/eleventh century.

Apart from *chilu* texts found in the Tengyur, Namkhai Norbu argues that ransom rites were already part of the indigenous Tibetan Bön religion before the first dissemination of Buddhism in Tibet around the seventh century C.E.[8] According to him, *lü* (*glud*) is a general Tibetan term for Bön ransom rites, a category that includes three different types of ransom rituals: (1) those that exorcise the danger of death, disease, and evil influences, called *dö* (*mdos*); (2) those that provide a gift to free oneself of disturbances, called *yé* (*yas*); and (3) those during which the substitute of a person is offered to a malevolent spirit, called *lü* (*glud*). The methods he describes for all three types of *lü* rites are very similar to what is found in *chilu* rituals.[9] I have not been able to find any Indian precedents for *yé* and *lü* (*glud*), but was able to locate one offering ritual in the Peking edition of the Tengyur with the word *dö* in its title, the *Ritual Cake Yantra (Dö) of the Crow-Headed Protector* (*Mgon po bya rog gdong gi gtor mdo*, Skt. *Nāthakā[kā] syabaliyantra*), written by Kṛṣṇa Nāgārjuna (Klu sgrub nag po). Lacking any biographical information about the author, it is impossible to date this text at present, but its existence in the Tengyur is proof enough of its Indian origin. In a footnote, Namkhai Norbu mentions that some Western scholars have recognized in the term *dö*, only the physical thread cross—a common part of such rites—but he claims that the term in fact denotes the broad category of rituals in which these devices are used as magical instruments.[10] In the Tengyur text mentioned earlier, the term *dö* is used to translate the Sanskrit *yantra* (literally, "instrument" or "support"). In the case of the *Nāthakākāsyabaliyantra*, when Buddhism entered Tibet, needing to find a Tibetan equivalent for the Sanskrit *yantra*, Tibetans most probably chose *dö* from the repertoire of their pre-Buddhist ritual terminology.

A comparison of *mṛtyu vañcana* texts in the Tengyur with Tibetan *chilu* rituals reveals obvious differences. Most striking, the texts in the Tengyur do not mention an effigy or any other substitute for the sick person's body, usually offered to harmful spirits as the core of Tibetan *chilu* rituals. Most *mṛtyuvañcana* texts in the Tengyur are short versions of Vāgīśvarakīrti's *Mṛtyuvañcanopadeśa*, which is a comprehensive summary of the activities that will prolong the life span and save one from untimely death. In general, Vāgīśvarakīrti states that death deception for "outer [signs of death] is done through bodily and verbal activities. For inner [signs it is accomplished] through meditative concentration." According to his system, jewels, mantras, and medicine are applied when there are outer signs of death, and the yogic powers (*rnal 'byor gyi nus pa*) are resorted to when there are inner signs.

Vāgīśvarakīrti also considers faith to be the prerequisite for practicing death deception. "Death deception with diligence can be practiced by believers. Therefore, have steadfast faith! Otherwise the effort will be pointless."[11] The first type of *chilu* is prolonging life through virtuous actions (*bsod nams las ni tshe 'phel zhing/ de 'phel bas ni 'chi ba bslu*). The text instructs the adept to refrain from the ten nonvirtuous actions, to take refuge in the Buddha, Dharma, and Saṅgha, and to observe the five and eight precepts; in this way "death will be banished afar." He gives the following example: "by saving the live of birds, fish, wild animals, thieves (*rkun ma*), snakes and so on—everything that is an object to be killed—though [one's] life span is short, it will instantly be extended."[12] Other merit-based, life-prolonging methods include: respect for parents, for older or wiser masters, and for one's tutelary deity (*rang gi 'dod lha*); repairing damaged *stūpas*; making *tsatsa* (*tsha tsha*, clay statuettes made from molds). Many more are given. The second *chilu* method mentioned by Vāgīśvarakīrti involves physical contact with jewels. He claims, for example, that there is no doubt that death will be deceived by touching precious jewels like sapphires.[13] Death deception by the power of jewels is followed by the third means: recitation of mantras that range in length from a single letter *a* to longer mantras which have to be repeated up to 100,000 times. Tārā mantras recited in front of a Tārā image—all the while burning the tip of a *kuśa* grass sprout saturated in yoghurt and honey, while pointing it to the east and north—is supposed to even ward off death that is the result of former karma.[14] Vāgīśvarakīrti concludes the section by praising mantras with the following verses:

> Whatever other phenomena exist in the world,
> There is nothing that cannot be achieved by mantras.
> For a person striving with true faith,
> Mantras are like wish-fulfilling jewels.[15]

The last *chilu* method mentioned in the text, that is to be used when there are outer signs, involves alchemy—the power of medicinal substances—the knowledge of which Vāgīśvarakīrti certainly acquired from Indian medical treatises studied during his time. To mention just some examples, the text recommends that at places where hunger predominates, substances from the medicinal *letré* (*sle tres*) tree should be used, either separately, or mixed with other medicine. This will strengthen the body and will prevent one from having to witness the gateway to the kingdom of the Lord of Death.[16] A yogi who takes the general combination of the three (medicinal) fruits (*aa ru ra*, *ba ru ra*, and *skyu ru ra*) or who extracts the essence of the five nectars together with *posocha* (*po so [cha]*) and *bhingarāja* (?) will be devoid of wrinkles and white hair. His vajra body—that is, his transformed human body—will become an excellent body, and death will be averted even for eons.[17]

We should recall that when death is revealed through inner signs, it must be counteracted through mantra repetition and meditative means. Vāgīśvarakīrti first mentions the recitation of mantras to forestall obstructing forces and enemies. The text lists examples of these mantras, which can also be accompanied by burnt offerings. The author reassures his reader that "by properly reciting hundreds of thousands of mantras against obstructing forces and enemies and by performing ten thousand fire offerings, all obstructing forces will be warded off."[18] The second practice involves yogis' meditation on diverse deities, which secures for them various positive effects, depending on the nature and appearance of the visualized deity. For instance, "by meditating on white Vairocana with the *mudrā* of supreme enlightenment (*uttarabodhi mudrā*), radiating white light rays, there is no need to ever die in *saṃsāra*."[19] Likewise, even the mighty gods Brahma, Viṣṇu, the gods of the Sun and Moon, the wrathful guardians of directions, and the gods of the desire realm will be unable to damage a single hair on the head of a practitioner who contemplates Tārā for six months while reciting her mantras. The yogi will, in this way, overcome death, but gray hair, wrinkles, misfortune, disease and poverty will also be eradicated, and the eight major kinds of fear (the fear of lions etc.) will be dispelled.[20] Anticipating a question about the secret behind rescuing oneself from death by visualizing a mighty deity, the text gives the example of meditation on the yoga of Heruka. After having fully transformed (*yongs gyur*) oneself into Heruka, one visualizes oneself as a manifestation [holding] a skull-cup, as a skeleton, or else holding a tantric staff (*khaṭvāṅga*). "Since it would not be right to kill [a deity as mighty as Heruka or a person who has become Heruka by transformation], death becomes impossible for that meditator."[21] Toward the end of his text, Vāgīśvarakīrti stresses again that these techniques will bring the anticipated effects solely when practiced with diligence, reinforcing his argument with the following metaphors. "Even a soft stream can bore through flat stones at some points when it constantly flows over them. When wood is rubbed, fire arises. When the soil is dug, water flows. When a person strives, there is nothing he or she will not [be able to] achieve. All appropriate effort bears fruit. Thus, even if you know a great number of death deceiving [methods], if you don't practice them, you will die in bed stained with excrement."[22]

In another text in the Tengyur, that is authored by Tathāgatarakṣita, the Sanskrit title reads not *mṛtyu vañcana* but *mṛtyuṣṭhāpaka*, "causing to stand or fixing (*sthāpaka*) the Lord of Death (*mṛtyu*)." Not only does the Sanskrit title of this ritual differ from that of the other *chilu* texts in the Tengyur, so too does its contents. Visualizing Tārā and reciting her mantras, a wheel with seven spokes is painted with saffron on birch bark. One recites, "May the sins of [the person] named so and so be eliminated!" and so forth. Tārā mantras and *dhāraṇīs* are also written down. The rolled-up birch bark with the wheel drawn on it is placed in a box made of precious substances, new terracotta, *kha sar* (?), horn or wood. The container is wrapped several times with a red thread and covered with a coating of white silk or cloth. It is then bound (*bcings*) on a tree near a temple belonging to a large monk community, or on a tree by a stūpa. The box has to be worshipped with great offerings on special occasions, and one must meditate and then recite Tārā mantras, *dhāraṇīs*, and eulogies.

It becomes apparent from Vāgīśvarakīrti's and Tathāgatarakṣita's compositions that death-deceiving methods in India neither involved a conversation between a yogi and death-causing spirits, nor any kind of effigy offered to these spirits as ransom for the life of a dying person. Effigies and spirits may have played a role in other types of Indian rituals, but in *chilu* rites, these two aspects of the ritual seem to be a Tibetan innovation. Though at present it is not possible to say exactly when and where in Tibet the offering of effigies was first practiced, we do know from reports of missionaries and anthropologists of the early twentieth century who pursued fieldwork in Tibet that in some parts of the country there existed a living tradition of human and animal sacrificial rituals. These may well date back to a pre-Buddhist period.[23] Animal sacrifice exists in certain parts of the Tibetan ethnic world to the present day, even if it is often condemned by Buddhists and Bönpos alike. The core aim of these practices was probably, as it is in many cultures, to avert disasters by pleasing spirits through the offering of a living being. *Chilu* may well represent a sublimated form of these sacrificial rituals, where the body of a dying person is ransomed not by offering another living creature in its place, as happens with sacrifice, but through the offering of a substitute effigy that is supposed to be superior to any human body. These sacrifices were performed to protect individuals or a whole community from a wide range of misfortunes, including disease, drought, meager harvest, natural disasters, and attacks from evil spirits. The existence of sacrificial rituals proves that Tibetan culture has always been familiar with propitiatory sacrifices, but it remains doubtful whether we can conclude from this that there is a pre-Buddhist Tibetan origin to the *chilu* rites, that is, to the specific rituals used to reverse the dying process in a sick person.

What Types of Rituals Are *Chilu* Rites?

Both etic and emic classification schemes are useful to understanding the place of *chilu* rituals vis-à-vis other rituals. In a now standard work on ritual, Catherine Bell provides a taxonomy of rituals, distinguishing between six basic categories: (1) rites of passage, (2) calendrical rites, (3) rites of exchange and communion, (4) rites of affliction, (5) feasting, fasting, and festivals, and (6) political rites. In this classification system, death-deceiving rituals would appear to fall in two categories: "rites of exchange," defined as a human–divine interaction by means of religious rituals "in which people make offerings to a god or gods with the practical and straightforward expectation of receiving something in return," and "rites of affliction," which Bell says seek "to mitigate the influence of spirits thought to be afflicting human beings with misfortune."[24]

A Tibetan indigenous categorization of (at least certain) rituals according to their function is to be found in the so-called four activities (*phrin las rnam bzhi*): (1) pacifying (*zhi*), (2) increasing (*rgyas*), (3) overpowering (*dbang*) and (4) subjugating (*drag*). (See chapter 7 by Cuevas in this volume.) *Trinlé* (*phrin las*) refers to the action the deity is requested to perform during the ritual.[25] In the index to Jamgön Kongtrül's *Rin chen gter mdzod*—a huge collection of varied rituals—death-deceiving rituals are grouped under the rubric "increasing/enriching activities or rites" (*rgyas pa'i las*), indicating the deity's role as the one who increases the life span of the afflicted person.

Chikyen (*'chi rkyen*): The Causes of Death

The ritual methods described in this chapter are said to reverse the process of dying, "deceiving death" and restoring the health of a sick person. But one should not expect death-deceiving rituals to be a panacea, capable of rescuing *any* person from his or her impending death. Rather, the texts warn that there are circumstances that make such ritual interventions *a priori* ineffective. *The Tibetan Book Of The Dead,* for example, makes a distinction between a natural condition of death—the natural exhaustion of one's life span as the result of growing old—and an *un*natural condition that leads to untimely death, further indicating that it is only "untimely or sudden death [that] may be avoided." In the case of "death due to the [natural] exhaustion of the life span," however, "there is no way of averting [death] through 'ritual deception' and thus...one should make preparations to depart."[26]

Another text mentions a different set of three conditions leading to death and offers a remedy for each of them. (1) Exhaustion of life should be counteracted by a long-life ritual; (2) exhaustion of karma should be remedied by the recitation of a ransom for life; and (3) persons whose merit is exhausted should be cured by accumulating new merit through offerings.[27]

When I asked Gehlek Rinpoché about the significance of *chilu* rituals, he briefly mentioned that there are three causes of death: karma, lack of merit (*bsod nams*), and "interferences" or "obstacles" (*bar chad*). Only in cases where death is caused by interferences will a *chilu* ritual be potentially successful.[28] This threefold differentiation seemed problematic to me since, on the one hand, karma is the commonly accepted and inescapable cause of *any* death; and, on the other hand, obstacles like disease, evil influences, and many others also result from negative karma. Likewise, a distinction between karma and merit is surprising since exhaustion of life is the exhaustion of good karma, which is nothing other than the exhaustion of merit. Another Tibetan informant, Geshe Tenzin Sherab, explained to me his understanding of the relation between karma, merit, and obstacles as causes of death in relation to *chilu* rituals. If negative karma is too strong, he said, it cannot be overcome by the power of ritual, and the intended goal will not be achieved. If the level of positive karma (i.e., merit) is low or if one's merit has been exhausted, this will again mean that rituals will be of no avail. The success of a death-deceiving ritual, he continued, is guaranteed only if one is dealing with obstacles (*bar chad*), rather than with negative karma or lack of merit, as the cause of the life-threatening condition.[29]

Dorjee Tseten comes to similar conclusions concerning the effect of rituals, the relationship of this to a person's karma, and the function of merit acquired from offerings.[30] He emphasizes that "rituals will not change a person's karma" but instead "can stimulate a 'latent positive potential'" in a person which is capable of prevailing over "the cause of an impending misfortune." At this point he adds that, conversely, if one's own karma is stronger than one's "latent positive potential," a ritual will fail and will not achieve its purpose. He adds that merit gained through offerings and gifts to monks have the same ability as rituals to activate "the forces of latent positive potential." According to him, then, for a ritual to be successful the "latent positive potential" has to be stronger than one's karma. Though the "latent positive potential" may be stronger, in some cases it has to be stimulated by the ritual or by merit gained through offerings. In other words, rituals and merit are capable of achieving results, but they are not capable of increasing the power of one's "latent positive potential." Why in some persons this "positive potential" has to be activated at all—why it is not already functioning by itself—prompts yet other questions.

Another exposition of how lack of merit, wrongdoings, and bodily conditions can have a negative impact on practices, which otherwise could prolong life is given by Tsongkhapa in his *Great Treatise on the Stages of the Path* (*Lam rim chen mo*):

> Because this is a time [i.e., because we live in a time] when the five impurities are rapidly spreading, there are extremely few persons who accumulate the great power of virtuous deeds that enable a long life. Also, since the medicinal power of our food and such is weak, we have little resistance to disease. The provisions we do use are not easy to digest and thus have diminished power for enhancing the body's great elements. Further, since you have done little to amass the collection of merit and your wrongdoings are very potent, practices such as mantra recitation have little efficacy. All of this makes it extremely difficult to prolong your life.[31]

The ritual texts see themselves as responding to obstacles, which may manifest in a variety of ways, the most prominent being diseases and evil influences, *dön* (*gdon*). One *chilu* ritual text, for example, includes the following entreaty: "May my own, the beneficiary's, and also the master's and his retinue's sicknesses, the evil influences [that harm us], and [other] obstacles resulting form former karma and immediate conditions be pacified."[32] Diseases arise when the five bodily elements—earth, water, fire, air, and space (*sa chu me rlung nam mkha'*)—are unbalanced, leading to traditional medical diagnoses such as wind (*rlung*), bile (*mkhris pa*), or phlegm (*bad kan*) diseases. A combination of the three is also possible. The *chilu* ritual text called *Bestowing the Bliss of Immortality* mentions that there are 424 possible illnesses caused by former karma or temporary conditions, *trelkyen* (*'phrel rkyen*) (injuries, infections etc.).[33] The same text states that 84,000 evil influences can be traced back to spirits, including gods (*lha*), *nāgas* (*klu*), demigods (*lha ma yin*), *gandharvas* (*dri za*, literally "scent-eaters"), Elemental Spirits (*'byung po*), and King Spirits (*rgyal po*); whereas the same number of obstacles (*bgegs*) are caused by demons of the categories Dü (*bdud*), Tsen (*btsan*), Gyalpo, Pehar (*pe har*), Mu (*dmu*), Mamo (*ma mo*), Shinjé (*gzhin rje*), Damsi (*dam sri*), and many others.[34] It is these various types of mundane gods (*'jig rten pa'i lha*) or spirits—usually associated with the land (mountains, rivers, lakes)—as opposed to the supramundane gods or deities (*'jig rten las 'das pa'i lha*), that are responsible for diseases and obstacles.[35] As mentioned in the Introduction to this volume, the majority of these spirits are malicious, excitable, and easily offended. When slighted, they frequently take revenge by attacking human beings with misfortune and disease. They can also obstruct the healing process and leave those afflicted vulnerable to further attacks by other evil spirits, including the Lord of Death (*gshin rje, 'chi bdag*). Just as predators target the sick and weak members of a herd, evil spirits find it easy to prey on individuals whose life-energy or *la* (*bla*) has become feeble.

Soteriological Significance of Death-Deceiving Rituals

Why do Tibetans not simply accept the death threatening them as the effects of karma and surrender to the internal and external forces at work? One answer is given by Loter Wangpo (Blo gter dbang po, 1847–1914) in his introduction to a death-deceiving ritual based on White Tārā, where he cites a stanza by the master Vāgīśvarakīrti:[36]

> There exists absolutely nothing in *saṃsāra*
> That is more significant than life (*srog*).
> Therefore, practice "death deceiving" immediately
> Using various means.[37]

Commenting on this verse, Loter Wangpo adds that it is a long life span (*tshe ring ba*) that ranks foremost among the "seven qualities of a high rebirth" (*mtho ris yon tan bdun*). Since all goals—both temporary and ultimate [i.e., enlightenment]—depend on long life, it is very important to exert oneself in regard to the various means for prolonging life.[38]

According to *The Tibetan Book of the Dead*, failure to perform a *chilu* ritual when this is called for is even more sinful than committing one of the "five inexpiable crimes" (*mthams med pa lnga*):[39]

> [However], when the external, internal, and secret signs of death do occur,
> If one does not perform the *Ritual Deception of Death*,
> One will incur the downfall of abandoning the assemblies of the Peaceful and Wrathful Deities,
> Who are the Conquerors, present within one's own body.
> As a result, one's commitments will degenerate, and one will proceed to the hells.
> It is said that this is even more negative than the [five] inexpiable crimes.
> Therefore, one should diligently persevere in the practices of the *Ritual Deception of Death*.[40]

What are the differences between "death-deceiving" rituals and other long-life rituals like the *tsedrub* (*tshe sgrub*), "establishing life," and the prayers requesting a spiritual master to remain in the world called *tenzhug* (*brtan bzhugs*) and *zhabten* (*zhabs brtan*)?[41] Over and above procedural differences—for example, ransom images and the interaction with menial spirits are not part of *tsedrub* and *zhabten* rituals—the most significant distinction, perhaps, is that long-life rituals such as the recitation of longevity prayers are performed frequently, and in some cases even daily, and they are performed even when the person is still healthy, whereas "death-deceiving" rituals are a last refuge in attempting to avert impeding death.

Signs Indicating Death (*'chi ltas*)

Death-deceiving rituals have a strong connection to the literature explaining the interpretation of the signs of death.[42] More than that, an expert knowledge of signs that indicate imminent death is a *sine qua non* for determining if death can be warded off through ritual means. This is important, given that resorting to *chilu* when death is irreversible is considered a grave downfall. Hence, not only is it a heinous sin not to carry out a death-deceiving ritual when it is called for, it is also a heinous sin to do a death-deceiving ritual when it will be of no avail.

The Tibetan Book of the Dead provides a sophisticated distinction between seven different types of death signs. Five of the seven deal with death that can be reversed—that is, death that is reversible by means of a ritual. These five types of signs are: (1) external signs, the investigation of bodily signs; (2) internal signs, the examination of vital breath and dreams between dawn and daybreak; (3) secret signs, which includes examination of the flow of one's semen or menstrual blood; (4) signs of remote death, the analysis of the optical projection of one's life-span onto the sky; and (5) signs of near- death, a diverse list. The last two classes of signs—(6) miscellaneous signs of death, and (7) signs of being very near death[43]—indicate that death is inevitable; that it cannot be turned back through rituals. According to this work, it is important to gain expertise in reading all of these signs correctly so as to avoid two mistakes: (1) not to perform a *chilu* ritual when there is a chance of averting death, and (2) to cause the dying person's consciousness to leave the body too early. The relevant verses read as follows:

> [Furthermore], if consciousness is transferred [too soon],
> When [only] one or other of the external or internal signs of death is present,
> This is called the 'slaying of the deities.'
> One must not allow this to occur, because the downfall will be extremely great.[44]

The *Kālacakra Tantra* also cautions against applying ritual methods to ward off malevolent spirits when signs of irrevocable death appear. According to Wallace, two reasons are mentioned. The first is the aforementioned ineffectiveness of ritual in such a case, and the second that "this situation may create temptation for the Tantric healer to perform the rites simply for the sake of his own material gain, while knowing that they will be of no benefit to the patient."[45]

Vāgīśvarakīrti also emphasizes the importance of familiarity with death signs. In his *Pith Instructions on [the Rite of] Deceiving Death* (*'Chi ba bslu ba'i man ngag*), mentioned earlier, the first two chapters, comprising thirty-one pages, introduce the reader to a wide range of external (*phyi yi mtshan nyid*) and internal signs (*nang gi 'chi ba yi mtshan nyid*) of death, along with methods for determining the time at which death is supposed to occur. For example, when a person hears the ringing of a bell at the time he engages in sex, even if he be like Brahma—that is, very strong—he will die after three months.[46] The sensation of a piercing pain between the eyebrows on the forehead at any time is a sure indication of immediate death.[47]

Death prognostications are also found in the huge literary corpus of the fourteenth century Nyingma scholar Longchen Rabjam (Klong chen rab 'byams pa Dri med 'od zer, 1308–64). In his article "Dying, Death and Other Opportunities," David Germano introduces three sets of signs of death found in Longchenpa's *The Sun and the Moon's Intimate Union* (*Nyi zla gza' bral*). Germano calls these (1) physical observations, (2) projecting one's shadow's afterimage into the sky, and (3) visual phenomena.[48] It would be an arduous but fruitful enterprise to compare the manifold signs found in the different sources to determine if there is any consistency or overlap. Was there a universally accepted range of signs that can be traced back to a common Indian origin, or did practitioners resort to different systems of death prognostication, some of which may have been unknown in India?

Related to the complex system of death prognostication are dreams. Concerning the importance of dream-signs, one text states:

> Though no dreams are real,
> It is foolish not to believe in them.
> Gods show us things in dreams,
> And, moreover, people who see the truth of dreams,
> Who come to trust in dreams,
> Should be on the lookout for signs of death![49]

To mention just one example of a dream-sign requiring a *chilu* ritual, Namchö Mingyur Dorje (gNam chos mi 'gyur rdo rje, 1645–67) has written:

> Dreaming of being led by a man on foot or on a horse towards the west, in the shade of trees, where one cannot be escorted by others and, once there, hearing [someone] crying behind one: this is a sign of death and it is necessary to perform a ritual to ransom oneself from death.[50]

Divination is another practice used to determine if a person is truly on the brink of death. In the predictive technique given by Ju Mipam,[51] when interpreting a pair of numbers on two dice, the combination of the numbers two (*ra*) and three (*pa*) are a sign of the demon of death (Ra pa).[52] In such a case, rituals should be performed immediately.

Description of Tibetan *Chilu* Rituals

One *chilu* text mentions that a precise number of ritual performers—one ritual master (*cho ga mkhan po*) and four monks—is required.[53] The person on whose behalf the ritual is performed is referred to as the beneficiary (*bsgrub bya*), literally "the one for whom [the goal] is to be realized." The "patron" (*sbyin bdag*) is the individual who sponsors the ritual, an individual who may of course *be* the sick person or beneficiary, but may also be a relative or friend.

Most rituals are performed in three successive phases: (1) preparation (*sbyor ba*), (2) the actual rite (*dngos gzhi*), and (3) the concluding rituals (*rjes/mjug*).[54] The preparatory phase of *chilu* rituals is concerned with the arrangement of a wide variety of offerings that include sacrificial cakes, *torma*, of different types[55]; food offerings like the three white substances (curd, milk, and butter) and the three sweet substances (sugar, molasses, and honey); liquids like *néchang* (*nas chang*), barley beer; bowls of water, representing the offering to the senses; the painting of a *maṇḍala* of the five elements or an offering *maṇḍala;* small clay votive tablets, *tsatsa*, of *stūpas* or of deities[56]; dough offerings in the form of an effigy (*ngar mi, ngar glud, ngar phye, srog glud*) (see Figure 5.1), dough squeezed within the hand (*chang bu*), dough buttons (small round pieces of dough flattened with the thumb, *mtheb skyu*), or small simple dough balls (*ril bu*). Some ritual texts mention that one should choose a house located in a solitary place as the site of the ritual, that one should clean the inside by sprinkling fragrant water, mend the mud floor, and decorate the room with a canopy (*bla bre*), umbrella (*gdugs*), offering banner (*ba dan*), victory banner (*rgyal mtshan*); and, of course, that one should display representations of the Buddha's body, speech, and mind, or painted *tangkas* (*thang kas*) depicting lamas, protective deities, Buddhas, bodhisattvas, and dharma protectors.

The ritual *Conquering Untimely Death* also incorporates a cleansing ritual and lists the twenty five substances found in a vase (*bum rdzas nyer lnga*) as requisites.[57] When preparing for the ritual *Bestowing the Glory of a Long Life*, half of the water collected after ritually cleaning the body of the sick person is to be poured into a clay vessel and mixed with milk. The other half is to be mixed with the earth of an old stūpa, ashes of a cremated body (*ro thal*), black earth (*sa nag*), clay dust (*rdza thal*) and "black words" (*tshig nag*). A fifteen-inch-high black body of the Lord of Death with the head of a buffalo is sculpted from this mixture; as implements, Death holds a stick and a lasso, and he is covered with a black garment.[58]

The employment of feces in the preparatory stage of the *Turning Away the Face of the Lord of Death*[59] proves its close affinity to Indian tantric practices. To present the sick person as unattractive as possible to the spirits threatening his or her life, a large carpet is saturated with various bodily substances belonging to the beneficiary, including stool, urine, nasal mucus, spittle, nails, and hair. A twenty-inch-high effigy (*ngar phye*)—to be offered in place of the foul carpet—is then created from flour mixed with various precious ingredients and infused

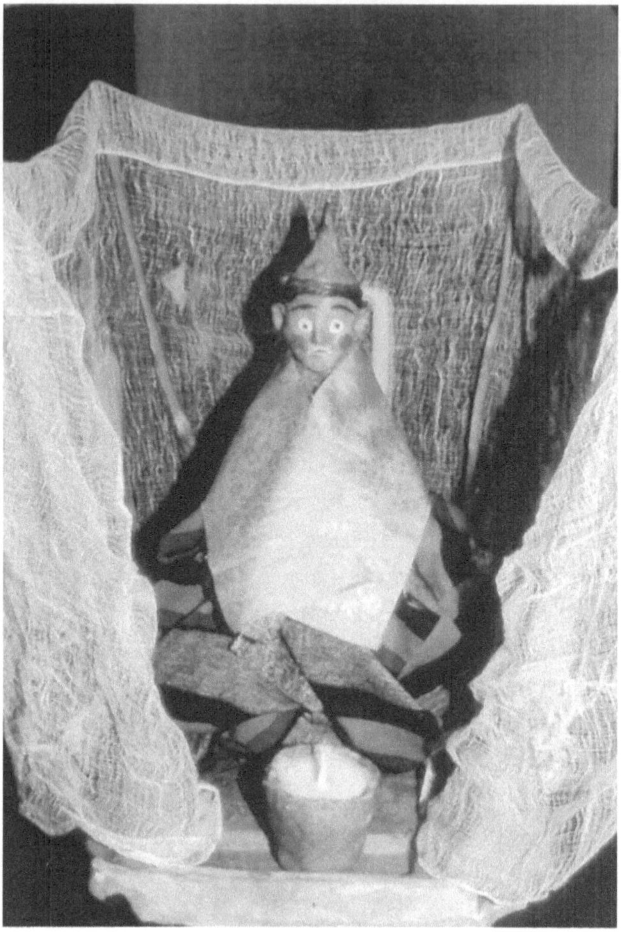

FIGURE 5.1. An effigy of the form typically used in substitution-type rituals. Photo J. Cabezón, Sera Monastery, Bylakuppe, India (1982).

with the breath (i.e., life-force) of many different species of sentient beings like humans and animals.[60] The effigy has blind eyes (*long tang gi mig*) etc., its sense organs still being in the process of developing. Into its belly is inserted a new clay vessel filled with drawn *maṇḍalas* of the five elements and wrapped with a cross *vajra* design (*rgya gram*) made of threads of five colors.[61] A red syllable (of the five elements), *raṃ*, drawn on paper and rolled up, is inserted into the effigy's eyes, a green *yaṃ* into its ears, a white *khaṃ* into its nose, a yellow *laṃ* into its tongue, and a blue *aḥ* into its heart.[62]

All the ritual objects and substances just mentioned are just a small selection of possible items described in the texts. The texts also frequently tells us that the number of offerings of a particular type—like *torma, tsatsa, changbu,* etc.—should be equal in number to the age of the sick person.

Stage two, the performance of the actual rite (*dngos gzhi*) generally begins with the common procedure of taking refuge and arousing the proper altruistic motivation (*bodhicitta*). Then the ritual master dissolves himself into a state of emptiness from which he visualizes the emergence of protector deities as supporters of the ritual. He then performs a number of other subrituals typically embedded into the *chilu* rite, including cleansing and purification rituals for offerings, and for images or the sick person's body, as well as consecration rituals of objects and substances to be offered to the deities.[63] One of the most detailed structural analysis of the main part of the ritual is found in the *Wisdom Sword Cutting the Lasso of the Lord of Death,*[64] where it is divided into fourteen individual steps numbered and named as follows:

1. taking refuge (p. 3.3),
2. training the mind in the four immeasurables[65] (p. 3.5),
3. consecrating the offerings (p. 3.5),
4. consecrating the ground (p. 5.3),
5. inviting the field of refuge (p. 6.2),
6. requesting the field to remain (p. 7.1),
7. offering a seat (p. 7.3),
8. bathing ritual (7.4),
9. wiping off the bodies of the deities after the bath (p. 8.3),
10. offering garments and jewelry (p. 8.4),
11. *maṇḍala* offering (9.4),
12. paying homage (p. 12.3),
13. reading the ten king *sūtras*[66] once and formulating the request to ward off the danger of death for the dying person (p. 13.4), and
14. offering the "*torma* of subsequent karmic connection" (*las kyi rjes 'brel gtor ma*) (p. 14.2).

The second or main stage of another *chilu* text, *Liberating the Lotus,*[67] also incorporates several other subrituals like consecration (*rab gnas*) and bathing (*khrus gsol*). The offering of *tsatsa*—a method of rectifying the imbalance of the five elements in the body of someone in danger of dying—plays an important role in this ritual. Eventually, the *tsatsas* have to be brought to the *tsatsa* house or *tsakhang* (*tsha khang*), a building where *tsatsas* are kept, or else placed at the shore of a river. Especially during the consecration ceremony of *tsatsas* of the five elements, the master performing the ritual has to engage in a far more detailed visualization/meditative practice—more complex, that is, than in other parts of the *chilu* ritual:

First, in order to consecrate the *tsatsa*, [the ritual master] recites the mantras of the deity [represented in] the *tsatsa*, and throwing mustard seeds, he exorcises obstructing spirits. [Then he] cleanses [the *tsatsa*]. He performs the bathing [ritual] by reciting "Just as, as soon as he was born... (*ji ltar bltams pa*)," and he recites the [bathing] mantra. Reciting *oṃ svabhāva* and so forth, he purifies the *tsatsas* by [seeing them] as empty. From within a state of the emptiness of all phenomena, on top of a lion throne, lotus and moon seats, from the [syllable] *oṃ* a wheel manifests marked by *oṃ*. From [the wheel], a white Vairocana [appears] with the *mudrā* of supreme enlightenment, decorated with all kinds of silk and jewels; he sits in the *vajra* posture with both legs [crossed]. Vairocana completely transforms into *dharmakāya stūpas* with perfect qualities. In the "vases" [i.e., the bulbous cavity] of these *stūpas*, on thrones lifted in the middle by a lion, in the east by an elephant, in the south by a horse, in the west by a peacock, and in the north by Garuḍa, on the five petals of the moon-lotus [the Five Wisdom Buddhas] appear: in the middle, from the [syllable] *oṃ*, a white Vairocana with the *mudrā* of supreme enlightenment; in the east, from the [syllable] *hūṃ*, a blue Akṣobhya with the earth-touching meditation *mudrā;* in the south, from the [syllable] *tāṃ*, a yellow Ratnasambhava, performing the meditation and supreme generosity *mudrās;* in the west, from the [syllable] *hrī*, a red Amitābha with two hands joined [in the meditation *mudrā*] (*phyag gnyis mnyam gzhag*); in the north, from the [syllable] *āḥ*, a green Amoghasiddhi with the refuge-granting *mudrā*.[68] Each of them is decorated with jewels. They all sit with both legs in the *vajra* posture. They are everywhere surrounded by throngs of Buddhas and bodhisattvas. All of them have at their three spots [i.e., at the head, throat and heart, the syllables] *oṃ āḥ hūṃ*. Light radiates forth from the [syllable] *hūṃ*, encircling the family of the Five [Wisdom Buddhas] together with the Buddhas and their spiritual sons. Come here. [Saying,] "*Ba dzra sa mā dzaḥ dzaḥ hūṃ baṃ hoḥ sa*," they dissolve inseparably [into the visualized replicas]. In the [*stūpa*] vases, from the [syllable] *oṃ* at the foreheads of whole group of gods, [there appears] a wheel [marked] with [the syllable] *oṃ*. From [the syllable] *āḥ* at their throats [there appears] a lotus with [the syllable] *āḥ*. From [the syllable] *hūṃ* at their hearts [there appears] a *vajra* with [the syllable] *hūṃ*. [At this point the ritual master recites a prayer.] The offering should be made by reciting the verse:

"I offer to all Buddhas and bodhisattvas drinking water, water for bathing their feet, flowers, incense, butter-lamps, scent, food and music. After accepting the offering, I request you to bring about the goals of sentient beings."[69]

As discussed earlier, temporary conditions that lead to untimely death are disease, evil influences, and obstacles. One may thus expect that any *chilu* ritual will counteract all three conditions as a whole, or else that there should exist specific rituals focussing on each of the three individually. The texts themselves do not indicate the specific condition of untimely death to which they are responding. Nonetheless, rituals like *Liberating the Lotus* pay apparent attention to the reinforcement of the five elements in the body, a clear indication that here it is health that is the chief concern. Other rituals chiefly consist of a direct negotiation with the Lord of Death and other evil spirits. In these cases, the goal is to persuade the spirits that the offerings being made by the ritualist is superior to the human body of the beneficiary. In this way, the person is freed from the grasp of demons. In the ritual *Quelling the Lord of Death,* the ritual master visualizes a host of evil spirits (*'byung po*), including the Lord of Death, appearing before him and first reminds them of their former vows with the following words:

All you powerful spirits,
According to the vows you accepted in a former life
In the presence of the Great Glorious Heruka,
You committed yourselves not to violate the vows.
If you violate your vows,
Your power and strength will decline.[70]

The ritual master then requests the king of the Lords of Death ('Chi bdag gshin rje'i rgyal po) and all evil spirits from the upper, lower, and intermediate realms to listen to him, the yogi, for a moment. He asks them to accept the effigy as a substitute for the sick person by praising the effigy's qualities: originating from the five elements, and possessing all five elements, the mental and physical aggregates and all the sense faculties, and because of various unique qualities, it is superior to the flesh and blood body of a human being. After taking the offerings, the spirits are asked to relax their grip on human beings: to liberate the ritual master and other yogis, the generous beneficiary (i.e., the sick person requesting and paying for the ritual), together with his or her family and friends. The master urges the spirits to take the food, small *tormas,* and butter-lamps as provisions for their journey and, without lingering, to instantly return to the other side of the vast ocean.[71] *Liberating the Lotus* is another example of a ritual that is responding to the influence of evil spirits who may be harming and bearing a grudge against the beneficiary. These include sickness-causing demons (*nad bdag*), the Lord of Death (*'chi bdag*), *lü* (*glud = klu? bdag*), and pollution-causing demons (*grib 'dre*). They are summoned by the ritual master to receive an effigy as replacement for the body of the afflicted person. During the exchange, the ritual master addresses the spirits with the following verses:

> This ransom effigy (*glud kyi ngar mi*) [composed of] the five elements
> Has a beautiful face, eyes and clothes.
> Foods like *chang bu* and raw meat,
> Luxuries, and possessions are piled up [as high as] a mountain.
> [I further] increase them using the *samādhi* mantra.
> Here, today, I offer them as ransom
> For the life and life-force (*tshe dang srog*) of [the person] named so and so.
> Take this ransom and give back his/her life!
> Relax your grasp and liberate him/her!
> Don't harm him/her from now on![72]

A third group of ritual texts attempts to thwart the danger of dying by seeking the support of protector deities, Buddhas, and bodhisattvas. In an example of this from the system of Ngog Lotsāwa Londen Sherab (Rngog lo tsā ba Blo ldan shes rab, 1095–1109), the offering is not made directly to the malevolent spirits, but primarily to the protective deity Black Flaming Mouth (Kha 'bar ma nag po), relying on her supernatural powers to rescue the dying person. That the offering may also satisfy the Lord of Death is mentioned as a side effect of the ritual.[73] The relevant verses of the ritual read as follows:

> In order to ward off the danger of Shinjé, the Lord of Death,
> I request the body emanation of the queen Flaming Mouth to come.
> The large *torma* comprising all five sense pleasures,
> Dough buttons (*theb kyu*), balls (*ril bu*), handprints (*chang bu*) and the ransom effigy (*gzugs glud*)—
> This offering decorated with red flesh and blood—
> I offer to the queen Flaming Mouth and her entourage.
> May it also satisfy the host of Lords of Death.[74]

Later, the text reveals the origin of the practice and the great power of the ritual by telling the story of how "Mo ha lo ma," the son of Ngogpa (Rngog pa), was sick and how his father respectfully beseeched the goddess Black Flaming Mouth for help. The goddess ordered him to hurry and perform her death-deceiving ritual. By doing as ordered, his son came back to life from the dead. When the son was asked what he had experienced, he replied:

> I dreamed that a red person led me to a thorny plain in the south. Then a girl of pure blue color arrived and told me, "You and I have to return

from that wrong path." She carried me inside a castle. Then I regained consciousness.[75]

Conclusions

Indian death-deceiving rituals (*mṛtyu vañcana*) were translated into Tibetan around the eleventh century, and at this point became accessible at least to the literate part of Tibetan population. The Indian idea of cheating death is based on a variety of methods to accumulate merit, and on meditational, yogic, and alchemical techniques that prevent aging and extend the life span. When introduced into Tibet, some aspects of these rituals—like the accumulation of merit, the recitation of *mantras, mudrās,* meditation practices and visualizations—were likely incorporated into already existing Tibetan indigenous rituals centered on sacrifice. One may speculate that, after the introduction of Buddhism, human and animal sacrifices were to a great extent replaced by the offering of dough substitute effigies, which became the most characteristic element of Tibetan *chilu* rituals. Another purely Tibetan aspect of *chilu* rituals is the direct conversation between the ritual master and evil spirits gripping the body of a dying person. *Dö* (*mdos*), *yé* (*yas*), and *lü* (*glud*) are most likely the oldest examples of ancient Tibetan ransom rites preserved in the Bön tradition. The sophisticated practices and techniques in reading signs of death as presented by Vāgīśvarakīrti seem to be of Indian origin, and were fully adapted by Tibetans, who in the course of time developed their own systems of death prognostications by including evil influences due to the mundane spirits populating the Tibetan landscape. Finally, the relation between rituals and the trio of karma, merit, and obstacles raises several questions concerning the doctrinal distinction between untimely death and a natural exhaustion of one's life span. As shown earlier, the influence of rituals on karma is explained in manifold, sometimes contradictory, and not always convincing ways. It may well be that these are attempts to make these rituals, which have been practiced long before the advent of Buddhism, conform to Buddhist concepts and principles.

NOTES

1. This involves the purchase of one or more animals—for example, sheep, goats, or yaks—to prevent their being killed for the meat. The animal will then usually be marked in some way to set it apart from the rest of the flock, and will be allowed to roam freely for the rest of its natural life.

2. Krang dbyi sun et al., *Bod rgya tshig mdzod chen mo*, 864: *'chi bslu, 'chi ba zlog pa byed pa'i thabs shig.* Sarat Chandra Das, *Tibetan-English Dictionary* (Kathmandu: Ratna

Pustak Bhandar, 1985), 444: "*'chi ba bslu ba*, Skr. *Mṛtyuvañcana*, to deceive death, to ransom the life of a dying person." In the *Sambotha Dictionary*, CD ROM (Seattle: Nithartha International, 2008 ed.), which compiles entries from several different sources (e.g., James Valbe = JV and Rangjung Yeshe = RY), we find: "*'chi ba bslu ba*, save one from death by paying ransom, deceive death, ransom life of a dying person [JV]"; "*'chi bslu*, ritual for "ransoming" from impending death [RY]." The latter has for *bslu ba* "to ransom; deception, fraudulent, to deceive, to lure; ft. of {*slu ba*} misleading [RY]." In Monier Monier-Williams, *Sanskrit-English Dictionary* (New Delhi: Munishram Manoharlal, 1988), we find: "*mṛtyu vañcana*, death-cheater" (828), and "*vañcana*, cheating, deception, fraud" (914).

3. *'Chi ba bslu ba* (*Mṛtyuṣṭhāpaka*), Sde dge Bstan 'gyur, Toh no. 1702, Rgyud 'grel *sha*, ff. 58a.3–5: *de'i rjes gro ga la gur gum gyis 'khor lo rtsibs bdun pa bris la che ge mo'i sdig pa zhi bar gyur cig la sogs pa spel la snying po dang gzungs dgod par bya'o/ de nas rin po che'am rdza sar pa kha sar ram/ rwa'am shing gi za ma tog gi nang du 'khor lo dril la skud pa dmar pos snod lan mang du bcing/ dar ram ras dkar po'i na bzas gyogs la dge 'dun gyi sde chen po'i gtsug lag gi shing ngam/ mchod rten gyi shing la bcings la/ dus khyad par can la mchod pa chen pos mchod cing bsgom pa dang snying po dang gzungs dang bstod pa rnams brjod par bya'o.*

4. Ritual texts contained in the Bstan 'gyur concerning deceiving death (*'chi bslu*) include: (1) *'Chi ba bslu ba*, Skr. *Mṛtyuṣṭhāpaka*, authored by Tathāgatarakṣita and translated by Mya ngan med pa'i dpal (Aśokaśrī), Sde dge Bstan 'gyur, Toh. no. 1702, Rgyud 'grel *sha*, ff. 57b.5–58a6 [TBRC Bstan 'gyur sde dge par ma, *vol.* 28, ff. 114.5–115.6]. (2) *'Chi ba blu ba'i man ngag*, Skr. *Mṛtyuvañcanopadeśa*, authored by Vāgīśvarakīrti (Ngag gi dbang phyug grags pa), Sde dge Bstan 'gyur, Toh. no. 1748, Rgyud 'grel *sha*, ff. 118b.7–133b.3; for a revision by Si tu paṇ chen of Atiśa's (b.972/982) and Rin chen bzang po's (958–1055) earlier translation, see Si tu paṇ chen Chos kyi 'byung gnas, *Ta'i si tu pa kun mkhyen chos kyi 'byung gnas bstan pa'i nyin byed kyi bka' 'bum: Collected Works of the Great Ta'i Si tu pa kun mkhyen chos kyi 'byung gnas bstan pa'i nyin* byed (Sansal, Kangra, HP: Palpung Sungrab Nyamso Khang, 1990), vol. 7, 1–61; TBRC Bstan 'gyur sde dge par ma, *vol.* 28, ff. 236.5–266.3. (3) *'Chi ba blu ba'i bsdus don*, Skr. *Mṛtyuvañcanapiṇḍārtha*, also authored by Vāgīśvarakīrti, Peking Bstan 'gyur, no. 4806, Rgyud 'grel *zhu*, ff. 146a2–147b7. (4) *'Chi ba slu ba'i sgrol ma dkar mo'i sgrub thabs*, Skr. *Mṛtyuvañcanasitatārāsādhana*, authored by the chief disciple (*slob ma thu bo*) of Vāgīśvarakīrti, Sde dge Bstan 'gyur, Toh. no. 3496, Rgyud 'grel *mu*, ff. 150a.1–150b.3; TBRC *Bstan 'gyur sde dge par ma*, *vol.* 77, ff. 299.1–300.3. (5) *Mi pham mgon po la bstod pa'i 'chi slu ma zhes bya ba*, Skr. *Ajitanāthastutimṛtyuvañcanā nāma*, authored by Abhayakīrti ('Jigs med grags pa), Peking *Bstan 'gyur*, no. 4605, vol. *pu*, 4a.1–4a.8. (6) *'Chi ba slu ba'i gdams pa*, Skr. *Mṛtyuvañcanāmnāya*, unknown author, Peking Bstan 'gyur, no. 3660, Rgyud 'grel *nyu*, ff. 210a.5–211a.2; Sde dge Bstan 'gyur, Toh. no. 2839, Rgyud *nu*, ff. 180b.1–181a.4; TBRC Bstan 'gyur sde dge par ma, *vol.* 73, ff. 360.1–361.4. (7) *'Chi blu'i bsdus don*, Skr. *Mṛtyuvañcanapiṇḍārtha*, unknown author, Peking Bstan 'gyur, no. 4807, Rgyud 'grel *zhu*, ff. 147b.7–150b.8. (8) *'Chi ba slu ba'i sgrol ma'i sgrub thabs*, Skr. *Mṛtyuvañcanatārāsādhana*, unknown author, Sde dge Bstan 'gyur, Toh. no. 3495, Rgyud 'grel *mu*, ff. 149b.4–150a.1; TBRC Bstan 'gyur sde dge par ma, *vol.* 77, 298.4–299.1. (9) *'Chi ba slu ba'i man ngag gi sgrol ma'i sgrub thab*, Skr.

Mṛtyuvañcanopadeśatārāsādhana, unknown author, Sde dge Bstan 'gyur, Toh. no. 3504, Rgyud 'grel *mu*, ff. 154a.3–154b.5; TBRC Bstan 'gyur sde dge par ma, vol. 77, ff. 307.3–308.5. (10) *'Chi ba slu ba*, Skr. *Mṛtyuvañcana*, unknown author, Peking Bstan 'gyur no. 4864, Rgyud 'grel *zu*, ff. 173b.1–174a.7.

5. I have Prof. Phillip Stanley to thank for his help with the dating these two texts.

6. He also wrote and co-translated another text in the Tengyur entitled *A Discourse on the Proper Conduct of [with?] a Yoginī*. Tathāgatarakṣita, *rNal 'byor ma kun tu spyod pa'i bshad sbyar*, Peking Bstan 'gyur, no. 2139, Rgyud 'grel *na* ff. 139b.5–160a.7; Sde dge Bstan 'gyur, Toh. no. 1422, Rgyud 'grel *wa*, ff. 120a.5–139a.3.

7. Si tu paṇ chen, *Collected* Works, vol. 7, 61.2–3.

8. Namkhai Norbu, *Drung, Deu and Bön: Narrations, Symbolic Languages and the Bön Tradition in Ancient Tibet* (Dharamsala: Library of Tibetan Works and Archives, 1995), 80.

9. Namkhai Norbu, *Drung, Deu and Bön*, 77: "In any case, after having prepared the prescribed ritual objects and empowering them with *mantras*, *mudrās* and meditation, they are dispatched to the specific instigators of the disturbances."

10. Namkhai Norbu, *Drung, Deu and Bön*, 252n4.

11. Vāgīśvarakīrti, *'Chi ba blu ba'i man ngag*, in Si tu paṇ chen, Collected Works, vol. 7, 32. 2: *'bad pas 'chi ba bslu ba ni/ dad pa nyid kyis bya bar nus/ de bas dad pa brtan par bya/ gzhan du ngal ba don med 'gyur*. In the rest of this chapter, all references to the *'Chi ba blu ba'i man ngag* is to the Si tu edition.

12. Vāgīśvarakīrti, *'Chi ba blu ba'i man ngag*, 33.4: *bya nya ri dags [dwags] rkun ma dang/ sbrul sogs gsad bya'i phyogs gyur rnams/ srog bskyabs pa yis 'phral du ni/ tshe thung ba yang tshe ring 'gyur.*

13. Vāgīśvarakīrti, *'Chi ba blu ba'i man ngag*, 37.2–4: *indranīla rin chen sogs/ nor bu chen po gzhan dag kyang/ bcangs pas 'chi ba thams cad ni/ bslu bar 'gyur ba the tshom med.*

14. Vāgīśvarakīrti, *'Chi ba blu ba'i man ngag*, 38.4: *sgrol ma'i spyan sngar bzlas nas ni/ zho dang sbrang rtsis sngar sbags pa'i/ dårva'i myu gu'i rtse mo ni/ shar dang byang bstan sbyin sreg bya/ sngon gyi las las skyes ldang ba'i/ 'chi ba 'ang nges par zlog par byed.*

15. Vāgīśvarakīrti, *'Chi ba blu ba'i man ngag*, 41.4–6: *'jig rten na ni dngos gzhan gang/ sngogs kyis mi 'grub de yod min/ yang dag dad pas 'bad pa las/ sngags rnams yid bzhin nor bur mtshungs.*

16. Vāgīśvarakīrti, *'Chi ba blu ba'i man ngag*, 41.6: *bkres shas che ba'i sa phyogs su/ sle tres gcig pu'am yang na ni/ sman gzhan dag dang lhan cig tu/ rtag tu shin tu spyad par bya/ de yis lus ni brtan gyur pas/ gshin rje'i sgo ni mthong mi 'gyur.*

17. Vāgīśvarakīrti, *'Chi ba blu ba'i man ngag*, 43.4–6: *'bras bu gsum ni spyir bsdus pa'am/ po so bhingarāja bcas/ rnal 'byor pa yis rtag spyad na/ bdud rtsi lnga yi bcud len te/ gnyer ma skar dkar rnams dang bral/ rdo rje'i lus ni gzugs bzang ldan/ bskal ba la sogs grangs kyis ni/ 'chi ba'ang nges par zlog pa yin.*

18. Vāgīśvarakīrti, *'Chi ba blu ba'i man ngag*, 45.6–46.1: *bgegs dgra'i gsang sngags 'bum phrag ni/ legs bzlas sbyin sreg khri byas pas/ bgegs rnams thams cad bzlog par bya.*

19. Vāgīśvarakīrti, *'Chi ba blu ba'i man ngag*, 47.4: *byang chub mchog gi phyag rgyar ldan/ 'od zer dkar po'i tshogs 'phro ba'i/ rnam snang dkar po bsgoms na ni/ 'khor srid du ni 'chi 'os min.*

20. Vāgīśvarakīrti, *'Chi ba blu ba'i man ngag*, 49.4–6: *tshangs dbang khyab 'jug nyi zla dang/ drag po phyogs skyong 'dod lhas kyang/ ba spu'i rtse mo'ang mi gcod par/ 'chi bdag lta bur 'chi las rgyal/ skra dkar gnyer ma skal ngan dang/ nad dang dbul ba ku zad byed/ seng ge la sogs 'jigs chen brgyad/ sdug bsngal tshogs ni 'jig par byed.*

21. Vāgīśvarakīrti, *'Chi ba blu ba'i man ngag*, 50.6: *he ru ka yi rnal 'byor bsgoms/ byas nas de yongs gyur pa ni/ ka pā la yi rnam par bsgom/ keng rus kyi gzugs bsgom pa'am/ yang na khaṭvāṅga ru bsgom/ gsad par 'os pa ma yin phyir/ 'chi ba nyid ni mi 'byung ste.* Vāgīśvarakīrti states that this meditation technique is contained in the *Cakrasaṃvara Tantra* (*'Khor lo sdom pa'i rgyud*).

22. Vāgīśvarakīrti, *'Chi ba blu ba'i man ngag*, 55.2–4: *rtag tu 'bab na chu rgyun 'jam pos kyang/ dus su rdo leb dag kyang rnam par 'big/ gtsubs na shing las me ni 'byung 'gyur zhing/ brkos par gyur na sa la hu 'byung 'gyur/ mi yis rtsol ba byas na mi 'grub med/ de 'dir 'os pa'i 'bad kun 'bras bur 'gyur/ 'di na 'chi ba bslu ba rnams/ shin tu mang po shes nas kyang/ nyams ma blangs na mal du ni/ bshang bas gos zhing(?) khyod 'chi 'gyur.*

23. Rev. Walter Asboe, "The Scape-Goat in Western Tibet," *Man* 36 (1936): 74–75, and "Sacrifices in Western Tibet," *Man* 36 (1936): 75–76. On the use of effigies in magical rites described by a nineteenth-century Tibetan author, see chapter 7 by Cuevas in this volume.

24. Catherine Bell, *Ritual: Perspectives and Dimensions* (New York: Oxford University Press, 1997), 93–137.

25. Richard Barron, tr. and ed., *The Autobiography of Jamgön Kongtrul: A Gem of Many Colors* (Ithaca: Snow Lion Publications, 2003), 521–26.

26. Graham Coleman with Thupten Jinpa, ed., *The Tibetan Book of The Dead: The Great Liberation by Hearing in the Intermediate States*, tr. Gyurme Dorje (New York: Viking, 2005), 156.

27. This distinction is found in 'Be lo Karma tshe dbang kun khyab, *Yi dam zhi ba dang khro bo'i tshogs kyi sgrub thabs nor bu'i phreng ba'i lo rgyus chos bshad rab 'byams*, block print, 87 folios, Og min mtshur mdo'i chos grwa (no other bibliographical information given), f. 83a. Beyer refers to this passage from 'Be lo's text in *The Cult of Tārā*, 368.

28. Gehlek Rinpoche, private communication, 2007.

29. Geshe Tenzin Sherab, private communication, 2007.

30. Dorjee Tseten, "Tibetan Art of Divination."

31. Tsong-kha-pa, *The Great Treatise on the Stages of the Path to Enlightenment: Lam rim chen mo of Tsong kha pa* 3 vols., tr. The Lamrim Chenmo Translation Committee, eds., Joshua W. C. Cuttler and Guy Newland (Albany, NY: Snow Lion Publications, 2000), 1: 156.

32. Zhu chen Tshul khrims rin chen, *Kha 'bar ma dkar mo la brten nas 'chi ba bslu zhing bar gcod bzlog pa'i thabs 'chi med bde ster* (Bestowing the Bliss of Immortality: A Method to Avert Obstacles and Deceive Death Based Upon the White [Goddess] Flaming Mouth), in his Gsung 'bum (Kathmandu: Sachen International, Guru Lama, 2005), vol. 6, 342.1: *bdag dang sbyin bdag dpon slob 'khor dang bcas pa'i sngon gyi las dang 'phral gyi rkyen las gyur ba'i nad gdon bar du gcod pa thams cad zhi bar gyur cig.*

33. Zhu chen Tshul khrims rin chen, *'Chi bslu 'chi med bde gter*, 342.5–6: *sngon gyi las dang 'phrel gyi rkyen las gyur pa'i nad kyi rigs su gyur pa rlung las gyur pa dang/ mkhris*

pa las gyur pa dang/ bad kan las gyur pa dang/ 'dus pa las gyur pa ste nad bzhi brgya rtsa bzhi.

34. Zhu chen Tshul khrims rin chen, *'Chi bslu 'chi med bde gter*, 342.6–343.2: *gdon gyi rigs su gyur pa lha'i gdon dang/ klu'i gdon dang/ dri za'i gdon dang/ 'byung po'i gdon dang/ rgyal po'i gdon la sogs pa gdon stong phrag brgyad cu rtsa bzhi'i gdon thams cad zhi bar gyur cig/ bgegs kyi rigs su gyur pa bdud/ btsan/ rgyal po/ pe har/ dmu/ ma mo/ gshin rje/ dam sri la sogs bgegs rigs stong phrag brgyad bcu rtsa bzhi'i gdon thams cad zhi bar gyur cig.*

35. Celestial gods dwell in three distinct heavenly spaces: from the "top" down, the formless realm, form realm, and desire realm. Mundane spirits inhabit the landscape residing in places like mountains, rivers, and lakes. Tibetan tradition often divides up the huge number of these gods and demons into eight classes (*lha srin sde brgyad*). Samuel, *Civilized Shamans: Buddhism in Tibetan Societies* (Washington,DC: Smithsonian Institution Press, 1993), 162–63 adds two more, distinguishing between ten classes of local and regional gods for a total of ten: (1) aquatic deities or *klu*; (2) badly intentioned, illness-causing spirits or *gnyan* (See chapter 2 by Karmay in this volume); (3) rock spirits or *btsan*; (4) king spirits or *rgyal po*; (5) disease-causing spirits or *gza'*; (6) guardian deities or *gnod sbyin*; (7) ferocious female deities or *ma mo*; (8) malevolent spirits or *bdud*; (9) lords of the soil or *sa bdag*; and (10) spirits who are benevolent toward human beings or *lha*. At present, it is difficult to determine if the huge number of Tibetan gods and spirits found in Tibetan literature can all be categorized into one of these ten classes. A precise classification becomes indeed arduous when one and the same class of god is depicted in the texts with opposite characteristics. A case in point is the *lha*, commonly described as spirits benevolent toward humans but, occasionally also accused of being the cause of evil influences (*lha'i gdon*). See Zhu chen Tshul khrims rin chen, *Bestowing the Bliss of Immortality*, 342.6.

36. Vāgīśvarakīrti, *'Chi ba blu ba'i man ngag*, 119a.4–5. Beyer traces the origin of the cult of White Tārā in Tibet back to Vāgīśvarakīrti's *'Chi bslu* texts translated in the *Bstan 'gyur*. See Beyer, *The Cult of Tārā*, 12.

37. Blo gter dbang po, *Rje btsun sgrol ma dkar po la brten pa'i bla slu'i cho ga ring 'tsho'i dpal gter* (*Bestowing the Glory of a Long Life: A Death Deceiving Ritual Based upon the Noble White Tārā*) in 'Jam dbyangs mkhyen brtse'i dbang po and 'Jam dbyangs blo gter dbang po (compilers), *Sgrub thabs kun btus: A Collection of Sādhanas and Related Texts of The Vajrayāna Traditions of Tibet* (Dehradun: G.T.K. Lodoy, N. Gyaltsen & N. Lungtok, 1970), vol. 1, f. 637.2: *'khor bar srog las gces pa ni/ ci yang yod pa ma yin te/ de bas myur du thabs mang pos/ 'chi ba slu ba kun tu spyad.*

38. The other six qualities are noble family (*rigs bzang ba*), beautiful body (*gzugs mdzes pa*), health (*nad med pa*), good fortune (*skal ba bzang ba*), abundant wealth (*nor phyug pa*), and great intelligence (*shes rab che ba*). Blo gter dbang po, "Bestowing the Glory of a Long Life," f. 637.2–3: *mtho ris yon tan bdun gyi gtso bo tshe ring ba nyid yin la/ de la brten nas gnas skabs dang mthar thug gi don thams cad bde blag tu 'grub pas na/ ring 'tsho'i thabs la 'bad pa gal che.*

39. The *mtshams med pa lnga* or "five inexpiable sins" are matricide (*ma gsod pa*), killing arhats (*dgra bcom pa gsod pa*), patricide (*pha gsod pa*), creating schism in the saṅgha (*dge 'dun gyi dbyen byas ba*), and drawing blood from a tathāgata's body (*bde bzhin gshegs pa'i sku la ngan sems kyis khrag 'byin pa*).

40. Coleman and Thubten Jinpa, *The Tibetan Book of the Dead*, 180.

41. For a historical approach to the *zhabs brtan* and its precursor, the *brtan bzhugs* literary genre, see José I. Cabezón, "Firm Feet and Long Lives: The Zhabs brtan Genre of Tibetan Buddhism," in *Tibetan Literature: Studies in Genre*, edited by José Ignacio Cabezón and Roger R. Jackson (Ithaca: Snow Lion, 1996), 344–57.

42. A few examples of texts examining a wide range of signs of death include: Dri med 'od zer, *'Chi ltas dran pa'i me long* (TBRC W12787); Karma gling pa, *'Chi ltas mtshan ma rang grol*, translated in Colemen and Thubten Jinpa, *The Tibetan Book of the Dead*; Rol pa'i rdo rje, *'Chi ltas brtag pa dang 'chi bslu tshe khrid bcas* (TBRC W2777); and Dge 'dun grub pa, *'Chi ltas brtag pa dang tshe bsring ba* (TBRC W814).

43. Coleman with Thupten Jinpa, *The Tibetan Book of the Dead*, 151–80. Beyer, *The Cult of Tārā*, 368–75, translated and annotated a selection of a text in which these signs are mentioned.

44. Coleman with Thupten Jinpa, *The Tibetan Book of the Dead*, 180.

45. Vesna Wallace, "Buddist Tantric Medicine in the Kālacakratantra," *Pacific World*, New Series 11 (1995): 161–62.

46. Vāgīśvarakīrti, *'Chi ba blu ba'i man ngag*, 9.4–6: *'khrig spyod tshe na dril bu yi/ sgra ni rna bar thos gyur na/ gal te tshangs pa dang mnyam yang/ de tshe zla ba gsum nas 'chi.*

47. Vāgīśvarakīrti, *'Chi ba blu ba'i man ngag*, 8.4–6: *mdzod spu'i gnas su phug snyam na/ nges par 'phral du 'chi bar 'gyur.*

48. Germano gives an excellent translation and description of these signs in his article. See David Germano, "Dying, Death, and Other Opportunities," in *Religions of Tibet in Practice*, ed. Donald S. Lopez, Jr. (Princeton: Princeton University Press, 1997), 458–93.

49. Vāgīśvarakīrti, *'Chi ba blu ba'i man ngag*, 20.2–4: *rmi lam thams cad bden min yang/ de la mi dad rig ma yin/ rmi lam dag tu lhas bstan dang/ yang na rmi lam bden mthong mis/ rmi lam yid ches byas nas su/ 'chi ba'i mtshan ma lta bar byos.*

50. Robin Cooke, tr. from the Italian, and Enrico Dell'Angelo, tr. from the Tibetan, *Namchö Mingyur Dorje: The Interpretation of Dreams in a 17th Century Tibetan Text* (Arcidosso GR: Shang Shung Edizioni, 1996), 13.

51. On Mipam, see Cuevas's chapter in this volume.

52. Jay Goldberg and Lobsang Dakpa, tr., *Mo: Tibetan Divination System [by] Jamgon Mipham*, (Ithaca, NY: Snow Lion, 1990), 53–55.

53. 'Jam dbyangs mkhyen brtse'i dbang po, *Bzang po spyod pa'i cho ga'i sgo nas 'chi bslu ba'i gdams pa gsal byed* (*Elucidating the Instructions for Deceiving Death Based upon the Ritual of the 'Excellent Conduct' [Prayer]*) in 'Jam dbyangs mkhyen brtse'i dbang po and 'Jam dbyangs blo gter dbang po, *Sgrub thabs kun btus*, vol. 1, 602.1–2.

54. The three-part division mentioned here is based on Martin Brauen's description of a Bon po death ritual. See Martin Brauen, "A Bon-po Death Ceremony," in *Tibetan Studies: Presented at the Seminar of Young Tibetologists, Zürich, June 26–July 1, 1977*, ed. Martin Brauen and Per Kvaerne (Zurich: Völkerkundemuseum der Universität Zürich, 1978), 54.

55. These include *gtor mas* of different shapes (e.g., *zlum gtor*, round cakes), sizes (*bshos bu/ gtor chung*), and colors—depending on whether they are being offered to tutelary deities deities (*yi dam*), local deities (*gzhi bdag*), or if they are *gtor mas* for blocking karmic debts (*lan chags bgegs kyi gtor ma*).

56. The mud for these clay tablets should have been obtained from a clean place. After they are pressed using a mold, they should be consecrated by reciting the Essence of Interdependence (*rten 'brel snying po*) mantra and the mantra *oṃ hūṃ tāṃ hrī a*. Some *tsha tsha* are molded by mixing the clay with the hair, nails, and clothing of the sick person.

57. Blo bzang nor bu shes rab, *Bzang po spyod pa'i sgo nas 'chi bslu ji ltar bya tshul gyi cho ga'i ngag 'don dus min 'chi 'joms* (*Conquering Untimely Death: A Text in Recitation Format of a Ritual Procedure of Deceiving Death Based on Excellent Conduct [Prayer]*), in his *Collected Works* (Beijing: Yellow Pagoda, 1996/97), vol. 2, 42–43.

58. Zhu chen Tshul khrims rin chen, *Rje btsun sgrol ma dkar mo la brten pa'i 'chi [b]slu'i cho ga ring 'tsho'i dpal ster* (*Bestowing the Glory of a Long Life: A Death Deceiving Ritual Based upon the Noble White Tārā*) in 'Jam dbyangs mkhyen brtse'i dbang po and 'Jam dbyangs blo gter dbang po, *Sgrub thabs kun btus*, vol. 1, 475.2–4.

59. Bdud 'joms 'Jigs bral ye shes rdo rje, *Tshe sgrub 'chi med srog thig dang 'brel bar 'chi ba bslu ba'i cho ga 'chi bdag gdong zlog*, (*Turning Away the Face of the Lord of Death: A Death Deceiving Ritual Connected with the Life Drop [of] Longevity [and] Immorality]*), in *'Chi med srog thig: Gter mas and Ritual Texts Collected by Bdud 'joms 'jigs bral ye shes rdo rje* (Varanasi: Deepak Press, 1973), 249–59.

60. Germano, who describes a very similar ritual, correctly states that inviting humans and animals to breathe on the dough infuses it with their life-force. Germano, "Dying, Death, and Other Opportunities," 469.

61. Bdud 'joms rin po che, *'Chi bdag gdong zlog*, f. 252.2–3: *nam mkha' rlung me chu sa'i rim pas 'khor lo rnams brtsegs te/ rdza phor so ma kha sbyor du bcug/ tshon skud lngas rgya gram du dkris.*

62. Bdud 'joms rin po che, *'Chi bdag gdong zlog*, f. 252.3–5: *gdan gzhi rgya che ba zhig gi steng du bsgrub bya'i dri che chung/ skra sen kha sna'i chu la sogs pa dri mas sbags shing/ rin po che sna tshogs bsres pa'i ngar phye dud 'gro dang mi la sogs pa'i sems can rigs mi mthun pa du mar bgres [bsres] shing dbugs la bdugs pa'i zan la 'dra glud khru gang ba long tang gi mig sogs skye mched dod pa 'gro ba la rings pa 'dra ba zhig bcos pa'i lto bar sngar gyi 'khor lo'i rdza phor de nyid steng 'og ma log par bcug/ mig tu raṃ dmar po/ rna bar yaṃ ljang gu/ sna la khaṃ dkar po/ lce la laṃ ser po/ snying gar aḥ sngon po rnams shog bur bris pa dril te bcug.*

63. These subrituals are found in many other Tantric rituals: for example, in consecration ritual; see, for example, Yale Bentor, "Literature on Consecration," in Cabezón and Jackson, *Tibetan Literature*, 290–311; and "The Horse-Back Consecration Ritual," in Lopez, *Religions of Tibet in Practice*, 234–54.

64. See Gter slob mkhan ming 'dul 'dzin (Gter slob karma ratna), *Rgyal po'i thugs dam mdo bcu la sogs la bsten pa'i 'chi bslu 'chi bdag zhags gcod ye shes ral gri* (*Wisdom Sword Cutting the Lasso of the Lord of Death: A Death Deceiving [Ritual] Based on the Ten King Sūtras and Others*), in *Brgya bzhi sdong brgyan kha 'bar ma rnams kyi mdos chog la nye bar mkho ba'i bdag mdun bskyed chog: Collected Rituals of the Rnying-ma-pa and Ris med traditions for Use in Funerals, Death Ransoming, and Averting Ceremonies, etc.* (Byllakuppe: Pema Norbu Rinpoche, 1985).

65. The four immeasurables (*tshad med bzhi*) are compassion (*snying rje*), love (*byams pa*), joy (*dga' ba*), and impartiality (*btang snyoms*).

66. The ten king *sūtras* are: (1) *Bzang po spyod pa'i smon lam gyi mdo*, (2) *Rdo rje rnam 'joms khrus kyi mdo*, (3) *Shes rab snying po lta ba'i mdo*, (4) *'Da' ka ye shes sgom pa'i mdo*, (5) *Bya ba ltung bshags bshags pa'i mdo*, (6) *Phag tu med pa tshe ring mdo*, (7) *Gos sngon can ni gzungs kyi mdo*, (8) *Gtsug tor gdugs dkar bzlog pa'i mdo*, (9) *Nor rgyun ma ni nor gyi mdo*, and (10) *Yi ge gcig ma snying po'i mdo*.

67. Zhu chen Tshul khrims rin chen, *'Byung ba lnga'i tsha tsha bskrun pa'i mchod sbyin la brten pa'i 'chi bslu'i cho ga grub pa'i zhal lung 'dab brgya 'grol byed* (*Liberating the Lotus: Oral Instruction for the Performance of a Deceiving Death Ritual Based upon the Offering of Molding Tsha tsha of the Five Elements*) in his *Gsung 'bum*, reproduced from Luding Rinpoche's exemplar of the *Gsung 'bum* (New Delhi: B. Jamyang Norbu, 1972), vol. 6, 319–37.

68. The *mudrās* described here are the classical *mudrās* of the Five Buddhas (*sangs rgyas rigs lnga*).

69. Zhu chen Tshul khrims rin chen, *'Byung ba lnga* (*Liberating the Lotus*), ff. 322.1–324.1: *de nas thog mar tsha tsha rab tu gnas pa'i phyir/ tsha tsha lha sngags zlos shing yungs dkar gyis brab ste bgegs bskrad/ ji ltar bltams pa sogs sngags dang bcas pas khrus byas la/ oṃ sva bhāva sogs kyis tsha tsha rnams stong par sbyangs/ chos kun stong pa'i ngang nyid las/ seng khri padma zla ba'i steng/ oṃ las 'khor lo oṃ gyis mtshan/ de las rnam par snang mdzad dkar/ byang chub mchog gi phyag rgya can/ sna tshogs dar dang rin chen brgyan/ zhabs gnyis rdo rje skyil krung bzhugs/ de nyid yongs su gyur pa las/ chos sku'i mchod rten mtshan nyid rdzogs/ mchod rten rnams kyi bum pa'i nang/ dbus su seng ge shar glang chen/ shor rta nub tu rma bya dang/ byang du mkha' lding bteg pa'i khrir/ padma zla ba'i 'dab lnga la/ dbus su oṃ las rnam snang dkar/ byang chub mchog gi phyag rgya can/ shar du hūṃ mi bskyod pa/ sngon po sa gnon mnyam gzhag can/ lho ru tāṃ las rin 'byung ser/ mchog sbyin mnyam gzhag phyag rgya mdzad/ nub tu hrī las 'od dpag med/ dmar po phyag gnyis mnyam gzhag can/ byang du a las don yod grub/ ljang gu skyabs sbyin mnyam gzhag can/ kun kyang dar dang rin chen brgyan/ zhabs gnyis rdo rje'i skyil krung bzhugs/ kun gyi mtha' skor sangs rgyas dang/ [byang chub] sems dpa'i tshogs kyis bskor bar gyur/ kun gyi gnas gsum oṃ āḥ hūṃ/ hūṃ las 'od 'phro la rigs lnga la/ rgyal ba sras bcas kyis bskor ba/? tshur byon ba dzra sa mā dzaḥ dzaḥ hūṃ baṃ hoḥ sa dbyer med thim / bum nang lha tshogs thams cad kyi/ dpral bar oṃ las 'khor lo oṃ/ mgrin par āḥ las padmar āḥ/ thugs dkar hūṃ las rdo rje hūṃ/* [...] *mchod pa snyod bya ba ni/ rgyal ba sras bcas thams cad la/ mchod yon zhabs bsil me tog sbos/ mar me dri bshos rol mos mchod/ bzhes nas sems can don mdzad gsol.*

70. Mkha' khyab rdo rje, *Chi ba bslu ba'i cho ga mdor bsdus pa 'chi bdag g.yul 'joms* (*Quelling the Lord of Death: An Abbreviated Death Deceiving Ritual*), in *Rgyal dbang mkha' khyab rdo rje'i bka' 'bum* (Paro: Lama Ngodrup, 1979–81), vol. 14, ff. 124.6–125.1: *'byung po stobs chen khyed rnams kyi/ sngon tshe dpal chen he ru ka'i/ spyan sngar khas blangs dam bcas ltar/ dam las ma 'da' sa ma ya/ gal te dam las 'das gyur na/ khyod kyi mthu rtsal nyams par 'gyur.*

71. Mkha' khyab rdo rje, *'Chi bdag g.yul 'joms*, ff. 125.4–126.6: *'chi bdag gshin rje rgyal po dang/ steng 'og bar gsum 'byung po rnams/ dar gcig rnal 'byor bdag la gson/* [...] *glud kyi 'gyung gnas 'byung ba lnga/ khams lnga phung po skye mched tshang/ mi yi sha khrag lus po las/ khyad par du mas 'phags pa'i glud/* [...] *bzhes nas rnal 'byor bdag cag dang/ rgyu sbyor yon bdag 'khor bcas rnams/ bzung ba thongs la bcings pa khrol/* [...] *zhal zas bshos bu mar*

me rnams/ lam rgyags lta bur bzhes nas su/ shul ring mgron po ma dal cig/ mtha' med rgya mtsho'i pha rol du/ da lta nyid du 'gro bar gyis.

72. Zhu chen Tshul khrims rin chen, *'Byung ba lnga* (*Liberating the Lotus*), vol. 6, ff. 332.4–5: *'byung lnga glud kyi ngar mi 'di/ zhal bzang spyan bzang gos kyang bzang/ chang bu sha rjen bza' ba sogs/ 'dod yon longs spyod ri ltar spungs/ ting 'dzin sngags kyis rgya cher spel/ deng 'dir che ge mo zhes pa'i/ tshe dang srog gi glud du 'bul/ glud 'di longs la tshe srog byin/ bzung ba thong la bcings pa khrol/ phyin chad gnod pa ma byed cig.*

73. Rngog Blo dlan shes rab, *Kha 'bar ma nag mo'i 'chi bslu bsdus pa* ("*An Abbreviated Death Deceiving Ritual of the Black [Goddess] Flaming Mouth*") (Sukhia Pokhari, 1996).

74. Rngog Blo dlan shes rab, *Kha 'bar ma nag mo'i 'chi bslu*, 1.6–2.2: *'chi bdag gshin rje'i 'jigs pa bzlog slad du/ kha 'bar rgyal mo'i sku sprul gshegs su gsol/ 'dod yon lnga ldan gtor ma rgya chen dang/ theb kyu ril bu chang bu gzugs glud bcas/ sha khrag dmar gyis brgyan pa'i mchod pa 'di/ kha 'bar rgyal mo 'khor dang bcas la 'bul.*

75. Rngog Blo dlan shes rab, *Kha 'bar ma nag mo'i 'chi bslu*, 3.1–3: *'di rngog pa'i sras mo ha lo ma sku snyung ba'i tshe rngog rin po ches lha mo la gus pas cher bskul ba'i tshe lha mo'i 'chi bslu 'di myur bar gyis gsungs/ de ltar bgyis pas lcam 'chi ba las sos/ khyod gang 'dra byung smras pas mi dmar po gcig gis lho phyogs tsher ma'i thang zhig tu khrid byung bas/ bu mo sngo sangs ma zhig slebs byung nas nga dang khyod lam nor log gsungs pas mkhar gyi nang du bskyal ba rmis pas dran pa sos byung zer ro.*

6

Representations of Efficacy

The Ritual Expulsion of Mongol Armies in the Consolidation and Expansion of the Tsang (Gtsang) Dynasty

JAMES GENTRY

Most Tibetan Buddhist ritual is premised on the intimate contiguity between persons, landscapes, and hosts of landscape spirits of all kinds.[1] Such contiguity assumes that human bodies, habitations, and settlements are impinged upon by the nonhuman forces that surround and inhabit them. Safeguarding the health and integrity of the corporate entities of human body, household, and community from the threats posed by contact with the capricious spirit world thus constitutes a major preoccupation for Tibetan Buddhist ritual specialists. Clergy have at their disposal a repertoire of ritual treatments to subjugate these threatening presences, exorcise them from the precincts of body, home, or territory, and restore internal health and cohesion.

Ritual exorcism, or *dogpa* (*zlog pa*), "that which turns back, out, or away," is one of the most popular Tibetan Buddhist ritual forms enacted for this purpose.[2] In addition to their performance for a single individual or community, the function of exorcism rites to protect against, or drive away, the dangerous impurities of contiguous entities, and to thereby consolidate corporate boundaries has had clear geopolitical ramifications as well. With the emergence of a shared Tibetan ethnic and cultural identity rooted in Tibet's imperial past,[3] foreign armies threatening Tibetan territories were often interpreted in terms analogous to demonic possession. To confront such martial threats, Tibet's ritual specialists frequently performed countrywide exorcisms, thus giving rise to the ritual subgenre of army expelling rites, or *magdog* (*dmag zlog*).[4]

The ostensible reason for such rituals was to "protect the doctrine" (*bstan srung*), or in other words, to preserve the geopolitical integrity of Tibet so that Buddhist institutions could thrive there unabated. And in addition to such conservative, protective functions, the ritualized expulsion of armies entailed the clear demarcation of territorial boundaries, and consequently can also be understood as a factor that contributed to the formation of a strong sense of communal, corporate identity. The pervasiveness of army averting rites in Tibetan Buddhist polities from the period of the Tibetan empire to the present[5] thus seems to indicate, among other things, that these rituals have performed a vital symbolic function in the construction and reaffirmation of Tibetan Buddhist state configurations.

Since the thirteenth century, Mongol armies frequently posed the most dangerous military threat to Tibetan survival. Outnumbered and overpowered, Tibetan political leaders often commissioned ritual specialists to supplement more conventional means of national defense with the magical protection promised by *magdog* rites. It is well known, for instance, that the rulers of the Tsang (Gtsang) dynasty (1565–1642) maintained very close connections with a number of important sectarian leaders, most notably the lamas of the Kargyü (Bka' brgyud), Jonang (Jo nang), and Sakya (Sa skya) schools, who regularly administered to the state's ritual needs.[6] The Nyingmapa figure Sogdogpa Lodrö Gyaltsen (Sog bzlog pa Blo gros rgyal mtshan, 1552–1624) was also particularly active during this period in driving Mongol forces from Tibet via *magdog* rites, as his nickname, "the one who repelled" (*bzlog pa*) "Mongols" (*sog*[7]) attests. In his text, the *History of How the Mongols Were Turned Back* (*Sog bzlog bgyis tshul gyi lo rgyus*[8]), Sogdogpa narrates his own thirty-two-year endeavor to rid Tibet of Mongol forces based on his guru Tertön Zhigpo Lingpa's (Gter ston Zhig po gling pa, 1524–83) treasure cycle, *Twenty-five Ways of Averting Armies* (*Dmag bzlog nyer lnga*). In a style that is part autobiography and part history, Sogdogpa candidly relates his self-proclaimed ritual success story as the culmination of Tibet's historic struggle with Mongol military intervention, and the many attempts of Tibet's leading ritual specialists to address such threats.

The existence of a history *cum* autobiography authored by a Buddhist cleric to demonstrate his successful performance of rituals intended to expel or kill invading foreign armies elicits a host of deeply perplexing questions that are not easy to resolve. Leaving aside for now a discussion of this text's most striking feature, namely, its seeming advocacy of rituals that violate the fundamental Buddhist tenet of nonviolence, let us turn instead to the issue of how these kinds of rituals were believed to function. Sogdogpa narrates that his rituals actually "worked" to produce the desired "outcome" of ridding Tibet of Mongol invaders. But what were the notions of efficacy underlying Sogdogpa's account?

In other words, how, precisely, did Sogdogpa represent the workings of his rituals, what were the various effects that he attributed to them, and what, by promoting their efficacy in writing, did he hope to achieve?

This chapter represents an initial foray into this set of questions through an analysis of Sogdogpa's depiction of events in the *History*. An examination into issues related to ritual efficacy is both amply rewarded and significantly complicated by a close reading of Sogdogpa's account. Sogdogpa is concerned throughout the *History* to present his rituals as powerful, magical manipulations of the cosmos done for tangible geopolitical ends. And as part of this presentation, Sogdogpa also obliquely implies a number of social and political functions for his rites, such as the power to consolidate and fragment resources, populations and territories, functions which seem to have more to do with the social, economic, and political power of ritual actions to produce a sense of solidarity among participants and patrons in the creation or affirmation of a bounded corporate identity.

As a first step toward determining how Sogdogpa might have understood all of these diverse elements as part and parcel of his ritual workings, I attempt to delineate the component features of the *History*'s ritual episodes. In particular, I hope to demonstrate how Sogdogpa represented the efficacy of his rituals through an elaborate interpretative process in which he linked his ritual performances to geopolitical events, prophecy texts, meditation signs, and dreams. I argue that it is through the strategic combination of these public and private discourses of meaning on the pages of the *History* that Sogdogpa locates himself at the center of interpretive authority, thus enabling him to claim ultimate responsibility for some of the most pivotal political events that transpired during his lifetime, including the unification of Tsang (west central Tibet) under the Tsang Desi (Gtsang sde srid)[9] and the expansion of Tsang Desi power into Ü (Dbus, central Tibet) and beyond. I close with a presentation of five of the most significant ritual episodes related to the rise and spread of Tsang Desi rule, illustrating how Sogdogpa further develops his interpretative authority through the act of designating diverse social and political events as outcomes of his own ritual proceedings.

The Blurred Genre of Ritual Memoir: Personal Reflections, Collective Histories, Prophesied Lives

The Tibetan term *logyü* (*lo rgyus*),[10] often translated as "history," which appears in the title of *The History of How the Mongols Were Turned Back* (*Sog bzlog bgyis tshul gyi lo rgyus*), is a broad genre label for any narrative account of something's or someone's past. In this instance, however, Sogdogpa explicitly frames his narrative through its opening verses as though it is an autobiography, and indeed, the final half of the *History* is Sogdogpa's own autobiographical account of his thirty-two-year ritual career of expelling Mongol armies from Tibet through ritual sorcery.[11] Moreover, given that the author's popular nickname, Sogdogpa, "the one who turned back the Mongols," was acquired through the execution of such rituals, the title self-refers to Sogdogpa the figure as much as it refers to the wider historical phenomenon of turning back Mongols through sorcery. The title thus resonates on the registers of personal autobiography and collective history with equal weight. The title might even alternatively be rendered as *The Story of How I Turned Back the Mongols*, or more loosely, *The Story of How I Became Sogdogpa*.

The fluidity witnessed here between narratives of collective historical events (*lo rgyus*) and autobiographical records of personal past events (*rang gi rnam thar*) also reflects an essential feature of Sogdogpa's legitimacy as a ritual expert, namely, the role of prophesies in authenticating Sogdogpa's personal role as the rightful heir to a military sorcery campaign foretold by Padmasambhava (b. eighth century) and enacted over the centuries in times of need.[12] Prophecies that were presumably first articulated and concealed by Padmasambhava and Yeshé Tsogyal (Ye shes mtsho rgyal) (b. eighth century) in the form of treasures (*gter ma*) were excavated and touted by later figures as guides for determining the proper times and places of foreign military invasions, and most importantly, the requisite persons and actions capable of preventing, or delaying such events, or at least mitigating damage.[13] Thus, the proper interpretation and implementation of treasure prophecies is central to how Sogdogpa represents his army repelling rituals as doing what they are intended to do.

The logic of how prophecies connect historical and personal events is explicit in the structure and content of the *History*. The only available edition of the text is divided into two main chapters: "previous lifetimes" (*sngon byung ba yin pa'i skyes rabs:* 206.1–217.3), and "stages of how it was done" (*ji ltar bgyis pa'i rim pa:* 217.3–259.6). Recounting past lives is a typical opening maneuver in Tibetan autobiographical writing. Here however, rather than relate elaborate details, Sogdogpa only makes cursory mention of his recognition as the speech incarnation of the translator Nyag (Gnyags) Jñānakumara (b. eighth century), who was in turn a reincarnation of king Songtsen Gampo's (Srong btsan sgam po, seventh century) minister of internal affairs, Nachenpo (Sna chen po, seventh century).

Then, with little transition, he shifts into a detailed account (207.3–217.3) of his unwilling reception of treasure revealer Zhigpo Lingpa's injunction to lead the ritual expulsion of prophesied Mongol military advances via Zhigpo

Lingpa's treasure ritual cycle, the *Twenty-five Ways of Averting Armies* (*Dmag bzlog nyer lnga*). This ten-folio section presents a rich guru–disciple dialogue in which Zhigpo Lingpa relates several prophecies, personal visionary experiences, and arguments to counter Sogdogpa's reluctance to shoulder the immense responsibility of confronting one of most ferocious military powers on earth.

This conversation with Sogdogpa, otherwise known as the healer (*'tsho byed*) of Dongkar (Gdong mkhar/dkar),[14] is set within the context of Sogdogpa's medical and ritual treatment of Zhigpo Lingpa for what would prove to be a fatal illness. In the course of the treatment, Zhigpo Lingpa reveals through the presentation and interpretation of prophecy texts that Sogdogpa is none other than the reincarnation of Gewa Bum (Dge ba 'bum, b. twelfth century),[15] the famed physician whose reincarnation was prophesied by Padmasambhava to be an instrumental figure in repelling invading Mongol armies.[16] Sogdogpa expresses some skepticism about his newfound identity, but upon realizing that Zhigpo Lingpa's request is indeed his dying guru's final wish, he promises to fulfill the role of protector and departs. Zhigpo Lingpa dies shortly thereafter.

The second chapter, "Stages of How it Was Done," consists of three subsections divided according to a threefold periodization of Mongol intervention in Tibet. Sogdogpa states that this threefold schema is based on a prophecy text which describes three occasions throughout the history of Tibet–Mongolia interactions in which Mongol armies attempt to invade Tibet.

The first subsection of this chapter (217.3–219.4) shifts from the autobiographical mode of the first chapter to describe the history of the first Mongol invasion of Tibet during the final two decades of the thirteenth century, and how Tibet's powerful ritual experts responded to the crisis.[17] The second subsection, which describes the second Mongol threat to Tibet, relates events that purportedly transpired during the final few years of treasure revealer Pema Lingpa's (Padma gling pa, 1450–1521) lifetime and the decade following his passing. This brief section (219.6–228.3) provides much detail concerning Pema Lingpa's instrumental role in interpreting various prophecy texts to warn of an impending Mongol invasion. Just prior to his death, Pema Lingpa passed the responsibility for preventing this disaster to his close disciple Chogden Gönpo (Mchog ldan mgon po, 1497–1557). The section goes on to describe Chogden Gönpo's failure to garner the requisite support for success. Pema Lingpa's injunction to repell the Mongols thus fell to Pema Lingpa's son, Dawa Gyaltsen (Zla ba rgyal mtshan, 1499–1587), who managed to accomplish all the prophesied activities except for the final, most important one—leaving his remains at Zabpu Lung (Zab bu lung).[18] Alternatively, Sogdogpa narrates that another source reports the performance of rites by Ngari Paṇchen (Mnga' ris paṇchen) and the Rigdzin Chenpo (Rigs 'dzin chen po) brothers, students of Chogden Gönpo, thus pushing pack the arrival of Mongol forces several years.

The series of events reported in this second subsection, and especially the dates of the figures involved, enables Sogdogpa to seamlessly connect his chronological narrative with the third and final period of Mongol threat, his own lifetime. In the third subsection, Sogdogpa switches back into a candid autobiographical style to relate his own thirty-two-year ritual endeavor dedicated to driving Mongol military forces from Tibet. This thirty-one-folio (228.3–259.6) memoir begins in 1583, when at 32 years of age Sogdogpa was first charged with performing the *Twenty-five Army Ways of Averting Armies*, and ends in 1614, when, at age 63, Sogdogpa led a group ritual which buried an entire army of Mongols under snow, and by Sogdogpa's account, ended Mongol violence in Tibet for the time being.[19] The memoir thus provides a chronological record of approximately twenty army-averting ritual episodes that he performed between the years of 1583 and 1614. With some variation, each episode includes a date, prophecy, place, corresponding contemporary event, ritual response, names of ritual specialists, participants, and sponsors, as well as successes and/or failures. The text closes with a calculation of the resources and materials that Sogdogpa himself expended toward the project; a list of political and religious figures who either did not follow through with pledges to contribute, or rejected the project outright; and gratitude in the form of a list to everyone who contributed in various ways.

Turning briefly to the rituals themselves, the ritual cycle that Sogdogpa performs in his autobiographical section of the *History*, the *Twenty-five Ways of Averting Armies*, is said to have been revealed by Zhigpo Lingpa in 1544 at Eagle Nest Rock (Khyung tshang brag).[20] The *Twenty-five Ways* consists of twenty-five techniques, each of which, when performed according to prophecies dictating who, where, and when to perform them, were thought to be capable of repelling advancing foreign armies from Tibet. To my knowledge, all that remains of this treasure cycle is a collection of five texts now found in the *Rinchen Terdzö* (*Rin chen gter mdzod*) collection.[21] Although these five documents represent only a fraction of the textual materials that Sogdogpa is said to have received from Zhigpo Lingpa, they nonetheless offer valuable insight into the nature of the rituals concerned. The first text in the collection, the *Sequenced Classification of Means for Averting a Whole Regiment, from the Twenty-five Ways of Averting Armies* (*Dmag zlog nyi shu rtsa lnga las spyi ru zlog thabs kyi rim pa sde tshan du byas pa*[22]), lists the twenty-five means as follows:

1–3. Repelling by supplicating lamas, tutelary deities, and ḍākiṇīs
4. Repelling through white mustard seed
5. Repelling through spells
6. Repelling through construction (*bcas*)

7. Repelling through the practice of Yamāntaka and Vajrakīlāya
8. Repelling an army, compelling it with magical substances in water (*chu la rdzas kyis ngar blud de zlog pa*)
9. Repelling an army with magical substances

10–13. Repelling through *yé* (*yas*)[23] materials (*zang zing yas*), *mdos* rituals, burnt offerings, and magical *torma* weapons (*gtor zor*)

14. Repelling through controlling the elements
15. Repelling through three mantrins of degenerate tantric commitments[24]
16. Repelling through three [mantrins] of nondegenerate tantric commitments
17. Repelling through three monks of degenerate monastic discipline
18. Repelling through three [monks] of nondegenerate [monastic discipline]
19. Repelling with a wand of invisibility (*sgrib shing*) [over] the valley
20. Pith instruction for the regional guardian (*yul 'khor srung gi man ngag*)
21. Protecting the country doing the practice of Hayagrīva (*rta mgrin*)
22. Subduing gods and demons in order to make them paralyze troops (*dmag dpung jag 'ching*) and cut off their route
23. Crumpling a paper effigy of a general (*dmag dpon yig gcu pa*)
24. Repelling through resounding the enlightened speech of dharma
25. Repelling through enforcing a ban on hunting and fishing, and through practicing.[25]

A detailed analysis of each item would lead us too far afield. At a glance it can be noticed that the list of twenty-five ways consists of a variety of activities and ritual types, several of which—the supplication of lamas, tutelary deities, and ḍākiṇīs, and the propitiation of the fierce Buddhist deities Yamāntaka, Vajrakīlāya, and Hayagrīva, for instance—are ordinary dharma practices yoked here to specifically martial ends. Indeed, the list seems to include anything and everything thought to be capable of successfully repelling armies, down to even the meritorious act of restoring and constructing sacred architecture. Yet, as we shall see, determining whether or not these rituals hit their intended mark was no simple matter.

The Logic of Efficacy: Reading Events, Interpreting Signs, and Writing Outcomes

It is immediately clear from just the title of Sogdogpa's text alone, *The History of How the Mongols Were Turned Back*, that a central concern in its authorship was to present a persuasive account of the efficacy of the rituals concerned, and the power of the actors involved. The rhetorical thrust of Sogdogpa's narrative is especially evident in his autobiographical account, where in episode after episode, he consistently attributes to his performance of the twenty-five means, the destruction, rerouting, or impeding of Mongol armies and warlords encroaching upon Tibetan territories. Yet, when investigating such accounts further, Sogdogpa appears to be just as concerned with demonstrating his interpretative authority to adjudicate the matter of ritual efficacy as he is with establishing the workings of the particular rituals concerned.

A closer look into the literary mechanisms by which Sogdogpa attempted to demonstrate that military events were the outcomes of his rites reveals a number of elements at work. First, as noted earlier, each episode in Sogdogpa's autobiographical account includes a date, prophecy, place, corresponding geopolitical event, ritual response, names of ritual specialists, participants and sponsors, and the dreams and/or signs of success that occurred in the context of ritual performances. Second, Sogdogpa carefully structures all these elements into a fivefold sequence that reflects the complex interpretative procedure through which he gave literary expression to the efficacy of his rites. This fivefold sequence proceeds as follows: (1) interpretation of a passage from a prophecy text in light of contemporary events, (2) appropriate ritual performance, (3) resultant signs and/or dreams, or lack thereof, (4) interpretation of signs and/or dreams, and (5) coordination of signs, dreams and prophecies with geopolitical events as ritual outcomes. Clearly then, ritual effects do not unambiguously follow from ritual performances without mediation. Rather, such outcomes emerge from an intersection of textual interpretations, group ritual performances, communal sensory experiences, private dreams, and semiotic operations in which public and private, discursive and embodied practices converge to produce the gestalt of ritual success. Furthermore, it should be noted that this memoir is the principle medium through which Sogdogpa worked out the precise terms of these correspondences. Thus, the designation of events as "outcomes" has everything to do with Sogdogpa's retrospective formulation and presentation of these events in writing.

Perhaps it is the function of prophecy texts in Sogdogpa's memoir which best epitomizes the hybrid, intertextual quality of his narrative. Tibetan Buddhists often represent all of history as a sprawling narrative that unfolds according to the prophecies that the Indian Buddhist master Padmasambhava hid within Tibetan soil; these are found in texts left for destined disciples in future incarnations to uncover and interpret anew according to specific contextual exigencies. Tibetan prophecy texts are therefore marked by an equal measure of cultural authority and textual ambiguity, thus enabling successive generations of Tibetans to interpret diverse contemporary events and legitimate their specific reactions to them in light of an ever-compelling cultural script. Yet, since Tibetan Buddhist prophecies are also often rich in specific personal details and events concerning the lives and contexts of the "future" incarnations of individuals, they might be productively construed as biographical and autobiographical writings specifically concerned with future histories.[26] Thus, as communal narratives (which nonetheless partake of an autobiographical and/or biographical character) prophecies are an ideal medium through which to bring private lives into the public sphere and appropriate public discourses to serve personal ends. It is little wonder then that Sogdogpa consistently uses the forum of prophecy to articulate and legitimate his ritual actions, signs and dreams in the public arena of his memoir. Indeed, communal Tibetan prophecies serve for Sogdogpa as the cultural matrix of significations through which he constructs the public ramifications of his personal actions, and in turn personalizes prophecies that concern the entire Tibetan public.

The importance of prophecies for Sogdogpa in legitimating the outcomes of his rituals is explicit in the opening episode of the *History's* first chapter, and in the opening passages of the autobiographical section of the *History's* second chapter. In both sections, Sogdogpa narrates Zhigpo Lingpa's lengthy explanations of personal prophetic visionary experiences along with his interpretations of the prophetic visions of Sangyé Lingpa (Sangs rgyas gling pa, 1340–96) and Pema Lingpa in demonstrating the urgency of turning back the Mongols during Sogdogpa's generation, as well as Sogdogpa's necessary role in this endeavor. These passages relate how Zhigpo Lingpa correlated his and others' prophecies to reflect a single coherent message, and thus offer considerable insight into the knotty process of prophecy interpretation. To give a taste of how these prophecies predict a general scenario of ritual efficacy, here is a section of a prophecy from Pema Lingpa's *All-Illuminating Mirror* (*Kun gsal me long*),[27] which Zhigpo Lingpa cites to convince Sogdogpa of his necessary role in turning back Mongol armies:

> At that time, by the power of the great merit of sentient beings and
> The Buddha-dharma not being extinguished,
> One with the name of Space (*nam mkha'*) will arouse the
> circumstancial cause, and
> One with the name of Famous (*grags pa*) will act as patron.
> An *ārya*, who is an emanation of Songtsen Yulzung (Srong btsan yul
> zung),
> And a healer, who is the [re-]birth of the doctor Gebum (Dge 'bum),
> With an emanation of myself assisting them,

Will, having gathered all the materials, perform burnt offerings.
They will focus intently on the tsen/gong (btsan/'gong) red Yamshü (Yam shud).[28]
Within the skulls of nine murdered Chinese generals
Will be inserted the effigies (*ling ga*) of nine demon generals.[29]
These should be burried underneath Śākyamūni.[30]

This prophecy provides only the barest information in the form of general names and vague descriptions of events. And even when Zhigpo Lingpa consulted other prophecies to provide dates and more complete descriptions of places and events, the phrasing is, at best, ambiguous. In the end, Zhigpo Lingpa correlated this passage with other passages that specify dates and other temporal clues to interpret the "one with the name Famous" as the political leader of Bang-khar (Bang mkhar), which judging from descriptions in the *History*, was in Uyug ('U yug) valley north of the Brahmaputra river; the "emanation of Songtsen Yulzung," one of Srong btsan sgam po's chief ministers, as Zhigpo Lingpa himself; and the "rebirth of Gebum," the famed twelfth-century physician and protector of Lhasa from flood waters, as Sogdogpa—a triad that Zhigpo Lingpa insisted must work together to ensure the aversion of Mongol armies through sorcery.

In this vein, the *History* reports that Zhigpo Lingpa's authoritative, interpretative acumen, and visionary insight enabled his tersely phrased collection of prophecy texts to function for Sogdogpa as a loose discursive map that provided crucial guidance throughout his ritual career on when, where, with whom, and how to avert Mongol forces. It must be recalled, however, that in order for successive generation to use and reuse prophecies for divergent purposes within differing contexts, prophecy texts must retain a certain degree of ambiguity. Sogdogpa's narration of Zhigpo Lingpa's interpretative work thus leaves multiple lacunae that resist precise identification.

Textual citations from relevant prophecy texts also appear in nearly every ritual episode within Sogdogpa's autobiographical section. These passages are used in two primary ways. First, as just noted, they are presented as providing Sogdogpa with loose guidelines on when, where, with whom, and how to perform the appropriate rituals. In keeping with their nebulous character, passages here only give years according to the duodenary calendrical cycle, rather than the more specific years of the sexegenary cycle (i.e., dog year as opposed to iron dog year), and only include laconic descriptions of military and political events, and vague or general place names and geographical descriptions, thus allowing Sogdogpa significant interpretive latitude.

The second major function of prophecies is to legitimate ritual outcomes, the ultimate litmus test of ritual efficacy by Sogdogpa's account being whether or not events corroborate authoritative prophecies—whether or not negative or positive events reported in prophecies "came to pass" (*thog tu khel*). Rituals therefore "work," according to Sogdogpa, when they have been executed in accordance with specifications outlined in prophecies, and when later events corroborate those guiding prophecies.

Sogdogpa's uses of prophecies can perhaps better be understood through turning to their occurrence in the ritual episodes themselves. The manner in which Sogdogpa cites prophecies in connection with ritual performances, signs and dreams, and geopolitical events to interpret ritual outcomes is well-illustrated in the following two episodes, which are reported as having occurred ten years apart:

1. It is stated in the prophecy of Gyalwa Düpa (Rgyal ba 'dus pa):[31]

> In the Fire-Female-Pig [year], a Hor[32] army will come to Tibet. Initially, it will mete out suffering to Drigung ('Bri[gung]) and Taglung (Stag[lung]).

Accordingly, when many Mongol troops led by one called Khathasu arrived that Pig year (1587), they rushed from Oyug[33] up to Nyugda.[34] At that time, I had no aquaintance with the one from Bangkhar (*bang mkhar nas*). [I] restored the *stūpa* at Dro ('Bro) [and] threw several thread-cross *tormas* (*mdos gtor*). Having performed the final rite of the lord of life,[35] there was a positive sign (*rtags mtshan bzang*) and I had a dream vision (*rmi lam mthong*) that pleasant news would soon come. Autumn of that [year], according to the words of the leader (*sde pa*) Bönpö Lapa (Bon po'i La pa), who had returned [from the east]:

> In China, several of the Mongol petty kings and ministers (*sog po'i rgyal blon*) were mass poisoned (*dug yoms*), had diarrhea (*'khrus*) of several animals, such as frogs, snakes, scorpions, and so forth, then died. At Mang Kölwa (Mang bskol ba), several divine hand emblems, such as flesh cutting blades, and so forth, emerged from within the boils of Gyagmi Rajang Wong's (Rgyag mi=rgya mi? Ra byang'ong) body, and he died. There is a great commotion [there] that these [events] were due to the sorcery of Tibetan dharma communities.

Beyond this, nothing happened. However, in *Nyidé Gyachen* (*Nyi zla'i rgya can*)[36] it is said:

> Then, in the Fire-Female-Pig year, Hor troops will burst forth. At that [time], one with the name of Rigdzin Trashi (Rigs'dzin Bkra shis), who abides on the [bodhisattva] levels, will appear in Uruzho (Dbu ru gzho). He will turn them back.

Thus, accordingly, Drigung Zhabdrung[37] gathered the choicest roasted barley in his jurisdiction, and yarn and sticks for thread-cross rites (*mdos*), and turned back [the army]. Thus,'Bri[gung] and Stag[lung] incurred no damage. Neither could [the army] severely harm the lands of Shangs,[38] 'O [yug] and so forth, as several men and horses died during their return journey.

2. Then, as related in the [prophetic] statement:

> In the Fire-Monkey and Rooster [years] there will be fighting in Tö,[39]

Khathan's army reached Mü,[40] Purang,[41] Karbum (Dkar dum), Lowo,[42] Mya Shug Tro (Rmya shug khro), Tesé,[43] Latö,[44] Jang,[45] and so forth. It sacked the [people of] Dolpo,[46] Nagtsang,[47] Pönpo (Dpon po) and so forth.

That year (1596) I initiated the *Great Means of Averting of Armies* (*Sog bzlog chen mo*). Consequently, I dreamt that a voice ordered the Mongols who were advancing from Ngari in Tö[48] up to Gyalmorong in Mé Dokham[49] to turn back. Even though it had been prophecied that during that year Sakya,[50] Ngari, Dzongkha,[51] and Jang Ngamring[52] would be destroyed, the ritual aversion seemed to help; the Hor Mongols then arrived in the vicinity of Drompa Gyang (Grom pa rgyang), and despite having rushed from Zangzang Lhadrag[53] all the way to the upper end of Ngamring, no casualties were seen.[54]

A cursory analysis of these two passages reveals the following rationale at work in Sogdogpa's representations of ritual outcomes: First, to establish the appropriate occasions to stage his rituals, Sogdogpa interprets contemporary events in light of the duodenary years mentioned in the relevant prophecy passages—the Pig year, and the Fire-Monkey and Rooster years, respectively—and the vague descriptions of events foretold there. Sogdogpa then mentions and sometimes describes the rituals he performed in response to such events. He then notes the occurence of auspicious signs and/or dreams in the context of his ritual performances as circumstantial evidence indicating ritual efficacy. Finally, he returns once again to the prophecy passages and interprets contemporary events by their light to determine the final success or failure of his ritual actions. To represent events as outcomes of rituals, he retrospectively connects these geopolitical events to their ostensive dreams, signs, and prophecies.

Here, and throughout the memoir, "signs" refer to auspicious events that occur in the context of ritual performances and function as indicators of ritual efficacy. Far from unambiguous gauges of ritual success, signs require considerable interpretation. Sometimes sign interpretation takes the form of reading events in light of textual descriptions. On one occasion Sogdogpa notes that "signs emerged exactly in accordance with the text."[55] And elsewhere, he ended a ritual practice "once the signs explained in the text had appeared in full."[56] Often, however, the interpretation of signs is an event which gains legitimacy through the consensus of the group of ritual participants. In one episode, Sogdogpa and six others performed fumigation rites and burnt offerings and "the entire area was permeated with the stench of Mongols," thus eliciting conviction among everyone present in the success of the ritual.[57] In two other episodes, the appearance of a skull of a fallen Mongol general and the discovery of a geneaological record of leading Mongol warlords, both materials used in the performance of effigy rites,[58] are read by Sogdogpa as signs of the success of previous rituals.

On more than one occasion, the public, consensual dimension of sign interpretation opens up the possibilities for alternate, competing interpretations from a wider demographic than ritual specialists alone. In one episode, Sogdogpa recounts the public denunctiation of the leader of Uyug by his citizens for the leader's sponsorship of a *stūpa* just prior to the onset of a countrywide drought. The citizens of Uyug used the logic of sign interpretation against their leader through positing a deliberate causal relationship between the *stūpa* project and the natural disaster, and thereby accused their leader of black magic.[59] During another ritual, the security guards of the ritual enclosure mistakenly interpreted a *torma*'s flaming wick as a sign that the ritual was succesful in killing the Mongol warlord Khathan.[60]

In each instance of what he considers to be sign misinterpretation, Sogdogpa provides for his readers the "correct" interpretation. Thus, when sign interpretation becomes public domain, the text of the *History* itself serves as the medium through which Sogdogpa makes the connections and sets the records straight. And of course the "public domain" described in Sogdogpa's narrative is none other than the textual domain of his memoir, in which he publicly narrativizes events through their careful selection and ordering, thereby affirming once again his interpretive authority to adjudicate such matters.

Like signs, auspicious dreams that occur in the context of ritual performances also serve as indicators of ritual efficacy. Needless to say, however, Sogdogpa's dreams differ from auspicious signs in being understood as entirely private experiences. Perhaps owing to their private character, Sogdogpa's dreams prove to be slightly more elusive for him than signs. On more than one occasion, Sogdogpa struggles to make sense of his dreams in light of later events. Once, he even doubts the authenticity of a potent visionary dream when no event unfolds to corroborate it.[61]

More often than not, however, Sogdogpa reports and intreprets dreams to demonstrate the efficacy of related rituals. Moreover, like signs, dream content in the memoir is drawn largely from communal cultural meanings, thus strategically enabling the discourse of private dream experiences to serve in authenticating the efficacy of rituals in the public arena, and most significantly perhaps, reaffirm Sogdogpa's personal role as a vital and authoritative intermediary and interpreter of events with public, and even statewide importance.

To move full circle, signs and dreams, and indeed also the rituals that elicit them, gain significance throughout Sogdogpa's memoir within the context of an overarching vision of Tibetan history as an ever-unfolding drama foretold in prophetic revelations. Signs and dreams here provide the critical epistemological link between ritual performances and prophesied events, thus enabling geopolitical events to be interpreted as ritual effects. However, it should be noted that signs and dreams are common indicators of ritual efficacy in Tibetan Buddhist ritual proceedings even when rituals have no explicit connection with prophecies. The memoir, which situates rituals and their outcomes within the prophetic narrative of Tibet's ongoing struggles with Mongol violence, therefore casts signs and dreams in a slightly different light. In other words, Sogdogpa's signs and dreams, as provisional suggestions of ritual success sensible to only himself or his immediate circle are meaningful indicators of ritual outcomes only in relation to the collective prophecies that concern the Tibetan populace as a whole. Linking signs and dreams with prophecies thus serves as an instrument enabling Sogdogpa to promote the authority of his personal experiences, and thereby read his private and interpersonal personae onto the communal prophetic record. The ultimate effect is a personalization, or rather, an "autobiographization" of communal prophecies, which works to locate Sogdogpa at the epicenter of interpretative authority over events and actions which impacted the fate of all Tibetans.

Geopolitical Unification, Expansion, and Other Outcomes

The thirty-two-year period of 1583–1614 during which Sogdogpa executed his army-averting ritual program was witness to significant shifts in the sociopolitical climate of the Ü and Tsang provinces of Tibet.[62] To begin with, the sixteenth century was perhaps one of the most tumultuous centuries in Tibetan history. It was a time of extreme political fragmentation and sectarian violence characterized by ongoing military conflicts between rival factions in Ü and Tsang over land and resources. A significant change of affairs took place in 1565, when the first Tsang ruler, Zhing Shagpa Karma Tseten (Zhing shag pa Karma tshe brtan), seized control of the strategic stronghold of Samdrubtse (Bsam grub rste) in Zhikatse (Gzhis ka rtse) from the Rinpungpa (Rin spungs pa) aristocracy, the family that had ruled much of Ü and Tsang from the year 1435. Zhing Shagpa then initiated a campaign to bring all of Ü and Tsang under his control, an endeavor that would only bear fruit with the concentrated efforts of his children and grandchildren several decades later.

During this period, Mongol tribes were also mired in civil war,[63] and hearing of the weakened state of Tibet's frontiers, losing Mongol armies often fled southwest to try their luck in Tibet.[64] The presence of Mongols in Tibet, and their sporadic show of military and financial support for one or another of Tibet's aristocratic families or religious schools, introduced a wildcard into local struggles over land and power. Focused as he was on ridding Tibet of Mongol military intervention, Sogdogpa was at cross purposes with several Tibetan factions, such as Ganden (Dga' ldan) and Drepung ('Bras spungs), who were actively courting Mongol favor to bolster their own financial and sectarian interests.[65] Moreover, Sogdogpa's sorcery campaign entailed his involvement with diverse and sometimes competing geopolitical, sectarian, and clan formations, which made him a vortex for the whirlwind of forces vying for supremacy at this time. Consequently, Sogdogpa suffered harsh criticisms from those whose fortunes depended on Mongol warlords, or who saw in Sogdogpa's ritual efforts selfish and careerist attempts to acquire wealth, power, and renown.[66]

Sogdogpa's representation of ritual efficacy outlined in the earlier section of this chapter portrays rites as magical techniques to manipulate the cosmos for tangible geopolitical results. According to this picture, rituals produce the real geopolitical outcome of repelling Mongol forces from Tibet, that is, when all the requisite conditions of prophecy are fulfilled and these coincide with the occurrence of meaningful signs and/or dreams. Yet, when turning to the diversity of events that Sogdogpa designates as ritual outcomes, it becomes evident that Sogdogpa envisioned the magical efficacy of his rituals as responsible not only for the direct expulsion of Mongol forces, but also for the creation of political and military circumstances within Tibet that would have facilitated their expulsion.

Indeed, one striking feature of Sogdogpa's account is his consistent effort to co-opt internal Tibetan political and military developments by designating them as outcomes of his rituals. Almost every episode in the *History* illustrates in some way a concern to encapsulate diverse internal, political, military, and economic developments and events within the magical functionality of his army averting rites. Ritual outcomes in Sogdogpa's account thus also include the consolidation of Tibetan polities, the increased influence and power of Tibetan rulers, and the increased authority and wealth of Sogdogpa and his colleagues, to name but a few.

Most significantly, Sogdogpa's narrative reveals that he was aware that the broad-based support necessary to execute his large-scale rites required disparate Tibetan polities to work together, perhaps resulting in a unified front that might stand a better chance in military confrontations with Mongol forces. Participation in Sogdogpa's ritual program would have therefore been a way to show support for the growth and reinforcement of a politico-military establishment that could successfully "protect the doctrine," or more precisely, its institutions and patrons. In Sogdogpa's time, such an establishment was none other than the Tsang Desi government based in Samdrubtse. Thus, Sogdogpa not only presents the efficacy of his rites in terms of their power to magically kill, repel, or render helpless enemy Mongol troops, but he also frames them as instrumental in the formation of a unified geopolitical entity centered on the Tsang Desi, which was committed to maintaining Mongol forces at a safe distance through a combination of diplomacy and martial force. Sogdogpa even goes so far as to lay claim to the gradual consolidation of Tsang and the subsequent expansion of Tsang Desi control into Ü and beyond.

Although several of the *History's* passages reflect the central role Sogdogpa assigns his rituals in the consolidation and growth of Tsang Desi power during the late sixteenth and early seventeenth centuries, the present chapter allows space for only a few examples.[67] In five episodes interspersed throughout his accounts of ritual activities between the years 1590 and 1605, Sogdogpa directly links the political unification of the Tsang region and the subsequent expansion of Tsang Desi rule with his army-averting rites. The first of these episodes attributes a pivotal event in the rise of Tsang political power—the end of internal strife in Tsang—to the might and authority of Sogdogpa's sorcery campaign.

> At that time,[68] most of the nobility and commoners of Rong were saying, "he (Sogdogpa) is perpetrating such boundless deceit." The people of Tsang were telling all the aristocrats, such as Chugpo Adar (Phyug po a dar), Bongkarné (Bong mkhar nas), Kudün Mönkipa (Sku mdun smon skyid pa), and the like that the prophecies were fabricated.[69] Even Nangtsené's[70] disciples were saying that things such as this do not exist at all in Nangtse's treasure teachings and that it was totally

> fraudulent. Some of great experience stated that [the message] seemed to have been altered from having correlated several prophecies. No one came forth who would hold them as authentic.
>
> At that [time], Kudün Mönkiné (Sku mdun smon skyid nas) told me to come to Gang Tsang.[71] I showed him the text of Turning Back Armies (dmag zlog), and he thus gained confidence in it and issued a request encouraging virtue to Tsedong.[72] Thereupon, the restoration of the shrine (lha khang) on the bank of the Brahmaputra river in Yeru[73] was accomplished. Then, just as the stream of earlier and later wars had become like water reaching a boil, [the prophecy] stating "the polity of Tsang will become a stable aliance" (*gstang gi rgyal srid mdun ma gru bzhi 'ong*) came to pass. Thus, since the peace and happiness within the Tsang region up to the present is due to his kindness, the benefit [of that act] is obvious.[74]

Here, Rong and Tsang are shorthand for the Rinpungpa aristocracy based in the region of Rong[75] in eastern Tsang and the Tsang Desi faction based due west of Rong in the citadel of Samdrubtse, Zhikatse, also in Tsang. This episode thus depicts the end of approximately twenty-five years of warfare between the Rinpungpa aristocracy who ruled much of Ü and Tsang beginning from 1435, and the new Tsang leadership of the Desi that first rose to power in 1565. The unification of Tsang described here as having taken place in 1590 via the formation of a "stable alliance" was surely a major contributing factor in the Tsang Desi government's eventual expansion of territory to include all of Ü and Tsang. Based on other episodes, Kudün Mönkiné seems to have been a leader with some influence in the court of the Tsang Desi. Tsedong refers to an influential Sakya monastery in Tsang that had close ties with the Tsang Desi government throughout this period.[76]

One of the greatest oppositions to Tsang rule over central Tibet came from Drepung and the burgeoning Ganden Potrang (Dga' ldan pho brang) government, who had been courting Mongol military assistant since well before the Third Dalai Lama Sönam Gyatso's (Bsod nams rgya mtsho) expedition to Mongolia in 1577 and 1578.[77] It is not surprising then that in the wake of Tsang unification Sogdogpa directed his rituals against divisions of Mongol forces which Drepuing had raised in retaliation for a previous attack on an affiliated faction. After providing extensive citations of relevant prophecy texts, Sogdogpa relates the following:

> In short, effigies were formed of the soldiers of the six Chakhar[78] divisions (*gzhung*) and their horses. Through practicing for one month, an auspicious sign emerged. That year[79] the Drepungpa had roused an army; in response to the western Hor having attacked the Sermyog (Ser

> myog),[80] an army headed by the king of the three Thümed[81] divisions had been approaching for about one month. They turned back.[82]

The year 1599 was particularly important for Sogdogpa; it marked his first encounter with the Tsang Desi.[83] Despite Sogdogpa's reputation as a Rasputinesque charlatan responsible for poisoning his patron, the leader of Bongkhar, in the midst of promoting a sorcery campaign for the acquisition of wealth and fame, the Desi nonetheless offered Sogdogpa the venue and patronage necessary to continue his ritual program after the death of his patron. Through this connection with the Tsang Desi Sogdogpa seems to have risen to the level of a state-sponsored ritualist, one of many, no doubt, responsible for the performance of rites integral to the security of the kingdom. In the process, the prophecied rituals, which had been time, place, and event specific up to that point, became embedded within the annual ritual calendar of the state.

> Then, in the Dog year (1598), the memorial service (*dus mchod*) for the leader [Bongkharné] came to pass and I was exiled from the land. Subsequently, in the Pig year (1599), the Ruler (*sde srid*) took possession of Lingkhar.[84] At the behest of Kudün Mönkiné, [the Tsang Ruler] also gave me a monastery. So, even though some Hor and Tibetans had previously offered him slanderous rumors [about me], from that time on, he nurtured me with his kindness. He interrogated me much, stating the following:
>
>> I have been wondering whether you lamas of the Ancient school are only show-offs. But you are a humble, simple monk. Someone said that you built *stūpas* as means to turn back border troops. Where are they?
>
> He told me:
>
>> Now that I have given you a monastery, by means of the monastic estate (bzhis=gzhis), you must henceforth take up the burden of turning back the Mongols.
>
> Thus, I performed each type (*rig=rigs*) of Mongol averting [ritual] annually, without interruption. There were also many *stūpas*, [protection] circles, and the like that were supposed to be placed at the upper end of each and every small valley (*lung tshan*), but the slander that I was employing malicious spells and poisoning [people] did not abate, [so I could not do these things].

Starting from the Pig year (1599), in observation of the annual ritual calendar of the territory as a whole, I performed the seven day accomplishment [rite] in connection with the *maṇḍala* for accomplishing Vajrakīlāya, annually without interruption. In accordance with the [prophetic] statement:

In the Earth Pig and Dog [years, they] will return to their own land," There was calm for those two years (1598–1599).[85]

Two years later, Sogdogpa used his new influence to restore *stūpas* along the northern frontier that were deemed capable of defending the Ü and Tsang provinces of Tibet against Mongol attacks. He was assisted in this project by a certain Garwangpa (Gar dbang pa). Given the exchange with the Ninth Karmapa Wangchug Dorje (Dbang phyug rdo rje, 1556–1603) that follows the restorations, Garwangpa probably refers to the Sixth Shamar Garwang Chöki Wangchug (Zhwa dmar Gar dbang Chos kyi dbang phyug, 1584–1630), whose biography relates his brokerage of a peace treaty between the Tsang Desi government and a group of unnamed Mongols just a year prior.[86] Moreover, the Mongol warlord Kathan mentioned in this episode figures prominently in the Sixth Shamar's biography, not as a foe, but as an influential patron who lavished great wealth on the Kargyu hierarch.[87] In addition, the Sixth Shamar's father was the twentieth hierarch of Drikung Til ('Bri gung mthil) monastery, Tsungmé Chögyal Püntsog Trashi Pelzangpo (Mtshung med chos rgyal Phun tshogs bkra shis dpal bzang po, 1547–1602/1626), a close associate of Sogdogpa's guru Zhigpo Lingpa,[88] and as Sogdogpa's first autobiographical ritual episode bears witness, an active performer of Mongol averting rituals in his own right.

The Shamar's role as political envoy to the Tsang Desi during this time,[89] along with his ties to the Mongol warlord Khatan and his father's participation in Mongol averting rites, all suggest that Sogdogpa conceived his ritual program to function in combination with the Tsang Desi government's more conventional strategies of diplomacy and national defence. Moreover, given the role of the Karmapa incarnation series as preceptors to the Tsang royal family,[90] Sogdogpa's mention of the Ninth Karmapa Wangchug Dorje's enthusiastic approval for his Mongol expelling ritual activities can be seen as a reflection of, or even a further bid for, Tsang Desi support.

In the Ox year (1601), from Zabu[91] I sent a letter via Drung Garwangpa (Drung Gar dbang pa) to the Nagtsangpa (Nag tshang pa)[92] leaders (*mi dpon*), and to master Tropuwa (Khro phu ba) and his disciples in Jang Dangra (Byang dang ra) [stating] the need to restore the northern

> *stūpas*. Thus, the master Tropuwa and his disciples, together with Garwang, and with Kyedar (Skyes dar) acting as sponsor, restored the *stūpa* at Gurmo (Mgur mo). Garwang roused patronage and restored the 108 *stūpas* of Tsikü-khug (Rtsi skud khug). And overseen by the sponsor Trobo Dar (Khro bo dar), he restored the *stūpas* in both Rigu (Ri gu) and Sheltsa (Shel tsha). Along the way, [they] were also able to restore the 108 stūpas and [the *stūpa*] in Shurutso (Zhu ru 'tsho = mtsho). Consequently, while Khatan was deceiving the Nagtsangpa leaders and plotting to murder them by asphyxiation, a message (*bya*) leaked out and [they] were able to flee.
>
> Later, a regional nomad council took place (*mdun ma lding*[93] *khel*), due to which a letter from the Nagtsangpa leaders arrived, as well as their acceptance of me as a treasure revealer (*gter byin* = *gter 'byin*). Thereafter, both Karpo (Dkar po) and Lhatrug (Lha phrug) from among the Pönpowa (Dpon po ba); and Kyedar (Skyes dar), Lhachug (Lha phyug), and Serpo (Ser po) [from] among the Nagtsangpa were planning to restore the Kungkhung Tsal (Kung khung tshal) [temple?] as well as other *stūpas*. However, the community migrated to the east (*smad*), so it was not accomplished.
>
> From that year until the Hare [year] (1601–03), I myself accomplished a little over 100,000 recitations of *The Heart of Wisdom, Averter of Demons* (*shes snying bdud bzlog*) with the aim of turning back the Mongols.
>
> At Namling, Garwangpa told Gyalwé Wangpo (Rgyal ba'i dbang po, the Ninth Karmapa Dbang phyug rdo rje) the story of how he had restored the northern *stūpas*. [The Karmapa] thus replied:
>
> > At the glorious copper colored mountain of Zabu,
> > A temple for turning back the Mongols has also been made.
> > You, Sogdogpa, and disciples seem to be of benefit to Tibet.
> > You still have to go to the north and restore the *stūpas* that require restoration. I will provide (*gter=ster*) the materials and ritual supplies.
>
> Gyalwé Wangpo passed away soon thereafter (1603), so this was not done.[94]

Sogdogpa relates that just a few years later, his rituals played a role in enhancing the power and authority of the Tsang Desi considerably, such that the leader was capable of military success against an invading Mongol army. Note that in the following episode Sogdogpa also enlists the assistance of Bönpo ritualists, suggesting that the justification of "protecting the dharma," the stated motive for the performance of these violent rites, included more than Buddhist institutions alone. Indeed, the rites described in these episodes appear to be more about protecting Tibet's frontiers and populace from the ravages of warfare than saving Buddhist monasteries, reliquaries, and shrines, although those two sets of concerns were no doubt seen as very much interrelated. Nevertheless, such inclusiveness suggests that rituals purportedly intended to "protect the dharma" were at times conceived more broadly as strategies for safeguarding Tibetan territorial, ethnic, and religious integrity, regardless of Bönpo or Buddhist affiliation. Also of note, the date of this episode, 1605, is roughly contemporaneous with Sogdogpa's composition of the *Thunder of Definitive Meaning* (*Nges don 'brug sgra*) and *Dispelling Mental Darkness* (*Yid kyi mun sel*), his two lengthiest compositions, perhaps indicating that the paper he acquired on this occasion went for more than printed effigy rites alone.

> Now, that year (1605), I thought to once again start repelling [rites]. When there was not enough paper, this corresponded with when the Ruler had led a large army into Ü.[95] [The ruler then said]: "Come to Panam Lhundrub Tse[96] to [perform] the rites for my health and longevity (*sku rim*) and for turning back the Mongols!"[97] An endless supply of paper was available there, so we printed about 150,000 effigies (*linga*). Then, in the course of the nine day accomplishment rite, several signs (*rtags mtshan*) of [the accomplishment of] violent [activity] occurred for everyone involved in the practice, which seems to have been due to the auspicious circumstance that the Ruler's power would expand (*sde srid mtshan don rgyug pa*).
>
> At that [point], Zhabdrung Chen-nga Rinpoché (Zhabs drung Spyan snga rin po che)[98] gave the order: "For accomplishment in this rite, it is very important to extend the session." Once signs had emerged, I requested permission to end [the practice]. It is said within the document: "Bönpos are to hurl one third of the effigies as magical weapons." Thus, [I had] three skilled Bönpo from Rizhingpa (Ri zhing pa) hurl magical weapons (*zor 'phang*). I performed a burnt offering (*sbyin bsregs*). The skull of a Mongol [then] appeared as a vessel for suppression [rites] (*mnan pa*), which was an auspicious circumstance (*rten 'brel bzang*).

> When (*rtsa=tsa*) considered afterwards, that was the day the Mongols were defeated in battle at Rama Gang (Ra ma sgang), and the following day they retreated from Gyang Tang Gang (Rgyang thang sgang). That our own health and longevity rites (*sku rim*) got the credit (*ngo so*) for the expansion of the Ruler's authority (*mtshan lung rgyug pa*), which was due to his own exalted merit, seems to have been due to the compassion of the [three] jewels.[99]

Beyond the mere expulsion of Mongol armies from Tibet, the effects described in the aforementioned five episodes range from the political unification of Tsang, the defeat of armies with ties to rival Tibetan factions, the consolidation of borders, and the expansion of Tsang power, to Sogdogpa's acquisition of a monastery, paper, skulls, and infamy. Implicit in Sogdogpa's inclusion of these diverse outcomes in his ritual episodes, although not stated as such, is the notion that broad-based support for these rites functioned as a catalyst for the unification of disparate polities and their material resources around a common cause. By thus subsuming these political and martial causes for Tsang Desi success within his ritual espisodes, Sogdogpa effectively credits to the magical functionality of rites a diversity of events that theoretically could have, in and of themselves and without the help of sorcery, contributed to the consolidation and expansion of Tsang Desi power, and the consequent expulsion of Mongol armies from Tibet.

Conclusions

Sogdogpa's rhetorical strategy of representing ritual outcomes as events foretold and authenticated by prophecies, signs, and dreams allowed him the interpretative leverage and authority to retrospectively claim a significant role for his rituals in the defining geopolitical events of his day. Indeed, when considering together the five episodes outlined earlier, it becomes clear that Sogdogpa envisioned his sorcery program as a decisive factor behind the Tsang Desi government's consolidation and expansion of power throughout Tsang and Ü. Associating ritual successes with the successes of the Tsang polity, and thereby reading the Tsang dynasty onto the prophetic record enabled Sogdogpa to legitimate Tsang rule and his own controversial ritual activities in a single stroke.

Although the *History* is without a colophon, its final episode takes place in 1614, ten years prior to Sogdogpa's death in 1624.[100] Composed sometime during this ten-year window, the *History* emerged at the apex of Tsang Desi power.[101] By 1614, the government of the Tsang Desi had made significant headway in the consolidation of Tsang and Ü, was actively engaged in diplomatic missions with the neighboring polities of Nepal, China, and Yunnan,[102] and was having some success in addressing Mongol threats with a combination of diplomacy and force.[103] The political climate was ripe during the final decade of Sogdogpa's life for him to publicly promote his ritual career as having been the major force behind the rise of Tsang power.

We learn from the colophon of Sogdogpa's correspondence, *Abandoning Objections to "Buddhahood Without Meditation": A Response to Lama Gojo's Query* (*Bla ma go 'jo'i zhu lan ma sgom sangs rgyas kyi btsod spong*),[104] that this short text was composed on the first day (*dga' ba*) of the seventh month of the Water Male Rat year, 1612, at Samdrubtse palace, the headquarters of Tsang Desi rule, thus indicating that Sogdogpa continued to nurture a relationship with the Tsang rulers during the years leading up to his composition of the *History*. Moreover, Sogdogpa's many depictions of the malicious gossip that circulated about his ritual activities further demonstrates that the *History* was in part a strategy to legitimate his ritual career and clear his name in the eyes of influential peers, most notably the Tsang royalty. The candor and hesitancy with which Sogdogpa relates his interpretation of events as ritual outcomes, coupled with the descriptions of failed rituals and scandals, combine with the citation of prophecies and the accounts of dreams and signs to lend the *History* a persuasive air of authenticity and honesty. What could be more convincing as proof of altruistic intent than the positive implications each prophesied episode had for the legitimacy of Tsang rule, articulated with a rare combination of humility, audacity, and humor?

The structure and content of Sogdogpa's ritual episodes—with their skillful combination of public prophecies, geopolitical events, signs, and dreams—gives thematic form to what is perhaps a necessary component of all storytelling, the retrospective structuring of experiences and events to conform to an authoritative, public discourse of meaning. And yet, as illustrated earlier, Sogdogpa does not narrate his story through simply organizing his private experiences according to the standards of a public, textual format. Rather, Sogdogpa crafts his story by strategically deploying a set of culturally significant discourses inclusive of dreams, signs, prophecies, rituals, and geopolitical events, varying in terms of their respective private and public scopes of experience, so as to move the reader to accept the mutual interanimation and implication of these discourses, and in turn, the private and public domains of which they partake. The resultant text is a "hybrid construction,"[105] which illustrates considerable fluidity between private and public discourses of experience, knowledge, and authority.

Ultimately, this careful blending of public and private discourses works to legitimate Sogdogpa's ritual actions, establish his interpretive authority over those actions, and thereby fashion him in the public image of the foremost state ritual specialist of his time (even if only in his own mind). The interpretative act of designating "outcomes" on its pages thus renders Sogdogpa's *History* a magical text in its own right.[106] It is, after all, Sogdogpa's act of writing the *History* that makes his sorcery so powerful, creating the potency and efficacy of his rites through the ritual act of instantiating these events within the public sphere of textual discourse.

NOTES

I thank Professors Ana Cristina Lopes and Janet Gyatso for their many insightful comments and suggestions on earlier drafts of this chapter and Yangga for his help in clarifying difficult Tibetan passages.

1. The material presented in this chapter forms part of my Ph.D. dissertation for the Committee on the Study of Religion at Harvard University.

2. For details on *zlog pa* and other similar types of protective rituals, see Beyer, *The Cult of Tārā*, 363–467; Donald S. Lopez, *Elaborations on Emptiness: Uses of the Heart Sūtra* (Princeton, NJ: Princeton University Press, 1996), 216–38; Stan Royal Mumford, *Himalayan Dialogue: Tibetan Lamas and Gurung Shamans in Nepal* (Madison, WI: University of Wisconsin Press), 117–39; René de Nebesky-Wojkowitz, *Demons and Oracles of Tibet* (1956; reprint, Kathmandu, Nepal: Book Faith India, 1996), 507–37; and Sherry Ortner, *Sherpas through their Rituals* (Cambridge: Cambridge University Press, 1978), 91–127.

3. This confluence of ethnic, religious, and state identity is perhaps most clearly expressed in the *Maṇi Bka' bum, bKa' thang* literature, and other treasure narratives related to the Tibetan imperial period. Such treasure stories began to surface in the twelfth century. See Matthew Kapstein, *The Tibetan Assimilation of Buddhism: Conversion, Contestation and Memory* (Oxford: Oxford University Press, 2000), 32–37, 38–50, 141–62, for insightful discussions of the rhetorical, literary dimensions of the *Sba' bzhed, Maṇi Bka' bum* and other narratives of the imperial period.

4. For more on state rituals intended to protect against foreign armies, see Nebesky-Wojkowitz, *Oracles and Demons of Tibet* (1996), 493–500.

5. Perhaps the most notable example is the Dga' ldan pho brang government's performance of annual army-averting rites as an integral part of its state ritual apparatus from the time of its inception in 1642. For details concerning some of the dGa' ldan pho brang government's martial state rites, see Nebesky-Wojkowitz, *Oracles and Demons of Tibet* (1996), 493–500. Also of note is that Bhutanese ritual specialists down to the present commemorate the expulsion of Dga' ldan pho brang government forces during the formation of the kingdom of Bhutan through the annual performance of army averting rites (Françoise Pommaret, personal communication, May 14, 2007). For a related discussion, see her article "Protectors of Bhutan: the Role of Guru Rinpoche and the Eight

Categories of Gods and Demons (*lHa srin sde brgyad*)," in *Written Treasures, Hidden Texts* (Thimpu: National Library, forthcoming). There, Pommaret discusses the symbolic role of a wrathful form of Padmasambhava in the protection of the nation of Bhutan.

6. It should be noted that *dmag bzlog* rituals were by no means the sole preserve of lay Rnying ma ritual specialists. Sa skya, Bka' brgyud, Jo nang, and Dge lugs ritual specialists of varying ordination statuses also engaged in rituals aimed at protection against bellicose neighbors. For ample evidence of pan-sectarian involvement in *dmag zlog* rites during the late sixteenth and early seventeenth centuries, see Kun dga' blo gros, *Sa skya gdung rabs ngo mtshar bang mdzod kyi kha skong* (Chengdu: Mi rigs dpe skrun khang, 1991); Che tshang sprul sku Bstan 'dzin padma'i rgyal mtshan, *Nges don bstan pa'i snying po 'bri gung pa chen po'i gdan rabs chos kyi byung tshul gser gyi phreng ba*, ed. Chab spel Tshe brtan phun tshogs, Gangs can rig mdzod 8 (Lhasa: Bod ljongs bod yig dpe skrun khang, 1989); and Ngag dbang blo bzang rgya mtsho, *Rje thams cad mkhyen pa Bsod nams rgya mtsho'i rnam thar dngos grub rgya mtsho'i shing rta*, *Collected Works of Vth Dalai Lama Ngag-dbang-blo-bzang-rgya-mtsho* (Gangtok, Sikkim: Sikkim Research Institute of Tibetology, 1991–95) vol. 8, among countless other examples.

7. The term Sog was an abbreviated ethnonym for Sogdians (Sog dag) during the imperial period and became an ethnonym for Mongols (Sog po) after their rise to power in the thirteenth century. For a general discussion of Tibetan ethnonyms, see Rolf Alfred Stein, *Tibetan Civilization* (Stanford: Stanford University Press, 1972), 34.

8. Sog bzlog pa Blo gros rgyal mtshan, *Collected Works of Sog bzlog pa blo gros rgyal mtshan* (New Delhi: Sanje Dorji), vol. 1, 203–59.

9. The Gtsang sde srid, or Gtsang rulers, featuring throughout Sog bzlog pa's account, were most likely Karma bstan srung dbang po (d. 1611?), the third Gtsang sde srid and son of the first Gtsang sde srid, Zhing shag pa Tshe brtan rdo rje, and Karma bstan srung dbang po's son, Phun tshogs rnam rgyal (1586–1632?). Although Karma bstan srung dbang po's exact dates remain unknown, Sum pa mkhan po Ye shes dpal 'byor, *Chos 'byung dpag bsam ljon bzang* (Lanzhou, PRC: Gansu Nationalities Publishing House, 1992), 893, records that the fourth Gtsang sde srid Karma phun tshog rnam rgyal assumed control in the Water Rat year of 1612, presumably following the death of his father. Gene Smith follows Bsod nams don grub's *Gangs can mi sna grags can gyi 'khrungs 'das lo tshigs re'u mig* to give 1597 as the birth date for Karma phun tshogs rnam rgyal; see www.tbrc.org. The Gtsang sde srid law code, *Gtsang pa sde srid dang karma bstan skyong dbang po'i 'dus su gtan la phab pa'i khrims yig zhal lce bcu drug*, recently republished in Bsod nams tshe ring, ed., *Snga rabs bod kyi srid khrims* (Chengdu: Mi rigs dpe skrun khang, 2004), 165–219, gives (on p. 167) the Iron Dog year (*lcags khyi lo*) as this figure's birth date. However, this year corresponds to 1550 or 1610, which are too early and late, respectively, for him to have ascended to the throne in 1612, seized Yar rgyab at age 25 (*Snga rabs bod kyi srid khrims*, 167) and defeated Mongol armies shortly thereafter in the Earth Horse year (*sa rta lo*) of 1618 (*Snga rabs bod kyi srid khrims*, 167). Given such inconsistencies, it is perhaps more likely, as concluded by Giuseppe Tucci, *Tibetan Painted Scrolls*, 2 vols (Rome: Libreria dello Stato, 1949), 2: 697, that Karma Phun tshogs rnam rgyal was born some time around the Fire Dog year of 1586, twenty-five years prior to his seizure of Yar rgyab in 1610.

10. Krang dbyi sun et al., *Bod rgya tshig mdzod chen mo*, 2807, defines *lo rgyus* as "a record of past events/circumstances" (*gnas tshul byung rabs*).

11. Sog bzlog pa, *Sog bzlog lo rgyus*, 204.6–206.1. Here, Sog bzlog pa twice refers to his work as a biography (*rnam thar*). And it is clear from his opening remarks that he means autobiography (*rang gi rnam thar*).

12. Sog bzlog pa also attempts to illustrate the precedence for such rituals by including in his biography of Padmasambhava, *Yid kyi mun sel*, key episodes where Padmasambhava performs "army averting rites" (*dmag zlog)* for the Tibetan court, rites that resemble Sog bzlog pa's own. For details, see Sog bzlog pa Blo gros rgyal mtshan, *Slob dpon sangs rgyas gnyis pa padma 'byung gnas kyi rnam par thar pa yid kyi mun sel*, in Sog bzlog pa Blo gros rgyal mtshan, *Slob dpon sangs rgyas gnyis pa'i rnam thar yig kyi mun sel* (Delhi: Chos spyod Publications, 2005), 113–17.

13. For a notable nonmartial point of comparison, see the detailed discussion of the role of prophecy in the autobiographical account of the treasure revealer 'Jigs med glingpa in Janet Gyatso, *Apparitions of the Self: The Secret Biographies of a Tibetan Visionary* (Princeton, NJ: Princeton University Press, 1991).

14. Sog bzlog refers to himself as the "healer of Gdong mkar" (*gdong dkar/mkhar 'tsho byed*) in the colophon of *Rdzogs chen pa sprul sku zhig po gling pa gar gyi dbang phyug rtsal gyi skyes rabs rags bsdus dang rnam thar*, in *Collected Works of Sog bzlog pa*, vol. 1, 109; and in the colophon of *Rig 'dzin gyi rnam dbye*, in *Collected Works of Sog bzlog* pa, vol. 2, 310. Gyurme Dorje and Kapstein locate Gdong mkhar in Gtsang along the northern bank of the Brahmaputra river, at the southern end of the Shangs valley due north of Gzhis ka rtse. For their map of Gtsang, see Dudjom Rinpoche, *The Nyingma School of Tibetan Buddhism*, tr. Gyurme Dorje and Matthew Kapstein (Boston, MA: Wisdom Publications, 1991), vol. 2, map 6.

15. Dge ba 'bum was the twelfth-century physician and student of Bla ma Zhang Brtson grus grags pa responsible for restoring the dikes of the Brahmaputra river to prevent flooding in Lhasa. For more details on this figure, see Ko shul grags pa 'byung gnas and Rgyal ba blo bzang mkhas grub, *Gangs can mkhas grub rim byon ming mdzod* (Lanzhou: Kan su'u mi rigs dpe skrun khang, 1992), 1848.

16. Sog bzlog pa writes that Zhig po gling pa cited this prophecy from Padma gling pa's treasure prophecy *Illuminating Mirror* (*Kun gsal me long*). This text can be found in Rig 'dzin padma gling pa, *Rig 'dzin Padma gling pa yi zab gter chos mdzod rin po che* (Thimphu: Kunsang Tobgay, 1975–76), vol. 1, 19–138.

17. Sog bzlog pa, *Sog bzlog lo rgyus*, 218, describes that the Mongol invasion was presaged by the death of 'Phags pa in 1281 and led to the destruction of 'Bri gung in 1290. For historical details concerning the first Mongol conquest of Tibet see Luciano Petech, *Central Tibet and the Mongols: The Yüan-Sa skya Period of Tibetan History*, Serie Orientale Roma 65. (Rome: Istituto Italiano Per il Medio ed Esremo Oriente, 1990); and Turell Wiley, "The First Mongol Conquest of Tibet Reinterpreted," *Harvard Journal of Asiatic Studies* 37, Issue 1 (1977): 103–33.

18. Zab bu lung is a valley associated with Padmasambhava located in Shangs, a region in Gtsang, north of the Brahmaputra River from Myang. See Dudjom, *Nyingma School of Tibetan Buddhism*, vol. 2, map 6.

19. These dates are based on the dates of Sog bzlog pa's birth and death found in Lo chen Dharmaśrī's (1654–1717) history of the *Mdo dgongs 'dus* empowerment lineage, *'Dus mdo dbang gi spyi don*, in *Rnying ma bka' ma rgyas* (Kalimpong, West Bengal: Dupjung Lama, 1982–87), vol. *pha*, 130.

20. For an elaborate account of this event, which was Zhig po gling pa's first treasure revelation, see Sog bzlog pa, *Zhig gling rnam thar*, 48–53. There, Sog bzlog pa refers to this treasure cycle as *Ways of Averting Border Armies* (*Mtha' dmag bzlog byed*). However, Kun bzang nges don klong yangs, *Bod du byung ba'i gsang sngags snga 'gyur gyi bstan 'dzin skyes mchog rim byon gyi rnam thar nor bu'i do shal* (Dalhousie, H.P.: Damchoe Sangpo, 1976), 297, calls it the *Twenty-five Ways of Averting Armies* (*Dmag zlog nyer lnga*). Gu ru bkra shis ngag dbang blo gros, *Gu bkra'i chos 'byung* (Beijing: China's Tibetan Culture Publishing House, 1990), 447–48, recounts this treasure revelation episode but does not include the *Twenty-five Ways of Averting Armies* among the treasures found on that occasion.

21. 'Jam mgon Kong sprul, *Rin chen gter mdzod* (Paro, Bhutan: Ngrodrup and Sherab Drimay, 1978), vol. 44 (*phi*), 57–136. The titles of these five texts are as follows: *Spyi ru zlog thabs kyi rim pa sde tshan du byas pa gter gzhung* (57–72), *Rgyal chen sde bzhi'i mchod phreng gter gzhung* (73–92), *Sgo srung dang 'phrang srung gi gtor chog gter gzhung* (93–104), *Drag bskul gter gzhung* (105–22), *Mgon po bdun bcu rtsa gnyis mdos bca' thabs bskur pa dang bcas pa chog gter gzhung* (123–36). Also under the heading of *Dmag zlog nyer lnga* are five other ritual texts authored by later figures as addenda to Zhig po gling pa's revelations. These include a *skong gsol* ritual reported to have been based on Sog bzlog pa's own visionary experience (137–68); *Rgyal chen mchod thabs gtor zlog mdos rnams kyi lag len*, by Rin chen rnam rgyal (169–216); a *srog dbang* ritual, by 'Jam mgon Kong sprul Blo gros mtha' yas (217–46); *Yul 'khor srung gi mchod rten las 'jug gter gzhung*, by Klong gsal snying po (247–60); and *Phyag rdor gtum po'i dmag zlog rgyal chen sde bzhi'i sgrub thabs gter gzhung*, by Nag gi rdo rje (261–75).

22. 'Jam mgon Kong sprul, *Rin chen gter mdzod*, vol. 44 (*phi*), 57–72.

23. Krang dbyi sun, *Bod rgya tshig mdzod chen mo*, 2561, defines *yas* as "the effigy substance, thread-crosses, ritual cakes, and so forth, of Bon po" (*bon po'i glud rdzad mdos gtor sogs*). Nebesky-Wojkowitz, *Oracles and Demons of Tibet* (1993), 371, describes *yas* as symbolic treasures kept in the thread-cross (*mdos*) residence of a god or goddess, made from "small pieces of cloth, semi-precious stones, and small weapons and harnesses, the latter objects being made of dough with the help of *zan par*."

24. Unfortunately, the obscurity of items 15–18 is not clarified through separate descriptions in the body of this text. However, the following directions on how to repel "through resounding the enlightened speech of dharma" (62–63) may shed some light on what is intended by these items:

Those reciting the scriptures should be as follows:

11 monks (*bande*) with ethical discipline (*khrims*)
7 [monks] without ethical discipline
11 mantrins with tantric commitments
7 [mantrins] without tantric commitments

The row should be headed by a ruler whose dominion has not yet declined (*btsad po mnga' thang ma nyams pa gcig*). At the head of them all should be a pure, fully ordained monk (*dge slong*). They should face the direction from which the army is coming and chant the scriptures. A spiritual friend with the view of enlightened mind should make the aspirations. (63)

25. Zhig po gling pa, *Dmag zlog nyi shu rtsa lnga las spyi ru zlog thabs kyi rim pa sde tshan du byas pa*, in 'Jam mgon Kong sprul, *Rin chen gter mdzod*, vol. 44 (*phi*), 58.1–59.1.

26. For discussions of prophecy as autobiography in the Tibetan religious context, see Gyatso, *Apparitions of the Self*, 240–41; and Janet Gyatso, "Autobiography in Tibetan Religious Literature: Reflections on its Modes of Self-Presentation," in *Tibetan Studies: Proceedings of the 5th International Association for Tibetan Studies, Narita 1989*, ed. Shōren Ihara and Zuihō Yamaguchi, 2 vols. (Narita-shi, Chiba-Ken, Japan: Naritasan Shinshoji, 1992) 2: 473.

27. Sog bzlog pa, *Sog bzlog lo rgyus*, 224.2–224.5, refers to the *All-Illuminating Mirror* (*Kun gsal me long*) as one of Padma gling pa's treasure prophecies.

28. Btsan 'gong yam shud dmar po is the name of a dharma protector, otherwise known as Yam shud dmar po, or red Yam shud. Nebesky-Wojkowitz, *Oracles and Demons of Tibet* (1996), 168–70, notes that some Tibetans regard this being to be a mixture between a *bstan* and a *'gong po*, two classes of spirits.

29. For a general discussion of the various functions of skulls in Tibetan rituals, including their use with effigies in exorcism rites, see Andrea Loseries-Leick, "The Use of Human Skulls in Tibetan Rituals," in *Tibetan Studies: Proceedings of the 5th International Association for Tibetan Studies, Narita 1989*, ed. Shōren Ihara and Zuihō Yamaguchi, 2 vols. (Narita-shi, Chiba-Ken, Japan: Naritasan Shinshoji, 1992) 1: 159–73.

30. Sog bzlog pa, *Sog bzlog lo rgyus*, 228.6–229.2.

31. *Rgyal ba 'dus pa* is the treasure cycle revealed by Sog bzlog pa's guru Zhig po gling pa. The cycle of the *Rgyal ba 'dus pa* appears in 'Jam mgon Kong sprul, *Rin chen gter mdzod* (1978), vol. 8 (*nya*).

32. Hor, or Hor pa, a Tibetan ethnonym originally associated with the Uighurs during the imperial period, was later used to identify Mongols in general beginning from the thirteenth century. Later still the term was used to designate specific Mongol tribes that underwent varying degrees of Tibetanization and settled in the regions east and northeast of central Tibet (Stein, *Tibetan Civilization*, 34). Here, and throughout the prophecies cited in the *History*, the term Hor seems to refer to Mongols in general. However, in the autobiographical episodes composed by Sog bzlog pa, it is clear that he uses the ethnonym Hor to refer to Mongols in general and to the partially Tibetanized Mongol groups that settled in the frontier zones along the eastern and northeastern peripheries of central Tibet. Although deciphering the exact referents of the various ethnonyms appearing in Sog bzlog pa's account is clearly a necessary step for a more complete appreciation of the dynamics described in the *History*, this lies beyond the scope of the present chapter.

33. 'O yug, or 'Od yug is an incorrect spelling for 'U yug, in Gtsang. This is the river valley of the 'U yug river tributary due north of the Brahmaputra from Rin spungs. For more details on this location, see Turrell Wiley, *The Geography of Tibet According to*

the 'Dzam gling rgyal bshad, Serie Orientale Roma 25 (Rome: Istituto Italiano Per il Medio ed Esremo Oriente, 1962), 71, 121, 140 and 141.

34. I could not locate Nyug mda' in any of the three place name indexes at my disposal—Turrell Wiley's *The Geography of Tibet According to the 'Dzam gling rgyal bshad;* Turrell Wiley's *A Place Name Index to George N. Roerich's Translation of 'The Blue Annals,* Serie Orientale Roma 15 (Rome: Istituto Italiano Per il Medio ed Esremo Oriente, 1958); and Alphonsa Ferrrari's *mK'yen brtse's Guide to the Holy Places of Central Tibet,* Serie Orientale Roma 14 (Rome: Instituto Italiano Per il Medio ed Esremo Oriente, 1958). The identification of each place name that appears in the *History* is an especially challenging enterprise that will require a substantial research effort. Unfortunately, such an effort lies beyond the scope of the present chapter. Throughout the remainder of this chapter I attempt only to provide annotations for as many place names as time and resources allow.

35. Shes rab rdo rje, the head Mkhan po at Bka' rnying bshad grub gling in Boudhanath, Nepal, informed me that this might refer to the tradition of ending a series of rites with a long-life ritual, specifically either a *tshe dbang* or *tshe 'gugs*, because the performance of rites is believed to shorten the life span of ritual specialists.

36. I have yet to identify this text.

37. 'Bri gung Zhabs drung is most likely the twentieth hierarch of 'Bri gung mthil monastery, Mtshung med chos rgyal phun tshogs Bkra shis dpal bzang po (1547–1602/1626), who was very close with Sog bzlog pa's guru Zhig po gling pa, and the father of the Sixth Zhwa dmar incarnation, Gar dbang Chos kyi dbang phyug (1584–1630).

38. Shangs refers to the river valley of the Shangs tributary of the Brahmaputra river, which runs north of the Brahmaputra and due west of the 'U yug river valley. For details see Wylie, *The Geography of Tibet*, 71, 129, 135, 140, and 141.

39. Stod. It should be noted that by itself Stod is highly ambiguous as a place name, but it can be taken to refer to far western Tibet, as Sog bzlog pa does in this episode.

40. Mus refers to the Mus valley, which is located north of the Brahmaputra river and upstream, or west of Shangs valley (Ferrari 1958: 68, 158).

41. Pu hrangs is a location in the far western region of Tibet known as Stod mnga' ris. For more details see Wylie, *The Geography of Tibet*, xix, xxxii, xxxiv, 56–64, 81, 96, and 120–21.

42. Glo bo is Klo bo sman thang, otherwise known as Loh Manthang, or Mustang in northwestern Nepal. See Wiley, *The Geography of Tibet*, 63 and 127.

43. Te se is probably an alternative spelling for Gangs ri Ti se, the popular pilgrimage destination more commonly known as Mount Kailash, located in far western Tibet. See Wiley, *The Geography of Tibet*, 53–62, 114, 121, and 123.

44. La stod is western Gtsang extending from Glo bo. See Wiley, *The Geography of Tibet*, 64.

45. Byang here probably refers to the Byang myriarchy, of which Ngam rings was the capital. See note 52 for more details.

46. Dol po most likely refers to contemporary Dolpo in northern Nepal.

47. Nag tshang is the region due north of Gtsang. See Wiley, *The Geography of Tibet*, 88 and 164.

48. Mnga' ris is a district in the far western region of Tibet known as Stod. See Wiley, *The Geography of Tibet*, xix, xxxii, xxxiv, 56, 60, 61, 63, 64, 81, 96, 120, 121, 126, 127, 130, 140, 145, 147, and 163.

49. Rgyal mo rong is a district in the far eastern region of Tibet known as Smad mdo khams. See Wiley, *The Geography of Tibet*, xix, 98, 102, 103, 105, 118, 163, and 184.

50. The area of Sa skya, which is the location of Sa skya monastery, is in western Gtsang south of the Brahmaputra river. See Wiley, *The Geography of Tibet*, 66, 67, 127, 133, 134, 143, 145, and 187.

51. Given the mention of Rgyal mo rong in Sog bzlog pa's dream, Rdzong kha here might possibly refer to Rdzong 'ga, one of the eighteen kingdoms of Rgyal mo rong. See Wiley, *The Geography of Tibet*, 102 and 184.

52. Byang Ngam ring, otherwise known as Ngam ring, was the capital of the old Byang myriarchy located in the northwestern edge of Gtsang along the northern bank of the Brahmaputra river. See Wiley, *The Geography of Tibet*, 67, 131, 132, 135, and 145.

53. Zhang zhang lha brag is a locale bordering Byang Ngam ring on the northern bank of the Brahmaputra river in far western Gtsang. Ferrrari, *mK'yen brtse's Guide*, 65 and 153.

54. Sog bzlog pa, *Sog bzlog lo rgyus*, 244.6–245.3.

55. Sog bzlog pa, *Sog bzlog lo rgyus*, 253.

56. Sog bzlog pa, *Sog bzlog lo rgyus*, 254.

57. Sog bzlog pa, *Sog bzlog lo rgyus*, 241.

58. Sog bzlog pa references the use of Mongol skulls and names in effigy rites several times throughout the *History*. For more on the use of skulls and effigies in rituals of black magic and exorcism, see Loseries-Leick, "The Use of Human Skulls in Tibetan Rituals," 168–69.

59. Sog bzlog pa, *Sog bzlog lo rgyus*, 241.

60. Sog bzlog pa, *Sog bzlog lo rgyus*, 244.

61. Sog bzlog pa, *Sog bzlog lo rgyus*, 233.

62. The following paragraph is paraphrased from Giuseppe Tucci, *Tibetan Painted Scrolls*, 39–56.

63. Charles Bawden, *The Modern History of Mongolia* (London/New York: Kegan Paul International, 1989), 23–24.

64. This is according to Sog bzlog pa's record in *Sog bzlog lo rgyus* of the reasons for the Mongol military presence in Tibet during this period.

65. See, for example, Sog bzlog pa, *Sog bzlog lo rgyus*, 251.1–251.3. Here, Sog bzlog pa cites a certain *'Bras spungs sprul pa'i sku'i rnam thar* that describes the Third Dalai Lama Bsod nams rgya mtsho's death, and his subsequent rebirth among Mongol aristocracy. Sog bzlog pa then laments this fact in light of his mandate to turn back encroaching Mongol armies, stating: "I became discouraged thinking that if the birth of such a sublime being in Mongolia was due to sentient beings' lack of merit, how could a single ordinary person like me, with the thought of turning back the Mongols, help them."

66. There are multiple episodes in the *History* where Sog bzlog pa reports accusations to this effect. Such charges were later echoed more vehemently by the Fifth Dalai Lama throughout his autobiographical and biographical writings, thus indicating that these episodes in the *History* were not produced solely for literary effect.

67. I intend to elaborate on this finding in much greater detail in my Ph.D. dissertation on the life and times of Sog bzlog pa Blo gros rgyal mtshan and his guru Zhig po gling pa.

68. The preceding passage gives 1590 as the date of this episode.

69. Thus far, I have been unable to identify the offices and locations of these three figures.

70. Snang rtse nas refers to Zhig po gling pa in his role as political leader of the region of Snang rtse, west of Lhasa.

71. I was unable to identify Gang tshang in the place name indexes available to me.

72. Rtse gdong is the famous Sa skya monastery located in Gtsang. Judging by descriptions in the *Sa skya gdung rabs kha skong* of trips made by the Rtse gdong hierarchs between there and Sa skya, the Gtsang rulers' stronghold of Bsam grub rtse is located between the two Sa skya monasteries. Thus, we have no reason to doubt that the old location of Rtse gdong corresponds with its current location on the northern bank of the Brahmaputra River in the Rnam gling area of Gtsang.

73. G.yas ru is the "left," or eastern quarter of the "four units" (*ru bzhi*), the old imperial military/administrative divisions of Dbus and Gtsang. G.yas ru corresponds to a segment of eastern Gtsang. See G. Uray "The Four Horns of Tibet According to the Royal Annals," *Acta Orientalia (Hungarica)* (1960): 31–57, for a discussion of the *ru bzhi*: *g.yon ru, dbu ru, g.yas ru, ru lag*. Uray (55) concludes that "the horns were the units of both military and economic (financial) administration as early as the 7th century and the beginning of the 8th," with *ru lag* added as an ancillary unit (*yan lag*) in the year 733.

74. Sog bzlog pa, *Sog bzlog lo rgyus*, 233.3–234.2.

75. Wylie, *Geography of Tibet*, 72.

76. For details concerning this relationship, see the biographies of the Rtse gdong hierarchs active between 1565 and 1642 in Kun dga' blo gros, *Sa skya gdung rabs kha skong*.

77. Tucci, *Tibetan Painted Scrolls*, 1: 39–56. For an analysis of Tibetan and Mongolian records of Bsod nams rgya mtsho's visit to Mongolia in 1577 and 1578, see Hidehiro Okada, "The Third Dalai Lama and Altan Khan of the Tümed," *Journal of International Association of Tibetan Studies* 5 (1989): 645–52. Okada concludes, based on Mongolian sources, that the Fifth Dalai Lama fabricated and omitted details pertaining to this visit.

78. The "six Chakhar divisions" are an eastern-Mongolian socio-political structure that was first established by Dayan Khan in the early sixteenth century. Johan Elverskog, *The Jewel Translucent Sūtra: Altan Khan and the Mongols in the 16th Century* (Leiden, Netherlands: Brill, 2003), 3–11, for a discussion of the relevant historiographical issues.

79. Earlier in this episode the Iron Female Rabbit year of 1591 is mentioned.

80. Evinced by the usage of the term in another passage, Ser myog appears to be an ethnonym.

81. The Thümed was a Mongol tribe whose prince, Altan Khan, is said to have been converted by the Third Dalai Lama Bsod nams rgya mtsho during a trip to Mongolia in 1577 and 1578. For more details, see Tucci, *Tibetan Painted Scrolls*, 1: 39–56; and Smith, *Among Tibetan Texts*, 121.

82. Sog bzlog pa, *Sog bzlog lo rgyus*, 239.5–239.6.

83. The Gtsang sde srid referred to in this and the following episodes are most likely Karma bstan srung dbang po.

84. Gling mkhar rdzong was the traditional stronghold of the 'U yug region north of the Brahmaputra river. It is listed as one of the thirteen myriarchies (*khri skor*), or constituencies consisting of 10,000 household-units. For a detailed account of the Mongol administrative division of Tibet into thirteen myriarchies, and a full list of these thirteen, see Petech, *Central Tibet and the Mongols*, 50–61.

85. Sog bzlog pa, *Sog bzlog lo rgyus*, 246.3–247.2.

86. Si tu paṇ chen Chos kyi 'byung gnas, *Sgrub brgyud karma kaṃ tshang brgyud pa rin po che'i rnam par thar pa rab 'byams nor bu zla ba chu shel gyi phreng ba* (New Delhi: D. Gyaltsan and Kesang Legshay, 1971), 259.4.

87. Si tu paṇ chen, *Gser phreng*, 260–63.

88. Mtshung med chos rgyal Phun tshogs bkra shis dpal bzang po's biography in Che tshang sprul sku, *'Bri gung gdan rabs*, 219–31, describes this figure's birth as having been prophesied by Zhig po gling pa. Moreover, both the biography in *'Bri gung gdan rabs* and Zhig po gling pa's biography describe a close student/disciple relationship between these two figures.

89. The Sixth Zhwa dmar's biography (Si tu paṇ chen, *Gser phreng*, 255–99) provides copious details concerning the Sixth Zhwa dmar's trips to neighboring states as diplomatic envoy for the Gtsang rulers.

90. Bsod nams tshe ring, ed., *Snga rabs bod kyi srid khrims*, 167.

91. For the location of Zab bu valley see note 18.

92. Nag tshang is known as one of the "Four Communities of Northern Tribes" (*byang rigs sde bzhi*) situated north of Dbus and Gtsang. More specifically, it is the region due north of 'U yug and Shangs in northern Gtsang. For details on this region see Wiley, *The Geography of Tibet*, 88 and 166.

93. Krang dbyi sun, *Bod rgya tshig mdzod chen mo*, 1453, defines *lding* as "a community in a nomadic herding region" (*yul 'brog tsho pa*).

94. Sog bzlog pa, *Sog bzlog lo rgyus*, 248.4–249.5.

95. Sog bzlog pa, *Sog bzlog lo rgyus*, 252. This is the first instance when Sog bzlog pa recognizes a wholly new political authority on the scale of the Gtsang sde srid government described in later sources. Sog bzlog pa's depiction of the Gtsang sde srid government's gradual expansion of power is confirmed in the Gtsang sde srid law code *Gtsang pa sde srid dang ka.rma bstan skyong dbang po'i 'dus su gtan la phab pa'i khrims yig zhal lce bcu drug* (Bsod nams tshe ring, ed., *Snga rabs bod kyi srid khrims*, 164–219). It is reported there that the Gtsang sde srid defeat of opposition in western Gtsang (*gtsang stod*) occurred only under the leadership of the third Gtsang sde srid (*Snga rabs bod kyi srid khrims*, 167). It further states that it was not until the fourth Gtsang sde srid, Karma Phun tshogs phyogs las rnam rgyal (1586–1632?), that this line was successful in bringing all of Dbus Gtsang under its control (*Snga rabs bod kyi srid khrims*, 168–69). Gtsang sde srid rule over all of Gtsang and Dbus was therefore not fully actualized until several decades after the first Gtsang sde srid Zhing shag pa Karma tshe brtan rdo rje's seizure of Bsam grub rtse in 1565.

96. Spa rnam lhun grub rtse citadel is situated in Gtsang, east of Gzhis ka rtse and west of Myang stod. For more details see Wiley, *The Geography of Tibet*, 70.

97. This episode happened one or two years after the son of Zhing shag pa Karma tshe brtan rdo rje, Sde srid Gtsang pa Karma bstan srung dbang po's seizure of Spa rnams in 1605 during the Gtsang ruler's gradual march toward Dbus to consolidate the Tibetan territories east of Gzhis ka rtse. For more details on this event, see Gene Smith's entry (www.tbrc.org) for Sde srid Gtsang pa Karma bstan srung dbang po.

98. I am unable to identify this figure with any certainty, but based on his title, Spyan snga, we can perhaps assume he was a 'Bri gung Bka' brgyud lama.

99. Sog bzlog pa, *Sog bzlog lo rgyus*, 252.4–253.3.

100. The date of 1624 for Sog bzlog pa's death is based on Lo chen Dharmaśrī's (1654–1717) history of the *Mdo dgongs 'dus* empowerment lineage, *'Dus mdo dbang gi spyi don*. There, Lochen states that he passed away sometime after his seventy-third birthday, in the Wood Rat year of 1624, based on the colophon of Sog bzlog pa's text *'Chi ba brtags bslu'i yi ge* composed that year. Unfortunately, this text is no longer extant.

101. The biographies of Padma dkar po and Rje btsun Tāranātha, along with the biographies of their contemporaries found in Kun dga' blo gros's *Sa skya gdung rabs kha skong* and Si tu paṇ chen Chos kyi 'byung gnas's *Gser phreng*, offer substantial evidence that during the reign of Gtsang sde srid Phun tshogs rnam rgyal, who probably died sometime after 1623 (Si tu paṇ chen, *Gser phreng*, 282.6), Gtsang rule was secure enough domestically to allow for increased diplomatic relations with neighboring states. Despite the continued presence of separatist elements within Tibet, this nonetheless suggests that by the middle of the second decade of the seventeenth century, the Gtsang rulers had more or less successfully consolidated control throughout most of Dbus and Gtsang.

102. See the Sixth Zhwa dmar's biography (Si tu paṇ chen, *Gser phreng*, 255–99) for more details concerning these diplomatic missions.

103. See also the Sixth Zhwa dmar's biography for specific details concerning Gtsang diplomacy with Mongol warlords during this period.

104. Sog bzlog pa Blo gros rgyal mtshan, *Ma sgom sangs rgyas kyi rtsod spong bla ma go 'jo'i dris lan*, in *Collected Works of Sog bzlog pa Blo gros rgyal mtshan* (New Delhi: Sanje Dorji, 1975) vol. 2, 191–212.

105. The term "hybrid construction" I draw from Mikhail Bakhtin, *The Dialogical Imagination: Four Essays*, tr. Caryl Emerson and Michael Holquist (Austin, TX: University of Texas Press, 1981), 358. There, Bakhtin defines a "hybrid construction" as "a mixture of two social languages within the limits of a single utterance, an encounter, within the arena of an utterance, between two different linguistic consciousnesses, separated from one another by an epoch, by social differentiation or by some other factor."

106. For the notion of "history as sorcery" I am indebted to Michael Taussig's discussion in *Shamanism, Colonialism and the Wild Man: A Study in Terror and Healing* (Chicago, IL: University of Chicago Press, 1986) 366–92.

7

The "Calf's Nipple" (*Be'u bum*) of Ju Mipam ('Ju Mi pham)

A Handbook of Tibetan Ritual Magic

BRYAN J. CUEVAS

Throughout the centuries there has been enduring anxiety among Tibetans about certain types of Buddhist practices and the books that describe them. These are the guarded secrets of Tibetan Buddhism, Tibet's occult lore. One major category of such literature in Tibet, and one that has yet to attract much scholarly attention beyond a few footnotes, is the *be'u bum*. This peculiar Tibetan term means "calf's nipple" and implies something that nourishes, something good for maintaining life and health. As a label for a type of text, the term seems to be rather old, dating back to at least the eleventh century, but probably much earlier. Per Sørensen has argued that the term *be'u bum* may actually be a corruption, perhaps through homophonic error, of *pe bum* (*dpe 'bum*) or "collection of exempla, parables" serving the purposes of edification, instruction, and exhortation.[1] In this light, some have even suggested that the genre label may be an early Tibetan equivalent of the Chinese *bianwen* or "transformation text," known largely from manuscripts discovered at Dunhuang. These are texts associated with oral narration accompanied by paintings of the events described, hence "picture tales" (cf. *etoki* in Japan, *yamapaṭa* in India).[2] In his fourteenth-century *Mirror Illuminating the Royal Genealogies* (*Rgyal rabs gsal ba'i me long*), Sönam Gyaltsen (Bsod nams rgyal mtshan, 1312–75) refers to 108 picture texts bearing the title *be'u bum* that were supposedly used in the consecration of the Lhasa Jokhang

(Jo khang) temple during the reign of Songtsen Gampo (Srong btsan sgam po, ca. 605–50).[3] Here it is clear that these *be'u bum* were a type of model book depicting images of protective deities and religious heroes from Buddhist tales and legends. It is recorded that these books of images were used as a point of reference for painting various murals inside the temple. We assume that some of the Buddhist tales and legends depicted in such books were derived from stories that were also narrated orally and sung by professional bards (episodes from the *Jātaka,* for example). The tradition of public oral recitation of the deeds of Buddhas and famous heroes hearkens back to the earliest recorded period in Tibetan history when the great ruling families relied on professional minstrels to preserve and transmit the clan's genealogies and the records of past glories. R. A. Stein and others have suggested that from the eleventh century onward the old oral tales of the bardic storytellers (*sgrung, lde'u*) gave shape to and were incorporated into "an edifying literature of anecdotes and moral maxims" that preserved a large body of popular ancient lore, some elements of which were indigenous to Tibet and others inherited from India.[4] From the eleventh century onward a great many of these anecdotes and proverbs began to be incorporated into collections bearing the name *be'u bum.* One of the most famous of such collections is the eleventh-century *Blue Calf's Nipple* (*Be'u bum sngon po*) by Dölpa Sherab Gyatso (Dol pa Shes rab rgya mtsho, 1059–1131), which comprises sayings of the early Kadampa (Bka' gdams pa) teachers, and is linked both by content and structure to the genre of *lojong* (*blo sbyong*), "mental training," and by extension also to the *lam rim,* or "stages of the path."[5]

But the term *be'u bum* covers more than just these little model books of edifying tales and good advice. The label was also used early on to identify a type of practical handbook compiling a variety of useful prescriptions drawn from both oral and written sources. In some of these little volumes we find instructions for the production of medicines and the treatment of disease—an example being the *be'u bum* of the fourteenth-century physician of Drongtsé ('Brong rtse), Lhabtsün Rinchen Gyatso (Lha btsun Rin chen rgya mtsho).[6] In other books we find collections of charms, incantations, and elaborate diagrams for conjuring spirits and executing a variety of magical rites, such as the early twelfth-century *be'u bum* of Bari Lotsāwa (Ba ri lo tsā ba, 1040–1111).[7] So what is it that unites the variant types of Tibetan text bearing the unusual label "calf's nipple"? In all cases, it would appear that the Tibetan *be'u bum* are compilations of useful material, perhaps we might even say recipes, selectively assembled from an array of sources to be quickly accessible and readily on hand for the purpose of educating and inspiring, or for performing operations that can either help or harm. And this leads us to the main focus of the present chapter, on the *be'u bum* as a handbook of Tibetan practical magic, a Tibetan grimoire as it were. Here I wish to briefly consider the category of ritual magic and its practice in Tibet as documented in one particular magical *be'u bum* from the early twentieth century: the *Calf's Nipple* of the Nyingma polymath, Mipam Namgyal (Mi pham rnam rgyal, 1846–1912).

Mipam's *Be'u 'bum*

Described as "one of the most imaginative and versatile minds to appear in the Tibetan tradition,"[8] a "luminary of the nineteenth century Rnying ma renaissance and *ris med* ecumenical movement,"[9] and "an indefatigable scholar, debater, and meditator,"[10] Mipam has secured in the eyes of many students of Tibetan Buddhism a rare and lofty position among a select group of Tibet's most recognizable Buddhist intellectual figures. To date, scholars interested in Mipam have been largely attracted to his philosophical work, his writings on emptiness and other Madhyamaka conundrums, and his polemical defenses of Nyingma scholasticism.[11] Although most have acknowledged in passing Mipam's skill in more practical matters—his mastery of the arts and sciences, his interest in Tibetan folk traditions, and his proficiency in astrology, divination, magic, and sorcery—with only one recent exception, few seem to have been interested in this aspect of Mipam's work, or at least not curious enough to study these particular writings or to assess the significance of this work vis-à-vis his more abstract scholastic output.[12] Here I hope to contribute something to this alternative project by introducing one of the more intriguing of Mipam's nonphilosophical works.

Three versions exist of Mipam's *Calf's Nipple [Handbook] of Magic Rites and Spells. A Good Treasure Pot from which Emerges All that is Needed and Desired* (*Las sna tshogs pa'i sngags kyi be'u bum dgos 'dod kun 'byung gter gyi bum pa bzang po*): two manuscript editions reproduced in the 1970s through the United States Public Law 480 program, and a modern typeset edition recently published in Hong Kong.[13] The text was not included in Mipam's *Collected Works* (*Gsung 'bum*), as it was never intended for wide distribution. The tradition keeps books of this sort secret, and attempts to restrict their distribution, presumably because the books themselves are believed to be as dangerously potent as the magical rites they contain. The *Calf's Nipple [Handbook] of Magic Rites and Spells* was compiled in 1907 and is one of three *be'u bum* attributed to Mipam—the other two being his *Handbook of Illusions* (*Sgyu ma'i be'u bum*), compiled in 1904, and the *Introductory Handbook* (*Lde mig be'u bum*), which to my knowledge is not extant. The reason Mipam put these handbooks together and under what circumstances is unclear. I have yet to find extended reference to the texts in his biographies and, aside from the compiling dates, the colophons provide no relevant information.

Mipam's *Calf's Nipple* is devoted to a series of abbreviated magic rites, totaling to approximately 225 individual operations (see table at the end of this chapter). All the ritual actions fall into three main categories grouped appropriately according to their basic functions: (Group 1) protection and pacification, (Group 2) enhancement and augmentation, and (Group 3) subjugation and control. These categories should be familiar to most students of Tibetan ritual as comprising three of the standard set of four mundane rites, simply called the "four actions" (*las bzhi*): (1) pacification (*zhi*), (2) augmentation (*rgyas*), (3) subjugation (*dbang*), and (4) ferocity (*drag*). Technically speaking, and in typical Buddhist fashion, the four actions are distinguished not by their specific ritual performance, but by their intended goals. Gönpo Wangyal's (Mgon po dbang rgyal) recent *Dictionary of Buddhist Enumerations* (*Chos kyi rnam grangs*) lists the fundamental purpose of each of the four activities as follows: "[1] Pacification of illness and demonic obstructions; [2] augmentation of lifespan, merit, and pleasures; [3] control over the three realms; and [4] the fierce actions of killing, dividing, and paralyzing."[14] These four activities, characterized as "lower acts" (*smad las*), designate a wide assortment of ritual actions, including those that some might call "magical," and function in contrast to the so-called higher acts (*stod las*) that have liberation from *saṃsāra* as their goal. There are abundant primary resources on the topic of the four actions in Buddhist Sanskrit and Tibetan literature, and a relatively thorough treatment in secondary scholarship, particularly in terms of the relationship of the four acts to the standard "six acts" (Skt. *śaṭkarmāṇi*) of Hinduism and the Indian tantric traditions.[15] The topic is extremely complex and impossible to review in this short study. Instead, I wish to comment briefly on the basic character of these ritual activities, as well as on the category of Tibetan practical magic in general and its terminology, as reflected in Mipam's little handbook. Let us start with magic.

Tibetan Magic

In what follows I cannot address the long, convoluted history of the term *magic* or the huge theoretical questions surrounding it—whether magic exists or can be defined, whether the term is useful as a category of analysis outside a European framework, how magic relates to religion and to science, and so on—but I do want to point out that Tibetans do have an understanding of "magic" as a definitive category of knowledge and expertise, and that their understanding does not differ all that greatly from the definitions of anthropologists and intellectual historians beginning with James Frazer (1854–1941). It was Frazer who, extending the insights of E. B. Tylor (1832–1917), made familiar the idea that all magic is based on the law of sympathy; that is, the assumption that things act on one another at a distance because of being linked together by invisible bonds.[16] Sympathetic magic is governed by two basic principles, imitation and contagion. Perfect examples of imitative or mimetic magic in Tibetan practice are the forming of the *liṅga*—molded effigies in the likeness of an enemy or designs drawn on paper into which the practitioner directs the divine or demonic powers that he controls (see Figure 7.1).[17] Contagious magic may be exemplified by wrapping this *liṅga* in a piece of cloth procured from some garment owned by the object of the ritual or by the intended victim in the belief that some essence of the person wears off on, and abides in his or her clothing.[18]

We can further subdivide the magical laws of sympathy into the laws of similarity, antipathy, and contiguity. The law of similarity, as just illustrated, rests on the assumption that "like attracts like," "like produces like," also "like cures like" (homeopathy); this is the "analogy of attraction" in Tambiah's terminology.[19] The law of antipathy rests on the assumption that the application of a certain material object—a plant, herb, mineral, drug, etc.—expels its contrary. And the law of contiguity is based on the notion that whatever once formed part of an object continues to form part of it; the parts relating to the whole through an operation of synecdoche. So if the ritualist can obtain a portion of a woman's hair, for example, he can begin to manipulate her through the invisible bonds that are supposed to extend between the woman and the hair in his possession. Another example well-known in Tibet, and dramatically illustrated, for instance, in episodes from the epic of Gesar (Ge sar), is that if the animal totem of an enemy—or an analogous mountain (*bla ri*), tree (*bla shing*), or stone (*bla rdo*), turquoise (*bla g.yu*) in particular—can be damaged or retrieved, in effect weakening the enemy's soul or *la* (*bla*), then that enemy can be in a sympathetic

FIGURE 7.1. Examples of *liṅga* used for silencing gossip from Mipam's *Calf's Nipple* (texts A and B).

manner constrained or even destroyed.[20] Another widespread belief, which we find represented throughout Mipam's handbook, is that a person's name (*bla dwags*) can be used to gain control over him. The assumption here is that the name of an individual and the individual himself are identical. The spells (Skt. *dhāraṇī*, Tib. *gzungs*) and mantras in rites of magic, and in tantric practices more broadly, are connected with this idea,[21] and we know, of course, that with these acoustic formulas are associated the gestures of *mudrā*, which are also mimetic in function and tend to accentuate the spoken word during ritual.[22]

These laws of sympathy, as well as the system of correlations they presume, are very clearly evoked in a common Tibetan word for magic, *lé-jor* (*las sbyor*). This is the term often used in designating the four actions. *Lé* (*las*) simply means "action" (*karma* in Sanskrit); *jor* (*sbyor*, from the verb *sbyar*) "to join, affix," means a bond, a connection. Together, *lé-jor* translates literally as an "action of correlation" or "correspondent action," perhaps even "sympathetic action." Sanskrit equivalents are *karma yoga* (practical application), *karma bandha* (bonds of action), and even *karma nibandha* (the consequence of actions). So with this we see that magic exists in Tibet as a definitive category, designated by the term *lé-jor*, and that in Tibet magic as a category is understood to turn on an ideology of correspondence, of sympathy. In Mipam's age, to be sure, few in Tibet would have ever doubted that it was possible for someone to ritually manipulate and coerce other people, animals, spirits, and so forth; and various techniques for achieving these ends were recognized and instituted, some indigenous to Tibet and others derived from traditions long established in India and China. In Tibet's traditional religious imaginaire, as is well-known, cosmos and human being were understood as integrated at multiple levels and all operating interdependently within a vast organic network of macro- and microcosmic correspondences—in Buddhist terms, the law of interdependent causality (Skt. *pratītyasamutpāda*). Among the myriad macrocosmic influences widely thought in particular to affect the microcosmic lives of human beings were the planets and stars (*gza' skar*), as well as a host of divine and demonic forces of the earth and sky, embodied as gods and spirits (*lha 'dre*).[23] These correspondences, astrological influences (*rtsis*), and divine and demonic energies gave meaning to human affairs, good and bad, and did well to explain the functioning (and malfunctioning) of the world and society. It was also commonly assumed that all this could be manipulated, and that harmonies between levels could be sympathetically exploited by anyone who could recognize the correlations and know precisely how the system worked. Indeed, it was conventional wisdom in Tibet that there had always been specialists who knew these secrets and had actually developed the skills to effectively work the cosmos for their own ends, to provide assistance or to inflict harm.

Mipam's *Calf's Nipple [Handbook] of Magic Rites and Spells* is a product of this worldview. It operates within the same systematic conceptual framework and renders practical this sense of magic as encompassing the laws of sympathy, of a science of correspondences (and I invoke science here intentionally), and of the possibility of the very real manipulation of cosmos and human being. So what do we find inside this little magical book?

Structure and Content of Mipam's *Be'u 'bum*

As noted earlier, the *Calf's Nipple* is broken up into three main sections, with rites and spells grouped according to their basic functions. The first section deals with rites of pacification, which are basically rites of healing and protection. It is the longest section, compiling approximately 111 individual operations. Among the rites and spells of this group we find in Mipam's text are means to be used against snakes, rodents, bedbugs, insects in the fields, bandits and thieves, fever and plagues, ghosts (*shi 'dre*) and possessing demons (*gson 'dre*), and catastrophes of nature such as snow, fog, wind, and rain. There are also protective measures for pregnant women, embryos, and infants, and a number of ways to become invisible and to effect release from captivity. For these measures, Mipam draws on an array of scriptural sources, including various canonical and noncanonical tantras, and operations extracted from indigenous "treasures" (*gter ma*). Some of the more repeated sources in this section include the *Mahākāla Tantra* (*Nag po chen po'i rgyud*),[24] the *Caṇḍamahāroṣana Tantra* (*Gtum po dpa' gcig gi rgyud*),[25] the *Maṇibhadra-yakṣasena-kalpa* (*Gnod sbyin nor bu bzang po'i rtog pa*) and accompanying *dhāraṇī*[26]; also *tantras* from the Collected Tantras of the Ancients (Rnying ma rgyud 'bum), such as the *Tantra of the Mirror of Magical Display* (*Sgyu 'phrul me long gi rgyud*),[27] the *Tantra of All Activities* (*Las thams cad pa'i rgyud*)[28]; and the treasures of the celebrated visionaries (*gter ston*) Sangyé Lingpa (Sangs rgyas gling pa, 1340–96), Ratna Lingpa (Ratna gling pa, 1403–1478), Pema Lingpa (Padma gling pa, 1450–1521), and Namchö Mingyur Dorje (Gnam chos Mi 'gyur rdo rje, 1645–67) (see Figure 7.2).

Section two covers rites and spells for enhancement and augmentation, comprising about 64 individual operations. They may be used for any of a variety of purposes—to increase merit, buildup physical strength, prolong life, enhance the pleasures of living, sharpen intelligence, develop swift feet, win arguments and defuse sarcasm and ridicule, win at archery or at a game of dice. Included are also means to help detect thieves and recover stolen goods, to determine the location of hidden treasure, and to develop clairvoyance. So in short, this group of rites is intended to enhance the body and mind—physical

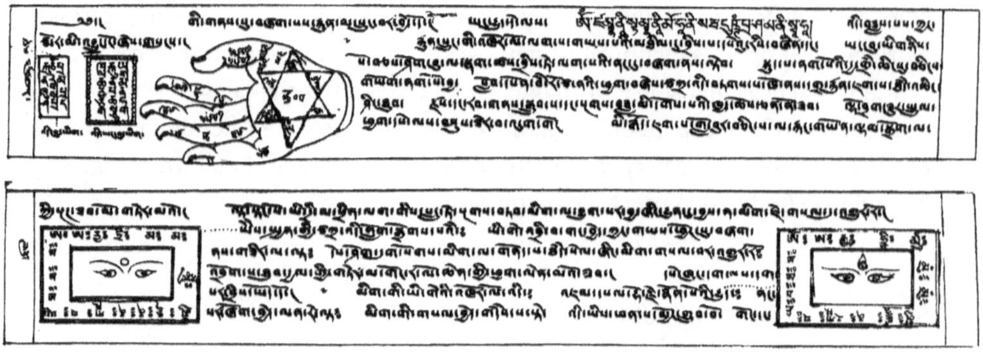

FIGURE 7.2. Diagrams for protection and augmentation from Mipam's *Calf's Nipple* (text B).

strength, dexterity, and speed; pleasant and persuasive speech, and rhetorical skills; clarity and depth of vision (while awake and during sleep), perspicuity, mindfulness, and so forth. Associated with these last measures we also find in this section various means of catoptromancy or divination with mirrors (*pra dbab/phab*).[29] Again, Mipam gathers these particular rites and spells from numerous sources, many of them from the same works cited in the first section, but with the addition of scriptures like the canonical Yamāri/Yamāntaka *tantras* (*Gshin rje'i gshed kyi rgyud*),[30] and from the Collected Tantras of the Ancients, the *Tantra of the Old Flat-maned Hayagrīva* (*Rta mgrin rngog ma leb rgan gyi rgyud*).[31]

The third and shortest section, comprising approximately fifty-one operations, details various rites and spells for control and subjugation. These include, in my opinion, some of the most interesting operations in Mipam's handbook, and ones that perhaps most closely resemble what we tend to think of as magic or even sorcery. The overall purpose of these measures is to manipulate living beings, to bring others under one's control. In this sense, we might broadly characterize the activities of subjugation as psychological in their intent because they aim to influence people's minds or constrain their wills—actions, for example, to gain the favor of kings and queens, to demoralize one's enemies, to arouse the love of a woman, or to persuade or coerce a potential tantric consort. From one perspective, these actions to control others could be seen as narcissistic and rather hostile toward others, so much so that we might be tempted to react to these practices as some sort of "black magic."[32] From another angle, Tibetan literature on this subject (including Mipam's *Calf's Nipple*) does tend to make a clear distinction between these actions of control and those measures that are more overtly hostile. The latter comprise the standard fourth group of magical acts, namely, fierce destructive rites (*drag po mngon spyod gyi las sbyor*, Skt. *abhicāra*)—Buddhist sorcery in the truest sense of the term—which as a ritual category Mipam explicitly chooses not to include in his little handbook.[33] This means there are no rites or spells in Mipam's *Calf's Nipple* aimed at killing (*bsad*) or "liberating" (*bsgral*),[34] expelling (*bskrad*), or suppressing (*mnan*).[35] For the record, there are *be'u bum* that do contain such rituals—for example, the tenth-century *Handbook of the Moon's Mystery* (*Zla gsang be'u bum*), known also as *Yama's Handbook* (*Gshin rje be'u bum*), by Nubchen Sangyé Yeshé (Gnub chen Sangs rgyas ye shes) and Jampel Shenyen ('Jam dpal bshes gnyen) (see Figure 7.3), or more recently, the politically controversial and widely banned *Handbook of Dorjé Shugden* (*'Jam mgon rgyal ba gnyis pa'i bstan srung rgyal chen rdo rje shugs ldan rtsal gyi chos skor be bum*) compiled by Trijang Lozang Yeshé Tendzin Gyatso (Khri byang Blo bzang ye shes bstan 'dzin rgya mtsho, 1901–81).[36] But although Mipam admits to excluding methods for killing, expelling, and suppressing other people or for inflicting physical harm on them, he does nevertheless include at the end of his handbook a few so-called minor (*phran tshegs*) operations that he identifies as wrathful acts—for example, means used to paralyze wild animals, to bind thieves, and measures to deal with disrespectful women. In the earliest version of the text we have (text A), this last section of minor rites is rather extensive, providing multiple operations for harming and turning away one's enemies, as well as a host of erotic techniques to coerce women into sex using a mysterious enchantment Mipam calls "vagina power" (*stu mthu*).

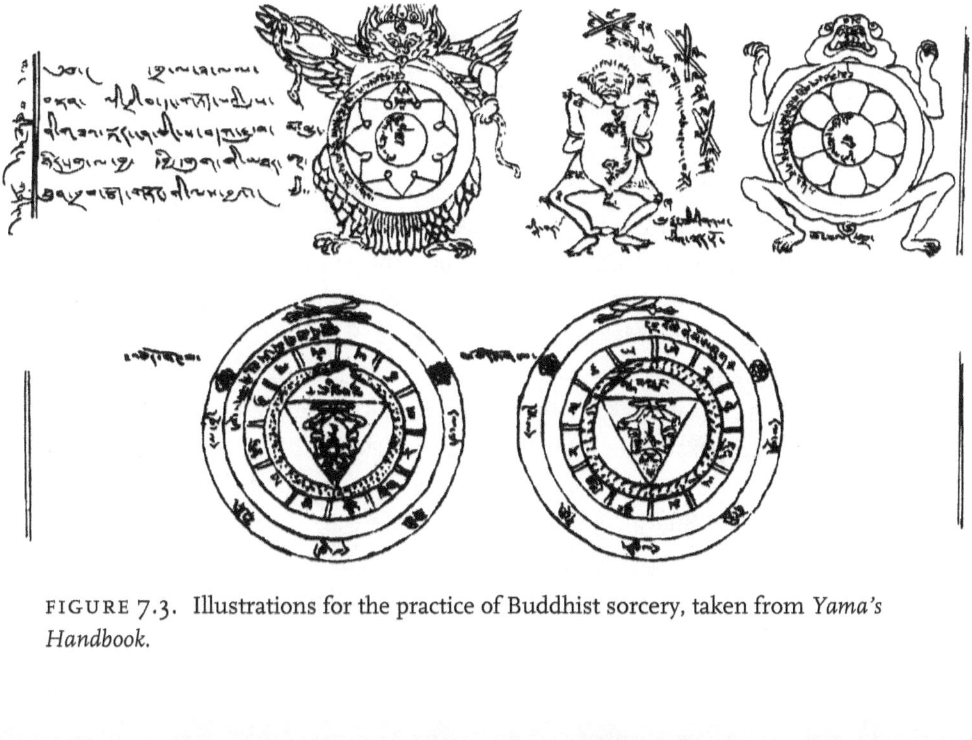

FIGURE 7.3. Illustrations for the practice of Buddhist sorcery, taken from *Yama's Handbook*.

Tibetan Sorcery

So what are the differences between the ritual actions of subjugation (*dbang*) and those of assault (*drag*)? Or another way to ask the question, using perhaps a more familiar but equally vague terminology: What is the difference between magic and sorcery in Tibet? While acknowledging that terms like these have a tendency to be thrown about indiscriminately, we might look for one key difference in Tibetan practice between magic and sorcery in the explicit and implicit motivation of the ritualist and in the intended outcome of the operation. This relates to the state of mind of the performer and also to the ultimate purpose of the performance, but not to the specific techniques utilized in the performance itself. Those procedures are all basically the same for each of the four actions—for example, the use of certain spells and mantras, plants, and other material substances, diagrams, effigies, talismans, and so on. And, as I have already suggested, all these types of ritual are performed in line with the analogical principles of sympathy. So we return to motivations and attitudes.

In actions of subjugation, the magician is not overtly hostile and anticipates that the intended subject or victim (*bsgrub bya*) of his rites and incantations will in the end be attracted to him without feeling harmed in any way. In destructive rites, we presume, the attitude of the sorcerer is explicitly hostile, perhaps also angry, hateful, or jealous, and he aims to harm the object of his wrath, causing all manner of mental and physical suffering, even death. But the attitude of the ritualist in this latter case may not be as antagonistic as the extreme nature of the actions would seem to indicate, and thus distinctions of attitude or distinctions between friendly and unfriendly intent may not be the most accurate gauge of the differences between the two types of ritual. The literature that describes aggressive rites invariably justifies such actions as acceptable, forceful but benevolent, by acknowledging that there are in fact legitimate persons against whom violent rites and spells may be performed; these are individuals who are thought to be profoundly deluded or confused, and hence in need of immediate and dramatic help (an intervention, in today's terminology). They are included among the so-called ten fields (*zhing bcu*) worthy of "liberation"—those who subvert the teachings of the Buddha, for example.[37] From this point of view, rites of assault are only to be executed with the purest of compassionate intentions, as any good bodhisattva savior would, and only by practitioners with the requisite skill to lead the "liberated" victim's consciousness to a Buddha's pure land. But the warning always follows: the sorcerer without this skill or without the right motivation is assured a rebirth in the lowest hell.[38] A ritualist of such corrupt character, the tradition assumes, must certainly be practicing a very sinister sort of magic; a *maleficium* so evil it transcends categorization, unable even to find its place in the fluid typology of the four actions. Perhaps, then, to stay within the accepted categorical boundaries, we might better express the distinction between magic and sorcery in Tibet as a difference of function between attraction (*'gugs pa*) and repulsion (*bzlog pa*).

So, in the end it is understandable why the tradition tries to keep these books secret and restricts their distribution. No one wants an arsenal of potentially deadly rites and spells to end up in the hands of the wrong people. The irony, of course, is that this pretense to secrecy tends always to pique popular interest, resulting in almost certain diffusion. But, nevertheless, why were these books compiled? Why did Mipam, the consummate scholar and luminary of the nineteenth-century ecumenical movement, put together a magical cookbook like this in the first place? What was the process that led to it being copied and circulated in manuscript form so that someone like me could one day check it out from a university library or buy a modern paperback edition from a bookstore in Lhasa? These are important historical questions that must await future consideration. For now I will assume that books of this sort filled with an array of occult techniques were produced in Tibet for actual use, and that the "calf's nipple," the *be'u bum*, offered a particularly convenient repository of practical information for that purpose.

The Rites of Magic in Mipam's *Be'u bum* (1907)
Text A: manuscript belonging to B. Jamyang Norbu. New Delhi, 1972.
Text B: manuscript belonging to Lama Jurme Drakpa. New Delhi, 1974.
Text C: modern typeset edition. Hong Kong, 1999.

No.	Purpose	Text
	I. *Pacification and Protection*	
1.	For maintaining happiness	A:4.1; B:79.2; C:1
2.	Protective measures against harm [caused by] various living creatures	A:5.4; B:80.3; C:2
3.	Protection against poisonous snakes	A:9.4.; B:83.1; C:5
4.	Protection against rabbits in the fields	A:10.2; B:83.4; C:5
5.	Protection against hooved animals	A:11.3; B:84.2; C:6
6.	Protection against insects in the fields	A:11.4; B:84.3; C:6
7.	For clearing away other [types of] insects	A:12.3; B:85.2; C:7
8.	Protection against lotus[-shaped] body parasites	A:14.6; B:87.3; C:9
9.	Protection against bedbugs	A:15.1; B:87.3; C:9
10.	For appeasing jackals	A:17.2; B:89.3; C:11
11.	For protecting sheep against jackals	A:17.3; B:89.3; C:11
12.	For protecting horses and cattle against the harm of carnivorous animals	A:18.4; B:90.2; C:12

(Continued)

(*Continued*)

No.	Purpose	Text
14.	For clearing away little mice, rats, and birds inside the house	A:24.6; B:95.4; C:14–15
15.	Protection against ghosts and demons	A:29.3; B:99.4; C:15
16.	Protective measures against obstacles and faults	A:30.4; B:100.5; C:16
17.	Māra's protection [against demonic obstacles]	A:31.4; B:101.5; C:17
18.	Maheśvara's protective knots	A:35.2; B:104.4; C:19
19.	Maheśvara's protective threads	A:37.2; B:106.2; C:20
20.	Protection against bad luck	A:38.1; B:106.5; C:21
21.	Protection against obstacles	A:39.1; B:107.4; C:21
22.	Protective measures against bandits, etc.	A:40.1; B:108.3; C:22
23.	For protecting one's wealth, horses, and cattle	A:54.1; B:119.3; C:30
24.	For binding thieves	A:56.4; B:121.3; C:31
25.	For binding enemies and thieves	A:57.3; B:121.6; C:32
26.	Protection against enemies on the road	A:59.4; B:123.5; C:32
27.	For reversing bad directions	A:60.1; B:124.2; C:33
28.	For achieving invisibility	A:60.5; B:124.5; C:33
29.	Wand of invisibility (*sgrib shing*) for wherever one goes, for not being seen by carnivorous animals, bandits, etc.	A:64.2; B:127.5; C:36
30.	Padmasambhava's wand of invisibility	A:67.1; B:130.1; C:37
31.	For concealing one's consort during secret practices	A:68.2; B:131.1; C:38
32.	For protecting one's wealth from thieves	A:70.4; B:133.1; C:40
33.	For achieving invisibility	A:70.6; B:133.3; C:40
34.	Padmasambhava's wand of invisibility	A:71.2; B:133.5; C:40
35.	For concealing a talisman	A:80.2; B:140.6; C:41
36.	For protecting one's reserves (*sris*), yoghurt, and beer, etc.	A:82.4; B:143.1; C:43
37.	Protection against ghosts	A:82.6; B:143.3; C:43
38.	For protecting one's reserves against thieves	A:83.1; B:143.4; C:44
39.	For protecting [supplies of] yoghurt and beer	A:83.3; B:143.6; C:44
40.	Pha dam pa's yoghurt protection	A:83.6; B:144.1; C:44
41.	For not giving away cow's milk	A:85.4; B:145.4; C:45
42.	For protecting [one's supply of] beer	A:87.5; B:147.1; C:46
43.	Protective measures against animals	A:90.2; B:148.6; C:48
44.	Pacification of evil oaths and counteractive measures against curses	A:94.1; C:49
45.	For [causing one] to fall asleep and counteractive measures [against such method]	A:96.1; B:152.4; C:51
46.	For insomnia due to [the influence of] demons, etc.	A:96.5; B:153.1; C:51
47.	For protecting sleep	A:97.5; B:153.6; C:52
48.	For protecting the seminal drop, the womb, and women	A:99.2; B:155.2; C:53
49.	For protecting the climbing seminal drop	A:99.5; B:155.4; C:53
50.	For protecting one's own woman against other men	A:100.2; B:156.1; C:54
51.	Protection against adultery	A:100.5; B:156.4; C:54
52.	For contraception	A:104.1; B:159.1; C:55
53.	For protecting children from crying	A:104.5; B:159.5; C:56
54.	Protective measures against plagues of men and livestock and against wild animals	A:105.4; B:160.2; C:56
55.	Protection against plagues of men and livestock	A:106.4; B:161.2; C:57

56.	For curing plagues that have already occurred	A:108.1; B:162.5; C:58
57.	For entrapping wild animals	A:108.6; B:163.3; C:58
58.	For muzzling hunting dogs	A:109.3; B:163.6; C:59
59.	For binding the kill of the hunt	A:109.5; B:164.2; C:59
60.	For breaking free of restrictive bindings	A:110.2; B:164.4; C:59
61.	For releasing iron [chains]	A:113.2; B:167.1; C:60–2
62.	For calming anger	A:116.1; B:169.5; C:62
63.	Pacification of contamination and illness	A:117.5; B:171.1; C:63
64.	For misgivings about tainted food and dirty clothing	A:118.1; B:171.4; C:63
65.	Protection against the impurity of corrupt [behavior] and release [from such impurity]	A:118.2; B:171.5–6; C:63
66.	Protection against impurity	A:118.5; B:172.2; C:64
67.	For increasing the variety of mantras that cure illness	A:119.6; B:173.3; C:64
68.	Edible letters for pacification (*zhi ba'i za yig*)	A:126.1; B:174.5; C:65
69.	Protection against poison	A:128.4; B:176.3; C:67
70.	Protective measures against weapons, planetary demons, etc.	A:130.6; B:176.4; C:67
71.	For muzzling rifles	A:132.2; B:179.6; C:68
72.	Protection against planetary obstacles	A:135.2; B:181.2; C:69
73.	For curing planetary illnesses	A:135.6; B:181.6; C:70
74.	Protection against king demons	A:138.2; B:184.3; C:72
75.	Protection against disturbance by demons (*rgyal, bsen, 'byung-po*)	A:139.1; B:185; C:72
76.	Protection against harm of serpent deities	A:139.4; B:185.1; C:73
77.	Protection against harmful ghosts and possessing demons	A:141.3; B:186.5; C:73
78.	Protection against zombies	A:141.5; B:187.1; C:73
79.	For calling birds to a corpse	A:142.1; B:187.3; C:74
80.	Protective measures against other harms	B:188.3; C:75
81.	For severe fever or omens of impending death	A:143.2; B:189.4; C:76
82.	For repelling and protecting against apparent enemies	A:143.6; B:189.6; C:76
83.	Protective measures against fear of the elements, etc.	A:146.2; B:192.1; C:78
84.	Protection against fear of fire	A:146.2; B:192.2; C:78
85.	Protection against harm [caused by] fire	A:146.6; B:192.4; C:78
86.	Protection against water spirits	A:149.5; B:194.5; C:78
87.	Protection against snow and rain	A:152.6; B:197.5; C:79
88.	For stopping rain and snow	A:153.3; B:198.2; C:80
89.	For clearing fog	A:154.1; B:198.5; C:81
90.	Protection against wind	A:154.5; B:199.3; C:81
91.	For controlling wind	A:154.6; B:199.4; C:81
92.	For suppressing wind spirits	A:155.6; B:200.1; C:81
93.	For riding Vayu's deer	A:156.3; B:200.3; C:82
94.	For summoning wind	A:159.1; B:202.5; C:84
95.	Protective measures against annual threats such as meteorological [events], hailstorms, etc.	A:160.4; B:203.6; C:85
96.	Protection against lightning and thunder	A:161.6; B:204.6; C:85
97.	Protection against untimely frost	A:163.5; B:206.2; C:87
98.	Coincidence upon the sudden gathering of clouds	A:164.4; B:207.1; C:87
99.	Protection against hailstorms	A:165.2; B:207.4; C:88
100.	For turning back hailstorms	A:165.6; B:208.1; C:88

(Continued)

(Continued)

No.	Purpose	Text
102.	For turning back floods [*1 in list of five]	A:169.2; B:210.4; C:90
103.	Protection against loss of young livestock [*2 in list of five]	A:169.6; B:211.2; C:90
104.	Protection against "enemy years" (*lo dgra*) [*3 in list of five]	A:170.5; B:211.6; C:91
105.	Protection against changelings [*4 in list of five]	A:171.4; B:212.4; C:92
106.	Protection against thunder called "sky-enemy" [*5 in list of five]	A:172.4; B:213.3; C:92
107.	For averting nightmares and reversing negative astrological [signs]	A:174.2; B:214.5; C:93
108.	For restricting gossip and slander	A:182.3; B:220.1; C:97
109.	For turning back gossip and slander	A:183.2; B:220.6; C:98
110.	For instantly turning back curses and evil omens	A:178.6*; B:221.5; C:98
111.	For pacifying all faults	A:184.2; B:223.1; C:100
	II. *Enhancement and Augmentation*	
1.	For enhancing the pleasures of life and merits	A:187.6; B:225.2; C:103
2.	For prolonging life	A:188.1; B:225.2; C:103
3.	For augmenting merit	A:192.1; B:228.4; C:105
4.	Edible letters for enrichment (*rgyas pa'i za yig*)	A:204.5; B:232.2; C:108
5.	For increasing the wealth of commerce, food, etc.	A:198.4*; B:237.5; C:111
6.	For protecting children and "turning the navel" (*lte bsgyur*)	A:222.2*; B:242.4; C:115
7.	For [causing] the existent to descend, turning its navel [=controlling its sex], and nourishing the womb	A:224.6; B:244.6; C:116
8.	For [augmenting] conception and [fetal] development	A:225.3; B:245.2; C:116
9.	For turning the navel	A:229.1*; B:245.6; C:117
10.	For increasing physical strength	A:210.4; B:252.5; C:121
11.	For obtaining a pleasant voice	A:214.5; B:256.1; C:124
12.	For increasing intelligence	A:217.4; B:259.3; C:124
13.	For meeting friends and achieving wishes	A:248.5*; B:261.4; C:126
14.	For loving all people	A:249.2; B:261.6; C:127
15.	For meeting pleasant friends wherever you are	B:262.2; C:127
16.	For achieving all goals whatever they are and whenever	A:251.2; B:263.1; C:127
17.	For swift-footedness, discovering treasures, and shape-shifting	A:301.3*; B:269.2; C:132
18.	For swift-footedness	A:301.3; B:269.2; C:132
19.	For finding underground treasures	A:305.2; B:271.5; C:134
20.	For seeing clearly in thick darkness	A:306.1; B:272.2; C:135
21.	For swimming [like a fish] and flying like a bird	A:306.3; B:272.4; C:135
22.	For changing bodies	A:307.1; B:273.1; C:135
23.	For [creating] rain and fog [etc.]	A:233.3*; B:274.1; C:136
24.	For causing rain	A:234.3; B:274.5; C:137

25.	For bringing fog	A:240.2; B:279.5; C:140
26.	For opening springs/fountains	A:241.3; B:280.4; C:141
27.	For growing flowers	A:241.6; B:281.1; C:141
28.	For increasing the lease of cattle and [the production of] milk	A:243.2; B:282.1; C:142
29.	For achieving clairvoyance and [ability] to interpret dreams	A:256.5; B:287.5; C:144
30.	For [achieving] clear vision	B:287.5; C:144
31.	For [achieving] clairvoyance	A:283.5*; B:288.4; C:145
32.	For clarifying dreams	A:264.4; B:289.1; C:145
33.	For seeing everything above and below the earth	A:266.2; B:289.3; C:145
34.	For mirror divination	A:268.4; B:289.6; C:146
35.	For envisioning the face of one's tutelary deity and ḍākinīs	A:270.2; B:290.4; C:146
36.	For bringing down the blessings of the ḍākinīs	B:291.1; C:147
37.	For accomplishing dream and meditation training	B:291.4; C:147
38.	For grasping the meaning of dreams	B:292.2; C:148
39.	For [achieving] sharp vision, clairvoyance, etc.	A:272.5; B:296.1; C:151
40.	Ear strap (*rna sgrog?*) that illuminates clairvoyance	A:275.1; B:298.3; C:152
41.	For sharp vision	A:277.1; B:300.2; C:154
42.	For divining [information from a] mirror	A:287.5*; B:302.1; C:155
43.	Khros [ma] nag [mo]'s mirror divination	B:302.1; C:155
44.	Dpal ldan lha mo's mirror divination	A:289.3; B:302.5; C:155
45.	For achieving the clairvoyance of Lha mo Tshe ring-ma	A:278.3*; B:304.1; C:156
46.	For achieving the clairvoyance of the samaya ḍākinīs	A:282.1; B:306.1; C:158
47.	For identifying thieves	A:290.2; B:306.5; C:158
48.	For identifying thieves according to the Brahmanic system	A:294.3; B:309.5; C:160
49.	For identifying thieves according to Pha dam pa's system	A:296.3; B:311; C:162
50.	For finding [whatever] has been lost [or] destroyed	B:313.3; C:162
51.	For bringing back wealth stolen by thieves	B:313.6; C:162
52.	For recovering stolen goods in this and in future lives	B:314.5; C:163
53.	For assistance [in regaining] wealth that has been stolen	B:316.2; C:164
54.	For examining the signs of [impending] death	B:317.1; C:165
55.	For disarming ridicule, winning arguments, etc.	A:307.5; B:319.5; C:167
56.	For winning arguments	A:309.2; B:320.5; C:167
57.	For winning disputes and rising above sarcasm and ridicule	B:321.3; C:168
58.	For suppressing the speech of enemies	B:323.2; C:169
59.	For binding the mouths of others	B:323.5; C:170
60.	For winning quarrels with enemies	A:311.2; B:324.4; C:170
61.	For winning at dice	A:315.3; B:326.6; C:171
62.	For winning at archery	A:327.1; B:332.2; C:174
63.	For conquering all regions	A:328.4; B:333.4; C:175

(*Continued*)

(*Continued*)

No.	Purpose	Text
	III. *Subjugation and Control*	
1.	For controlling human beings, hunger, and thirst, etc.	A:333.4; B:339.1; C:179
2.	For controlling the dharma	B:342.6; C:182
3.	For coercing kings	A:341.1; B:343.2; C:182
4.	For coercing queens	A:341.3; B:343.3; C:182
5.	For pleasing and taking care of all people	B:343.5; C:182
6.	For [making] all beings obey one's orders	B:343.6; C:182
7.	For coercing enemies and exploiting them as servants	A:341.5; B:344.2; C:183
8.	For coercing living beings	B:344.4; C:183
9.	For coercing women	A:342.5; B:345.2; C:183
10.	For pleasing all people and controlling food and drink	A:345.4; B:345.5; C:184
11.	For controlling appearances	B:349.6; C:187
12.	For coercing public crowds	A:344.5; B:350.4; C:187
13.	For coercing others, minor [activities]	B:350.6; C:188
14.	For controlling women	B:351.2; C:188
15.	For coercing beautiful women	B:351.2; C:188
16.	For knowledge about summoning a [tantric] consort	A:387.2; B:352.4; C:189
17.	For gathering and coercing disciples and consorts	B:354.1; C:190
18.	For controlling whomever/whatever one wishes	B:356.2; C:192
19.	For subjugation	B:359.5; C:194
20.	For stirring up and affecting minds one-pointedly	B:360.1; C:195
21.	For controlling wealth	B:361.1; C:195
22.	Edible letters for subjugation (*dbang gi za yig*)	A:351.4; B:361.4; C:196
23.	For controlling the three spheres [heaven, earth, netherworld]	B:362.4; C:197
24.	For summoning the karma ḍākinīs	A:389.3; B:366.4; C:200
25.	Iron hook that summons the subjugation of appearances	A:391.1; B:367.5; C:200
26.	For controlling friends, food, and wealth	A:373.4*; B:369.5; C:202
27.	For coercing ḍākinīs and exploiting them as servants	A:360.2; B:370.2; C:202
28.	Instructions of Indian scholars guiding all beings to the profound dharma	B:372.3; C:204
29.	For charming all living beings and gathering food for the ḍākinīs	B:374.2; C:205
30.	For coercing people	B:374.5; C:205
31.	For making others reveal their secrets	A:403.2; B:378.4; C:208
32.	For bringing people into compliance [with oneself]	A:403.4; B:379.1; C:208
33.	Minor activities [belonging to the category of fierce rites]	B:380.3; C:209
34.	For binding thieves and making them uncomfortable	A:407.2; B:380.4; C:209
35.	For paralyzing (stag, male deer, etc.?)	A:408.2; B:381.3; C:210
36.	For binding thieves	A:410.3; B:382.1; C:210

37.	For muzzling dogs	B:382.4; C:211
38.	Very profound binding [activities]	B:383.3; C:211
39.	For binding others such as enemies, thieves, etc.	A:411.5; B:384.1; C:212
40.	Bon po instructions on deceiving thieves	B:388.5; C:215
41.	For deceiving thieves	B:389.3; C:216
42.	For binding thieves	B:390.3; C:217
43.	For making people sleepwalk	B:391.3; C:217
44.	For keeping enemies paralyzed temporarily	A:418.2; B:392.5; C:218
45.	For sexual intercourse with a woman	A:457.3; B:397.2; C:221
46.	For [dealing with] evil and disrespectful women	A:456.3; B:398.2; C:221
47.	For transforming demon food	B:398.5; C:222
48.	For turning away enemies	A:430.5–435
49.	For dividing enemies and hindering the abilities of evil people	A:438.2–452
50.	For performing "vagina magic" (*stu mthu*) on a woman	A:454.4–456
51.	For [dealing with] enemies and depleting their merit	A:458.1–470

IV. *Destruction*

Note: Harmful acts, such as ritual killing, expulsion, divisiveness, suppression, etc. are not discussed [see III.33–51]

NOTES

1. Per Sørensen, *Tibetan Buddhist Historiography—The Mirror Illuminating the Royal Genealogies: An Annotated Translation of the XIVth Century Tibetan Chronicle: rGyal-rabs gsal-ba'i me-long* (Wiesbaden: Harrassowitz Verlag, 1994), 292n892. In fact, for what it is worth, we do find this spelling, *dpe (')bum*, in the title of the sixteenth-century *be'u bum* of the Sixth Zhwa dmar Chos kyi dbang phyug (1584–1630), see *Nyer mkho sna tshogs kyi dpe bum phan de rab ster* (Delhi, 1977).

2. For a discussion of *bienwen* and popular Chinese storytellers, including extended comparisons across Asia, the Indian *yamapaṭa* and so on, see Victor H. Mair, *Tun-huang Popular Narratives* (Cambridge: Cambridge University Press, 1983), *Painting and Performance: Chinese Picture Recitation and Its Indian Genesis* (Honolulu, HI: University of Hawai'i Press, 1988), and *T'ang Transformation Texts: A Study of the Buddhist Contribution to the Rise of Vernacular Fiction and Drama in China* (Cambridge, MA: Harvard University Press, 1989). On *etoki* and medieval Japanese storytellers, see Barbara Ruch, "Medieval Jongleurs and the Making of a National Literature," in *Japan in the Muromachi Age*, ed. John W. Hall and Toyoda Takeshi (Berkeley, CA: University of California Press, 1977), 279–309; Ikumi Kaminishi, *Explaining Pictures: Buddhist Propaganda and Etoki Storytelling in Japan* (Honolulu, HI: University of Hawai'i Press, 2006). For consideration of possible examples of the *bienwen* genre in Tibet, see Matthew Kapstein, "A Dunhuang Tibetan Summary of the Transformation Text on Mulian Saving His Mother from Hell," in *Dunhuang wenxian lunji*, ed. Hao Chunwen (Shenyang: Liaoning Renmin Chubanshe, 2001), 235–47, "Mulian in the Land of Snows and King Gesar in Hell: A Chinese Tale of Parental Death in Its Tibetan Tranformations,"

in *The Buddhist Dead: Practices, Discourses, Representations*, ed. Bryan J. Cuevas and Jacqueline I. Stone (Honolulu, HI: University of Hawai'i Press, 2007), 345–77, and "The Tibetan *Yulanpen jing*," in *Contributions to the Cultural History of Early Tibet*, ed. Matthew Kapstein and Brandon Dotson (Leiden: Brill, 2007), 219–46.

3. Bsod nams rgyal mtshan, *Rgyal rabs gsal ba'i me long* (Beijing: Mi rigs dpe skrun khang, 1981), 152.

4. R. A. Stein, *Tibetan Civilization* (Stanford, CA: Stanford University Press, 1972), 267; also Ulrike Roesler, "Not a Mere Imitation: Indian Narratives in a Tibetan Context," in *Facets of Tibetan Religious Tradition and Contacts with Neighbouring Cultural Areas*, ed. Alfredo Cadonna and Ester Bianchi (Firenze: Leo S. Olschki Editore, 2002), 155–57; Sørensen, *Tibetan Buddhist Historiography*, 582n3.

5. R. A. Stein, *Recherches sur l'Épopée et le Barde au Tibet* (Paris: Presses Universitaires, 1959), 475n5; Roesler, "Not a Mere Imitation," 151n3. For examples of the genre of *blo sbyong*, see Thupten Jinpa, *Mind Training: The Great Collection* (Boston, MA: Wisdom Publications, 2005); for *lam rim*, see Tsong-kha-pa, *The Great Treatise*.

6. Lha btsun Rin chen rgya mtsho, *'Brong rtse be'u bum/ Man ngag bang mdzod* (Beijing: Mi rigs dpe skrun khang, 2005).

7. Ba ri lo tsā ba Rin chen grags, *Be'u-bum of Ba-ri Lo-tsā-ba Rin-chen-grags* (Delhi, 1974). Only the first work in this collection is explicitly attributed to Ba ri lo tsā ba.

8. E. Gene Smith, *Among Tibetan Texts: History and Literature of the Himalayan Plateau* (Boston, MA: Wisdom Publication, 2001), 230.

9. Karma Phuntsho, *Mipham's Dialectics and the Debates on Emptiness: To Be, Not to Be or Neither* (London: Routledge, 2005), 13.

10. John Whitney Pettit, *Mipham's Beacon of Certainty: Illuminating the View of Dzogchen, the Great Perfection* (Boston, MA: Wisdom Publications, 1999), 1.

11. See Steven M. Goodman, "Mi-Pham rgya-mtsho: An Account of His Life, the Printing of his Works, and the Structure of his Treatise Entitled *mKhas-pa'i tshul la 'jug-pa'i sgo*," in *Wind Horse: Proceedings of the North American Tibetological Society*, ed. Ronald M. Davidson (Berkeley, CA: Asian Humanities Press, 1981), 58–78; Leslie S. Kawamura, "An Analysis of Mi-pham's *mKhas-'jug*," in *Wind Horse*, ed. Davidson, 112–26, "An Outline of *Yāna-Kauśalya* in Mi-pham's *mKhas-'jug*," *Indogaku Bukkyōgaku Kenkyū*, 29/1(1981): 956–61, and "The *Akṣayamatinirdeśasūtra* and Mi-pham's *mKhas-jug*," in *Contributions on Tibetan and Buddhist Philosophy*, ed. E. Steinkellner and H. Tauscher (Vienna: Arbeitkreis für Tibetische und Buddhistische Studien Universität Wien, 1983), 131–45; Kennard Lipman, "A Controversial Topic from Mi-pham's Analysis of Śāntarakṣita's *Madhyamakālaṃkāra*," in *Wind Horse: Proceedings of the North American Tibetological Society*, ed. Ronald M. Davidson (Berkeley, CA: Asian Humanities Press, 1981), 40–57; Katsumi Mimaki, "Le commentaire de Mipham sur le *Jñānasārasamuccaya*," in *Indological and Buddhist Studies: Volume in Honour of Professor J.W. De Jong on His Sixtieth Birthday*, ed. L. A. Hercus (Canberra: Australian National University, 1982), 353–76; Matthew Kapstein, "Mi-pham's Theory of Interpretation," in *Buddhist Hermeneutics*, ed. Donald S. Lopez, Jr. (Honolulu,HI: University of Hawai'i Press, 1988), 149–74; Pettit, *Mipham's Beacon of Certainty*; Thomas Doctor, *Speech of Delight: Mipham's Commentary on Shantarakshita's Ornament of the Middle Way* (Ithaca, NY: Snow Lion,

2004); Phuntsho, *Mipham's Dialectics*, and his "'Ju Mi pham rNam rgyal rGya mtsho—His Position in the Tibetan Religious Hierarchy and a Synoptic Survey of His Contributions," in *The Pandita and the Siddha: Tibetan Studies in Honor of E. Gene Smith*, ed. Ramon N. Prats (Dharamsala: Amnye Machen Institute, 2007), 191–209.

12. The one welcome exception to this general trend is the recent article by Lin Shen-yu, "Tibetan Magic for Daily Life: Mi pham's Texts on *gTo*-rituals," *Cahiers d'Extrême-Asie* 15 (2005): 107–25. On my more general point, consider Gene Smith's comment: "Mi pham belongs to an unusual tradition that goes back at least to Karma chags med in the seventeenth century. These teachers sought to incorporate into Khams pa Buddhism the beliefs and folklore treasured by humble nomads and agriculturalists. These teachers were almost anthropologically oriented... Mi pham was also keenly interested in the practical arts. He was a creative physician. Even if some of the methods he recommends smack of quackery, we can never accuse him of lacking imagination. His medical works continue to be highly regarded to this day"; Smith, *Among Tibetan Texts*, 231. See also the comments in Phuntsho, *Mipham's Dialectics*, 14.

13. *Sngags kyi be'u bum* [= *Las sna tshogs pa'i sngags kyi be'u bum dgos 'dod kun 'byung gter gyi bum pa bzang po*] (New Delhi, 1972; henceforth A); *Sngags kyi be bum* [= *Las sna tshogs pa'i sngags kyi be bum dgos 'dod kun 'byung gter gyi bum bzang*], published with *Sgyu ma'i be bum* [= *Rdzu 'phrul sgyu ma'i be bum ngo mtshar stong ldan*] compiled in 1904 (New Delhi, 1974; henceforth B); *Las sna tshogs kyi be'u bum* [= *Las sna tshogs pa'i sngags kyi be'u bum dgos 'dod kun 'byung gter gyi bum pa bzang po*] (Hong Kong: Zhang kang then mā dpe skrun khang, 1999; henceforth C).

14. Mgon po dbang rgyal, *Chos kyi rnam grangs shes bya'i nor gling 'jug pa'i gru gzings* (Delhi, 1993), 116: [1] *nad dang gdon bgegs zhi ba/* [2] *tshe bsod longs spyod rgyas pa/* [3] *khams gsum dbang du 'du ba/* [4] *bsad skrad dbye rengs drag po'i las rnams so.*

15. The rites included among the *ṣaṭkarmāṇi* are variously listed, but the most common set is given as follows: (1) pacification (*śānti*), (2) subjugation (*vaśya, vaśīkaraṇa*), (3) immobilization (*stambhana*), (4) causing dissension (*vidveṣaṇa*), (5) eradication (*uccāṭana*), and (6) liquidation/killing (*māraṇa*). Other activities alternatively listed include: delusion (*mohana*), attraction (*ākarṣaṇa*), acquisition (*puṣṭi*), agitation (*kṣobhaṇa*), piercing (*kīlana*), oppression (*pīḍana*), coercion (*nigraha*), binding/checking (*bandhana/pratibandhana*), intimidation (*trāsana*), kicking (*tāḍana*), crushing (*mardana*), devouring (*jambhana/jṛmbhana*), dessication (*śoṣaṇa*), teasing/showing/pleasant pastimes (*kautuka/vinoda*), making sick (*vyādhikaraṇa*), and power of resuscitation (*saṃjīvinī vidyā*). See Teun Goudriaan, *Māyā Divine and Human: A Study of Magic and Its Religious Foundations in Sanskrit Texts, with particular attention to a fragment on Viṣṇu's Māyā preserved in Bali* (Delhi: Motilal Banarsidass, 1978); H.G. Türstig, "The Indian Sorcery Called *Abhicāra*." *Wiener Zeitschrift fur die Kunde Südasiens* 29 (1985): 69–117; Gudrun Bühnemann, "The Six Rites of Magic," in *Tantra in Practice*, ed. David G. White (Princeton, NJ: Princeton University Press, 2000), 447–62.

16. James G. Frazer, *The Golden Bough: Abridged Edition* (1922; reprint, New York: Penguin, 1998), 13–57. On these categories, Stanley Tambiah has positively noted: "But there is some molten gold in Frazer's volcanic overflow. For example, the associational principles of similarity and contiguity as general features of the human mind have since Frazer's time found an elaborated use in other interpretive frameworks

stripped of their 'causal' connotations as applied to magic. Roman Jakobson has fruitfully exploited the terms 'metaphorical and metonymical associations' in his linguistic and literary studies, and after him Lévi Strauss has popularized them in the study of savage thought, particularly in the realm of mythology. In my own essay on 'The Magical Power of Words' [1968] I apply them (I hope productively) in the analysis of Trobriand ritual"; *Magic, Science, Religion, and the Scope of Rationality* (Cambridge: Cambridge University Press, 1990), 53. For Frazer, however, the two principles of magic, similarity and contagion, were mistaken principles that rested on incorrect assumptions about the laws of nature; magic, in his opinion, was nothing more than false science.

17. In the dictionary of Dge bshes Chos grags, *liṅga* (syn. *nya bo*) is defined as "whatever serves as a support for the 'liberation' of the one named as intended 'victim' during [the rite of] liberation [by] secret mantra"; *gsang sngags sgrol ba'i skabs su dmigs yul gyi ming rus can gyi bsgral rten gang yin pa'i linga lta bu;* Dge bshes Chos grags, *Dge bshes chos kyi grags pas brtsams pa'i brda dag ming tshig gsal ba* (Beijing: Mi rigs dpe skrun khang, 1995), 303. On Tibetan *liṅga*, see R. A. Stein, "Le *Liṅga* des danses masquées lamaïques et la théorie des âmes," *Sino-Indian Studies (Liebenthal Festschrift)*, 5/3–4 (1957): 200–34; Richard Kohn, *Lord of the Dance: The Mani Rimdu Festival in Tibet and Nepal* (Ithaca, NY: State University of New York Press, 2001), 75–78. For brief instructions on how to construct a *liṅga* image, see Padma gling pa, *Linga bri ba'i yig chung gsod byed gri gug rgya can*, in his *Collected Works (Gsung 'bum), The Rediscovered Teachings of the Great Padma-gliṅ-pa* (Thimphu: Kunsang Tobgay, 1975), vol. 3, ff. 365.1–367.3.

18. See Mengele's chapter in this volume for examples of the ways in which such effigies are used in the context of death-deceiving rituals.

19. Stanley Tambiah, "Form and Meaning of Magical Acts," in *Culture, Thought, and Social Action: An Anthropological Perspective* (Cambridge, MA: Harvard University Press, 1985), 67.

20. Consider, for example, Ge sar's defeat of the demon Klu btsan by first subduing his "soul residences" (*bla gnas*), a tree, a lake, a serpent, etc. Also, Ge sar's defeat of the Hor by first destroying the "soul stone" (*bla rdo*) of the kings of that country. The most convenient summary of the Ge sar epic remains Alexandra David-Neel, *The Superhuman Life of Gesar of Ling* (1933; reprint Boston, MA: Shambhala Publications, 1987).

21. Stanley Tambiah, "The Magical Power of Words," *Man* 3/2(1968): 175–208.

22. Jan Gonda, "Mudrā," *Studies in the History of Religions* 12 (1972): 21–31.

23. Anne-Marie Blondeau, "Le Lha-'dre bKa'-thaṅ," in *Études tibétaines dédiées à la mémoire de Marcelle Lalou* (Paris: Adrien-Maisonneuve, 1971), 29–126. On Tibetan astrology, see Alexander Berzin, "An Introduction to Tibetan Astronomy and Astrology," *Tibet Journal* 12/1(1987): 17–28; Philippe Cornu, *Tibetan Astrology* (Boston, MA: Shambhala, 1997); Gyurme Dorje and Sangye Gyatso, *Tibetan Elemental Divination Paintings: Illuminated Manuscripts from the White Beryl of Sangs-rgyas rGya-mtsho with the Moonbeams Treatise of Lo-chen Dharmaśrī* (London: John Eskenazi in association with Sam Fogg, 2001).

24. *Śrī Mahākāla Tantra* (Tib. *'Phags pa nag po chen po'i rgyud*); Sde dge Bka' 'gyur, Toh. no. 667, Rgyud *ba*, ff. 199a.6–201b.3.

25. *Ekavīrākhyā Śrīcaṇḍamahāroṣana Tantrarāja* (Tib. *Dpal gtum po khro bo chen po'i rgyud kyi rgyal po dpa' bo gcig pa*); Sde dge Bka' 'gyur, Toh. no. 431, Rgyud *nga*, ff. 304b.1–343a.1.

26. *Maṇibhadra Yakṣasena-kalpa* (Tib. *Gnod sbyin nor bu bzang po'i rtog pa*); Sde dge Bka' 'gyur, Toh. no. 765, Rgyud *wa*, ff. 56b.2–69a.6. See also *Ārya Maṇibhadra-nāma Dhāraṇī* (Tib. *'Phags pa nor bu bzang po'i gzungs*); Sde dge Bka' 'gyur, Toh. no. 764, Rgyud *wa*, ff. 56a.1 56b.2 and Sde dge Bka' 'gyur, Toh. no. 970, Gzungs *wam*, ff. 86a.4–86b.7.

27. Most likely an abbreviation for the *Rdo rje sems dpa'i sgyu 'phrul dra ba gsang ba thams cad kyi me long zhes bya ba'i rgyud;* NGB, Mtshams brag 441, vol. 22, *za*, text 5, ff. 480.6–692.6.

28. This is perhaps the *Ma mo las thams cad kyi las rgyud lung;* NGB, Mtshams brag 713, vol. 39, *ti*, text 6, ff. 638.5–677.5. Whatever it is, Mi pham cites this so-called *Las thams cad pa'i rgyud* copiously in this section.

29. Also included is a brief instruction on the mirror divination of Dpal ldan lha mo given to Mi pham by his teacher Dbang chen Dgyes rab rdo rje (b. 1832). See Section II.44. On Tibetan mirror divination more generally, see Nebesky-Wojkowitz, *Oracles and Demons of Tibet* (1993), 462–63; John Vincent Bellezza, *Spirit-Mediums, Sacred Mountains and Related Bon Textual Traditions in Upper Tibet: Calling Down the Gods* (Leiden: Brill, 2005), 437–38.

30. See the root cycle of the *Kṛṣṇayamāri Tantra* (Tib. *Gshin rje gshed nag po'i rgyud*); Sde dge Bka' 'gyur, Toh. no. 467, Rgyud *ja*, ff. 134b.1–151b.4; Sde dge Bka' 'gyur, Toh. no. 469, Rgyud *ja*, ff. 164a.1–167b.5; Sde dge Bka' 'gyur, Toh. no. 473, Rgyud *ja*, ff. 175a.1–185b.7. Commentaries and related texts are found in Sde dge Bstan 'gyur, Toh. nos. 1918–2089.

31. This would be the *De bzhin gshegs pa thams cad kyi dgongs pa'i khro bo 'dus pa/ bde gshegs spyir dril rta mgrin rngog ma leb rgan gyi rgyud;* Gting skyes 303, vol. 24, *ya*, ff. 110.2–212.4.

32. A possible equivalent term for black magic in Tibetan would be *mthu*, which means literally "force, power" and in this sense is similar to the word *drag* included among the "four actions." The term *mthu*, however, explicitly connotes something malevolent, an evil action of the sort we might more easily recognize as witchcraft. The distinction between *mthu* and *mngon spyod*—another common word for black magic (see note 35)—is not altogether clear.

33. *Sngags kyi be'u bum* B, f. 380.3; C, 209.

34. On the delicate distinction between ritual murder (*bsgral ba*) and liberation (*sgrol ba*), see Cathy Cantwell, "To Meditate upon Consciousness as *Vajra:* Ritual 'Killing and Liberation' in the Rnying-ma-pa Tradition," in *Tibetan Studies: Proceedings of the 7th Seminar of the International Association for Tibetan Studies, Graz 1995*, ed. Helmut Krasser, Michael Torsten Much, Ernst Steinkellner, and Helmut Tauscher (Vienna: Verlag der Österreichischen Akademie der Wissenschaften, 1997), 107–18; see also Peter Schwieger, "Schwarze Magie im tibetischen Buddhismus," *Studies in Central and East Asian Religion* 9 (1988): 18–36.

35. The Tibetan term for sorcery, *mngon spyod* (Skt. *abhicāra*), is defined in the *Tshig mdzod chen mo* as "fierce activities; the action of slaying ('liberating') enemies, demons, and obstructors through the power of mantra"; *drag po'i las te sngags mthus dgra bo dang gdon bgegs rnams bsgral ba'i las;* Krang dbyi sun, et al., *Bod rgya tshig mdzod chen mo*, 690. These rites are also collectively called *mnan sreg 'phang gsum*, referring to the

three primary methods for achieving the intended goal—pressing (*mnan pa*), burning (*bsreg pa*), and hurling (*'phang ba*). These are the same three categories of fierce ritual listed in the Chinese Imperial Edict of 1726, which was ratified for the sole purpose of prohibiting the practice of sorcery in Tibet, particularly among followers of the Rnying ma pa. See Mdo mkhar Zhabs drung Tshe ring dbang rgyal, *Mi dbang rtogs brjod* [= *Dpal mi'i dbang po'i rtogs brjod 'jig rten kun tu dga' ba'i gtam*] (Chengdu: Si khron mi rigs dpe skrun khang, 1981), 482 and the discussion in Luciano Petech, *China and Tibet in the Early XVIIIth Century* (Leiden: Brill, 1972), 106–12. Very soon after this pronouncement, in 1802, Thu'u bkwan disparagingly used the phrase *mnan sreg 'phang gsum* also in reference to the sorcery of the Rnying ma pa. He writes: "Nowadays, the Rnying ma pa merely put on a show of magic, chanting liturgical books, conjuring hosts of deities, pressing, burning, and hurling [the *gtor ma* and *zor* weapons], and so forth, but act [as if what they] do is crucial"; *da lta'i rnying ma ba rnams las byang gyer ba dang/ tshogs 'khor gyi yo lang dang/ mnan sreg 'phang gsum sogs las sbyor gyi gzugs bryan la snying por byed ba tsam mo; Grub mtha' shel gyi me long* (Lanzhou: Kan su'u mi rigs dpe skrun khang, 1984), 80. For a general overview of destructive rites in Tibet, see Nebesky-Wojkowitz, *Oracles and Demons of Tibet* (1993), 481–502; Martin J. Boord, *The Cult of the Deity Vajrakīla, According to the Texts of the Northern Treasures Tradition of Tibet (Byang-gter phur-ba)* (Tring: The Institute of Buddhist Studies, 1993), 197–206. On such rites in India, see again Türstig, "Indian Sorcery." For a discussion of these rites in China and Japan, see Michel Strickman, "Homa in East Asia," in *Agni: The Vedic Ritual of the Fire Altar*, ed. Fritz Staal, 2 vols. (Delhi: Motilal Banarsidass, 1983) 2: 418–55.

36. Gnubs chen Sangs rgyas ye shes and 'Jam dpal bshes gnyen, *Zla gsang be'u bum* (Dehra Dun, 1975). The so-called *Shugs ldan be'u bum* is extant in two versions, the New Delhi edition (Mongolian Lama Guru Deva, 1984) and the Lhasa edition (1991), both in two volumes.

37. The ten fields are listed by Klong rdol Ngag dbang blo bzang (1719–94) in his *Gsang sngags rig pa 'dzin pa'i sde snod las byung ba'i rgyud sde bzhi'i ming gi rnam grangs* as follows (Lhasa: Bod ljongs bod yig dpe rnying dpe skrun khang, 1991), 110: [1] those who subvert the teachings of the Buddha; [2] those who blaspheme the Three Jewels; [3] those who rob the goods of the monastic assembly; [4] those who slander and condemn the Mahāyāna; [5] those who attack the guru/lama; [6] those who slander their tantric brothers; [7] those who hinder an evocation; [8] those who have neither love nor compassion; [9] those who break their vows and pledges; and [10] those who hold wrong views about karma and its effects"; *bsgral ba'i zhing bcu zhes pa ni/ sangs rgyas bstan pa bshig pa gcig/ dkon mchog dbu 'phang smad pa gnyis/ dge 'dun dkor ni 'phrog pa gsum/ theg chen smod cing sun 'byin bzhi/ bla ma'i sku la bsdo ba lnga/ rdo rje spun sum 'byin pa drug/ sgrub la bar chad byed pa bdun/ brtse ba snying rje gtan med brgyad/ dam tshig sdom pa bral ba dgu/ las 'bras log par lta ba bcu.*

38. Klong rdol Ngag dbang blo bzang, *Gsang sngags rig pa*, 109–10: *de ltar lta stangs bzhi po ni/ 'grub kyang mngon spyod drag las kyi/ zhing bcu tshang ba'i dgra bo yang/ bsgral na rang nyid sdig pa che/ 'o na mngon spyod drag las ni/ ji tsam zhig nas byed pa yi/ zhe na lta stangs bzhi po yis/ de ltar nus kyang de ma thag/ lta stangs mdzad pas* [110] *sngar mgo bzhin/ nus na gdug can bsgral ba dang/ de yi rnam shes mtho ris kyi/ rten bzang bskyal nus nges par 'ongs/ de lta'i sngags pas dgra bgegs bsgral.*

8

Rites of the Deity Tamdrin (Rta mgrin) in Contemporary Bön

Transforming Poison and Eliminating Noxious Spirits with Burning Stones

MARC DES JARDINS

My first encounter with the Bönpo deity Tamdrin (Rta mgrin) occurred in April 2004. Upon my arrival at the Yeshé (Ye shes)[1] Monastery in Nyagrong (Nyag rong, Xinlong xian) following two days of continuous travel from Chengdu, I suffered from exhaustion. The lama in whose quarters I was temporarily lodged became worried and decided that there were hindering spirits who were preventing me from functioning normally. Anyi Lama (A nyi bla ma), a senior monk, is one of the monastery's ritual experts. He took it upon himself to conduct a ritual of exorcism for my well-being, as well as for some other monks who were also suffering from recurring illnesses. The third day after my arrival, all the preparations for the ritual, including the special *torma* cakes and other offerings for the altar, had been completed before 10:00 a.m. The lama then conducted the "General Ritual of Tamdrin" (*Rta mgrin skor*),[2] and I was invited to join the other monks in his kitchen. It was close to noon. Little did I expect that the main part of the ritual was going to take place in the kitchen. I noticed that close to the hearth an acolyte was busy pumping air to fan an already well-established fire. On the stove was a cauldron with liquids. On the first fire was a receptacle containing stones that had been heated to bright red. We all sat on the floor or on the side bench and let Anyi Lama conduct the ritual. While he was intoning mantras, the acolyte manning the fire took one red-hot stone with tongs and put it directly on the open hand of Anyi Lama. There was a puff of smoke and flame which suddenly hissed upward. The lama, without stopping or flinching, continued to recite the mantras while circling his hand over all the participants, including me. He then threw the stone, still red, into the cauldron on the stove. This made the liquid boil violently and overflow with loud noises. Anyi Lama repeated this five more times with similar stones. After throwing the last one in, he then took a twig of juniper which he dipped into the cauldron and sprinkled each of us, one by one. This concluded the rite. At my request, Anyi Lama showed me his hand, which did not appear to have suffered any burns from the stones. I witnessed this dramatic ritual more than three times over the course of several years, while conducting research at Yeshé Monastery. It seems that it has become the specialty of about three of its monks, all disciples of Anyi Lama. The ritual can also be performed with more props, such as the drawing of a colored powder circle with two fires in its midst, the use of a ritual cauldron, repeated offerings of *torma*, use of colored threads, and many more ingredients and paraphernalia (Figure 8.1).

The tutelary deity invoked in this ritual was none other than Tamdrin or Hayagrīva, a member of the Bön as well as the Buddhist pantheon. Anyi Lama

FIGURE 8.1. The officiating lama takes hold of one of the burning stone. Yeshé Monastery. Photo: M. des Jardins (April, 2004).

possesses a painting (*thang ka*) made by a former master of the monastery which depicts Tamdrin in the center, red in color, with his outstretched right hand holding a sword in the *tarjanī mudrā* and the left hand in the same posture holding a skull cup. This sword is the identifying mark which differentiates it from the Buddhist iconography, which, by contrast, shows him holding a *vajra*. Below him on his left is Khyung (Garuḍa), stretching a snake between his two hands and his beak. Chagna Dorjé (Phyag na do rje, Vajrapāni), on his right and below, is holding a vajra in his right hand with the left hand at his heart in the *tarjanī mudrā*. Above Tamdrin are the Three Enlightened Ones of the past, present, and future. The assembly hall of Yeshé monastery also possesses a life-sized statue of red Tamdrin in a recessed alcove (Figure 8.2).

This chapter has a number of goals: (1) to provide some historical background for the chief deity of the ritual, Tamdrin, especially in the Bön tradition; (2) to provide a detailed description of the ritual cycle within which the Burning Stones ritual is found; (3) to explain the social context in which this rite is performed; (4) to reflect on what makes this rite so popular; and (5) to argue for the fact that rites like this one suggest the need for a more nuanced understanding of the relationship of Bön and Buddhism in Tibet.

Context

Hayagrīva is the well-known Indian horse-head deity commonly conceived as an incarnation or *avatāra* of Viṣṇu by a majority of Hindus. Kamala Nayar has clearly demonstrated in her study of Hayagrīva in India[3] that there is no single story of this important deity. Its *hauts faits* are attested to in a multiplicity of voices, religions, cultures, and worldviews. Hayagrīva's stories are found in the epics, such as the Mahābhārata (200–400 CE), and the Purāṇas, such as the Harivamśa, Skanda Purāṇa, Viṣṇu Purāṇa, the Viṣṇudharmottara Purāṇa, and the Kālikā Purāṇa. Among the Āgama, it is found in the Hayaśīrṣa Saṃhitā, Īśvara Saṃhitā, Pādma Saṃhitā, Sanatkumāra Saṃhitā, Sātvata Saṃhitā, Śeṣa Saṃhitā, Śrīpauṣkara Saṃhitā, Sāradātilaka Tantra, the Yoginī Tantra (ca. 16th century), and the Meru Tantra. It also appears in regional sectarian writings such as the Periya Tirumoḷi and the Tiruvāymoḷi of the Āḷvārs as well as in the Śata Dūṣaṇī of the Śrī Vaiṣṇava Ācārya, Vedānta Deśika (1269–1370).[4] Many indications point to the present-day cult of Hayagrīva as strongest in Assam, in northeastern India, where there are many entire temples dedicated to this deity. Of the various and sundry narratives of Hayagrīva, the ones that have gradually dominated, unified, and strengthened the core tradition centered on the narratives of him as an *avatāra* of Viṣṇu. Scholars have accounted for the

FIGURE 8.2. The statue of Tamdrin at Yeshé Monastery. Photo: M. des Jardins (April, 2004).

horse-head deity theme running throughout a long period of time in sacred Indian texts.

In Tibet, Hayagrīva is at the center of many "treasure" (*gter ma*) teachings and cycles, belonging for the most part to the Nyingma school. Sera monastery has, however, a peculiar tradition of the cult of the deity which is unique to this institution. This has been explored by Cabezón.[5]

Tamdrin in Bön

We may assert with much caution that the first authoritative scriptural reference to Tamdrin in Bön can be found in the long version of Tönpa Shenrab's (Ston pa gshen rab) hagiography, the fourteenth century *Precious Compendium: The Blazing Sūtra Immaculate and Glorious* (*Dri med gzi brjid*).[6] The particular section on Tamdrin has been reprinted separately in the Bön Tengyur (Brten 'gyur) under the title *The Lore of King Tamdrin from the Sūtra on the Teachings of Bön [Extracted] from the Concise [Teachings] in Terms of the Five Categories of Asuras Versus the Great Magic of the Gods from the Precious Compendium, the Immaculate and Glorious.*[7] This text begins by stating how the Teacher Shenrab, out of compassion for all sentient beings, taught on the top of the Excellent Mountain (*ri rab*, i.e., Mount Kailash) a method to subdue violent hindrances or hindering spirits (*drags gegs*) who could not be conquered by ordinary means. It is said that subduing these spirits with deities from the sphere of the Peaceful Ones (*zhi ba*) was not possible. Therefore, in order to accomplish their subjugation, the Teacher recited the mantra of Tamdrin (*bso oṃ vajra rag* (*sha?*) *khro da rab rab haya ghrī ba hum phat*). Shenrab then produces an emanation body (*sku sprul*) in front of himself as Hayagrīva, who appears with a flaming red body, one face, two hands, standing in the striding posture and holding a flaming red sword with gold ornaments. In the midst of his mane is a green horse head. He stands in mid-air, blazing.[8] As is common in other Tibetan literature of this genre, he then emanates rays of light that hook the beings to be called forth, drawing their principle of consciousness (*bla*) in front of him. He then intones a long mantra spanning over four folios.[9] This invokes the *devas, asuras*, the Great Ones of the cemeteries (*dur khrod chen po*), and the Fierce Fathers and the Mothers (*drags gegs pho mo*). A vast host of the beings are then brought into his presence through emanations of martial spirits. The list is very extensive and includes not only many grouped categories of eight gods and demons (*lha 'dre*), but also a variety of beings such as fire deities (*me lha*), neither-male-nor-female deities (*ma ning*), life-force deities of the Sinpo (Srin po) class, etc. This list is a mixture of deities of Indian origin, recognizable from their Sanskritized names, some corresponding to known categories, and others of a more popular nature, such as wind deities (*rlung lha*), city-gods (*grong khyer*), gods of various realms, various demonic lords (*dmu rje, bdud rje*), the Wealth God (*nor lha*) and many others difficult to identify.

There are no epic narratives in this short text. The account is closer to a roster of personalities witnessed at a royal court. In fact, the point might just be to affirm the reigning authority of Tamdrin over mundane and trouble-making deities. This work is concise, straightforward, and is not unique in its genre. There are a number of Buddhist texts dating from around the ninth century in Tibet, and earlier in China, that do not contain narratives. Scriptures, such as the *Mahāmāyūrī Sūtra*,[10] are lists of a wide array of divinities that are more often than not regrouped under various categories and classes. In China, a specific scriptural genre was in vogue from as early as the sixth to the ninth century which was referred to under the generic name of *Foming Jing* (*Scriptures of the Names of the Buddhas*).[11] These texts were primarily used for long rituals which consisted of reciting the name of each Enlightened One, worshipping it with incense, and prostrating while circumambulating the inner precincts of the temple. These grand rituals often lasted for several days and were physically so demanding that during its course followers would fall down, often in a trance. The rituals were very popular, and monastic institutions and masters would create their own version of *Foming Jing* to attract followers and generate financial and other forms of support. Thus, the various Chinese Buddhist Canons have many of these scriptures, which may contain from 100 to 30,000 names of deities. Taoism has also followed this trend with important scriptures such as the *Scripture of Universal Salvation*,[12] thus showing a ritual trend common not only to Tibet, but also to East Asia more generally.[13]

A Short History of Tamdrin in Bön

More research needs to be conducted in order to ascertain the age of the Tamdrin practices in Bön. The history of Yeshé Monastery's lineage suggests that it is a relatively recent practice, as gleaned from the records of the master Tsultrim Chog-gyal (Tshul khrims mchog rgyal, d. ca. 1978), who left terse but most informative accounts of the lineages of most of the empowerments and practices he received during his lifetime. Tsultrim Chog-gyal was the master and uncle of the late Ayung Lama (A g.yung bla ma, alias G.yung drung bstan pa'i rgyal mtshan, 1926–97). The latter organized the first printing of the Bön Canon (Bka' 'gyur) during the late 1980s, and with the present editor of the Tengyur, Sogden Tenpé Nyima (Sog ldan bstan pa'i nyi ma), collected many of the texts now available in this collection.

Tsultrim Chog-gyal's lineage explanations, which are today only available in an original manuscript, do not quite fill two folios, and are rather elliptical. He begins by stating that the lineage of the empowerment (*dbang*) and transmission (*lung*) of Tamdrin, Chagna and Khyung began when, in the distant past, the three root-deities appeared in a pure place where omniscient and enlightened ones abide. The emanation (*sprul*) of the Fierce King Tamdrin subdued wild demons (*bdud srin*) with oaths. The manifestation of Speech, pure son of the gods, could split deceivers into hundreds of pieces. The three manifestations of the Three Bodies were then realized by Sangwa Düpa (Gsang ba 'dus pa).[14] He then transmitted these to the nine great sorcerers (*mthu chen mi dgu*),[15] who then transmitted them to Drenpa Namkha (Dran pa nam mkha'), who in turn transmitted these to his two sons Tsewang Rigdzin (Tshe dbang rig 'dzin) and Pema Jungné (Pad ma 'byung nas).[16] These teachings were then entrusted to a wisdom ḍākinī. In the fifth month, during a Fire Dragon year, the protectors of these teachings entrusted them to Yungdrung Tenpé Gyaltsen (G.yung drung bstan pa'i rgyal mtshan, b. 1516) of the Kharag (Kha rag) Monastery in Pelyul (Dpal yul).[17] He transmitted these to his grandson Lama Yungdrung (Bla ma g.yung drung). From the latter, they passed successively to the Trülku Yungdrung Tenpa Yangpa (Sprul sku g.yung drung bstan pa dbyangs pa), to Yungdrung Döndrub (G.yung drung don 'grub), to Shengyal Tendzin (Gshen rgyal bstan 'dzin), to lama Yungdrung Bönten (G.yung drung bon bstan), and finally to Tsultrim Chog-gyal. From the first master of Kharag Monastery to our writer, there are seven generations. From Tsultrim Chog-gyal, the lineage passed to Ayung Lama, and from him to Anyi Lama, and other contemporary practitioners of the Tamdrin ritual cycle.

Tsultrim Chog-gyal[18] was a famous master of the Yeshé Monastery. In his early days, he traveled far and wide in Kham (Khams) to study with renowned Bönpo masters. One of his root-masters was the famous Shardzé Trashi Gyaltsen (Shar rdzas bkra shis rgyal mtshan, 1858–1934).[19] He also received lineages from another contemporary master, Sang-ngag Lingpa (Gsang sngags gling pa, b. 1864).[20] He kept meticulous records of his transmissions, which are invaluable sources for the study of contemporary Bönpo religious history. His records, as well as information found within the ritual texts themselves, allow us to ascertain that this ritual cycle belongs to the New Treasure (Gter gsar) or New Bön (Bon gsar) movement. Although this classification is used by some more conservative Bönpo masters, the Kham traditions of Bön, in concert with its Nyingma counterparts, accept new *terma* discoveries as well as the more traditional teachings from the Old Bön terma. This is in keeping with local religious trends.

The Fierce Ones of the Three Bodies

The corpus of texts used by Anyi Lama to propitiate Tamdrin, and which contains, among other texts, the ritual of the Burning Stones, is entitled: *The Armor of Everlastingness, by which the Fierce Kings of the Three Bodies Save and Destroy*

Hypocrisy and Defilements (*Sku gsum khro rgyal gyis ngo g.yo dri ma 'jig skyobs g.yung drung go cha*). It consists of a collection of eighteen texts with smaller prayers, praises, lineage accounts, and miscellaneous directives and recitations included in relevant sections. This small compendium was obviously created for ritual recitation. The more complete version contains the empowerment rites as well as other miscellaneous rituals such as the rite of Slaying (*bsad pa*) and the Burning Stone rites.

Although monks of Yeshé Monastery see this practice as related to Tamdrin, the rite involves more than just this one deity. The deities of the Three Bodies alluded to in the headings of the various texts and throughout the ritual are the three different deities already mentioned, namely Tamdrin, Chagna Dorjé (also known as Yungdrung Namjom, G.yung drung rnam 'joms), and Khyung—in other words Hayagrīva, Vajrapāni, and Garuḍa. These are the body, speech, and mind of enlightened activities and are also manifestations or emanations of the Three Masters of the ninth century, Drenpa Namkha and his two sons.

List of Texts and Sections in the Fierce Kings of the Three Bodies *Corpus*

1. *dug phyung me long g.ya' sel* (clearing away of defilements) *dbu phyogs*

   This text is a petition to the group of yidams requesting that they remove poisons and other noxious influences from the area in which the rite will take place.

2. *sku gsum khro rgyal gcig dril las cha lag las byang* (auxiliary rites) *don 'dus*

   This section starts with a lengthy introduction to the many offering practices and others which constitute the bulk of the rite. The main parts of the ritual are recited while offering a large number of ritual cakes (*gtor ma*) to nāgas (*klu*) and other spirits, bodhisattvas and enlightened beings, consecration of the vase where the deities will be invited to stay during the rite, verses for taking refuge, purification, generating bodhicitta, requests of blessings, and other rites which surround the propitiation rites addressed to the three main deities.

3. *sku gsum khro rgyal bskang ba* (mending ritual) *rin chen gter spyungs*
4. *shen rab sku sprul rta mgrin dpa' bo gcig pa sde brgyad rgyal bsen shi 'dre dregs pa zil gnon* (*shi 'dre dgra gegs pa'i gnya' gnon?*)

   This is the actual propitiation manual of Tamdrin the Solitary Hero. It contains the main visualization of the deity with its various mantras and prayers.

5. *gshen rab gsung sprul bcom ldan phyag na rdo rje* (Vajrapāni) *gza' gdon 'byung po ma rung 'dul ba'i gnyen po*

This is the propitiation manual of Vajrapāni proper, similar in many points to no. 4.

6. *gshen rab thugs sprul ye shes khyung nag* (Black Wisdom Garuḍa) *klu gnyan nad mdon gdug pa 'dul mdzad*

   This is the propitiation manual of Garuḍa proper.

7. *sku gsum khro rgyal bsrungs ba'i las byang* (manual of protection) *dbus phyogs*

   This booklet contains the consecration liturgies of various offerings to be made to protector deities.

8. *sku gsum khro rgyal las bzlog pa* (repelling) *byad ma 'bum zlogs dbu phyogs*

   This is the rite which repels the attacks from various ill-intentioned spirits such as the nāgas, cemetery sprites (*dur sri*), demons (*bdud*) from different quarters, Tsen (*btsan*), Mamo (*ma mo*), Za (*Gza'*), Shinjé (*gshin rje*, Skt. *yamas*), Sinpo (*srin po*), Gyalpo (*rgyal po*, lit. kings), Mara (*ma ra*), etc.

9. *ma cig bka' gsang lha mo'i bskul pa* (exhortation)

   This text consists of praises to the Sole Mother (*ma cig*), Sipa Gyalmo (Sri pa rgyal mo), the ruler of this world according to Bön.

10. *gshin rje'i gco 'khor* (the cycle on breaking Yama) *bskul pa nyung 'dus dbu phyogs*

    The prayers in this section placate the various spirits associated with death, such as the sprites of the cemeteries and others. It consists of entreaties, offerings, and exalting the power and virtues of the enlightened beings associated with Bön.

11. *bstan bsrung rdo rje legs pa srod bsgrub dam nyams srog gi thog mda'* (thunderbolt arrow) *dbu phyogs.*

    This text serves to incite to action a class of protectors subjugated in the past and bound by oaths, the *damchen* (*dam can*), as well as to remind them of their duty. The protectors include Dorjé Legpa (Dor rje legs pa), who was subjugated by Padmasambhava and became the protector of Nyingmapas in general.

12. *dam can rgya mtsho mkha' la rang bzhin gyis bsad gsol* (request to slay) *dbu phyogs*

    The *bsad pa* (slaying) rite is accomplished toward the end of a retreat, or in cases where offending spirits have to be "liberated" by severing their life-force and transferring their principle of consciousness to a better realm. At Yeshé Monastery, this rite is not one that is frequently performed. When it has to be done, a senior lama is usually requested to perform it. It is believed that the practice of this rite shortens one's life. This one in particular involves the participation of the *damchen* protectors, mentioned earlier. It is not yet clear to me whether this rite is also used to subjugate and bind by oath would-be *damchen* spirits. (See also the discussion of slaying rites in chapter 3 by Mayer and Cantwell in this volume.)

13. *grub mtha'i rgyal po sangs gyas gling pa'i lugs kyi nyer mkho* (requisites) *zur 'degs* (lifting of a part?) *sgron me dbus phyogs*

    The shortened title of this booklet should be *nyerkho* (*nyer mkho*) or "requisites," according the ritual tradition of Sangyé Lingpa (Sangs rgyas gling pa, b. 1705), the founder of the Bönsar tradition, regarded as the third incarnation of Loden Nyingpo (Blo ldan snyin po, b. 1360), and master of Kündrö Dragpa (Kun grol drag pa). Instead, it uses the enigmatic term of *zurdeg* (*zur 'degs*), whose exact meaning eludes me. The text in fact includes many different mantras that ought to be recited at various moments of the performance of selected rites; it also indicates the drumbeat and other ritual miscellanea.

14. *sku gsum khro rgyal las bsad pa dam nyams* (slaying meditation) *srog gshed*

    This is the actual rite of slaying using the "power" of the three deities of this cycle alluded to earlier.

15. *sde brgyad rgyal bsen kun phung sbyin bsreg* (*homa* or burnt offering) *dzwa dmar ba'i 'khyil pa*

    The burnt offering rite concludes all retreats, just as it does the full performance of the Tamdrin ritual involving the burning stone sequence described in this chapter.

16. *rma bya dug 'joms* (conquering poison, i.e., the white stone rite) *dzwa dbal chu bcas ba*

    This is the text of the rite of the burning stone described earlier in this chapter.

17. *dbal khyung nag po'i rgyud klu gnyan 'dul ba'i* (subduing of *nāgas* and *nyen*) *gdon khrol*

    As the title suggests, this text seeks to use the powers of the Black Garuḍa to subjugate offending *nāgas* and *nyen* spirits. (See chapter 2 by Karmay in this volume.)

18. *rta mgrin dpa' bo gcig pa'i dbang chog* (empowerment) *bde ba'i yan lag*

    This is the ritual of empowerment to the practices and meditations of this cycle of rites.

Five texts are essential during any general practice of the Tamdrin corpus. These are the auxiliary rites manual, the individual rites of the three deities, and that of the protectors. In keeping with the New Treasure tradition, these are fairly concise practices.

The Auxiliary Rites Manual

Text no. 2 in the aforementioned list (and the set of prayers from other sources that are to be added at key moments), the auxiliary rites manual (*cha lag las byang*), contains the basic elements that form the core of the ritual. It is a framework of miscellaneous rites that support whichever of the three central "root texts" is recited in a given context. The rites of this manual are used to introduce, as well as to conclude the general ritual. They are mandatory to the performance of more advanced practices, such as those involving the burning stones, the ritual slaying of hindering spirits, as well as fire offerings and others. The colophon of the auxiliary rites manual tells us that these "few words of great meaning, which are like wish-fulfilling gem, were obtained the 15th of the fifth month of a fire dragon year" (f. 128). This would correspond to the year spanning 1556 and 1557. It states that it is the secret heart of the exalted ones of both Bön and Chö (Chos, i.e., Buddhism), and makes references to the Teacher Shenrab and to the Buddha Śākyamuni. It is therefore a practice that is perceived as deliberately bridging the two creeds. This, the text continues, is to be kept secret from the kind of vow-violators who have wrong views.

The different sections of texts to be recited during the performance are quite standard—common to both Tibetan Buddhist and Yungdrung Bön (G.yung drung bon). One finds such rites as the offering of the white *torma* (*dkar gtor*) to mundane deities, to the guardians of the quarters, and to the heads of the eight classes of gods and demons (*lha srin*) (f. 18), offerings of a host of different *tormas* suited to the recipient beings, and ransom *tormas* (*glud gtor*) for ransom rites used to secure and protect the site of the performance from opposing spirits (f. 19). One also finds inner-offerings consecrations (f. 19), seven-limbed prayers and meditations (ff. 19–20), going for refuge, generating *bodhicitta*, confession of sins, prayer to the masters of the lineage, delimiting the sacred space (*mtshams bcad*) (f. 22), generation of the three central deities, and mantra recitations to control *nāgas*, *rakṣasas*, and other spirits, as well as rites for purification, etc. (ff. 26–29). It also contains concluding prayers and offerings to be recited after the main meditation or the practice of other rituals.

Propitiation

The next three texts, which correspond to texts nos. 4, 5, and 6 in the list mentioned earlier, are the root texts of each of the three deities of this corpus. These are, of course, Tamdrin as the manifestation of the enlightened body of Tönpa Shenrab, Chagna Dorjé as his enlightened speech manifestation, and Khyung as his mind manifestation. In the course of the acquisition of the lineage, the practitioner has to concentrate on one deity for a given period of time. This involves the repetition of mantras, visualizations, and other related meditation techniques. When the ritual is performed for patrons, all three texts are recited one after the other in each section. For example, when the officiant recites the "Requests to the Lamas of the Lineage," *Lagyü Söldeb* (*brgyud gsol 'debs*), of the Tamdrin text, at the conclusion of this section, he switches to the *Söldeb* of Chagna, and then to the Khyung *Söldeb* section. Once the recitations of the three different parts are completed, he passes on to the next sections of the rite in the Tamdrin manual and follows a similar procedure with the other texts. The whole recitation thus includes the propitiation of the three deities.

The three texts that constitute the central practices (*dngos gzhi*) in question are relatively short, no more than thirteen folios for Tamdrin, eleven folios for Chagna, and ten folios for Khyung. They are overall fairly homogeneous and follow similar, if not identical, developments in the unfolding of the different sections during the performance. That is, they follow the similar patterns of *torma* offerings, followed by the setting up of the sacred perimeter, then the self-generation (*bdag bskyed*) or front-generation (*mdun sbkyed*), and so on. There then follows the inevitable mantra recitations for accomplishment, followed by praises, hymns, and auspicious verses.

Protectors

The last required section or rite is the daily propitiation of the protective deities. These are of a general nature, but do contain verses addressed to the main general protectors of Bön such as Sipé Gyalmo (Srid pa'i rgyal mo). A common feature of all these are the constant offerings of *torma*. Here, lamas add offerings, praises, and requests to their own individual protectors and to those of their respective lineage or monastery. The practitioners again reestablish the sacred perimeter, then pray to the knowledge-holders (*rig 'dzin*), such as Tönpa Shenrab, consecrate offerings, invoke the main deity, Hayagrīva, erect the palace of the gods, then invite them to be present, make offerings, and finally request their activities.

The Rite of the Burning Stones

The ritual which brought us to this research was a form of exorcism using burning quartz stones carried in an open unprotected palm and then thrown into a cauldron of water mixed with nine poisons. The historical origin of this tradition is still to be determined. The text of the practice is *The Peacock Conqueror of Poison, Fiercely Stepping on the Waters* (*Rma bya dug 'joms dzwa dbal chu bcas*). It is uncertain whether or not Yungdrung Tenpé Gyaltsen was the author. There are no indications of its authorship or when it was written. The introduction to the ritual emphasizes that during the age of degeneration, to benefit sentient beings, following the practices of the faithful yogis, the yogi Pema Jungné went to the southwest to tame the *sin* (*srin*) demons of the cemeteries. At that time he was practicing the three deities, Tamdrin, Chagna, and Khyung. Then, the lord of the *sin* demons, Hadha(?)-one-eyed, was born. Transforming himself, he manifested nine snouts which were primarily ignorance and sloth. He manifested also as a black boar with nine heads, the cause being a *rakṣasa* of pride with nine heads, nine hands, nine feet, on his back. From his nine mouths and nine noses he spread allotments of covetousness and desires. His nine eyes spread allotments of epilepsy and poison. His nine heads spread allotments of poisonous warfare. He was subdued by Pema Jungné using the three deities: Tamdrin, Chagna, and Khyung.

The ritual describes the method to prepare oneself and the materials needed for the rite, and then proceeds through its various steps. The successive sections of this ritual follow a template common to other similar rites and begins with the delimitation of the sacred space; then going for refuge; prayers for realization; invitation and the bringing down of the deities; offerings; self-generation as the three deities; recitation of the mantras; the handling of the nine stones with mantras and visualization; the sprinkling of the patients with the transmuted, formerly poisonous water for the sake of purifying them; offering of praises; praising the body of Chagna; the offering *torma;* and request for activities.

The stones are heated to the point of becoming incandescent, and then one by one are put on the open, unprotected hand of the officiating lama. The latter then circles the patients with his palm while reciting a mantra. He then proceeds to throw the stones, as described earlier, into the cauldron filled with water in which nine poisonous substances have been placed. The poisons are believed to be transformed into a beneficent and curative substance by the stones. Using juniper twigs, the lama then sprinkles the patients with the water.

A later part of the rite consists of tying threads of five colors to poplar twigs and intertwining the other ends to the individual fingers of the patients. The threads are then cut while the lama intones prayers and entreaties. This is believed to cut off noxious influences from the five elements after transferring the evil spirits afflicting the patients to the poplar twigs. The twigs are then taken away and thrown or burnt without ceremony.

The following morning the final concluding prayers are performed after the rite is completed with a last propitiation of the three deities, who are then asked to leave. A proper full recitation of this ritual of Tamdrin lasts two days and a morning. Practitioners sometime hold impromptu sessions in their home, which may last only half a day. The elaborate powder fire altar is then replaced with the kitchen stove and "the five colored ribbons" rite altogether dispensed with. Such hurried application of the rite is conducted when it is performed for friends and fellow monks without remunerations, and in informal settings.

Reflections on the Practice

Reasons for the Performance

According to Anyi Lama and one of his most sought-after disciples, Tagbön (Stag bon, alias G.yung drung bstan 'dzin), there are various reasons why patrons request such rituals, most of them related to health issues. Problems mentioned by patrons range from general weakness, skin infections, symptoms resembling arthritis and rheumatism, to specific, previously diagnosed illnesses of all kinds. A less-frequent demand is to dispel a repeated series of bad luck events, repeated unfortunate incidents, and unhealthy living conditions. Tagbön has mentioned to me that in cases of bad luck, he usually first conducts a divination session in order to ascertain the nature of the offending spirits. In cases of malignant sprites, but not *lu/nāga*, he will use the Purba ritual.[21] Tamdrin is judged very efficacious for troubles caused by the *lu* water-spirits.

Patronage

Patrons who requested the performance of this ritual, more often than not at home, belong in the majority of cases to the Bönpo community. Each monastery receives the support of a certain number of households, which supply its sons to the institution, but which in return request ritual services for life. These requests are not, however, free. The amount of remuneration any given monk will receive is the result of the monk's seniority, expertise in the practice of the rite, as well as his station in the greater monastic hierarchy. For example, a reincarnate master (*sprul sku*) will definitely earn more than a nonreincarnate monk. Specialists like Tagbön will earn more than others who have not completed the proper retreat, but not as much as an abbot (*mkhan po*), a lama with higher administrative rank within the monastery's hierarchy, or a ritual master like Anyi Lama.

Patrons from other Bönpo communities apparently request the performance of the Tamdrin ritual with some regularity. Buddhist families also request it. The relationships between the Bönpos and lay Buddhists seemed in many respect to be one of perceived necessity. Buddhist families usually request rituals from monks of their own Buddhist communities. When these patrons are not satisfied with the outcome, or if they receive a divination that spirits are still plaguing them, Bönpo monks are asked to perform the rite. Although Bönpos do not object to this, it is relatively rare to have Bönpo monks come back to the same Buddhist household that has had other rites performed on its behalf, unless there has been a call specifically for Bönpos. Thus, in contemporary Tibet, Bönpos still fulfill some role within the larger Tibetan society.

On the Popularity of the Burning Stone Ritual

This ritual of Tamdrin may be unique among the arsenal of ritual weapons of contemporary Bönpos. However, there are oral traditions within this community which allude to similar dramatic rites involving the deity Belsé (Dbal gsas) and the manipulation of red-hot iron rods. I encountered anecdotes to this effect among the monks of Yeshé Monastery, and it may allude to other local rites similar to the Tamdrin one which are high in their dramatic content. Aside from the area around the Kharag Monastery in the Derge (Sde dge) region, perhaps, our ritual is not currently performed outside of Nyagrong. If it is, as it was a few years ago in the Amdo Sharkhog (A mdo shar khog) area, it was due to the presence of a Yeshé monk (namely Tagbön) who was on pilgrimage there.

The dramatic aspects of this practice—that is, the feat of a Bönpo monk handling red-hot stones with bare hands—definitely plays an important role in the perceived value and power of such a ritual. Even among the Bönpo monks who have supported its performance many times and have completed the requisite retreat, very few have the nerve to try handling the red-hot stones. This is undoubtedly why the main practitioners of this rite are seen as being entitled to some measure of charisma and ritual authority. I would argue that it is precisely this dramatic element that gives this rite its perceived value. This value is attributed to the ritual by its patrons, who recognize this sort of rite as being powerful and efficient. Its high demand in Nyagrong makes it lucrative for a monk who is seeking support for his livelihood. Whether it always fulfills the expectation of its clients is not the point here. There are many explanations that monks and patrons offer to explain the rite's failure to secure health or healing. On the one hand, then, the popularity of this rite has a great deal to do with its dramatic elements. One the other, this rite thrives in an environment which has either come to take the ritual for granted or else where the rite has attained the status of a fashion. The law of supply and demand might just be the very reason why some rites thrive and eventually cross the boundaries of creed and religion. This could help us to understand cross-sectarian ritual cycles such as Purba, Hayagrīva, and Severance or Chö (Gcod). This observation, however, takes us beyond the topic of this chapter and has to be addressed in subsequent publications.

Connection of this Practice to Buddhism

I should add that the presence of Buddhist elements in this rite as well as in other similar ritual traditions belonging to the Bön New Treasures movement might partially be explained by appeal to the just-mentioned phenomenon of a ritual's popularity. In addition, however, I feel that Buddhism, having permeated all aspects of Tibetan society and culture for such a long period of time, has transformed Tibetan culture to the point of being almost totally blended within it. Tibetans recognize as theirs Buddhist elements, symbols, deities, and practices. Contemporary Bön, on the other hand, is nativistic in principle. It identifies itself with the original indigenous religious culture, and portrays itself as the rightful heir to these traditions from antiquity. Given that Buddhism has been assimilated for well over a millennium in Tibet, it is not surprising to see a competing religion (Bön) restating aspects of it. In fact, a historical study of local traditions of Bön may help gage the level of assimilation of Buddhism throughout time in different areas of Tibet. Understanding Bön as borrowing or plagiarizing from Buddhism may in fact demonstrate a poor understanding of Tibetan culture. Buddhologists may well recognize phenomena pertaining to their specialty in all aspects of Tibetan society. This alone, however, does not make Tibetan society a Buddhist society *tout court*. Indigenous, non-Buddhist elements and cultural artifacts continue to be expressed. Although these expressions inevitably contain Buddhist themes, and references to Buddhist values, to see Tibet as a "Buddhist society" in any simple way may makes one blind to the layers and complexity present within it. This seems to me to be especially true when one examines popular cults and Bön. Similarly, to recognize Buddhist elements within Bönsar does not makes Bön any less Bönpo, nor does it make it either more Buddhist or a heterodox branch of Buddhism. Buddhist polemicists will readily push for the two latter conclusions, but their assertions have not changed Bönpos' beliefs or understanding of their religion, nor do the view of "experts outsiders" when they argue for this same agenda. Bönpos decide, in any case, what their practices and religion are. Our task as scholars should not be to support value-laden agendas—for example, that Bön is crypto-Buddhist—but to understand Bönpo religion in all its complexity, including its social functions, history, and other aspects. In this regard, a simple-minded reduction of Bön to Buddhism is counterproductive.

This being said, there are unmistakable symbols that exhibit Buddhist as well as Indian and Chinese influences in Bönpo rites. This particular cycle of ritual focuses on Hayagrīva (an undeniably Indian deity), Vajrapāni (definitely Buddhist), and Garuḍa (another pan-Indian and Southeast Asian popular deity). The different ritual stages of the complete rite follows a pattern that can be found in other contemporary Buddhist rituals of the same genre, with the exception of the burning stone element. The mantras of the three deities in this corpus are variants of those found in Buddhist *sādhanas*.

Conclusions

Tamdrin in Bön is present since at least the fifteenth century when the *Ziji* (*Gzi brjid*) was written. This corresponds to the height of Nyingmapa activities relating to the Hayagrīva, and it can reasonably be argued that the Bönpo phenomenon of Tamdrin is somehow related to the Nyingma practice, at least ritually. Bönpos considered Tamdrin to belong to their pantheon of enlightened beings, and to be an emanation of Tönpa Shenrab. In the ritual traditions of Yeshé Monastery in Nyagrong, the practice of Tamdrin comes from revelations imparted to a sixteenth-century lama from Kharag Monastery in Pelyul. Present masters of this lineage at Yeshé represent a seventh generation of practitioners. Their trademark is the practice of the burning stones that cure illnesses and transmute poisons. This rite involves the handling of red-hot quartz stones with bare hands and is a dramatic method of healing and exorcism. The practitioner of this ritual receives regular requests from Bönpo, local and translocal, and from Buddhist patrons, who request that the rite be performed in their houses for the benefit of afflicted members of the family. This unique rite guarantees a steady income for its officiating monks and masters, both from the local area and from the outside. It fulfills the important role of alternative spiritual care for suffering patients and their relatives. This particular rite also exhibits a degree of assimilation of Buddhist elements which may help in measuring the assimilation of Buddhism within a specific area of Tibetan culture and society.

NOTES

1. On this monastery, see Samten G. Karmay and Yasuhiko Nagano, eds. *A Survey of Bonpo Monasteries and Temples in Tibet and the Himalaya*, Bon Studies 7 (Osaka: National Museum of Ethnology, 2003), 420–25. Also Seng ge sprul sku rig 'dzin nyi ma, *Nyag rong ye shes dgon pa'i lo rgyus* (Chengdu: Privately Published, 2004).

2. This is my provisional title of a ritual compendium entitled *Sku gsum khro rgyal gyis ngo g.yo dri ma 'jig skyobs g.yung drung go cha* in 216 folios which is used at Ye shes monastery. The monks use the generic appellation of *Rta mgrin skor*. This is discussed later.

3. Kamala Nayar, *Hayagrīva in South India: Complexity and Selectivity of a Pan-Indian Hindu Deity* (Leiden: Brill, 2004).

4. Nayar, *Hayagriva in South India*, 27–28.

5. "The Cult of Peaceful and Wrathful Avalokiteśvara at Sera Monastery," in *Bodhisattva Avalokiteśvara (Guanyin) and Modern Society: Proceedings of the Fifth Chung Hwa International Conference on Buddhism*, ed. William McGee and Yi-hsun Huang (Taipei: Dharma Drum Publishing, 2007), 35–64.

6. *'Dus pa rin po che dri ma med pa gzi brjid rab tu 'bar ba'i mdo*, Bon po bka' 'gyur (Chengdu: Ha sa yon and Bon slob Nam mkha' bstan 'dzin, 1991, second print) vols.1–12. On the different versions of the Bon po bKa' 'gyur as well as a collated index of these, see Dan Martin (general editor), Per Kvaerne (project coordinator), Yasuhiko Nagano (series editor), *A Catalogue of the Bon Kanjur*, Bon Studies 8, Senri Ethnolgical Reports 40 (Osaka: National Museum of Ethnology, 2003).

7. *Lha mthu chen dang lha ma yin sde lnga dbang du bsdus nas bon bstan pa'i mdo las rta mgrin rgyal po'i gzungs*, Bon po brten 'gyur chen mo (Lhasa: Sod ldan Bstan pa'i nyi ma, 1998), vol. 106, no. 59, ff.1489–1512, hereafter *The Lore of the King Rta mgrin*. See also Samten G. Karmay and Yasuhiko Nagano, eds., *A Catalogue of the New Collection of Bonpo Katen Texts—indices*, Bon Studies 5, Senri Ethnolgical Reports 25, with CD-ROM (Osaka: National Museum of Ethnology, 2001), and Samten G. Karmay and Yasuhiko Nagano, eds., *A Catalogue of the New Collection of Bonpo Katen Texts*, Bon Studies 4, Senri Ethnolgical Reports 24 (Osaka: National Museum of Ethnology 2001).

8. *The Lore of King Rta mgrin*, ff. 1492–93.

9. *The Lore of King Rta mgrin*, ff. 1493–96.

10. The Taishō versions are: *Da kongque mingwang huaxiang tanchang yigui* (Taishō 983), *Kongque wang zhoujing* (Taishō 984), *Da kongque wang zhoujing* (Taishō 985), *Da jinse kongque wang zhou* (Taishō 986); *Da jinse kongque wang zhoujing* (Taishō 987); *Kongque wang zhoujing* (Taishō 988); *Kongque wang zhoujing* (Taishō 988). The Tibetan versions are found in the *rgyud* section of the Bka' 'gyur, *Rig sngas kyi rgyal mo rma bya chen mo*, in Daisetz T. Suzuki, ed., *The Tibetan Tripiṭaka, Peking Edition* (Kyotō: Tibetan Tripitaka Research Institute, Otani University), vol. 7, Rgyud XV, no. 178, 111–25. See also The Digital Sanskrit Buddhist Canon website at http://www.uwest.edu/sanskrit-canon/; The University of the West, Los Angeles, Nagarjuna Institute of Exact Methods (A Center For Buddhist Studies) Chakupat, Lalitpur, Nepal, catalogued as: K 303, K 304, K 305, K 306, K 307, K 373, K 1293, and K 1375. See also its study by des Jardins, *Le Sūtra de la Mahāmāyūrī: rituel et politique dans la Chine des Tang (618–906)* (Québec: Les Presses de l'Université Laval, forthcoming).

11. Kuo, Li-ying, "La recitation des noms de BUDDHA en Chine et au Japon," *T'oung Pao*, no. 81 (1995): 230–68, and for an example of such scriptures, see MS 2153 of the Schøyen Collection in London: http://www.schoyencollection.com/china.htm.

12. *Lingbao wuliang durenpin miao jing*, Zhentong daozang 1. See also Kristofer Schipper and Franciscus Verellen, eds., *The Taoist Canon: A Historical Companion to the Daozang* (Daozang tongkao) (Chicago: University of Chicago Press, 2004–05).

13. See Michel Strickmann, *Mantras et mandarins: le Bouddhisme tantrique en Chine*, Bibliothèque des sciences humaines (Paris: Gallimard, 1996).

14. Gshen gsang ba 'dus pa is understood in Bön as the main teacher during the first eon of the propagation of Bön. He is considered the main transmitter of the secret teachings of the Tantra.

15. Karmay, *A Treasury of Good Sayings*, 42–43.

16. This is, of course, Padmasambhava. On Padmasambhava in the New Terma movement of Bön, see Samten G. Karmay, *Feast of the Morning Light: The Eighteenth Century Wood-engravings of Shenrab's Life-stories and the Bon Canon from Gyalrong*, Bon Studies 9, Senri Ethnological Reports 57 (Osaka: National Museum of Ethnology, 2005); and Anne-Marie Blondeau, "Mkhyen-bre'i dba-po: la biographie de Padmasambhava selon la tradition du bsgrags-pa bon, et ses sources," in *Orientalia Iosephi Tucci Memoriae Dicata*, ed. G. Gnoli & L. Lanciotti, 2 vols. (Rome: *Istituto italiano per il Medio ed Estremo Oriente* 1988), 1: 111–58.

17. See Karmay and Nagano, *A Survey of Bonpo Monasteries*, 396–400.

18. His biography was written by Seng ge sprul sku rig 'dzin nyi ma, *Bla ma a g.yung gi rnam thar dang mchog rgyal gyi rnam thar* (Chengdu: Si khrun lho nub mi rig slob grwa'i par khang, 2003).

19. See William M. Gorvine, "The Life of a Bonpo Luminary: Sainthood, Partisanship and Literary Representation in 20th Century Tibetan Biography," Ph.D. diss., University of Virginia, Charlottesville, 2006. His biography has been published separately: Bskal bzang bstan pa'i rgyal mtshan, *Shar rdzas ba bkra shis rgyal mtshan gyi rnam thar* (Chengdu: Si khron mi rigs dpe skrun khang, 1988).

20. See his autobiography, the *'Gro 'dul bstan gnyis gsar gling pa'i skye gnas bar do'i rnam par thar pa brjod pa sgyu ma'i 'khrul 'khor*, in Bon gyi brten 'gyur chen mo, vol. 149, no. 4, 443–798.

21. At Ye shes Monastery, the Phur gsar cycle of Gsang sngags gling pa is used most frequently. The Phur rnying is considered to be too complicated and lengthy for practicing at patrons' houses. On the Phur ba cycle of rites, see also chapter 3 by Cantwell and Mayer in this volume.

9

Texts as Deities

Mongols' Rituals of Worshipping Sūtras, and Rituals of Accomplishing Various Goals by Means of Sūtras

VESNA A. WALLACE

From an impressively large variety of Mongolian Buddhist rituals, I have selected for discussion in this chapter two types of rituals: (1) those involving the veneration of popular Mahāyāna *sūtras* that are accepted as tutelary deities (*yi dam*) by the Mongols and that promise various mundane and spiritual blessings to those who venerate, copy, and recite them, and (2) the protective and healing rituals that integrate the recitation of these *sūtras* for the sake of pragmatic aims. I hope that this brief analysis will shed light on some of the ways in which these rituals illuminate Mongolian Buddhist culture and prevailing attitudes toward ritual, particularly toward the ritual role of certain Mahāyāna scriptures.

The Sanctity of Sūtras, and Sanctification by Means of Sūtras

Before examining the rituals just mentioned, it may be useful to first provide a brief discussion of the Mongols' worldview concerning the scriptures whose worship will be examined later in this chapter. First of all, in the Mongolian language, the word *nom* (inherited from the Sogdian *nmw* through Uighur[1]) designates both a book and the Dharma, implying that the Mongols do not differentiate between the two. The second line in the salutary words found at the beginning of many Mongolian Buddhist texts states: "I pay homage to the Dharma (*nom*),"[2] implying one's homage to both the Dharma as an abstraction and to the physical book. The Mongols' reverence for Buddhist scriptures is also expressed in the texts prescribing the various methods of worshipping *sūtras* and *tantras*, making offerings to them, and even giving them alms as if they were living monks or *śrāmaṇas*.[3]

Traditionally, the most venerated Mahāyāna *sūtra* in Mongolia has been the *Aṣṭasāhasrikāprajñāpāramitā Sūtra*.[4] Reportedly, already in the thirteenth century, the Mongols obtained what has come to be known as "Nāgārjuna's copy" of this *sūtra*, which was written in the *lentsa* (*lan tsha, rañjana*) script on seventy birch wood leaves. Since then, the *Aṣṭasāhasrikā* has been copied, translated, and printed numerous times. As in Tibet, every Mongolian monastery contains a copy of the *Aṣṭasāhasrikāprajñāpāramitā*, which is placed on top of the *Kangyur* (*Bka' 'gyur*) collection in recognition of its preeminence over other texts. While the *Aṣṭasāhasrikāprajñāpāramitā* has been chiefly utilized by Buddhist clergy, almost every Buddhist household possesses numerous copies of the *Vajracchedikāprajñāpāramitā Sūtra*, *Suvarṇaprabhāsottama Sūtra*, and *Āryāpāramitāyurjñāna Sūtra*. The *Suvarṇaprabhāsottama*, popularly known as the *Altangerel*,[5] the *Vajracchedikā*, known as the *Ochiroor Ogtlogch*, and the *Aparamitāyurjñāna*, mostly known as the *Tsendü*, have been the most popular and most frequently recited Mahāyāna *sūtras* in Mongolia owing to their respective content, functions, and to the usages assigned to them by Mongolian Buddhist authors and rulers. The popularity of the first two aforementioned *sūtras* can be attributed to several political and religious factors.

In the case of the *Suvarṇaprabhāsottama*, its uniqueness lies in its sanctification of royal power, its call for the loyalty of subjects to their kings, and in its explicit and primary concern with the mundane well-being of society. It is for this reason that its translations were widely distributed, its significance for the courts of the Mongol *khans* being to strengthen their political power and to elevate their royal status to that of divine sons (*tengri-yin köbegün, devaputra*) and universal monarchs (*cakravartin*). On the basis of the data available in the colophons to Mongolian translations of the *Suvarṇaprabhāsottama*, Tsendiin Damdinsüren[6] and Shagdaryn Bira[7] tried to reconstruct the history of this *sūtra* in Mongolia. According to the colophons, the first Mongolian translation of the *sūtra* dates to the beginning of the fourteenth century, when the Sakya scholar Sharavsenge (Tib. Shes rab seng ge) translated it from Tibetan, while consulting Uighur and Chinese versions. Bira's analysis of the colophon of what Damdinsüren calls colophon "A," suggests the year 1332 as the exact date of Sharavsenge's translation. It may be especially significant that this was the period after the enthronement of Toγan Temür Khan, the last Mongol *khan* of the Yüan Empire, suggesting it may have been a last-ditch effort to preserve

Mongol reign. The colophon praises the *khan* for his support of the translation of the *sūtra*, deems him a Bodhisattva who has never abandoned the spirit of awakening (*bodhicitta*) and compares him to the Bodhisattva Avalokiteśvara in exhibiting the latter's qualities of peacefulness, tolerance, and gentleness.[8] This first translation of the *sūtra* instigated the first wave of its popularity.

Another important phase in the history of the worship of the *Suvarṇa-prabhāsottama* was the reign of Altan Khan (1507–81), who was responsible for its large-scale reproduction and its widest distribution among the Mongols. The colophon to the manuscript held in the Oriental collections of the Hungarian Academy of Sciences in Budapest and studied by György Kara mentions a ritual consecration of the printing of the *sūtra* by decree of Altan Khan in 1584.[9] Since the time of Altan Khan, thirty different Mongolian versions of the *Suvarṇaprabhāsottama* have been produced in Mongolia.[10]

In the case of the *Vajracchedikā*, one of the factors that contributed to its popularity in Mongolia was the decree of the Manchu emperor Kangxi (1661–1772). That decree mandated that all Mongolian households keep in their possession the *Vajracchedikā*, along with the other four texts: *Aṣṭasāhasrikā*, *Suvarṇaprabhāsottama*, *Pañcarakṣā*, and *Sangdui* (Tib. *Gzungs bsdus*, a collection of *dhāraṇīs*), also known in Mongolia as *Nuutsyn Khuraangui*. Another factor was the proliferation of Mongolian commentarial works on this *sūtra*, which began in the late sixteenth century, and which emphasized its unique significance and limitless powers.

Although the Mongols had encountered the *Vajracchedikā* at the latest in the fourteenth century, when they acquired a copy of the Kangyur, written in Tibetan and known as "Butön's copy," the earliest Mongolian translation of the *Vajracchedikā* dates back at least to the formation of the Mongolian Kangyur in the late sixteenth and early seventeenth centuries.

The catalogue of the archives of the St. Petersburg Branch of the Institute of Oriental Studies of the Russian Academy of Sciences alone lists fifteen Mongolian versions of commentaries on the *Vajracchedikā:* two consist of twenty-two chapters, one consists of thirteen chapters, and the rest consist of fifteen chapters.[11] Other versions with thirteen, fifteen, and twenty-two chapters are kept in the State Central Library in Ulaanbaatar and in the Royal Library in Copenhagen. The study of Mongolian commentaries on the *Vajracchedikā* reveals that their authors were not particularly intent on interpreting and elucidating the doctrinal points of the *sūtra*, but were almost entirely concerned with its magical powers and with the great benefits it procures for those who worship, recite, teach, and copy it. One of the most renowned of such commentaries is the text entitled *The Sūtra that Explains the Benefits of the Vajracchedikā* (*Včir-iyar oγtaluγči-yin ači tusa-yin nomlaγsan sudur*),[12] which was most likely composed in the late sixteenth century. In subsequent centuries, it appeared in numerous manuscript versions. Different versions of this commentarial text contain descriptions of the extraordinary powers of the *Vajracchedikā*, illustrated in the narratives depicting the ways in which various individuals and groups of people benefited from it. These stories provide the reader with some insight into the functions and uses of the *Vajracchedikā* in Mongolia and the reasons behind them. In the twenty-first chapter of a long version of this commentary, it is written that the god Indra, accompanied by a retinue of 80,000 gods, having attended and delighted in the Buddha's teaching on the *Vajracchedikā*, promised their help to those who recite the *sūtra*—so that they may accomplish any task both in the present and in future lives. To guarantee this promise, Indra sealed the *sūtra*, and for this reason the *Vajracchedikā* has ever since been referred to also as the "sealed *sūtra*" (*tamgat sudar*) that contains limitless blessings.[13] The twenty-second chapter of the same text explains twenty-two ways in which the power of this "sealed *sūtra*" can contribute to one's well-being by way of its transformative, curative, protective, and soteriological efficacy. It is the indestructible weapon that cuts off all forms of suffering at its root.

Like the *Suvarṇaprabhāsottama*, it facilitates rebirth in the heavens of Sukhāvatī and Tuṣita; it prevents wars, prolongs one's life span, and brings about Buddhahood. Yama, the lord of death, himself recognizing in his encounters with the dead that the powers of the *sūtra* exceed his own, desires that the *sūtra* be recited for his benefit as well. In one example, Lord Yama bestows a gift of silk to a dead monk who recites the *sūtra* for him in his palace, and he sends the monk back to the world of the living, where he enjoys a long life to the age of ninety-five. To benefit from the *sūtra*'s power, one is not required to fathom the depths of its meaning, but one is advised to have faith in it, venerate it, and make various offerings to it. The commentary strongly encourages one to worship the *sūtra* as one's own chosen deity (*yi dam, iṣṭa-devatā*) or to recite it to those who have accepted it as their chosen deity.

We know why the *Vajracchedikā* has gained the status of a chosen deity in Mongolia from accounts that have been handed down and preserved to this day in the oral tradition. According to this tradition, as the "king of the perfection of wisdom" (*prajñāpāramitā-rāja*), the *Vajracchedikā* contains the quintessence of the *prajñāpāramitā*. It is for this reason that the nineteenth-century author Davagjaltsan (Güüsh Girdi Duaz), in his *Explanation of the Vajracchedikā*, praises the *sūtra* as the highest among all the teachings of the Buddha.[14] As a container of the essence of the *prajñāpāramitā*, the *Vajracchedikā* has been viewed as a symbol of emptiness and as the quintessence of the *sūtrayāna* as a whole. As such, it has been treated as a counterpart to another highly esteemed and popular text in Mongolia, the *Guhyasamāja Tantra*, which, being a "king of *tantras*" (*tantra-rāja*) has stood as a symbol of bliss and as the epitome of the *tantrayāna*. These two texts traditionally have been bound together in a cloth cover (*bar-indag*), placed in the same box, and kept on the household altar as objects of veneration. Bound together in this way, as the *yab yum*, they signified the union of bliss and emptiness and the union of the *sūtrayāna* and *tantrayāna*.[15] Representing in this way the Buddha's *dharmakāya* understood as both the Buddha's mind and the body of his teachings, the presence of these two texts in one's home has indicated the blessing-bestowing presence of the Buddha and his Dharma, which consecrates and transforms one's ordinary dwelling into a shrine (*caitya*).[16] This accords with the passage of the *Vajracchedikā* in which the Buddha points out that any part of the world in which this *sūtra* is propagated will become like a shrine (*caitya*), honored by gods, men, and evil spirits. Therefore, every Mongolian home that contains the *sūtra* may at times function as a shrine. The twenty-second chapter of a long version of the *Sūtra that Describes the Benefits of the Vajracchedikā*[17] tells of people who showed their reverence to the *sūtra* by carrying it on their heads, while circumambulating their homes and *stūpas*.

Both texts, the *Vajracchedikā* and the *Guhyasamāja Tantra*, have been also used by Mongolian Buddhists as talismans. For this purpose, these two texts have been produced in small pocket-size copies (Figure 9.1). Traditionally,

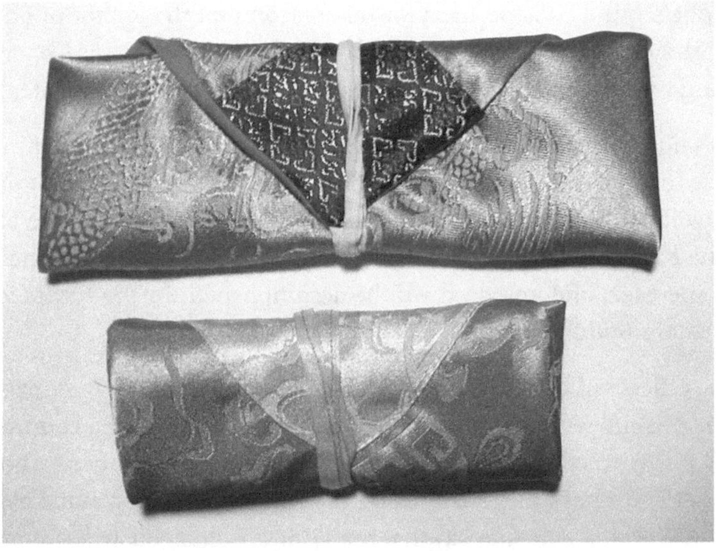

FIGURE 9.1. Two pocket-sized texts from Mongolia, one of the *Vajracchedikā* and the other of the *Guhyasamāja*, wrapped in their traditional cloth covers. Photo: J. Cabezón (2008).

Mongolian monks have carried the *Guhyasamāja* in the pockets of their robes, and lay people have carried the *Vajracchedikā*. In this way, the entire Mongolian Buddhist community has been divided into the carriers of the two aspects of the Buddha's mind—bliss and emptiness—symbolically transforming Mongolian society into the Dharma-body of the Buddha.

The *Guhyasamāja Tantra*, being a textual body of the Buddha, at times has also functioned as the body's preservative. For example, the following practice involving a use of the *Guhyasamāja Tantra* can be still encountered in Mongolia's countryside. When a person living in a remote area dies during the warm summer season and the corpse needs to be preserved from decay until all the relatives of the deceased arrive from different parts of the country, a long cord is wrapped around the *Guhyasamāja Tantra*, and the end of the cord is placed in the mouth of the deceased.

As for the *Vajracchedikā*, its words are deemed an expression of the Buddha's perfection of wisdom, and therefore, the power that dwells in a single page or in two lines of the *sūtra* is believed to have the same efficacy as the power of the entire text. According to the aforementioned commentary, a young servant girl came across a single page of the text and recited two lines from it; she found a wealthy husband and eventually took rebirth in heaven. Moreover, as a unique text that reflects the realm of the Buddha's perfection of wisdom, the *Vajracchedikā* itself comes to be reflected in the understanding of its interpreter, thus making a commentarial text yet another reflection of the Buddha's mind. It is perhaps for this reason that the author of one of the existing versions of the *Explanation of the Benefits of the Vajracchedikā*, a version containing twenty chapters, concludes his commentary with the statement:

> It is said that if one reads or causes others to read, and if one copies or causes others to copy this *Explanation of the Benefits of the Vajracchedikā*, one will surely gain the merit of accomplishing and praising the body of the 84,000 Dharmas; in this life, one's virtue, lifespan, and health will increase, and any deed will be accomplished. In the future, one will attain Buddhahood.[18]

Thus, the efficacy of the *Vajracchedikā* as the expression of the Buddha's awareness does not end with this *sūtra*, but continues in the texts and commentaries in which it is correctly reflected and in the consciousness of those who understand its effectiveness in transforming the mundane and spiritual aspects of life. Because of this, one may say that the *sūtra* simultaneously operates on two planes—the ultimate and conventional. It is the unmediated reality, a pure self-expression of the Buddha, which is unique and non-replicable; and at the same time, it is a reproducible text that has a second author—a person who copies, recites, or explains it, who may or may not correctly reflect the ultimate reality of the text and who inevitably brings to it the perspective of his Mongolian culture, mitigating the *sūtra*'s cultural accommodation. Thus, the *Vajracchedikā* is not to be seen as a static body of words, finalized in time. Rather, it is subject to a continuous process of reflecting the ultimate for as long as it is copied, recited, read, and explained.

In Mongolian Buddhist culture, the approach to a *sūtra* as a representation of the Buddha's mind and body traditionally has not been restricted to the aforementioned Mahāyāna *sūtras* alone, or even to Mahāyāna *sūtras* and *tantras* in general. In Mongolian Buddhist culture, the term *sudar* (Skt. *sūtra*) designates not only the Buddhist canonical sources containing discourses of the Buddha, but also any Buddhist work of Mongolian origin. Upon acquiring the Buddhist canon, the Mongols created their own tradition of the portion of the canon known as the *sūtra piṭaka*, which, according to Mongolian sources, can be classified into different categories—namely, philosophical, historical, prophetic, medical, and veterinary *sūtras*, *sūtras* of omens, *sūtras* of customs, *sūtras* of the signs of places, and *sūtras* of dream signs. To the Mongols, their own *sūtra* tradition constitutes a continuation and enrichment of the canonical *sūtra piṭaka*.[19]

Likewise, as evidenced by their ritual worship and usages, the Mongols' veneration of the book also extends to the summaries of the canonical *sūtras*, which were composed by Mongolian authors.[20]

Rituals of Worshipping *Sūtras* and Ritual Usages of *Sūtras*

The rituals of worshipping the texts discussed earlier and the rituals of accomplishing the desired goal by means of ritual recitation or copying of the texts reveal that one does not need to have a semantic understanding of the texts in order to derive benefits from them, for the extraordinary powers that are inherent in them are always present. However, it is only through the veneration of the *sūtras* and through their ritual recitation that one can set their powers in motion and navigate them in a particular direction.

When examining the sources relevant to the study of a ritual veneration of *sūtras*, one may at first wonder whether it is possible to differentiate clearly between the ritual and nonritual forms of *sūtra* worship. Some of them are easily recognizable as explicitly regulated and stylized performative actions that are characterized by formality and repetition, which are clearly ritualistic, while others appear to be only implicitly so on account of lacking the visible formality and stylization.

The rituals of venerating the *sūtras* can be classified into two groups: private and public. As one looks at the instructions on how to reverently copy or read a *sūtra*, which have traditionally been passed down from teacher to disciple, it becomes evident that the suggested ways of reading and writing down the *sūtra* are private, ritualized practices. For example, the guidelines for copying a text demonstrate that the act of copying is to be approached as the ritual practice of constructing a textual *maṇḍala*. When setting out to copy a text, one is to think of the Buddha Amitābha, and when writing down letters, one is to think of Avalokiteśvara. One should imagine the book's paper to be his incomparable palace and the ink and pen to be his skillful means and wisdom. Lifting the right side of the page is to be imagined as a token of one's respect for the nobility, and lifting the left side of the page as a sign of one's concern for commoners. The upper edge of the page represents the sky, and the lower edge of the page is the golden world, or the earth. The letters are to be imagined as the means of assisting sentient beings by means of one's own various incarnations. At the completion of copying the book, one is to generate the aspiration never to be separated from the Three Jewels in this and all future lives. Only such a way of copying a text is said to be auspicious.

Similarly, in the ritual of reading, or reciting, a *sūtra*, prior to unwrapping the book's cloth cover (*barindag*), one is to generate faith and meditate on the Four Immeasurables (*dörvön tsaglashgüi*). When unwrapping the book, one should imagine oneself as loosening the ties of spiritual ignorance. When placing the book on a table, one is to imagine the four Māras being crushed. The opening of the book should be seen as a meeting with the Buddha. One is to think of the book's hard cover as a Buddha's *maṇḍala*-palace, and the book's paper as his divine silken clothing. Likewise, one is to think of the words in the book as being of the nature (*mön činar, svabhāva*) of the Buddha's body, and the stanzas as being of the nature of spiritual awakening. One should also imagine the dots (Mong. *tseg*, Tib. *tsheg*) as being of the nature of *nirvāṇa* and the lines of the text to be the Bodhisattva path of training. Furthermore, one should look upon the circular pattern of letters as the Buddha's eye of gnosis (*belge bilgiin nüd*, Skt. *jñāna-cakṣu*), and upon the edges of the book as devoid of the two extremes of substantialism and nihilism. And finally, when reading the book aloud, one is to imagine it as the sounding of the Dharma-drum filling the three worlds with a Dharma-song.[21]

These stylized manners of copying and reciting a *sūtra* can be characterized as a regulative type of a ritual, which orients a preexisting activity of reading and writing to that which transcends the ordinary, everyday experience of these activities by transforming their aesthetic and performative styles. As such, they are a withdrawal from the ordinary world into extraordinary space, time, and action. Integrating two different, but simultaneously performed actions—the physical and the mental—these ritualized practices of reading and copying a text activate one's sense-faculties into a reorganization of the experience of the text and into a possible reformulation of knowledge regarding the transcendent nature of both the text and one's own mind and body. Imbued by symbols pointing to the ultimate, these two ritualized practices are the enactments of the idea of the unitary nature of one's own and of the Buddha's mind and body. As such, they function as the medium for the experience of the text not as a mere symbol of ultimate reality, but as the physical and textual embodiment of that reality. In this way, they are the means for replicating the ongoing process of spiritual awakening

While these explicitly formalized methods of venerating *sūtras* easily lend themselves to a ritual interpretation, other reverent modes of reciting or handling a *sūtra* may pose a challenge to the interpreter. Since the ritual's formalized style is only implicitly present in them, they may not at first appear to be ritual actions. Instances of such modes of veneration abound in copious Mongolian versions of texts that illustrate the benefits of worshipping the *Vajracchedikā Sūtra* as one's own tutelary deity. They recount the events in the lives of ordinary individuals who gained desired benefits from reciting the *sūtra* in a nonregulated manner when faced with the immediate dangers of demons, enemies, hell, and so on, or from handling it in a respectful manner, whether fully aware of it or not.[22]

In all the given instances of the recitation of the *Vajracchedikā*, the emphasis is placed on the fact that the utterance of the *sūtra* has mobilized its transformative power and actualized its hidden truth by altering the events, the states of mind, and experiences of everyone involved. In these instances, the recitation of the *sūtra* is not a mere verbalization of its content; it is an enactment of the *sūtra* as a tutelary deity.

Since in all the cases mentioned, the recitation of the *Vajracchedikā* transforms people and events, one can also categorize it as what J. L. Austin and John R. Searle call "an illucotionary act," or a "performative utterance"—that is, an utterance that does not merely say something, but also does something, and is therefore ritualistic. The recitation of the *Vajracchedikā* is an inexplicit performative utterance, which accomplishes things through both its operational and explicitly stated meanings. Therefore, I propose that even the nonstylized and less-formalized modes of reciting the *sūtra*, as exemplified in the various versions of the Mongolian texts on the *Benefits of Worshipping the Vajracchedikā*, can be considered ritualistic.

Furthermore, one also encounters in the Mongolian Buddhist tradition the rituals for worshipping *sūtras* through both offerings and recitations. These rituals do not stand by themselves, but are integrated into multiphased and multileveled rituals that have other functions as well. In these rituals, as in the aforementioned examples, the rites of worshipping the *sūtra* have pragmatic purposes and are not performed for the sake of mere worship. These rituals are not private; they are performed for others and in the presence of others.

An example of such rituals is found in the text called *A Summary of the Āyuḥsūtra or Āryāyurjñāna* (*Khutagt Tseden-ish Buyu Tsend-Ayush Khemeekh Sudryn Quraangui Orshvoi*), which is an abbreviation of the *Aparamitāyurjñāna-mahāyānasūtra*, popularly known among the Mongols as a "children's *sūtra*." The content of the *sūtra* itself predominantly consists of the enumeration of the rewards resulting from its veneration, among which the most emphasized reward is a long lifespan, bestowed by the Tathāgata Aparamitāyurjñānasuviniścayatejorāja, who resides in the Aparamitaguṇasaṃcaya ("Collection of Limitless Virtues") world-system (*loka-dhātu*). The *Summary* primarily functions as a ritual text of benediction for the blessings contained in the *Aparamitāyurjñāna*. It is ritually recited for the sake of the long life of infants and children, and for their protection from the fifteen types of spirits causing fifteen varieties of children's diseases.[23] It is also recited to prolong the life of the elderly who are nearing death. However, the recitation of the *Summary* also performs another function, without which, its main function could not be accomplished. As a container of the essence of the *Aparamitāyurjñāna*, this benedictory text itself is considered worthy of veneration, a fountain of the accumulation of manifold virtues and blessings. Therefore, it should be worshipped and performed on astrologically significant days. The introductory paragraph states this in the following way:

> If one worships, reads, and writes this benediction of the famous *Long-life Sūtra* during the years that coincide with one "black life-force stone" (*amiin chuluu*, Tib. *srog*), one "black body-stone" (*bieiin chuluu*), and one "black life-principle stone" (*süldnii chuluu*, Tib. *bla*), long life and merit will flourish through the line of one's descendents.[24]

In Mongolian astrology, the aforementioned black stones, which signify inauspiciousness, together with white stones as their counterparts, are used in preparing one's yearly horoscope to determine whether the juncture of the three types of significant factors—namely, the five bodily constituents,[25] the element of one's birth year,[26] and the element of a current year—is auspicious or not.[27]

The same paragraph also informs one of the types of offerings[28] that are to be given in the rite of worship that is followed by the recitation of the *sūtra*'s 108-syllable *mantra*.[29] Once the offerings to the *Summary* are made and the *mantra* is recited, the main part of the ritual consists of a recitation of the *Summary* as a benediction. Since a ritual of benediction is efficacious only when the text is properly worshipped, it is to be preceded by the worship of the text through offerings. However, the recitation of the benediction itself is also an act of worshipping the *Aparamitāyurjñāna*. Thus, one rite of worship must be performed so that the second rite of worship can take place. The ritual as a whole clearly has a dual function, which is reflected in its dual performative features—namely, in the performance using multiple media such as offerings intended for the text, and in the performative utterances of the text that are implicitly directed toward the life-determining karma and to the spirits causing illnesses.

A similar example of such a ritual is also presented by *A Summary of the Noble Suvarṇaprabhāsottama-nāma-mahāyānasūtra* (*Deed bütsen khölgön altangerel nert sudryn khuurangui orshivoi*), which is a benediction for the blessing of the *Suvarṇaprabhāsottama*. Its *Summary* begins with prefatory words declaring the protection of the State as a main purpose of the ritual benediction. It states: "Inherited by this pure lineage of the Father Sky above the Mother Earth below, the entire benediction, [which is] a eulogy and a decree of restoring, observing, pacifying, and uniting the noble principle of the state-family established by the Lord (*ezen*) Bogd Chinggis is contained here."[30] These opening words to the Buddhist benediction reveal the integrative character of a ritual, whose Buddhist identity is not separate from that of the Mongolian, pre-Buddhist religion of Tengerrism, according to which, the Father, Eternal Heaven destines all things from above—including the origin of the ruling lineage of Chinggis Khan and his rise to power—while, the earth goddess, Mother Etüken, protects the Mongols' ruling family.

This declaration precedes the two-phased ritual of worshipping the *Summary* itself. The first phase involves arranging specific types of offerings[31] to the text in the prescribed image of thirteen mountains; and the second phase involves a *sādhana* practice in which the performer purifies his body by imagining himself attaining the Buddha's body. He also recites the *mantras* for removing obstacles[32] and invites his tutelary deity into his mind in order to purify the offerings. Here too, a ritual veneration of the text through offerings must precede the actual ritual of benediction; but in this case, the ritual of veneration of the text is itself a multileveled ritual performance. As in the previous example, the multiple functions of this ritual correspond to its multiple performative features—the third being a formalized, mental performance, or *sādhana*.

In these two rituals that involve the veneration of the abridged versions of the *Aparamitāyurjñāna* and the *Suvarṇaprabhāsottama*, which consist chiefly of the *sūtras' mantras*, invocations, and prayers, the text, which is an object of a ritual veneration, also becomes a ritual subject, after being activated as a tutelary deity through worship and enacted through a performative utterance. Thus, one could say that there are two different, but mutually dependent agents in these two rituals: the person performing the ritual and a text as a tutelary deity that accomplishes things through the ritual.

The fact that the *Suvarṇaprabhāsottama* was not the only Mahāyāna *sūtra* considered appropriate for the recitation rituals for the protection of the state and nation is evidenced in the epistle of the Eighth Jebtsundamba (Tib. Rje btsun dam pa) Khutukhtu (1870–1924), the last theocratic monarch of Mongolia and the sixth in the line of the Khutukhtus chosen among Tibetans, to Khalkha Mongols, and other Mongolian ethnic groups. In his epistle, he exhorts the Mongolian nobility to recite the *Aṣṭasāhasrikāprajñāpāramitā* in all four seasons of the year and urges the assemblies of monks to recite the *Prajñāpāramitā* [*-hṛdaya-sūtra*] for deliverance from the great calamities threatening the Mongols and their livestock due to both the ongoing increase of Chinese population among them and Chinese economic and cultural dominance generally.[33]

Furthermore, the identity of the text and its related power become important in healing and protective rites. An examination of these kinds of rituals sheds light on the ways in which the Mongols conceptualized the distinct identities and related powers of the previously mentioned *sūtras*, and it further explains why several of these Mahāyāna *sūtras* were included in various *tantra* sections of the Mongolian Kangyur.[34] The textual sources that I have been able to access so far reveal that among all the Mahāyāna *sūtras* in the Mongolian Kangyur, only the *Suvarṇaprabhāsottama*, the *Aṣṭasāhasrikāprajñāpāramitā*, the *Prajñāpāramitā-hṛdaya Sūtra*, and the *Vajracchedikā*, together with various *dhāraṇis*, have been put to use in these rituals. As in the previously discussed rituals, here too the recitation of the *sūtras* does not require a semantic understanding of the texts, since their innate powers emerge merely through the reverent modes of reciting them or holding them in one's hands.

For example, according to the Tsepel Wangchug Dorje's (Tshe 'phel dbang phyug rdo rje) *Manual for Healing Diseases of Sheep* (*Rdzi bo sogs la phan 'dogs par bya rgyu lug thabs kyi rim pa rnams las spyi dang bye brag lug nad bcos pa'i bskor lags*), when a sheep becomes afflicted with the disease called *khorkhiroo*, one must recite the *Suvarṇaprabhāsottama* three times and perform the rite of purification with holy water (*rasiyan*, Skt. *rasāyāna*) three times both in the morning and evening.[35] Likewise, even today when Mongolian nomadic families wish to ensure the health and prosperity of their sheep and goats, they ceremonially carry the *Suvarṇaprabhāsottama* in their hands as they circumambulate their herd's shelter three times.[36]

Furthermore, a text that instructs a healer on how to interpret the signs on the horse he rides when he goes to examine a sick man and the manner in which the man summoning him has arrived,[37] advises the healer to do the following. If the person who has come to summon him sits down with one knee bent, he is to recite the *Suvarṇaprabhāsottama*, make incense offerings, and set out the body-substitute, clothes, and boots of the sick man. When a man who is summoning a healer sits in this manner, this indicates that that the sick man has eaten carrion that has been taken by some animal, on account of which he has been afflicted by demons, and will soon vomit and suffer from sharp abdominal pains.[38] Therefore, the recitation of the *Suvarṇaprabhāsottama* has to be undertaken as a remedial strategy for exorcising demons out of that sick man.

As in the past, in the contemporary period, when the *Aṣṭasāhasrikāprajñāpāramitā* is ceremonially recited in a healing rite on behalf of a person facing death, for the sake of enhancing the healing efficacy of both the text and its ritual recitation, a copy printed in the color red, the color of power and ferocity, is invariably used.

The Mongolian translation of the Tibetan text, *The Order of the Holy Panchen Erdeni, of His Gegeen the Dalai Lama, and of the Holy Chinggis Khan*, which was prepared at the time of the Eighth Jebtsundamba Khutukhtu when the epidemics of syphilis and hepatitis were afflicting the Khalkha Mongols, urges its readers to recite the *Prajñāpāramitā* and the mantra of the *Suvarṇaprabhāsottama* for the sake of the deliverance from these epidemics.[39]

Similarly, in his epistle to the Mongols, called the *Prophecy of the Holy Gegeen*, the Eighth Jebtsundamba Khututkhu urges the Mongols to recite the *Aṣṭasāhasrikāprajñāpāramitā* and the *Vajracchedikā* in order to deliver themselves from the sins of smoking various kinds of tobacco and drinking alcohol, which brought them "the black and red rulers of tuberculosis."[40]

As attested in the text called the *Examination of Shoulder Blades* (*Daluu üjilge orusibai*),[41] which was studied in detail by Charles Bawden, the recitation of the *Suvarṇaprabhāsottama* or the *Aṣṭasāhasrikāprajñāpāramitā* is also a part of the protective rites, and its performance is based on predictions received during a divination by scapulimancy.[42] For example, if the color of a certain topographical area on the bone appears pale like ashes, this is an omen indicating bad things to come. In that case, one is advised to recite the *Suvarṇaprabhāsottama* every month for a year. Similarly, if the neck on the topographical location on the bone breaks, this is a sign that grief and repentance will take place during that year. In that case, one should recite the *Aṣṭasāhasrikāprajñāpāramitā*, perform *pūjas*, and make prostrations at shrines and temples. Or if one notices a black crack in the left-hand corner of the shoulder blade, one must recite the *Prajñāpāramitā[hṛdaya Sūtra]*, together with the *Tsagaan Shukhert* (*White Umbrella*) *dhāraṇi*, numerous times, and one must perform the rites of inhibition (*qariγulγa*) and the rite for counteracting quarrels. Likewise, while examining the cracks that appear on the scorched left-hand shoulder blade in order to determine the outcome of an illness, if one notices an omen that predicts a success in finding a helpful healer, one must recite several times the *Suvarṇaprabhāsottama* or the *Aṣṭasāhasrikāprajñāpāramitā*. In addition to that, one is to make offerings of candles and incense to one's own shrines and monasteries and offerings of tea to the monks during temple ceremonies.[43]

So far, we have seen that not only the performative utterances of different *sūtras*, but also those of the very same *sūtra*, may have different functions according to the different ritual contexts in which they are used. Depending on the intended goal of its ritual context, the same *sūtra* can alter the experience of the ritual performer, prolong life, protect the state, exorcise demons, cure humans and livestock, and prevent possible unpleasant events in one's life. Although it retains its recognizable, divine identity throughout different types of rituals, it might not remain unchanged owing to the possible plurality of performative styles.

One could say, in conclusion, that the Mongolian ritual uses of the Mahāyāna *sūtras* mentioned in this chapter support other, extant evidence which show that certain Mahāyāna *sūtras*, having been deemed tutelary deities, could no longer be confined to the walls of monasteries or to the interiors of *stūpas*. They became an integral part of a daily religious life on the steppe. Once conceived as tutelary deities, their domains of influence and their functions expanded. A ritual, on the other hand, provided a technique for communicating their divinity and making it accessible to experiences that go far beyond the textual domains.

NOTES

1. The Sogdian *nwm* is related to the Greek *nomos*, and comes from the root meaning a "law." The word *nom* was originally used by Sogdians and Uighurs to denote the Buddha Dharma.

2. *Burqan-dur mörgümüi. Nom-dur mörgümüi. Bagsi-dur mörgümüi.*

3. One such example is the "Deed bütsen khölgön altangerel nert sudryn khuraangui orshivoi," in *Khünii nasan zayaany amydral ajil üilsiig devjen ösgökh Burkhany surgaaliin khuraangui*, compiled by Getsel Tüvdenvaanchüg (Ulaanbaatar: Uranbishrelt, 2004), 50.

4. It is the largest book in the Mongolian National Central State Library in Ulaanbaatar. It measures 32 × 91 cm, and is written on a black paper with ink made of gold, silver, and nine precious stones.

5. Its full title in the classical Mongolian translations most commonly appears as the *Qutuγtu degedü altan gerel-tü sudur-nuγudun qaγan neretü yeke kölgen sudur.*

6. Tsendiin Damdinsüren, "Two Mongolian Colophons to the *Suvarṇaprabhāsottama-sūtra*," *Acta orientalia Academiae scientiarum Hungaricae* (AOH) 33, fasc. 1 (1979): 39.

7. Shagdaryn Bira, "The Worship of the *Suvarṇaprabhāsottama-sūtra* in Mongolia" in *Mongolyn tüükh, soyel, tüükh bichlegiin sudalgaa*, ed. Ts. Ishdorj and Kh. Purevtogtokh, Studies in Mongolian History, Culture, and Historiography: Selected Papers 3 (Ulaanbaatar: International Association for Mongol Studies, Mongolian Academy of Sciences, Institute of History, International Institute for the Study of Nomadic Civilization, 2001), 322–31.

8. Shagdaryn Bira, "The Worship of the *Suvarṇaprabhāsottama-sūtra* in Mongolia," 2001, 323.

9. Shagdaryn Bira, "The Worship of the *Suvarṇaprabhāsottama-sūtra* in Mongolia," 2001, 325.

10. Tsendiin Damdinsüren, *Mongolyn Uran Zokhiolyn Toim*, 2 vols. (Ulaanbaatar: Bembi San, 1999) 2: 158. Pentti Aalto in his "Notes on the Altan Gerel," *Studia Orientalia Edidit Societas Orientalis Fennica*, 14/6 (1950): 4–26, analyzes three Mongolian versions of the text that are kept in the Ethnographical Museum in Sweden and points to the existing internal evidence that suggests that these translations were not based solely on Tibetan versions, but that their translators also utilized the Chinese version prepared by Yijing and certain Sanskrit versions.

11. Aleksei Georgievich Sazykin, *Katalog mongolskih rukopisei i ksilografov instituta vostokovodeniya akademii nauk SSSR* (Moskva: Nauka, 1988) 95–98. D. Tserensodnom, *Mongolyn Burkhany Shashny Uran Zokhiol*, 2 vols. (Ulaanbaatar: Shinjlekh Ukhaany Akademiin Khel Zokhiolyn Khureelen, 1997) 1: 282, mentions twenty versions listed in Sazykin's catalogue. However, I have found only fifteen. One of the fifteen texts is incomplete and consists of eleven chapters.

12. It was also known under the title *Gčodba-yin tayilburi.*

13. Tserensodnom, *Mongolyn Burkhany Shashny Uran Zohiol*, 1: 284.

14. The manuscript of the *Včir-iyar oγtaluγči-yin tailburi*, held at the State Central Library in Ulaanbatar was composed in 1871 and consists of fifteen chapters.

15. This information was provided by Munkhtaivan Lama during an interview conducted in July of 2005 in Ulaanbaatar.

16. Cf. the passage of the *Vajracchedikā* in which the Buddha points out that any part of the world in which this *sūtra* will be propagated will become like a shrine (*caitya*), honored by gods, men, and evil spirits.

17. Tserensodnom, *Mongolyn Burkhany Shashny Uran Zokhiol*, 1: 284.

18. *Ochiroor Ogtlogchiin Tus Erdem*, translated from Tibetan and transliterated from the classical Mongolian script into Cyrillic by G. Chantsal and L. Dulamsuren (Ulaanbaatar: New Mind Technology, 2000), 48: "*Bilgüün chanad khyazgaar khürsen Ochiroor ogtlogchiin tus erdmiin tailbar üüniig unshvaas, unshuulvaas, bichvees, bichüül-*

bees, nayiman tümen, dörvön myangan nomyn tsogtssyn tus erdmiig magtan unshsan, büteesnii buyanyg olj ene nasand nas buyan, erkhten khiimory delgerch, alivaa üils büteed, etses khoitod body khutiig olokh ny damjiggüi khemeen nomlojee."

19. See Lkhamsurengiin Khürelbaatar, *Sudar Shastir Bilig* (Ulaanbaatar: Institute of Language and Literature, Academy of Sciences, 2002), 342–43.

20. Summaries of the *sūtras* not only made the teachings of the *sūtras* available to the broader audience, but they also became commonly used in rituals requiring readings of *sūtras*. Probably the most popular summaries were those of the *Suvarṇaprabhāsottama*. Among the birch bark manuscripts discovered in the *stūpa* at Kharburkhyn Balgas in Bulgan *aimag* and dating from the later part of the seventeenth century, at least ten different copies are summaries of the *Suvarṇaprabhāsottama*. Those studied by Elisabetta Choido in *The Mongolian Manuscripts on Birch Bark from Xarbuxyn Balgas in the Collection of the Mongolian Academy of Sciences*, Part 1 (Wiesbaden: Harrassowitz Verlag, 2000), 71–87, contain passages reminiscent of the popular Mongolian folk religious texts invoking the spirits—guardians of mountains and other localities, and the elements of the Mongolian shamanic religion.

21. Ch. Narantuya, *Mongol Bichmel Sudryn Tovd* (Ulaanbaatar: Admon, 2002), 177.

22. This is illustrated by the story of a seven-year-old girl who walked seven steps with the *sūtra* on her head in order to free her father's hands as he tried to move a large stone from the road; she was consequently reborn seven times in the *trayastriṃśa* heaven and eventually attained spiritual awakening. One such texts is *The Sūtra that Explains the Benefits of the Vajracchedikā* (*Včir-iyar oɣtaluɣči-yin ači tusa-yin nomlaɣsan sudur*), most likely composed in the late sixteenth century.

23. Diseases range from eye-defects, intolerable diarrhea, spasms, bodily pains, fear attacks accompanied by crying, sore throat, squalling, cough, insomnia, enraged shrieks, impeded movement, aversion to the mother's breasts, and bodily chills, to producing various odors and forms. Commonly in the case of a sick child, and occasionally in the case of an old person facing impending death, its recitation is followed by the reading of another short ritual text called the *Tridaśa-cakra* (*Arvan Gurvan Khürden Orshvoi*), whose sole function is to expel and divert various types of malevolent spirits such as cause all sorts of difficulties in one's life.

24. "Khutagt Tseden-Ish Buyu Tsend-Ayush Khemeekh Sudryn Khuraangui Orshvoi," in Getsel Tüvdenvaanchüg, compiler, *Khünii nasan*, 207.

25. The five main life constituents are life force (*amy*), body (*bie*), sense-faculties (*erkhten*), wind-horse (*khiimori*), and life-principle (*süld*).

26. The element of one's birth year can be any of these five: fire, earth, iron, water, or wood.

27. When the juncture of these three factors coincides with a black life-force stone or with a black body-stone on the astrological chart, this is interpreted as an inauspicious sign indicating a threat to one's vital force or a serious physical illness during that year. At times, it is possible that even two or three black life-stones or black body-stone appear, in which case, it is seen as an indication of even a greater inauspiciousness in one's life-force or in the body. Similarly, if the juncture of those elements coincides with a black life-principle stone, it is an indication of the decline of one's life-principle and of the inauspicious omens that will soon start to appear in one's dreams or visions.

28. The offerings consist of *tsha tshas*, incense, rosary, perfume, and *enkhmel* flower.

29. The *mantra* is: *Oṃ namo bhagavate aparamitāyur-jñāna-suviniścita-tejo-rajāya thatāgatāya arhate saṃyaksaṃbuddhāya tadyathā oṃ puṇya-mahāpuṇya aparamitapuṇya aparamitāyur-puṇya-jñāna-saṃbhāropacite, oṃ sarvasaṃskāra-pariśuddhadharmate gagana-samudgate svabhāvapariśuddhe mahānayaparivāre svāha.*

30. "Deed bütsen khölgön altangerel nert sudryn khuraangui orshivoi," in Getsel Tüvdenvaanchüg, compiler, *Khünii nasan*, 50.

31. The text mentions the following nine kinds of offerings: tea, milk, water (or alcohol), five grains as nutrients of a soil, five types of food, five types of nutrients, nine kinds of the best quality objects, five purifying scents, five vital organs (the heart, liver, lungs, spleen, and kidneys) that produce nourishment to the body, six [offering] bowls, eight auspicious emblems (umbrella, fish, vase, flower, conch, lucky diagram, victorious banner, and wheel) symbolizing a group of five senses, and *dash* ceremonial scarves (*khadag*, Tib. *bkra shis kha btags*) of the five colors and folded three times.

32. The mantra "*oṃ āḥ hūṃ*" is recited three times. Thereafter, the following mantra is recited: *oṃ vajra amṛta kuṇḍali hana hana huṃ phaṭ. Oṃ svabhāva śuddha sarva dharma svabhāva śuddho 'haṃ.*

33. The Eighth Jebtsundamba Khutukhtu's preference of the Perfection of Wisdom *sūtras* over the *Suvarṇaprabhāsottama* is, perhaps, due to the fact that the *Suvarṇaprabhāsottama* never gained the same degree of popularity among Tibetans as it did among the Mongols. According to the report of the members of the Foundation for the Preservation of the Mahāyāna Tradition in Ulaanbaatar, given to me in the summer of 2006, when the Tibetan Buddhist missionary Lama Zopa Rinpoche came to Mongolia for the first time, he expressed his surprise that Tibetans have not resorted to the *Suvarṇaprabhāsottama* at the times of their need and worshipped it as the Mongols had done for centuries. He immediately ordered 2,000 copies of the text and distributed it to his centers in various parts of the world. Afterward, he wrote a short essay entitled "Benefits of the Sūtra of Golden Light," which was published on the foundation's website www.fpmt.org/Teachers/Zopa/advice/goldenlight_benefits.asp. He also had the *sūtra* translated into English for his Western students. For a complete translation of the epistle of the Eighth Jebtsundamba Khutukhtu see Alice Sárközi, *Political Prophecies in Mongolia in the 17th–20th Centuries* (Wiesbaden: Otto Harrassowitz, 1992), 127–32.

34. Two versions of *Aparamitāyurjñāna* appear only in the fifteenth volume of the *tantra* section of the Mongolian Bka' 'gyur, and its third version appears in the twenty-third *tantra* section of the Bka' 'gyur. Similarly, the *Suvarṇaprabhāsottama Sūtra* appears only in the fourteenth *tantra* section of the Bka' 'gyur.

35. Khürelbaatar, *Sudar Shastiryn Bilig*, 2002, 376.

36. This has been reported to me by Erdenebaatar Erdene-Ochir who has witnessed this event on more than one occasion while visiting his relatives in Zavkhan *aimag*.

37. The edition and analysis of the text is given by Charles R. Bawden in his article "The Supernatural Element in Sickness and Death According to Mongol Tradition," in *Confronting the Supernatural: Mongolian Traditional Ways and Means* (Wiesbaden:

Harrassowitz Verlag, 1994), 41–84. In that article, Bawden does not give the title of the text and designates it merely as "Text of Louvain 37."

38. Bawden, *Confronting the Supernatural*, 59.

39. See Alice Sárközi's edition and translation of the "Boγda bančin erdeni dalai blam-a-yin gegen boγda činggis qaγan-narun čarlig-un bičig" in her *Political Prophecies*, 71.

40. Sárközi, "Boγda gegen-ü lündüg," in *Political Prophecies*, 118–27.

41. This text was edited and analyzed by Charles R. Bawden in "On the Practice of Scapulimancy among the Mongols," in Bawden, *Confronting the Supernatural*, 111–42.

42. Scapulimancy is an ancient Mongolian method of prognostication by reading the cracks, colors, and breaks in bones that are produced by burning the bones in fire. A shoulder blade of a sheep has been the most commonly used bone in this type of divination.

43. Bawden, *Confronting the Supernatural*, 124–25, 136.

10

The Ritual Veneration of Mongolia's Mountains

JARED R. LINDAHL

Despite the obvious influence of Tibetan Buddhism upon the religious landscape of Mongolia, Mongolian Buddhism is not simply Tibetan Buddhism in Mongolia, just as Tibetan Buddhism is not simply Indian Buddhism in Tibet. Previous scholarship on the ritual manuals that engage Mongolia's local deities has tended to consider these rituals as instances of the corruption of Buddhism by "Shamanism."[1] Rather than argue that the introduction of Buddhism to Mongolia resulted in an unfortunate hybrid tradition of ritual practice, I suggest that ritual was an oblique strategy that Buddhists intentionally used "in order to emplace themselves within a local society"[2]—in the process, converting indigenous practices into Buddhist practices. Although ritual theorists unanimously acknowledge that place is a significant component to the understanding of ritual, there is a difference of opinion regarding exactly how significant place is. Jonathan Z. Smith argues that nothing is inherently sacred or profane; rather, things and actions are sacred only relationally—especially in relation to place.[3] Ronald Grimes, on the other hand, resists affording a privileged position to place, and instead situates place among other constituent elements such as time, actions, agents, and objects.[4] While I agree with Grimes that *in general* there is no ground for privileging place as the primary key to understanding ritual, I find unwarranted his claim that "sacrality becomes evident in *how* people act," which privileges action in much the same way that Smith privileges place.[5] Charting a middle way between these two theorists, I maintain that although we should not assume, in an a priori fashion, that place will be the primary variable of analysis for understanding ritual, nevertheless, when studying the ritual veneration of the features of Mongolia's landscape, place is of utmost importance. Such sites are deemed sacred by virtue of the presence of the deities that are considered to be either identical with, or inhabitants of the features of the landscape.[6] With respect to the tradition of mountain veneration rituals in Mongolia, the relevance of place logically precedes that of action because one must adhere to certain modes of ritual protocol at sacred places, and in the presence of the deities who inhabit them. This is not to say, however, that place is the *only* important feature of these rituals. Grimes is right to direct our attention to other facets of ritual, such as action, agents, time, and objects, and in this chapter I will demonstrate how examining these other facets of ritual processes help us understand particular relationships to place, and in particular to mountains and mountain deities.

Through a careful study of the genre of incense-offering rituals, *sang* (Tib. *bsang/s mchod*; Mong. *sang*), I argue that such ceremonies reinforce, and even reenact the historical conversion of the Mongols to Buddhism. Incense-offering rituals address many of the same pragmatic concerns that non-Buddhist ritual specialists addressed in pre-Buddhist Mongolia, such as petitions for the health of animals and humans, for good weather, for the protection of agriculture, and for the accumulation of wealth. Nevertheless, these rituals are decidedly Buddhist, and the most important mountains of Mongolia have highly developed ritual traditions that reveal significant influence from tantric *sādhanas*. The introduction of tantric ritual elements, in particular the tantric pantheon of deities, establishes a uniquely Buddhist relationship between ritual specialists and the local mountain deities. In particular, the ritual conversion of the local mountain deity to Buddhism serves as a reminder of both the historical conversion of the Mongols to Buddhism and the dominance of Buddhism over indigenous religious beliefs and practices.

Previous Scholarship on Mongolian Ritual Manuals

In the sixteenth century, imperial edicts issued by Altan Khan proclaimed Buddhism to be the national religion of Mongolia and outlawed prior forms of ritual practice.[7] This resulted in a period of great social and religious transformation. A good deal of scholarship on this topic depicts the transformation of Mongolia as beginning with the introduction of Buddhism, followed by the subsequent persecution of "Shamanism,"[8] and concluding with a syncretism in which either Buddhism was "corrupted" by "shamanic elements" or "Shamanism" was merely given a "Buddhist veneer."[9] For example, in her introduction to a ritual manual entitled "Cutting Off the Lasso," Alice Sárközi writes:

> The text now under consideration, though it is a hand-book of a shaman ritual to exorcise the evil spirits, has an overall touch of Lamaism, containing a number of Lamaist expressions and motives. So this short text in itself represents the complicated situation of Mongolian spiritual life, ruled by the Yellow Faith, that was full of shamanist practices deeply rooted in the everyday life of the people. The booklet belongs to the period, when pre-Buddhist cults and cult-figures were adapted to the new faith, older shamanist deities were transferred into the new pantheon, and old practices were dressed in the guise of Lamaist rituals.[10]

The ritual manual commences by prescribing the recitation of Buddhist texts if one is plagued by malevolent spirits.[11] Then, after outlining the preparation of a dough effigy as ransom to the malevolent spirits, the remainder of the ritual involves a visualization in which the ritual specialist identifies with the tantric deity Heruka in order to banish evil hindrances. The ritual concludes with the recitation of Sanskrit mantras. Throughout the ritual manual, there is no evidence that this is anything but a Buddhist text. Sárközi also notes that there is a Tibetan edition of the text, all of which would indicate that this text is neither "a text of popular religious belief" nor a "shaman text";[12] rather, it falls squarely within the purview of tantric Buddhism, which, contrary to her expectation, does in fact perform rituals to exorcise malevolent spirits.[13]

However, one of Alice Sárközi's translations, "Book of Filling Up the Hole," does seem to support her view that such ritual manuals are merely "Shamanist practices" and "folk beliefs... in the disguise of Lamaism."[14] She describes the text in question as a rite of exorcism, as the ritual functions to banish evil spirits from and confer blessing upon the patron. The only elements of the ritual manual that bear any resemblance to other Buddhist rites are the use of a few mantras, such as *oṃ āḥ huṃ*, the mention of a few ecclesiastical-sounding names, and an overt reference to the fact that "this performance is not a performance. It was taught by Buddha Śākyamuni."[15] Sárközi could be correct that "to mention their names certainly helped to camouflage this clearly shamanist text in Lamaism and, therefore, make it more acceptable by those who follow the Yellow Faith."[16] However, it is very difficult to determine if this practice originated with non-Buddhist ritual specialists and was then camouflaged as a Buddhist ritual so as to reassert indigenous ritual practices, or if it was composed by Buddhist ritual specialists in order to appropriate a non-Buddhist ritual and transform it into a practice that was deemed sufficiently Buddhist. In either case, it is clear that this practice is probably best characterized as being unique to *Mongolian* Buddhism. Previous scholarship, in tending to reduce everything to either "Shamanism," "Lamaism," or some syncretistic hybrid of the two, has failed to acknowledge that Buddhism in Mongolia may be different from Buddhism in Tibet precisely because of the transformations that took place during the widespread and forced introduction of Buddhism in the sixteenth century. That a ritual manual requests seemingly "mundane" things such as good weather, healthy animals, and wealth, and seemingly "supernatural" things such as the banishment of various classes of malevolent beings, does not imply that it is an assimilation of "Shamanic" or "folk religious" elements into a Buddhist ritual practice, nor does it imply that this is essentially a "Shamanic" text that is given a Buddhist veneer and structure so that the practice may survive. Rather, it is an indication of the breadth of Buddhist praxis and an expression of the local concerns that Buddhists had to address if their tradition was to thrive among the people of Mongolia.

Since the indigenous religious traditions of Mongolia were not overtly doctrinal, the emerging Buddhist traditions could not be localized solely through intellectual discourse; rather, Buddhism also had to be made appealing at the level of ritual practice. Because of the nature of the indigenous *habitus*—a deeply engrained system of practice that is "contrary to intellectualist idealism"—Buddhist missionaries focused on replacing the material culture associated with the practices of ritual specialists.[17] When two edicts, one issued in 1558 and the second in 1577, outlawed "Shamanism and other unorthodox creeds," Buddhist lamas confiscated and burned the paraphernalia of the ritual specialists: the clothing, drums, and in particular the shamans' *ongod*—ritual effigies that are inhabited by deities called *ongon*.[18] "Because of the conception of these *Ongghot* being inspirited by the magical forces of Shamanism, the first action of Lamaism was everywhere an iconoclastic purge."[19] The destruction of the *ongod* did not eliminate the indigenous *habitus*; rather, it left a void in the praxis of both the ritual specialists and their communities. The lamas could not simply destroy the *ongod*, for the local deities had to be petitioned or the crops would not grow, sickness would ravage the land, and the ancestral spirits would return to haunt the living. Because these considerations were part of the *habitus* of the Mongolian people, Buddhist lamas had to *replace* the *ongod* with images of their own deities. Thus, "statuettes of lamaist deities, mostly of fierce appearance, were substituted for the housegods and treated by the Mongols in the same way as the *Ongghot* had been formerly treated."[20]

In addition to transforming Mongolian material culture by introducing Buddhist statues and associated ritual implements, lamas also disseminated tantric practices among the Mongolian populous during this initial purge of non-Buddhist ritual practice. One important source for this controversial activity comes to us through the biography of the missionary lama Neyichi Toyin (1577–1653).[21] He distributed various practices pertaining to the tantric deity Yamāntaka without requiring the study of Buddhist scriptures or the most fundamental ritual initiations. Despite his eventual condemnation and banishment by orthodox Buddhists, he succeeded in converting a large number of people to Buddhism. In order to further eliminate the need for indigenous ritual specialists, the Mongol nobility offered material rewards to those who learned tantric ritual practices. By teaching them the recitation of Buddhist spells (*dhāraṇī*), divination, *mudrās*, and methods of exorcism and healing, Buddhist missionaries such as Neyichi Toyin encouraged lay people to act in the capacity of a ritual specialist themselves. To those accustomed to consulting a variety of indigenous ritual specialists to mediate their relationship with the local deities, tantra must have seemed particularly appealing, as Neyichi Toyin's teachings suggested that tantric practices offered an unmediated interaction with the deity.[22]

Scholars have also investigated the role of the ritual cairn (Mong. *ovoo* or *oboo*; Tib. *la rdzas*) (Figure 10.1) in the Buddhist appropriation of place; however, the origin of the Buddhist cult of the *ovoo* in Mongolia has yet to be conclusively established.[23] Although it is clear that Buddhists did engage in a thorough elimination of the *ongod*, as described earlier, there is no evidence that there was any attempt, let alone a failed attempt, to actually eradicate the cult of the *ovoo*. In his study of the *ovoo*-construction and *ovoo*-veneration rituals composed by Mergen Diyanchi (1717–66), Charles Bawden demonstrates how Mergen Diyanchi consciously absorbed the cult of the *ovoo* within the fold of acceptable

FIGURE 10.1. An *ovoo* for the local deity of the mountain, Arkhangai Province, Mongolia. Photo: J. Lindahl (2004).

Buddhist praxis. He concludes that "the intention of Mergen Diyanchi Lama was perhaps not so much...to suppress shamanistic elements of worship by incorporating them, suitably altered, into Buddhist ritual, as to strengthen the position of Buddhism in Mongolia by associating indigenous cult-elements with similar phenomena already established in Tibetan lamaism."[24] Insofar as Mergen Diyanchi attempted to establish specifically Buddhist ritual practices for the veneration of local deities at the already existing *ovoo*, his approach to the appropriation of place differs significantly from Neyichi Toyin, who confiscated all remnants of pre-Buddhist ritual practice and replaced them with Buddhist paraphernalia. Christopher Atwood also points out how Mergen Diyanchi saw the role of the Buddhist missionary in Mongolia as analogous to Padmasambhava's subjugation of the local deities of Tibet—that is, local deities are best controlled by having them swear an oath to protect the Dharma, not by destroying the ritual effigies and other implements associated with their worship.[25]

Common Ritual Practices Performed at the *Ovoo*

The *ovoo* is perhaps the most significant feature of Mongolia's sacred geography. These piles of rocks are ubiquitous throughout the countryside; they are found on nearly every mountain peak and mountain pass, on the shores of lakes and rivers, in the center of valleys, and in forests. They are often embellished by a birch branch flagstaff that is heavily bedecked with blue and white ceremonial scarves (Tib. *kha btags*; Mong. *khadag*) (Figure 10.2). In forested areas, an *ovoo* may be completely enclosed by birch branches. Since the *ovoo* is an altar and a site of cult practices for both laity and ritual specialists, one finds a multitude of assorted offerings scattered among its rocky base. In a brief typology of *ovoo*s, Ágnes Birtalan proposes that the *ovoo* serves two major roles: a marker of territory and a ritual altar.[26] It is primarily the latter role, in connection with the cult of ancestors, local deities, and burial practices, that will be the focus of this chapter.

The *ovoo* serves as a point of contact between ritual specialists and various classes of deities who inhabit the nearby landscape. In the Mongolian language, the words *ovoo* (ritual cairn) and *uul* (mountain) refer not only to the physical object, but also to the deities that inhabit those places, and Mongolian authors typically do not distinguish between the physical object and the local deity. An entire area of the landscape, and to some extent the entirety of the natural world, is viewed in this manner. For instance, in an introduction to *ovoo* rituals, Khatgin Sukhbaatar explains how "at the *ovoo* [that is the site] of the offering, the queens of the mountain, the guardian, and the protector who enriches the treasury are the [surrounding] peaks, hills and passes."[27] This indicates that the mountain upon which the *ovoo* is located is identified with the principal local deity, usually the "master of the area" (Tib. *sa bdag* and *gzhi bdag*; Mong. *savdag, gazaryn ezen*). It also tells us that the area surrounding the central peak is inhabited by other local spirits, namely "the entourage" (Tib. *'khor*; Mong. *nökhörlöl*) of queens and guardians surrounding the master of the area. Insofar as it is the abode of local deities, the *ovoo* demarcates a sacred region within which certain social behaviors are deemed taboo and a specific ritual protocol must be followed. While near its abode (Tib. *gnas*; Mong. *oron*), one must take care not to offend the local deity either through actions that damage and pollute the environment, or through actions that are considered socially offensive. One contemporary Mongolian author explains this as follows:

> Those who went to the ritual offering at any mountain, *ovoo*, or water did not kill any wild animals, drink any liquor, harbor any bad intentions, or upset any animals or people. Rather they devoted themselves to saying numerous recitations of the *mani* and *megdzem*[28] prayers... Having to stop and spend the night at the ritual site of the mountain and *ovoo* because you went there without a purpose, saying words that have bad causal connections,[29] "checking the horse"[30] wherever you please, chewing gum, going without a sash or naked, *Oṃ vajrapāni hūṃ phat!* These are seen as sinful [actions]![31]

Khatgin Sukhbaatar also enumerates the possible transgressions of ritual protocol that offend the local deity:

> At the time of the *ovoo* offering, it is not proper to drink too much vodka and other alcoholic drinks, to quarrel, fight or brawl, to leave your trash and so forth, because doing these things enrages the lords of the earth and water, and the master of the area (*gazaryn ezen*). It is better that each person very carefully controls his or her actions of body, speech, and mind... After the *ovoo* offering ritual, and in general, we have the custom of renouncing all harmful actions towards nature, such as disturbing the stones, fishing, hunting wild animals, and tearing the grass in the area surrounding the particular mountains and *ovoos* to which we make offerings... However, nowadays [people] place their rubbish, such as beer and liquor bottles and cans, crutches, staffs, and spare parts for their horse[32] [on the *ovoo*]. Because this is not an offering and is a bad deed, and because stopping this is a virtue, each person should strive to stop [such offerings].[33]

These contemporary Mongolian sources serve as general introductions to the mythology of Mongolia's sacred sites and instruct the reader on proper (and

FIGURE 10.2. An *ovoo* on a mountain pass along the border of Dzavkhan and Arkhangai Provinces. Photo: J. Lindahl (2004).

improper) behaviors in the proximity of the *ovoo* and local deity. The ritual protocol can be divided into two categories: actions directed toward other humans, and actions directed toward the environment. One must control one's actions of body, speech, and mind, in particular by avoiding drinking and slanderous speech, and by not carelessly pronouncing the name of the mountain and mountain deity. In most instances, mountains are respectfully referred to as *khairkhan* (beloved). Furthermore, one must refrain from damaging the natural environment by disturbing that which is already there, or leaving something that does not belong. In addition to these prohibitions, Sukhbaatar also summarizes the most common and fundamental offerings made at the *ovoo*: the offering of food, stones, and ceremonial scarves.

> In the morning and in the evening, you should make an offering in which you give the best part of your tea, milk, yogurt, and *airag*[34] to your own mountain and *ovoo*. Having come to the *ovoo*, it is also permitted to make an offering in which you say "Let me give to you the height of all the *ovoos*; bestow upon me the greatness of all the people. *oṃ āḥ hūṃ*." [Because] the majesty of an *ovoo* is [known] only through its height and its greatness, gather three stones from the lower and middle slopes of the mountain and offer your stones while circumambulating its *ovoo* three times... If there are no stones around that area, place a stone from the skirt[35] of the *ovoo* higher up. Having made [the ovoo] higher, people offer [hairs from] the horse's mane and tail, and

> ceremonial scarves. They come with their wind-horse flags and then fly their flags in the wind to revive [their luck force].[36]

Although these injunctions have elements that are noticeably Buddhist, similar ritual protocol governs the behavior at an *ovoo* in circumstances that are not overtly Buddhist.

Mongolian Conceptions of Deities of the Landscape

Perhaps the major difference between the Buddhist and non-Buddhist ritual practices at *ovoos* is the conception of the deity or deities involved. While space does not permit a thorough explanation of the pantheon and related ritual practices of pre-Buddhist Mongolia, there are a few concepts that are crucial by way of preamble. One of the most thorough accounts of indigenous Mongolian cosmology and ritual practice is Caroline Humphrey's ethnography of the Daur Mongols of Inner Mongolia. Unlike most scholarship on the indigenous traditions of Central and North Asia, Humphrey is unsettled by the use of the term "Shamanism" to categorically refer to the beliefs and practices of a pre-Buddhist culture, or a culture largely uninfluenced by Buddhism.

> The problem, with regard to 'shamanism,' was that a shaman's presence was quite unnecessary for the worship of the sky [*tenger*]. There were many other rituals too, sacrifices to mountain spirits at the *oboo* for example, where other ritual practitioners were dominant and shamans were even excluded... Theirs was never the only response to Daurs' views of existence, and shamans were never the masters of all religious life.[37]

Lest one think that these statements pertain only to the Daur Mongols, Humphrey forthrightly states that "there is no society in North Asia which has only the classic spirit-managing shaman as a religious specialist."[38] Among the Daur Mongols of Inner Mongolia, she finds the following ritual specialists: *bagchi* (ritualist, or elder), *barishi* (bone-setter), *bariyachi* (midwife), *kianchi* (sorcerer), *otoshi* (curer), and *yagdan* (shaman). These various ritual specialists had their own, often mutually exclusive, domain of practice, and we should not assume the existence of an overarching coherent system of belief or practice, as suggested by the use of the term "Shamanism."

Although these were not the only modes of ritual practice in pre-Buddhist Mongolia, Humphrey sets up an insightful comparison between a "chiefly" mode and a "shamanic" mode of ritual interaction with local deities.[39] The clan chiefs or elder ritual specialists were necessarily male and were nominated through patrilineal descent. The elders were masters of prayers and rituals directed toward the local deities. It was primarily the elders who propitiated the masters (Mong. *ezen*) of a particular place. Some of the other ritual specialists mentioned earlier were responsible for interacting with more volatile deities such as fox spirits and demons that afflicted humans with various illnesses. Women were usually excluded from the chiefly forms of ritual practice at the *ovoo*.[40]

By contrast, shamans could be either male or female and became shamans through a direct encounter with the spirits of their predecessor apotheosized as an *ongon*.[41] When shamans died, they were given two burials; during the second, their soul went through a metamorphosis into a local master, or *ezen*.[42] The *ezen* then became the *ongon* of the shaman of the following generation. In contrast to the elders, who would ritually petition the local deities, but never directly encounter them, shamans were distinguished from other ritual specialists due to their ability to have unmediated encounters with, and have control over both their tutelary deity and the local deities. Because they acted as intermediaries in this way, their conception of the local deities was more specific and personal than that of the elders. "The shaman thus cumulates varied external powers, while the chief, in his ritual role, and the lama unify, regulate, and rank them."[43] Humphrey also notes that the unique status of shamans resulted in the mutual exclusivity of the chiefly and shamanic paradigms for ritual practice: "Shamans were also excluded [from the *ovoo* ritual] in many places; though members of the lineage, they were destabilizing pretenders to a different and more direct access to the spirits."[44] I wonder if they were excluded because the local deity worshipped was in some sense the tutelary deity of the shamans themselves. For why would the shamans need to *propitiate* their own deity, with whom they have already demonstrated an unmediated relationship in their own ritual practices? This view is supported by some of Humphrey's later observations in which she writes that "the spirit of the Baragkhan *oboo* was a shaman, Solbon Khashkhi Noyon, who 'lives' on the mountain with a large household, cattle, and two servants, an Evenk and a one-eyed Russian."[45] Thus, although the elders and the shamans had different roles and different relationships with the local deities in terms of ritual practice, there is evidence to support the idea that the local deities were, in some instances at least, the transmogrified souls of deceased shamans, who were also the tutelary deities of contemporary shamans. These *ezen* were not so much "spirits *of* the tree, rock, or hill, but souls-turned-spirits located *in* them."[46] From this, we can understand that ritual practices at the *ovoo* and other sites in the landscape may be less about the features of the landscape and more "about a real human event."[47] It is important to bear this in mind as we begin to explore the ritual relationship to these local deities as presented in Buddhist ritual manuals for the veneration of mountains in Mongolia.

The Buddhist pantheon of deities is even more vast and complicated than the pantheon of the shamans, so the following presentation of local deities is necessarily incomplete. In Buddhist ritual manuals for the veneration of mountains, there are some deities that are found frequently, and others that make occasional appearances. Regarding the sacred geography of Tibet, Samten Karmay distinguishes between mountains that are pre-Buddhist sites for the cult of local deities (*yul lha*) and mountains that are associated with specifically Buddhist activity, the *neri* (*gnas ri*).[48] The *yul lha* cults follow the "chiefly" mode of ritual practice insofar as the rituals are performed by clan elders, not Buddhist monks. The deities petitioned in *yul lha* rituals include the master of the area (*gzhi bdag*), the master of the earth (*sa bdag*), the local deity (*yul lha*), the war-god (*dgra lha*), and the *nāga* (*klu*). Similar to the chiefly mode of ritual practice in Mongolia, which venerated ancestral deities as local masters, Karmay notes that the early Tibetan kings propitiated nine mountain deities that were regarded as the "soul of the body" (*sku bla*) of the relatives of the first Tibetan king.[49] There is an interesting parallel in the indigenous Tibetan conception of the soul (*bla*) with the metamorphosis of the soul of the Mongolian shaman into a local master deity.

> The *bla* may dwell, temporarily at least, in various places outside the body without risking any danger. Hence the expression *bla gnas* 'dwelling of the soul,' a place where the *bla* takes up residence. It can be a rock or a boulder (*bla rdo*), a tree (*bla shing*), a lake (*bla mtsho*), or a mountain (*bla ri*). These places are often considered as sacred.[50]

Neri sites, on the other hand, are deemed significant due to the previous or continuing presence of Buddhist yogis, relics, and treasures (*gter ma*). These sites are the object of pilgrimage and the locus of explicitly Buddhist ritual activity. While the same local deities associated with the *yul lha* cults can be invoked during rituals at a *neri*, *neri* sites are unique in often being conceived of as the *maṇḍala* of translocal tantric deities, which hierarchically subsumes local deities into a larger, Buddhist pantheon. Sites of *yul lha* cult practice and *neri* sites are not mutually exclusive insofar as one mountain can be the site for both modes of ritual practice. Toni Huber notes that:

> The older mountain gods and goddesses were incorporated into the expanding pantheons on two, frequently overlapping, levels: into higher Tantric initiatory categories as chosen meditational deities or as members of their retinues; and into service roles as "defenders of religion" or their local minions ... In some cases this assimilation process came to designate [*gnas ri*] as sites for Tantric practice, for worship of the defenders of religion, and for their local cults simultaneously.[51]

While more research needs to be done to determine which mountains in Mongolia might be considered *neri*, it is already clear that there are *yul lha* sites of various degrees of significance, many of which are the object of veneration by Buddhist ritual specialists.

In the genre of incense-offering rituals found in Mongolia, there are general ritual manuals that are not site-specific, and others that are particular to a mountain, lake, river, or spring. If the manual used is not site-specific, the ritual specialist is to insert the name of the local mountain deity at the appropriate time during the ritual. Thus, the same ritual can be performed at numerous mountains.[52] On the other hand, there are mountains of much greater importance, such as Bogd Khan Mountain, Khentii Khan Mountain, and Otgontenger Mountain, that do have site-specific ritual manuals. These manuals incorporate the iconography and narratives associated with the local mountain deity into the ritual practice. The complexity of the ritual is correlated to the significance of the mountain deity, such that ritual specialists engage the most clearly defined and most important mountain deities with ritual practices that are similar to the level of complexity of tantric *sādhanas*. In the case of Otgontenger Mountain, the mountain deity is Vajrapāṇi, a translocal tantric deity and the national deity of Mongolia. The mountains that are considered the abodes of translocal deities and that are the sites of tantric ritual practices are more likely to be the sites of other practices associated with *neri*, such as pilgrimage and hermitage traditions.

Whether the local deity is a nameless master of the area or a defined tantric deity, the presence of that deity is manifest in the special natural features of the site, especially its rock formations, flora, and fauna.

> Let me clarify what is actually so special about the juniper incense of Otgontenger Mountain. First, Otgontenger Mountain is the home of Vajrapāṇi. In regard to that, it is considered to be a good omen that the blessing of Vajrapāṇi has been infused into the juniper incense of that mountain. Because of this, it is superior to the juniper incense of other places... There is a tradition in which only the elderly are permitted to gather juniper incense from designated places on this mountain to the extent that they need it. [When so doing they] recite great Buddhist *dhāraṇī*, they bend at the knee, offer prayers to their *tenger*,[53] and express their wishes.[54]

Contemporary Mongolian sources also indicate that the local deity may be more or less present during certain times, and this too determines the degree of ritual protocol required:

> Our ancestors...made offerings on the 3rd, 8th, and 15th days of the new half of each month, the particular auspicious days of each month, and especially at the best hour of the day in which the *nāga*[55] comes. The majority of mountains and *ovoos* [have their own] incense offering [*sang*] to be recited, and not only that, their own traditions established [particular] days for making offerings, taking into account the characteristics of the banner area [in which they are located]...[Our ancestors] have the custom of publicly prohibiting [actions such as] making a fuss, quarrelling, hunting wild animals, or digging and disturbing the ground in the area [surrounding the mountains and *ovoos*] during the three, seven, nine, or thirteen days following the very day that the offerings to any mountains and *ovoos* were made, taking into account the sequence of the arrival of the *nāga*.[56]

After one makes an offering to the *nāga*, there is a period of three, seven, nine, or thirteen days during which the *nāga* may arrive to receive the offerings. It is during this time that the area is particularly sacred, due to the presence, even potentially, of the *nāga*, and thus the area must be kept in particularly good order so as not to offend the *nāga*. Establishing a relationship between natural resources and the local deity in these ways has provided the Mongols with a unique system of environmental protection for many centuries. Bogd Khan Mountain, for instance, is the world's oldest continuously officially protected area, beginning with the decree of the Manchu emperor in 1778.[57]

The Appropriation of Place via Mountain-Veneration Rituals

As Toni Huber has mentioned (see the passage cited earlier), *yul lha* cult sites were often subsumed into the mode of ritual practice associated with *neri* sites, with the local deities becoming incorporated into the limitless pantheon of Buddhism. Caroline Humphrey also indicates some of the paradigm shifts in discourse and practice that took place as the Mongolian nobility embraced Buddhism, particularly from the sixteenth through the nineteenth centuries. She argues that during this time "Buddhism allied itself with the chiefly sacred geography, and lamas became in effect priests for political leaders" such that "the effect of the centralized Buddhist system was to reduce imaginative variety and standardize the mountain rituals."[58] A few major changes were necessary if the Buddhists were to perform rituals at the *ovoos*. First, all animal sacrifices were prohibited.[59] Second, a new ritual practice was introduced in Tibetan, the dominant liturgical language of Mongolia.

Buddhists were not content simply to co-opt the chiefly paradigm for ritual practice; their appropriation of place was so thorough that the competing ritual paradigm, that of the shamans, also came to be usurped. In general, the conversion begins when "a Buddhist master makes the native spirit take an oath by displaying a *vajra* in order to make them [sic] protect Buddhist interests; and these spirits are then raised to the status of *chos skyong* (*dharmapāla*) and may even be admitted into a *maṇḍala*."[60] An incense-offering ritual[61] for Otgontenger Mountain is unique in that it presents Otgontenger as the center of a *maṇḍala* to which the local deities from other mountains in Mongolia are summoned.

> O great lord of victorious power, master of secrets,[62] come to this place! At the center of the *maṇḍala* of the vast expanse of the northern regions of the earth there is a mountain that is completely surrounded by a retinue of many millions. From this Mount Sumeru, which is endowed with auspiciousness and ten virtuous signs, come here to Otgontenger sacred mountain and guard this abode (*gnas*)! May the rain of possessions, food, wealth, and all desirables fall! May the bestower of the auspicious glory of this mountain abode and his entourage come to the snowy mountain renowned as Little Bogd,[63] which is endowed with power and dominion over all the earth. O great sorcerer, obey your great local deity. Grant beautiful longevity to the life of the mountains Myangan Sumbar, Bayandzurkh, Khukhu Onger, and so forth. O masters of the area (*gzhi bdag*) of a thousand mountains, come to this mountain abode! O great *nāgas* of rivers of lakes such as Badar Khongag, Bayanbolag mountain, Tsagaan Khokh Khar lake, Buyant river, and the Shiri stone, come to this mountain abode! O masters of the earth (*sa bdag*) from the direction of the steppe in places such as Tsagaan Tokhoi, Tasin Suudal, Botog Balgatai, Chandmani Urt Yombuu, and Tsagaan Bulan, come to this mountain abode! And in addition, O masters of the countryside and pasture lands, who lurk its soil, waters, trees, rocks, valleys, lakes, ponds, alpine meadows, springs, rock outcroppings, crossroads, mountains, and plains, come to this abode![64]

The invocation commences with the summoning of Vajrapāṇi, the tutelary deity for the ritual and the local deity of Otgontenger Mountain. After the invocation, which summons the local *zhidag* (*gzhi bdag*), *sadag* (*sa bdag*), and *nāgas* to the center of the *maṇḍala*, the ritual specialist offers incense to his lama, tutelary deity, and the various higher classes of deities, eventually reaching the lower local deities of the landscape previously summoned.

> Through our virtuous karma and aspirations, we offer purifying incense to the local deities, *nāgas*, masters of the area, and elemental spirits together with their retinue. We offer purifying incense to Otgontenger, the great deity who holds up our former lives along with this [present] life. In a word, we offer purifying incense to all those who are transformed into elemental spirits by dwelling in the lands which we claim as our own, in abandoned lands (*'tsher sa*) and estates, in landscapes with trees and landscapes with rocks, and in the mountains, rivers, valleys, and plains.[65]

This last sentence is particularly interesting in that it seems to acknowledge the metamorphosis of an ancestral spirit into a local deity of the landscape. While Buddhist rituals may not be overtly converting the souls of shamans to Buddhism, for centuries Mongols considered the local masters to be a metamorphosis of the shaman's soul. Given the close etymological connection between the Tibetan *zhidag*, its Mongolian equivalent *gazaryn ezen*, and the *ezen* that is the transmogrified soul of a shaman, these conceptions of the local deity must have, at times, overlapped.[66] It is certainly possible that integrating conversion narratives into the ritual practices was intended to reinforce and reenact the historical conversion of the Mongols to Buddhism by attempting to appropriate not only the chiefly *ovoo*-based ritual practices, but also the very conception of the local deities themselves. In Buddhist ritual manuals, these deities are visualized, invoked, presented with incense, and then reminded of their vows to protect the Dharma and refrain from harmful actions directed toward humans or animals. A ritual manual for the veneration of The White Old Man concisely presents these stages in a manner typical of other incense-offering rituals.[67]

> From the palace of the innate great bliss [emanates] the great power of heaven and earth, the sovereign master of the earth (*sa bdag*): the [White] Old Man. [The White Old Man has] white eyebrows, a white moustache, and white hair. His complexion is also white, and he has one face and two arms. In his right hand, [which has the] quality of a human being, he manipulates a rosary. In his left hand, he brandishes a dragon-head staff, and holds medicinal fruit from a mountain peak (*ri rtse mo*). There are twenty-four lands, waters, enclosures (*rwa*) and towns in which the great sovereign master of the earth dwells and lives encircled by his queen, sons, and a group of ministers. He promises to protect the Lord of the Sages,[68] with his ancient and stable eye, the teachings, and the adherents to the teachings. By virtue of the power of these commitments (*dam tshig*), we implore you to come to this abode (*gnas*)... We offer incense to the sovereign master of the earth and the

> retinue of his ministers, his queen, and his sons. We offer incense to the master of the earth and his retinue who dwell in the earth. We offer incense to the retinue of water deities who dwell in the water. We offer incense to the rock deities who dwell in the rocks. We offer incense to the tree deities who dwell in the trees. In brief, we offer incense to the deities, *nāgas* and *asuras* and elemental spirits such as the *nāgas*, the *kṣetrapālas* (*zhing skyong*), and the guardians of the four directions. Please accept this genuine and extensive incense offering ritual! May [you all] be contented and delighted, [endowed] with great bliss! We, the lama and disciples, benefactors and recipients, and our audience, [implore you to] pacify [our] sickness, obstacles, and negative influences. [Grant us] longevity and merit, extensive wealth and glory, and [enable us] to conqueror the three realms. Annihilate [our] enemies and hindrances [who cause us] harm and injury. In particular, may we always abide in this land with a kind and compassionate disposition in the same way as [our] parents, free from all dangers such as hail, drought, and famine of grain, quarreling and pain, wars and epidemics, enemies and thieves. In the meantime, also [grant us] long life without sickness. [Grant us] relief from quarreling, from being pursued by wolves, from sickness to herds or humans. Be an ally and effortlessly and spontaneously accomplish all our wishes without exception. Wherever we are, whether at home or abroad, may the rains be timely and may the herds and crops always prosper. Pacify others' curses, defamations, and disputes and establish enlightened activity . . . O great sovereign master of the earth, like [the attitude of] an affectionate mother towards [her] fair children, you and your retinue [should] always be an ally to those of us who are practitioners and to our disciples—not wandering [from us] day or night. Defend and protect the [Buddhist] teachings in general, and the precious teachings of Tsongkhapa in particular.[69]

Like the ritual manuals for mountain deities that are Dharma protectors of the highest rank or for tantric deities such as Vajrapāṇi, this text also commences with visualization. However, in comparison with other, site-specific mountain veneration rituals, the visualization for the White Old Man is not as detailed, and more rapidly segues into an extensive enumeration of the deities of the landscape. The incense-offering rituals for Bogd Khan Mountain, Choiriin Bogd Mountain, and Khentii Khan Mountain present a more extensive visualization ritual of their protector deities. The ritual manual for Bogd Khan Mountain commences by instructing the ritual specialist to meditate on his personal tutelary deity before visualizing the protector deity of the mountain, Dung-kyong Karpo (Dung skyong dkar po). Having dissolved into emptiness, he begins to visualize the phonemes *oṃ*, *aḥ*, and *hūṃ*, from which various visualized offerings arise. The various offerings are consecrated by means of mantras and *mudrās*. After an extensive description of the iconography of Dung-kyong Karpo to aid in visualization, the ritual specialist is to:

> Visualize [Dung-kyong Karpo] as being marked with *oṃ* at the head, *aḥ* at the neck, and *hūṃ* at the heart. From the *hūṃ* at the heart [of the deity] in front of you, [rays of] clear light similar to hooks strike and instantly invoke the great master of the area (*gzhi bdag*) together with his entourage from the diamond palace in which they reside. Then, recite [the following]: Vajradhāra, sovereign of the one hundred Buddha families, together with the eight root lamas, implore the great *upāsaka*, who is bound by oath and repeated empowerments, to come to this place together with his entourage. Great guardian for the lineage and the family of the royal place, master of magical power and heavenly seals, come to this place, where there is a round gently-sloping mountain.[70]

After the arrival of the master of the area, the great *upāsaka*, the ritual specialists are to recite mantras and contemplate the nonduality of the visualized image of Dung-kyong Karpo with the master of the area. The ritual manual for Choiriin Bogd Mountain follows nearly exactly this procedure, except that the visualization of the mantric phonemes and the deity are even more intricate. After the visualization,

> Rays of light like iron hooks radiate from the seed syllable at the heart of your tutelary deity. Abiding in the natural great bliss, contemplate this invitation of the protector of the sacred mountain, the war god along with his entourage...[Then recite the following:] Come, my protector of this sacred ground, right here, right now, dwell firmly upon the full moon seat. Because you have partaken of this murmuring incantation and sound of music, a portion of this complete *torma* offering, and these oblations of tea and barley wine, since you have subdued the very worst enemies, and because you are a Dharma protector of the Tathāgata, in this very moment, approach this very place. You have come to dwell [here] in order to destroy and cast away illness and death. Foremost of all the war gods and yogis, Dorje Öden (Rdo rje 'od ldan), I implore you to approach! Four Menmo[71] Sisters, consorts [of Dorje Öden], I implore you to approach! Entourage and

> assembly, [all of you] without exception, I implore you to approach! *Dzaḥ huṃ baṃḥ hoḥ* [sic]! Enter into and become one with the deity being visualized.[72]

The ritual manual for Khentii Khan Mountain also closely follows this paradigm. It commences by acknowledging Vajrapāṇi as the protector deity of Mongolia in general and then, from within emptiness, the ritual specialists are to visualize the arranged offerings arising from the seed-syllables *oṃ*, *aḥ*, and *hūṃ*. These offerings traverse infinite space to delight Samantabhadra in his Pure Land. After the offerings are consecrated by *mudrās* and mantras, one summons Samantabhadra "in order to tame the northern land of Mongolia."[73]

> In particular, we offer incense to all the praiseworthy *ḍākas* and *ḍākinīs*, guardian spirits, and oath-bound deities, who abide in the sacred sites of many royal mountains such as Khentii Khan, and Bogd Khan Mountain, with its formidable steep ridges. We make an incense offering to Samantabhadra, the great deity of Chinggis Khan's natal land,[74] who is endowed with the power to subjugate the class of demons of the dark side (*nag phyogs bdud*) and to guard and protect the class of deities of the good side (*dkar phyogs lha*), together with his mother and son and their retinue of attendants and messengers. We offer incense to the supernatural brigade (*dmag tshogs rdzu 'phrul*) of gods and demons who master wind, rain, snow, and heat, along with the horse gods, sheep gods, cattle gods, and wealth gods who propagate food and wealth along with the affluence and prosperity of cattle. We offer incense to the local deities, *nāgas*, *yakṣas*, and lake goddesses who control and abide in all mountain and valley [sites] such as the slate cliffs, grassy meadowlands, groves of trees, honey bearing flowers, caves, supports for the local deity (*lha rten*), stone cairns with a single tree staff, brooks, rivers, branching streams, springs, lakes, ponds, pools, and wells [upon] the mountain, all of which are part of the region of this sacred land.[75]

These ritual manuals for Otgontenger Mountain, Bogd Khan Mountain, Choiriin Bogd Mountain, and Khentii Khan Mountain are unusual in that the primary local deities of the mountain are first ritually visualized in a manner similar to tantric tutelary deities before being petitioned and given offerings. Ritual manuals that are not site-specific tend not to acknowledge any iconography of the local deity, and do not ritually conjoin the invoked local deity with a visualized image. Further research will hopefully reveal whether this major distinction in the genre of incense offering rituals is related to a distinction between mountains that fall into the category of *yul lha* cult sites and those that are *neri* sites.

Since Otgontenger Mountain, Bogd Khan Mountain, Choiriin Bogd Mountain, and Khentii Khan are four of the most important mountains in Mongolia, it is not surprising that they have been given the most attention by Mongolian ritual specialists and have the most elaborate ritual traditions. The ritual practices for these mountains establish the local deity of the mountain as being superior in rank to the other local deities of the landscape—a notion most explicit in the ritual manual for the veneration of Otgontenger Mountain. Furthermore, these ritual manuals serve as examples of how Buddhists appropriated the practice of the ritual veneration of the landscape by introducing a ritual tradition that addressed the same pragmatic concerns as the indigenous ritual specialists while operating within the framework of tantric Buddhism. This ritual tradition should not be seen as an unavoidable corruption of Buddhism by "Shamanism"; rather, Buddhist missionaries intentionally constructed a tradition that would appeal to potential converts to Buddhism while making the shamans and elders ritually obsolete in Mongolian society. To reinforce this, embedded in the ritual manuals themselves are narrative elements that describe the conversion of the local deity to the support of the Dharma. The performance of these rituals thus serves as a reminder that the sacred geography of Mongolia has been appropriated by, and thoroughly integrated into the Buddhist tradition.

NOTES

1. See, for instance, Henry Serruys, "Early Lamaism in Mongolia," *Oriens Extremus* 10 (1963): 181–216; Alice Sárközi, "A Text of Popular Religious Belief: Cutting off the Lasso," *Acta Orientalia* 39/1 (1985): 39–40; Alice Sárközi, "A Bon Funeral Rite in Lamaist Mongolia," in *Synkretismus in den Religionen Zentralasiens*, ed. Walther Heissig and Hans-Joachim Klimkeit (Wiesbaden: Otto Harrassowitz, 1987), 119; and Walther Heissig, "Banishing of Illnesses into Effigies in Mongolia," *Asian Folklore Studies* 45 (1986): 33–43. I discuss the problems with Sárközi's articles at length later.

2. Richard S. Cohen, "Nāga, Yakṣiṇī, Buddha: Local Deities and Local Buddhism at Ajanta," *History of Religions* 37/4 (May 1998): 377.

3. See Jonathan Z. Smith, *Imagining Religion: From Babylon to Jonestown* (Chicago, IL: University of Chicago Press, 1982), 55, and *To Take Place*, 104.

4. See Grimes, *Rite Out of Place*, 108–9.

5. Grimes, *Rite Out of Place*, 108.

6. There are a number of emic concepts that are more appropriate than "sacred" as means of describing the perception of a feature of the landscape. Concepts indigenous to Mongolia include the idea that a site is the abode of a *tenger* (deity), that it possesses *id shid* (magical power), and *sur* (splendor). Other emic concepts implying the

sacrality of a place or object were introduced to Mongolia via Tibetan Buddhism—concepts such as *byin rlabs* (blessing), *gnas* (abode), and *rten* (support), all convey a sense of the "sacred" that is entirely immanent.

7. See Walther Heissig, *The Religions of Mongolia* (London: Routledge and Kegan Paul, 1980), 25–26.

8. Although commonly used in the literature on Mongolian and Tibetan religions to refer to the pre-Buddhist indigenous matrix of religious beliefs and practices, when employed in this way "Shamanism" is a less-than-accurate category for understanding Mongolian religions, obscuring through the use of a single totalizing category the internal heterogeneity that exists among ritual specialists within Mongolian societies. For an excellent discussion of the diverse roles of Mongolian ritual specialists, see Caroline Humphrey, *Shamans and Elders: Experience, Knowledge, and Power Among the Daur Mongols* (Oxford: Oxford University Press, 1996), which is discussed in detail later.

9. For an insightful and thorough critique of this all-too-pervasive aspect of twentieth century scholarship on Mongolian religions, see Christopher P. Atwood, "Buddhism and Popular Ritual in Mongolian Religion: A Reexamination of the Fire Cult," *History of Religions* 36/2 (1996): 112–39.

10. Alice Sárközi, "A Text of Popular Religious Belief: Cutting off the Lasso," *Acta Orientalia* 39/1 (1985): 39–40.

11. Among such malevolent forces listed are *pretas*, a term nonexistent in pre-Buddhist Mongolia.

12. Sárközi, "A Text of Popular Religious Belief," 39, 43.

13. Christopher Atwood nicely sums up this problem when he notes that many scholars think that "a ritual with a practical function, for example, to ward off disease or jealous spirits, is ipso facto not Buddhist but rather shamanistic." Atwood, "Buddhism and Popular Ritual," 118.

14. Alice Sárközi, "A Bon Funeral Rite," 119.

15. Alice Sárközi, "A Mongolian Text of Exorcism," in *Shamanism in Eurasia*, ed. Mihály Hoppál (Gottigen: Edition Herodot, 1984), 328.

16. Sárközi, "A Mongolian Text of Exorcism," 334.

17. Pierre Bourdieu, *The Logic of Practice*, tr. Richard Nice (Stanford: Stanford University Press, 1990), 52.

18. Walther Heissig "A Mongolian Source to the Lamaist Suppression of Shamanism in the 17th Century," *Anthropos* 48 (1953): 493. Heissig uses "*ongghot*," the Classical Mongolian spelling of "*ongod*," in the quotes that follow.

19. Heissig, "A Mongolian Source," 511.

20. Heissig, "A Mongolian Source," 511.

21. Walther Heissig presents a synopsis of Neyichi Toyin's biography in "A Mongolian Source," and in *The Religions of Mongolia*.

22. Heissig emphasizes that Neyichi Toyin was criticized for openly disseminating tantric practices. Toyin defended himself against these charges by claiming that his aim was to convert as many Mongols as possible to Buddhism by enticing them with tantric ritual practices. He admitted that teaching tantra in this way would necessarily be superficial and ineffective. The widespread dissemination of tantric practices did not actually

result in the elimination of ritual specialists, whether shamans, lay Buddhist ritual specialists, or ordained ritual specialists. See "A Mongolian Source," 528–30.

23. Charles Bawden summarizes some of the positions Mongolists have proposed in "Two Mongol Texts Concerning Obo-Worship," *Oriens Extremus* 5/1 (1958): 23. Some scholars argue that the *ovoo* was ritually insignificant, or possibly even nonexistent, prior to the introduction of Buddhism and that the cult of the *ovoo* is of Tibetan origin and influence. However, there is ample evidence of ritual practices at stone cairns in cultures across the world; see F. Sierksma, "Sacred Cairns in Pastoral Cultures," *History of Religions* 2/2 (1963): 227–41. For another summary of the history and function of the *ovoo*, see Chaolu Wu and Kevin Stuart, "Rethinking the Mongol *Oboo*," *Anthropos* 90 (1995): 544–54.

24. Bawden, Two Mongol Texts," 40.

25. See Atwood, "Buddhism and Popular Ritual," 137–39.

26. Ágnes Birtalan, "Typology of Stone Cairn Obos," in *Tibetan Mountain Deities, Their Cults and Representations*, ed. Anne-Marie Blondeau (Vienna: Verlag der Österreichischen Akademie der Wissenschaften, 1998), 199–200.

27. Khatgin O. Sukhbaatar, *Mongolyn gazar usny neryn domog* (*Mongolian Legends of the Land*) (Ulaanbaatar: Alliance of Religions and Conservation, 2001), 13. All translations from Mongolian and Tibetan sources are my own, unless otherwise indicated. I am greatly indebted to Erdenebaatar Erdene-Ochir for guiding my translations from Mongolian.

28. The *mani* prayer is, of course, *oṃ maṇi padme hūṃ*. The *megdzem* prayer (Tib. *dmigs brtse ma*) is an homage prayer to Tsong kha pa Blo bzang grags pa (1357–1419) that has three forms: an outer version in which Vajrapāṇi is omitted, an inner version including Vajrapāṇi, and a secret version including Vajrapāṇi and Vajradhāra as the central Buddha.

29. Tib. *rten 'brel*; Mong. *bileg demberelgui*. This could also be understood as conveying the sense of bad omen or inauspiciousness.

30. That is, urinating.

31. Dambii, Sukhiin, "Uul ovoo rashaan usny takhilgand oroltsoj baisan Mongol ulamjlal" (The Mongolian Tradition that has Participated in Offerings to Mountains, Ovoos, and Sacred Mineral Springs) (Ulaanbaatar, pamphlet, 2003), 15–17.

32. This phrase is rather ambiguous. Perhaps it refers to accessories for one's horse, or, more likely, spare parts for one's automobile.

33. Sukhbaatar, *Mongolian Legends of the Land*, 14.

34. Fermented mare's milk.

35. This sentence parallels the previous sentence concerning offering stones from the lower and middle slope of the mountain. Here, the skirt refers to the pile of stones, which cascade outward and downward from the central flagstaff. The practice involves lifting a stone from the bottom of the *ovoo* and placing it nearer to the top and toward the central flagstaff, just as in the previous sentence the practice involves bringing a stone from the bottom of the mountain and placing it on the *ovoo* at its peak.

36. Sukhbaatar, *Mongolian Legends of the Land*, 14.

37. Humphrey, *Shamans and Elders*, 50.

38. Humphrey, *Shamans and Elders,* 51. By "classic spirit-managing shaman" she is referring to the general European theories of Siberian "Shamanism" that identify the shaman as a "wounded healer" who is capable of entering into an ecstatic trance in order to engage with deities and to ascend to heaven or descend to the underworld.

39. Caroline Humphrey, "Chiefly and Shamanist Landscapes in Mongolia," in *The Anthropology of Landscape,* ed. Eric Hirsch and Michael O'Hanlon (Oxford: Clarendon Press, 1995), 135–62.

40. Humphrey, "Chiefly and Shamanist," 148.

41. Elsewhere, Humphrey writes: "[*Ongon*] spirits were 'ancestral' in a different sense from the old man's ancestors. Shamanic spirits had previously belonged to an earlier shaman, but they were not inherited in the male line... The link could zig-zag from women to men and vice-versa, or branch off into temporary animal existence." Humphrey, *Shamans and Elders,* 36–37.

42. Humphrey, "Chiefly and Shamanist," 153. Walther Heissig also cites a Mongolian source on this: "The souls of the Shamans and Shamanesses who have died since a long time ago, becoming the masters, Ongghot and demons of these mountains, streams, brooks, lakes, and forests etc. are helpful as well as harmful to creatures." Heissig, "A Mongolian Source," 508–09. See also Magdalena Tatár, who writes: "The spirits of shaman forefathers are believed to take up residence on mountain tops after their death and the prayers addressed to them often start with a description of their 'dwelling places' "; Magdalena Tatár, "Two Mongol Texts Concerning the Cult of the Mountains," *Acta Orientalia* 30/1 (1976): 15.

43. Humphrey, "Chiefly and Shamanist," 151.

44. Humphrey, "Chiefly and Shamanist," 148.

45. Caroline Humphrey, *Marx Went Away—But Karl Stayed Behind* (Ann Arbor: University of Michigan Press, 1998), 423.

46. Humphrey, *Shamans and Elders,* 128.

47. Humphrey, *Shamans and Elders,* 128. The relationship between ancestors, local deities, and the landscape is highly idiosyncratic and site-specific. Nevertheless, it is possible to generalize: the deaths of unusual people (for instance, shamans) or unusual deaths result in the deceased becoming an ancestral spirit and taking up residence in the landscape. In some instances, the identity of the ancestral spirit becomes integrated with the local deities of the landscape. However, as Humphrey points out, the burial practices that resulted in the transformation of the shaman's soul into an *ongon* preserved a distinction between this type of ancestral spirit and other ancestral spirits or local deities of the landscape.

48. Karmay, *The Arrow and the Spindle* (1998) vol. 1: 432–33.

49. Karmay, *The Arrow and the Spindle* (1998) vol. 1: 441.

50. Karmay, *The Arrow and the Spindle* (1998) vol. 1: 314.

51. Toni Huber, *The Cult of Pure Crystal Mountain: Popular Pilgrimage and Visionary Landscape in Southeast Tibet* (Oxford: Oxford University Press, 1999), 27.

52. These generic texts often have simple titles such as *Klu'i bsangs* or *Sa bdag spyir gser skyems.*

53. *Tenger* is a Mongolian word for a deity as well as for a deified sky or heaven. Here it is used somewhat unusually to refer to one's tutelary deity.

54. O. Barsbold, *Otgontenger uulyn takhilga ba ochirvaani burkhan* ("The Offering [Ritual] to Otgontenger Mountain and Vajrapani Buddha") (Ulaanbaatar, pamphlet, 2004), 15.

55. Tib. *klu*; Mong. *lus*: a class of subterranean and subaquatic beings who are often the recipients of offerings at mountains and *ovoos*.

56. Dambii, "Uul ovoo rashaan us," 14.

57. UNESCO and the Mongolian Ministry of Enlightenment, "Mongolia's Tentative List: Cultural and Natural Heritage" (Paris: UNESCO/WHC, 1996), 39.

58. Humphrey, "Chiefly and Shamanist," 140, 148.

59. Although, to this day animals are killed and eaten during *ovoo* rituals; Buddhists tend to justify this by claiming that the animal is not actually ritually offered as a means of petitioning the deity.

60. Karmay, *The Arrow and the Spindle* (1998) vol. 1: 446. Many sacred sites in Mongolia follow the general pan-Asian paradigm of "mandalization." The Ulaanbaatar valley, which is surrounded by four sacred mountains, is considered to be a *maṇḍala* of Cakrasamvara. On mandalization, see Huber, *The Cult of Pure Crystal Mountain*, 26 and throughout.

61. This ritual manual, entitled *Lha chen od hong theng ker sogs la bsangs mchod 'bul tshul bde legs 'dod dgu'i char 'bebs* (*Praying for the Rain of All Auspicious Desires to Fall: Being the Method for Making Incense Offerings to the Great Deity of Otgontenger Mountain*), was composed by an abbot named Ngag dbang 'phrin las rgya mtsho (dates unknown). It is part of an important collection of ritual manuals published in facsimile by Mongolian scholar Khatgin O. Sukhbaatar in his *Mongolyn takhilgat uul usny sudar orshboi* (*Sacred Sites of Mongolia*) (Ulaanbaatar: WWF Mongolia/ARC, 2001).

62. An epithet of Vajrapāṇi.

63. The Tibetan reads *ba ka bog do* (Mong. *baga bogd*), meaning "little Bogd [mountain]." This is an important epithet for Otgontenger Mountain as it establishes a connection with Bogd Khan Mountain, the southern of four mountains encircling the Ulaanbaatar valley and one of the most important sacred mountains in Mongolia. There is a Mongolian legend that Otgontenger originated on the occasion of a severe drought in Zavkhan province. The famished people sent a strong man to Bogd Khan Mountain to bring part of the mountain, known for its abundant water, back to Zavkhan. The man lassoed the mountain, severing it in half, and took the top half with him, which became known as Otgontenger Mountain. See Sukhbaatar, *Sacred Mountains of Mongolia*, 92.

64. Ngag dbang 'phrin las rgya mtsho, *Lha chen od hong theng ker*, ff. 1b–2b.

65. Ngag dbang 'phrin las rgya mtsho, *Lha chen od hong theng ker*, ff. 3b–4a.

66. Eva Jane Neumann Fridman also found evidence of the Buddhist conversion of *ezen* in Buryatia. "Some shamanic [*ezen*] of *obos* were not 'dismissed from their duties' and instead were given new Tibetan names and even canonical lama portraits... The chief Buryat god, Bukha–Noyon, was changed by lamas into Rinchen-Khan... Other widely known shamanist gods were included in the lamaist pantheon and canonized." Eva Jane Neumann Fridman, *Sacred Geography: Shamanism Among the Buddhist Peoples of Russia* (Budapest: Akadémiai Kiadó, 2004), 137.

67. The text, composed by Blo bzang dpal mgon (dates unknown), exists in manuscript form and is entitled *Sa bdag rgyal po rgan po dkar po la bsangs mchod gtor cho ga*

(*The Torma and Incense Offering Ritual for the Sovereign Master of the Earth, The White Old Man*).

68. An epithet of the Buddha.

69. Blo bzang dpal mgon, *Sa bdag rgyal po rgan po dkar po*, ff. 1b–4b.

70. Dashravdan Unenbiligt, *Pho lha dung skyong dkar po'i gsol mchod* (*The Offering and Invocation to the Male Deity White Shell Protector*), in Sukhbaatar, *Sacred Sites of Mongolia*, 84–88, ff. 1a–2b. Sukhbaatar attributes authorship of this text to Dashravdan Unenbiligt, though the only name in the colophon is Gun dga' pang bde legs (dates unknown). I am grateful to Dr. Greg Hillis for patiently advising me on the many misspellings and opaque passages in this text. A similar ritual manual that exists in manuscript form, *Pho lha dung skyong dkar po klu dang bcas ba'i bsangs mchod* (*The Incense Offering Ritual to the Male Deity White Shell Protector and the Nāga*) by Blo bzang dpal ldan bstan pa'i nyi ma, eschews the visualization of the deity and instead commences with an elaborate visualization of *torma* to be presented to the deity. Blo bzang dpal ldan bstan pa'i nyi ma is the name of the Fourth Paṇ chen bla ma (1782–1853), who may be the author of this text.

71. Guardian deities of lakes.

72. Blo bzang tshul khrims rgya mtsho, *Byang phyogs khal kha'i yul gyi 'od gsel ri bo gnas skyong rdo rje 'od ldan gyi gsol mchod bdud rgyal dung gi sgra dbyangs* (*The Euphonious Conch Shell of the King of the Maras: The Offering and Invocation to Rdo rje 'od ldan, The Abode Protector of Choiriin Bogd Sacred Mountain in the Land of the Northern Khalkha Mongols*), ff. 2a–4a. TBRC P3096 lists a Blo bzang tshul khrims rgya mtsho (1841–1907) as having visited Mongolia. It is therefore possible that during his time there he composed this ritual manual.

73. Zava Damdin (Blo bzang rta mgrim = Blo bzang rta dbyangs, 1867–1937) *Kun tu bzang po zhes grags pa'i sa 'dzin dbang po'i lha klu gzhi bdag rnams la bsangs mchod 'bul tshul kun bzang dga' ston zhes bya ba* (*The Banquet of Samantabhadra: Being The Method for Making Incense Offerings to the Local Deity, Nāga, and Master of the Area of The Powerful Mountain Renowned as Samantabhadra*), in Sukhbaatar, *Sacred Sites of Mongolia*, 96–100, ff. 1b–2b.

74. At the beginning of this ritual manual (f. 1b), Chinggis Khan is identified as the *cakravartin* of the region of Khentii Khan Mountain. Sukhbaatar notes that this region is sacred on account of being a burial site of the great Khans (see Sukhbaatar, *Sacred Sites of Mongolia*, 96). This further supports the notion that the Buddhist ritual tradition that venerates sacred mountains and mountain deities has also integrated local ancestral spirits into the pantheon of deities venerated.

75. Zava Damdin, *Kun tu bzang po*, ff. 4a–5a.

11

Encounter with a Dream

Bhutanese Pilgrims in Tibet—Performing a Ritual?

FRANÇOISE POMMARET

In recent years Katia Buffetrille, Toni Huber, and Alex McKay,[1] among other scholars, have made breakthrough contributions to the field of Tibetan pilgrimage studies. This chapter does not pretend to be a thorough study of pilgrimage, comparable to the work of these colleagues. Its scope is rather more modest. In 2007, I had the good fortune to go for a week on a pilgrimage to Tibet with Bhutanese friends. Bhutanese pilgrimage has never been documented. This chapter is therefore meant as a contribution to the corpus of data on pilgrimage in the Tibetan and Himalayan world by adding some observations concerning the Bhutanese case, and how it might be considered a form of ritual.[2] First, I briefly place Bhutanese pilgrimage to Tibet in the context of religious history and geography. Then I propose to interpret the pilgrimage as a form of ritual, and present some salient features based on the fieldtrip to support my point.

Bhutanese Pilgrims in Tibet

For centuries and until 1959, Bhutanese used to go to Tibet for religious purposes as well as for trade. Because of their Drugpa ('Brug pa) and Nyingmapa (Rnying ma pa) long-standing religious affiliations, Bhutanese went mostly to south-central Tibet, including Lhodrag (Lho brag), Kongpo, Dagpo (Dwags po), and Kham (Khams); monks studied in the central Tibetan monasteries of Drug Ralung ('Brug Rwa lung), Mindröl

Ling (Smin grol gling), Dorje Drag (Rdo rje brag), as well as in several monasteries in Kham, especially Dzogchen (Rdzogs chen), Katog (Kaḥ thog), Pelyul (Dpal yul), and Pelpung (Dpal spungs). There are also records of Bhutanese monks studying in the Gelugpa (Dge lugs pa) stronghold of Drepung ('Bras spungs) near Lhasa in the 1920s.[3] Moreover, among many other examples, we know about reincarnation links between Bhutan and Tibet,[4] countless trips by Tibetan and Bhutanese lamas[5] and by the royal family in the early twentieth century[6] as well as of the large offerings made to religious masters, temples, and monasteries in Tibet.[7] All these religious interactions reinforced the sense of the two countries having a common religious base. The pilgrimage to Tibet was rarely seen as a political gesture of any sort, but rather as a form of worship at a common fountainhead, in the same way as Muslims from all over the world go to Mecca, Roman Catholics to Rome, or Jews to Jerusalem. In Tibet, the most common pilgrimage circuit done by the Bhutanese was Tsari in southern Dagpo, on the border with Arunachal Pradesh, India, and the expression *Tsari nyugma* (*Tsa ri snyug ma*), "the bamboo of Tsari," is still used in Bhutan in songs and literature. Unfortunately, there seems to be no written record of Bhutanese pilgrimage to Tsari.

Under the guise of pilgrimage, however, missions could be undertaken when required. One of the most famous examples is the mission to Tibet by Chung Rinpoché Ngawang Pekar (Chung rin po che Ngag dbang pad dkar, b. 17th century) at the end of the seventeenth century, as related in the biography of his brother Jamgön Ngawang Gyeltsen (Byams mgon ngag dbang rgyal mtshan 1647–1732), who himself was at the Derge King's court for several years:

> Desi Gedün Chöphel summoned to the capital Jamgön's brother Ngawang Pekar He instructed him to go to Kham under the pretext of conducting a pilgrimage and deliver a letter giving Jamgön permission to return, should he have fulfilled his mission there. The Desi considered this the best option—dispatch of a special envoy was not thought appropriate, since the prevailing relationship between Bhutan and Tibet was not harmonious.[8]

After the closure of the border in 1959, all interactions stopped. Although Bhutan is closer to central Tibet than, for example, Kham is, Tibet became a distant and fabled land as remote as the mythical Shambhala. It was almost forty years, toward the end of the 1990s, until the Bhutanese started going to Tibet again, and this time officially as tourists. For the Tibet Autonomous Region (TAR), there is no special financial concession available to the Bhutanese; they have to form a group and pay the same amount as Western tourists. Travel agents in Thimphu with connections in Kathmandu advertise groups meant as "Pilgrimages (*gnas skor*) to Tibet" in the Bhutanese media. Of course, to go to Tibet one has to be quite well-off, or make a special financial effort. A large part of the Bhutanese can afford to go to Nepal or Bodhgaya, which they do in winter, but Tibet is still too expensive for eighty percent of the population. Among the urban middle-class in their 40s, those who can afford the trip first offer it to their parents as a kind of thanksgiving gesture, with the view that their elderly parents should have priority. If the children have means, they accompany the parents; otherwise they wait for "their turn."

It is the dream of every Bhutanese to go to Tibet, and the trip is never envisaged as a simple trip but always as a *nekor*, a pilgrimage. The whole mental outlook concerning the journey is therefore very specific: the eventual hardships or personal inconveniences that may be encountered are never mentioned. It is a religious journey that is going to bring merit and help one's practice. The reality of geography or of politics has absolutely no relevance, and the history of the place visited is significant only insofar as a given site has some connection with renowned religious figures or important religious events.

The Dalai Lama's comments on pilgrimage apply perfectly to the Bhutanese pilgrims:

> They (Buddhists) visit places where a spiritual master once spent time meditating. His presence makes the place seem somehow blessed or charged, as if there is some kind of electricity around it. Pilgrims come to feel these mysterious vibrations. They try to share in the visions of the master. Along their road, they undertake hardship with no thought of material reward. Their every step, every movement, becomes filled with a sense of spiritual progress. Many intensify the sense of hardship along the way by going barefoot, or reciting prayers or mantras, and so increase the spiritual merit they gain.[9]

Although there is no written Bhutanese pilgrimage guide or *neyig* (*gnas yig*) of Tibet, our whole trip becomes an enacted *neyig*, and after such an experience, I would almost feel competent to write a traditional *gnas yig* of the places visited by the Bhutanese.

The Religious Geography of Tibet in the Bhutanese Mind: Lhasa, Samyé, Pö (Bod), and Kham

Most Bhutanese traditionally care very little about geography, and the Western obsession with the names of the mountains, passes, maps, etc. never ceases to astonish them. Instead, Bhutanese need to know how long a trip takes, where the evening stops for food and shelter will be, and when holy places are going to be encountered.

The notion of Tibet is in fact relatively recent, and for most Bhutanese Tibet is not defined in scientific or geographical terms. Tibet or Pö (Bod) means Lhasa and Samyé, which in their minds is somewhere near Lhasa. Pö—or rather Ütsang (Dbus Gtsang), central and western Tibet—is the region that is geographically close to Bhutan; Kham is very important in religious geography because of all the important Kargyu, Nyingma, and Rimé (Ris med) centers located there, but only a few people know where Kham is actually located, and how far it is from Lhasa.

Rather than being geographic entities on a map, names like Lhasa and Kham conjure up religious images. Bhutanese dream Tibet, but not a fantasy Tibet like that found in the Western imaginary. They dream the religious side of the place, and visit it with this perception—that is, with a sense of religious devotion and awe.

Therefore, to walk into this Tibet, a religiously imagined entity, in an age of permits, passports, and tickets, the Bhutanese need someone not only to organize the material side of the trip, but also someone to serve as a guide who will explain the meaning of the places. The tradition of having a person with a religious background in the group, and if possible someone who speaks Tibetan, is still an ideal; it is essential in order for the pilgrimage to have its full impact and for the full benefit to participants to be realized. The figure of the religious guide is in fact as central to the pilgrimage as it is to a ritual, and it is this aspect that I would like to now explore.

Pilgrimage as a Ritual

Toni Huber writes:

> Like many examples of Tibetan popular ritual, they [pilgrimages] are in fact a combination of different acts and rites . . . Tibetan pilgrimages can encompass mundane material concerns, complex social agendas, and both proximate and ultimate soteriological orientations and goals. Thus, as a general class of ritual activity, they are not amenable to either simple description and analysis or rigid classification.[10]

This might have deterred me from trying to write on the subject. However, Toni Huber's remarks refer to pilgrimages in general, and I am focusing here on the specific topic of Bhutanese pilgrimage to Tibet, which, as mentioned earlier, has not been previously documented in Western scholarly literature. I attempt to point out convergences between pilgrimage and ritual, without denying the multiplicity of approaches and the uniqueness of each pilgrimage.

Pilgrimage belongs to the ritual corpus in the sense that it is a religious action performed with a religious guide for defined aims with a right attitude and in a well- defined spatio-temporal dimension. It is sequenced like a ritual by a series of prerequisites, or features, which are also usually present in rituals, and that I now describe.

1. *Material Arrangements.* A number of material arrangements have to be made before departure. This includes the financial side of the journey, settling on an appropriate time so as not to disturb the agricultural calendar or other activities, the availability of people to look after the household while family members are away, and eventually the determination of the astrologically auspicious time, although the mere act of visiting Tibet appears to outweigh (in the sense of being more auspicious than) any impact of a negative date.

   Moreover, threads and modern religious objects such as small *vajras* or *cakras* (wheels) have to be purchased in order that these might be blessed in each of the holy places. This shopping is usually done at Boudanath in Nepal, a great pilgrimage place for the Bhutanese, who feel at ease here since they all speak Nepali. Lastly, gold or semiprecious stones belonging to the family might be taken along for "adorning"—that is, as offerings to—statues in Tibet. Other offerings include white scarves and money for offerings (*snyan dar*[11]) given by friends and family, homemade butter, and Bhutanese incense, reported to be highly valued in Tibet.[12]
2. *The Religious Guide.* For a Bhutanese going to Tibet, a religious guide is indispensable, and some would-be pilgrims would not go if such a person were not available. The person has to speak Tibetan, has to be able to explain the religious significance of the sites, and has to translate for the pilgrims the explanations given by Tibetan temple-custodians. It matters little if the religious guide has not previously visited the sites; the most important trait of the guide is that he or she provide explanations and impart a sense of religious values while visiting the sites. This is necessary in order to obtain the maximum benefit and merit. It also, of course, serves as teaching, which will ultimately enhance the personal practice of the pilgrim.
3. *Right Attitude.* The pilgrims should have a sense of commitment and not harbor any negative feelings or attitudes, something that is perceived as diminishing the spiritual benefit of the journey for the whole group. Squabbles and interpersonal conflicts therefore have to be avoided so as not to create negative feelings and distract the group

members from their spiritual enterprise. In addition, if the group encounters any hardship or obstacle on the way, this should be taken as a test of their determination. It should not affect their positive attitude.

4. *Correct Performance.* Again, as in the case of a ritual, the correct performance of the pilgrimage is of tantamount importance because its efficacy depends on it. This is where the religious guide plays an important role. The members of the group must also be aware of the series of duties that pilgrims perform at each place.

The "mandalization" of space in Tibetan culture has been well studied.[13] In the case of a holy site, even if the pilgrims are not highly educated, the site is, consciously or not, envisaged as a three-dimensional *maṇḍala*. However, at the sites, the physical movements are the reverse of those in the practice of the meditation in front of a *maṇḍala*. Thus, the pilgrims go straight inside the temple and prostrate in front of the main image; they then offer their monetary contribution and the incense bundles which they carried from Bhutan. Then they circumambulate the temple inside and listen to religious explanations of important statues, relics, as well as stone imprints and unusual rock formation or specific trees. They do not hesitate to collect water, earth, bark (see Figure 11.1),

FIGURE 11.1. Collecting bits of bark from a sacred site. Photo F. Pommaret (2007).

leaves, or small stones which have a special meaning, and are empowered by virtue of their association with different holy places.[14]

In the Jokhang Temple, pilgrims obtain, in return for monetary donations, a few ready-made packets containing pieces of the Jowo (Jo bo) statue's clothes; they also receive blessed pills. Upon their return, these mementos are placed in the family altar and also distributed, as we shall see. Wherever they go, the pilgrims touch the images and relics with their head for the blessing, and briefly place on the images the bag containing the cords and amulets purchased before departure so that the objects also get blessed. While doing so, they pray and place a small monetary contribution in front of each image and relic. They also offer the monetary contributions and scarves that friends and relatives have sent with them. After completing their visit, they go outside the temple and circumambulate it, spinning prayer-wheels as they go.

The holy sites have value, not only because of what they religiously embody, but also by virtue of the presence of the religious and mythical figures who visited or lived there. In a holy place, past and present, history and myth are transcended to become one forceful spiritual entity which ultimately benefits the pilgrims.

5. *Offerings.* Besides the monetary contribution made in each temple and in front of each image, Bhutanese pilgrims usually make special offerings at the Jokhang and at Samyé, the two most important sites for them. Bhutanese know the story of the construction of the Jokhang, as two of the "Temples for Subjugating [Spirits]" (*mtha' 'dul dang yang 'dul gyi gtsug lag khang*) are located in Bhutan: Kyichu (Skyid chu) in Paro valley and Jampa (Byams pa) in Bumthang valley. Moreover, the story of the Nepalese and Chinese spouses of King Songtsen Gampo is very popular in Bhutan, and the Jowo is the most revered image. Samyé is considered special because of the devotion that all Bhutanese have for Guru Rinpoché, and because of their fervent belief that Bhutan is protected by him. Pilgrims offer gold and stones to the images, or even flower arrangements. They also light 50, 100, or 1,000 butter-lamps for the benefit of their entire family.

A trip to Tibet is also an occasion to hang prayer-flags or *lungta* (*rlung rta*) for the well-being of the pilgrims. Their religious guide chooses the most appropriate day and place to do so. He then recites the short *lungta* prayer, considered a mind treasure (*dgongs gter*) of the revered Nyinmapa master Düjom Rinpoché (Bdud 'joms rin po che 'Jig dral ye shes rdo rje, 1904–87), which incorporates the *lotag* (*lo rtags*), the animal sign of the birth year of the person (Figure 11.2).

FIGURE 11.2. The religious guide at a prayer-flag site. Photo F. Pommaret (2007).

The visits as well as the offerings are accomplished by paying attention to the smallest details in order to gain the greatest religious benefit, but pilgrims are also careful not to do anything that could jeopardize or pollute the blessings thus acquired.[15]

6. *Sharing the Blessed Objects.* The objects collected at the sites as well as the prepurchased objects blessed during the pilgrimage are kept isolated and clean in the luggage. They are wrapped separately, and should not touch any clothing or shoes, which are considered dirty. They are usually carried as hand luggage on the plane. These objects are not only blessings for the pilgrim and empowered mementos that will be placed in the family altar, but they are also the living testimonies of the pilgrimage; they confer on the pilgrim an elevated status in the society. The protection cords, which everyone had brought in ample quantity, are distributed to the whole family, colleagues, and friends, with priority given to sick people. The small objects, such as the *vajras* and wheels or *cakras*, are given to monks and to young people, who often attach them onto their mobile phones. The blessed water and the small natural or vegetable mementos from the holy site are kept in the family altar, and will be used in minuscule quantities in times of need—for example, when someone is sick or dying.

> For the Bhutanese, another important testimony of having made the pilgrimage are photos, which are, like the objects, empowered by the different places visited, and are testimonies of their visits. These too confer prestige to the pilgrims. They pose in front of each temple and try to take a photo of the Jowo statue in the Jokhang as they are ushered by it. Taking photos is now a part of the pilgrimage ritual, one of the requirements for a pilgrimage to be successful. Photos of sites will be distributed to relatives and placed in the altar; albums will be put together; entrance tickets are added to the photos for visitors to the household to see. Each photo is then commented on, and religious explanations are given to people who did not have the chance to go. The audience, in turn, listens with admiration and envy.

The purposes of a pilgrimage are complex and multifaceted. The Dalai Lama provides one explanation:

> We Buddhists believe that merit is accumulated when you take part in something religious, with discipline and faith, because in doing so you shape a proper attitude within. With the right attitude, any journey to a sacred place becomes a pilgrimage. In our tradition, the Buddha advised that in times to come people interested in his teachings should be told about the places associated with the major events of his life. His purpose was not to ensure the aggrandizement of the person of the Buddha, but rather the welfare of his followers. We believe that expressing respect and admiration for the qualities of the Buddha—by making offerings or undertaking a pilgrimage—contributes to our own spiritual progress.[16]

Bhutanese pilgrims share the same beliefs and goals when they undertake a pilgrimage: not only cleansing, empowerment, gaining merit, but also increasing their determination for religious practice in their daily life. This aspect seems to be particularly important for them, and it is an occasion to take pledges to become better practitioners. It is seen as giving one the opportunity to take one more step in one's religious practice.

Like a ritual, pilgrimage is therefore the occasion to renew the faith of the person and to ask for protection. It is composed of a number of sequences and actions which have to be performed with the right attitude to have a maximum efficacy, whatever the complex personal aims of the pilgrims might be. They could be summarized as follows: preparations; performance, offerings, and liturgy (if we consider prayers examples of this); blessings; sharing of the objects.

Specificities of Bhutanese Pilgrims

It is a truism to say that people only see what they are familiar with and what has relevance for them. In the case of Bhutanese pilgrims, although all the religious sites are holy, because of the financial constraints, they usually cannot spend more than one week to ten days in Tibet. Because of this they have to prioritize, in accordance with their religious interests, which sites they will visit. Moreover, some of the sites that they would like to visit are out of bounds for foreigners (at least for the time being)—places like Ralung and Lhodrag.

For the Bhutanese, the most important accessible sites are Lhasa, Samyé, and Mindröl Ling. However, given the opportunity, they would also visit Kongpo, where several sites are associated with prestigious "treasure revealers" or *tertöns* (*gter ston*), and especially with the Second Düjom Rinpoché (Bdud 'joms rin po che), whose teachings (*gter gsar*) have been tremendously influential in Bhutan. In Kongpo, the sites visited are Tso Dzong (Mtsho rdzong) in Dragsum Tso (Brag gsum mtsho), Langma Ling (Glang ma gling), and Puchu (Spu chu), another "border taming" (*mtha' 'dul*) temple.

In Lhasa, where they do not usually spend more than two days, a selection again has to be made. The Potala, the Jokhang, and Ramoche (Ra mo che) temples, the Norbu Lingkha (Nor bu gling kha) summer palace, and at least one of the great Gelugpa monasteries are visited with great fervor, and in the case of the Potala, even awe. Time is also set aside for circumambulating the Jokhang along its Barkor (Bar skor) circuit as well as for special offerings inside the temple itself.

While on pilgrimage, the Bhutanese do not have an exclusive or sectarian view. All the sites are holy, and they would gladly spend two to three weeks in central Tibet, but as stated earlier, because of the financial cost of a pilgrimage, they select the sites which are most important for them.

Bhutanese are puzzled by the fact that in Tibet today the most famous holy sites are monuments at which one has to pay an entrance fee, as this does not exist in Bhutan. Coming from a society which is very traditional when it comes to religion, they are surprised that one does not have to remove one's shoes or hats when entering a temple, and that the protector deity chapels (*mgon khang*) are open to public viewing. My companions were happy to see that in the two temples associated with Düjom Rinpoché in Kongpo—Tsodzong at Dragsum Tso and Langma Ling—shoes had to be removed and that the temples were spotless. In fact, the relative untidiness of the majority of temples is something of a shock for the Bhutanese, who consider a clean temple to be a sign of respect, as well as being the tangible reflection of a nonpolluted space.

In a society like Bhutan where everyone has a personal contact, and where crowds are unknown, the masses of pilgrims and the pushing in the Jokhang and Potala were quite unsettling for the Bhutanese, who had problems concentrating on their prayers. They preferred to go round the Barkor at night when there were fewer people, and the atmosphere was more serene. Although they were happy to purchase small offering packets from the Jokhang to take back to Bhutan, the seeming lack of attention from the monks and the lack of private space for personal devotions disturbed them.

The Bhutanese do not prostrate full length like the Tibetans do, but I ignore the origin of this gestural difference. The encounter, on a road in Kongpo, with a whole family from Derge in Kham (Sichuan), including five children, who were prostrating all the way to Lhasa, amazed them and filled them with admiration. This style of worship and pilgrimage does not exist in Bhutan, and neither is there a tradition of prostrating around a monument or in front of it.[17] All prostrations are done inside a temple.

Another custom that does not exist in Bhutan is the throwing of small *lungta* papers and shouting, "Victory to the Gods!" (*lha rgyal lo*) at the passes, although some people say the words in a discreet manner. Bhutanese prefer to add a small stone to the cairn which are often found at the pass. Although Bhutanese found that throwing *lungta* papers was an auspicious custom, they thought it was damaging to the environment.

As mentioned earlier, photos sessions are very important for Bhutanese pilgrims. The difference in the living standard of Bhutanese and Tibetan pilgrims probably explains this major difference in modern pilgrimage practice.

There is, however, one aspect of the pilgrimage which has totally disappeared due to modern socio-economic circumstances: today Bhutanese do not trade when they go on pilgrimage to Tibet. In the past, Bhutanese, as many Tibetans still do, used to combine pilgrimage with petty trade, which financed their journey. The trade was based on the barter system. The Bhutanese carried paper, raw silk (*bu ras*), madder, and lac (*laccifer lacca*) as well as bamboo wares, textiles, and even rice. They came back with woolen cloth, gold, salt, borax, Chinese brick tea, and Chinese silk.

Conclusions

Alex McKay writes that "pilgrimage is a core element of religious practice in the Tibetan cultural world... Pilgrimage today remains not only an almost universal feature of Tibetan society but also serves as a prominent indicator of local and national cultural identity."[18] Bhutanese pilgrims, wandering in Lhasa in traditional costumes, are recognized as Drukpa ('Brug pa) and as kin in religion. Although the journey to Tibet was physically accomplished, it was as much a spiritual journey enacted through the mediation of religious and cultural markers—a magical–realist endeavor.

Bhutanese step into the spiritual geography, common to peoples of the Himalayas, Mongolia, and Tibet; they walk, pray, and prostrate with pilgrims from Kham, Amdo, or Kongpo, all with their distinctive languages and dress, but all going through the common ritual vocabulary of pilgrimage.

NOTES

1. Katia Buffetrille, *Pèlerinages tibétains aux montagnes sacrées* (Oslo: Norwegian University Press, The Institute for Comparative Research in Human Culture, forthcoming). Toni Huber, "Putting the *gnas* Back into *gnas-skor*: Rethinking Tibetan Buddhist Pilgrimage Practice," in Toni Huber, ed., *Sacred Spaces and Powerful Places in Tibetan Religious Culture* (Dharamsala: Library of Tibetan Works and Archives, 1999), 77–104, and *The Cult of Pure Crystal Mountain. Popular Pilgrimage and Visionary Landscape in Southeast Tibet* (New York and London: Oxford University Press, 1999). Alex McKay, ed., *Pilgrimage in Tibet* (London: Routledge Curzon, 1998).

2. The trip took place from January 2007 to February 2007.

3. Michael Aris, *The Raven Crown* (London: Serindia, 1994), 106.

4. Françoise Pommaret, "Historical and Religious Relations Between Lhodrak (Southern Tibet) and Bumthang (Bhutan) from the 18th to the early 20th Century: Preliminary Data," in *Tibet and Her Neighbours. Proceedings of the History of Tibet Conference St. Andrews University 2001*, Alex Mckay, ed. (London: Ed. Hansjörg Mayer, 2003), 91–106.

5. See, among others works on the subject: (1) John Ardussi, "Observations on the Political Organisation of Western Bhutan in the 14th Century as Revealed in Records of the 'Bra ra' ba Sect," in *Impressions of Bhutan and Tibetan Art, Proceedings of the 9th IATS Leiden 2000, Tibetan Studies III*, ed. John Ardussi and Henk Blezer (Leiden: Brill, 2002), 5–21. (2) "The Rapprochement Between Bhutan and Tibet Under the Enlightened Rule of *sDe srid* XIII Shes-rab-dbang-phyug (r. 1744–63)," *Journal of Bhutan Studies* 1/1 (December, 1999): 64–83 (reprinted with corrections from *Proceedings of the International Association of Tibetan Studies VII, Graz, 1995*). (3) "The House of 'Obs-mtsho—The History of a Bhutanese Gentry Family from the 13th to the 20th Century," *Journal of Bhutan Studies* 2/1 (Summer, 2000): 1–29. (4) Samten Karmay, "Dorje Lingpa and his Rediscovery of the 'Gold Needle' in Bhutan," *Journal of Bhutan Studies* 2/2 (Winter, 2000): 1–34. (5) Dorji Penjore, "Oral Construction of Exile Life and Times of Künkhyen Longchen Rabjam in Bumthang," *Journal of Bhutan* Studies 13/2 (Winter, 2005): 60–73. (6) Lham Dorji, "Religious Life and History of the Ematated Heart-son Thukse Dawa Gyeltshen," *Journal of Bhutan Studies* 13/2 (Winter, 2005): 74–104. (7) Yoshiro Imaeda, Karma Ura and Mynak Tulku, photographer Satoru Tabuchi, *Festival and Faith at Nyimalung* (Tokyo: Hirakawa, Shuppan Inc., 2002), 195–209. (8) Sarah Harding, *The Life and Revelations of Pema Lingpa* (Ithaca: Snow Lion, 2003). (9) Françoise Pommaret,

"The Fascinating Life of Lama Changchub Tsöngru (1817–1856) According to his Biography," in *The Spider and the Piglet. Proceedings of the 1st International Seminar on Bhutanese Studies 2003*, ed. Karma Ura and Sonam Kinga (Thimphu: Centre for Bhutan Studies, 2004), 73–89.

6. See, among others, Aris, *The Raven Crown*; Slob dpon Padma tshe dbang, *'Brug gi rgyal rabs slob dpon Padma tshe dbang gis sbyar 'Brug gsal ba'i sgron me* ("History of Bhutan by Lopön Padma Tshewang") (Thimphu: National Library, 1994).

7. David Jackson, "The 'Bhutan Abbot' of Ngor," in *Lungta* 14 (Aspects of Tibetan History), ed. Tashi Tsering, guest ed. Roberto Vitali (Dharamsala: Amnye Machen Institute, Spring 2001): 88–107. Padma tshe dbang, *'Brug gi rgyal rabs.* Yonten Dargye and Per K. Sorensen, with Gyönpo Tshering, *Play of the Omniscient: Life and Works of Jamgön Ngawang Gyaltshen, an Eminent 17–18th Century Drukpa Master* (Thimphu: National Library & Archives of Bhutan, 2008).

8. Yonten Dargye and Sørensen, *Play of the Omniscient*, 111.

9. The Dalai Lama, "The Path to Enlightenment," Web-exclusive Commentary, *Newsweek*, April 21, 2007, [Online] available at http://www. newsweek.com/id/35298.

10. Huber, *The Cult of Pure Crystal Mountain*, 12.

11. *Snyan dar*, contraction of *snyan zhu 'bul ba'i dar*, originally meant "the silk/scarf to inform/to pray"; verses could be written on it (Samten Karmay, private communication, July 2007). In Bhutan, *snyan dar* has also come to mean the money for the offerings.

12. Interestingly, the most valued Bhutanese incense is made from a recipe originally from Smin grol gling monastery.

13. For example, A. W. Macdonald, ed., *Mandala and Landscape* (New Delhi: DK Printworld, 1997).

14. Toni Huber, *The Cult of Pure Crystal Mountain*, 14: "The collection of stones, pinches of soil or dust (often called *nédo*, '*né* stones,' and *nésa*, '*né* earth'), plants, the drinking water, and so on in the physical environment of a *né* are all common, though subtle and thus often unnoticed, forms of ritual activity on pilgrimages. Such *chinlab* 'harvests' thus procure portable sources of a site's power to be directly consumed, or carried of for later use and further distribution."

15. Toni Huber, *The Cult of Pure Crystal Mountain*, 16–17, analyzes this situation in the following way: "Pilgrimage is seen by the Tibetans as a fundamental method of removing, purifying, or cleansing embodied *drib* and *dik* and is thus a ritual of relevance to a wide range of general material, social and salvational concerns, from which all levels of practitioner can benefit... Whether conceived of as washed, purified, or flooded by power in various ways, the ritually transformed body of the pilgrim attains a different status."

16. The Dalai Lama, "The Path to Enlightenment."

17. Prostrations are nowadays done in front of the memorial *mchod rten* in Thimphu, mostly by worshippers of Tibetan descent. However, since 2007, three cases of full prostrations from one holy place to another have been documented in Bhutan.

18. McKay, *Pilgrimage in Tibet*, 1.

Bibliography

A myes zhabs Ngag dbang kun dga' bsod nams, 'Jam mgon. *Bcom ldan 'das rdo rje gzhon nu'i gdams pa nyams len gyi chu bo chen po sgrub pa'i thabs kyi rnam par bshad pa 'phrin las kyi pad mo rab tu rgyas pa'i nyin byed*. New Delhi: Ngawang Sopa, 1972. Microfiche, The Institute for Advanced Studies of World Religions, *'Khon lugs Phur pa'i rnam bśad, 'Chams yig brjed byaṅ*, LMpj 012,223.

Aalto, Pentii. "Notes on the Altangerel (*The Mongolian Version of the Suvarṇaprabhāsa-sūtra*)." *Studia Orientalia. Edidit Societas Orientalis Fennica* 14 (1950): 14–26.

Abhayakīrti ('Jigs med grags pa). *Mi pham mgon po la bstod pa'i 'chi slu ma zhes bya ba* (Skt. *Ajitanāthastutimṛtyuvañcanā nāma*). Peking Bstan 'gyur, no. 4605, Rgyud 'grel *pu*, ff. 4a.1–4a.8.

Abu-Lughod, Lila. "Writing Against Culture." In *Recapturing Anthropology: Working in the Present*, ed. Richard G. Fox, 137–62. Santa Fe: School of American Research Press, 1991.

Amoghavajra (Pukong). *Da kongque mingwang huaxiang tanchang yigui*. Taishō vol. 19, no. 983a, 439–41.

Ardussi, John R. "The Rapprochement Between Bhutan and Tibet Under the Enlightened Rule of *sDe srid* XIII Shes-rab-dbang-phyug (r. 1744–1763)." *Journal of Bhutan Studies*, 1/1 (December 1999): 64–83. Also online at: http://www.digitalhimalaya.com/collections/journals/jbs/index.php?selection=1.

———. "The House of 'Obs-mtsho – The History of a Bhutanese Gentry Family from the 13th to the 20th Century." *Journal of Bhutan Studies* 2/1 (Summer, 2000): 1–29. Also online at: http://www.digitalhimalaya.com/collections/journals/jbs/index.php?selection=2.

Ardussi, John R. "Observations on the Political Organisation of Western Bhutan in the 14th century as Revealed in Records of the 'Ba' ra ba Sect." In *Impressions of Bhutan and Tibetan Art, Proceedings of the 9th IATS Leiden 2000, Tibetan Studies III*, ed. John Ardussi and Hank Blezer, 5–35. Leiden: Brill, 2002.

Aris, Michael. *The Raven Crown*. London: Serindia, 1994.

Ārya Maṇibhadra-nāma Dhāraṇī (*'Phags pa nor bu bzang po'i gzungs*). Sde dge Bka' 'gyur, Toh. no. 764, Rgyud *wa*, ff. 56a.1–56b.2; and Sde dge Bka' 'gyur, Toh. no. 970, Gzungs *wam*, ff. 86a.4–86b.7.

Asboe, Rev. Walter. "The Scape-Goat in Western Tibet." *Man* 36 (1936): 74–75.

———. "Sacrifices in Western Tibet." *Man* 36 (1936): 75–76.

Atkinson, Jane M. *The Art and Politics of Wana Shamanship*. Berkeley: University of California Press, 1989.

Atwood, Christopher. "Buddhism and Popular Ritual in Mongolian Religion: A Reexamination of the Fire Cult." *History of Religions* 36/2 (1996): 112–39.

Austin, J. L. *How to Do Things with Words*. New York: Oxford University Press, 1962.

Ba ri lo tsā ba Rin chen grags. *Lha pa'i lha rnams kyi sgrub thabs kun las btus pa ba ri brgya rtsa'i rgya gzhung rnams*, 14 vols. Dehradun, U.P., India: G. T. K. Jodoy, N. Gyaltsen, and N. Lungtok, 1970.

———. *Be'u bum of ba ri lo tsā ba rin chen grags*. Delhi: Jurme Drakpa, 1974.

Bagchi, S., ed. *Guhyasamāja Tantra (Tathāgataguhyaka)*. Buddhist Sanskrit Texts Series, no. 9. Darbhanga: The Mithila Institute, 1965.

Bakhtin, Mikhail. *The Dialogical Imagination: Four Essays*. Tr. Caryl Emerson and Michael Holquist. Austin: University of Texas Press, 1981.

Barron, Richard, tr. and ed. *The Autobiography of Jamgön Kongtrul: A Gem of Many Colors*. Ithaca: Snow Lion Publications, 2003.

Barsbold, O. *Otgontenger uulyn takhilga ba ochirvaani burkhan*. Ulaanbaatar, 2004. Pamphlet.

Bawden, Charles R. "Two Mongol Texts Concerning Obo-Worship." *Oriens Extremus*: 5/1 (1958): 23–41.

———. *The Modern History of Mongolia*. London, New York: Kegan Paul International, 1989.

———. "The Supernatural Element in Sickness and Death According to Mongol Tradition." In Charles R. Bawden, *Confronting the Supernatural: Mongolian Traditional Ways and Means*, 40–110. Wiesbaden: Harrassowitz Verlag, 1994.

———. "On the Practice of Scapulimancy Among the Mongols." In Charles R. Bawden, *Confronting the Supernatural: Mongolian Traditional Ways and Means*. Wiesbaden: Harrazowits Verlag, 1994, 111–42.

———. *Confronting the Supernatural: Mongolian Traditional Ways and Means*. Wiesbaden: Harrassowitz Verlag, 1994.

Bdud 'joms 'Jigs bral ye shes rdo rje. *Tshe sgrub 'chi med srog thig dang 'brel bar 'chi ba bslu ba'i cho ga 'chi bdag gdong zlog*. In Bdud 'joms 'Jigs bral ye shes rdo rje, *'Chi med srog thig: Gter mas and Ritual Texts Collected by Bdud 'joms 'jigs bral ye shes rdo rje*, 249–59. Varanasi: Deepak Press, 1973.

———. *'Chi med srog thig: Gter mas and Ritual Texts Collected by Bdud 'joms 'jigs bral ye shes rdo rje*. Varanasi: Deepak Press, 1974.

———. *'Chi med srog thig gter ma*. In Bdud 'joms 'Jigs bral ye shes rdo rje, *The Collected Writings and Revelations of H. H. bDud-'joms Rin-po-che 'Jigs bral ye shes rdo rje*, 25 vols, vol. *pha*: 75–554. Kalimpong: Dupjung Lama, 1979–85.

———. *The Collected Writings and Revelations of H. H. bDud-'joms Rin-po-che 'Jigs bral ye shes rdo rje*, 25 vols. Kalimpong: Dupjung Lama, 1979–85.

———. *Gnam lcags spu gri las byang*. In Bdud 'joms 'Jigs bral ye shes rdo rje, *The Collected Writings and Revelations of H. H. bDud-'joms Rin-po-che 'Jigs bral ye shes rdo rje*, vols. *tha* and *da*. Kalimpong: Dupjung Lama, 1979–85.

'Be lo Karma tshe dbang kun khyab. *Yi dam zhi ba dang khro bo'i tshogs kyi sgrub thabs nor bu'i phreng ba'i lo rgyus chos bshad rab 'byams*, block print, 87 folios, Og min mtshur mdo'i chos grwa.

Bell, Catherine. *Ritual: Perspectives and Dimensions*. New York and Oxford: Oxford University Press, 1997.

Bellezza, John Vincent. *Spirit-Mediums, Sacred Mountains and Related Bon Textual Traditions in Upper Tibet: Calling Down the Gods*. Leiden: Brill, 2005.

Bentor, Yael. "Literature on Consecration." In *Tibetan Literature: Studies in Genre*, ed. José Ignacio Cabezón and Roger R. Jackson, 290–311. Ithaca: Snow Lion, 1996.

———. "The Horse-Back Consecration Ritual." In *Religions of Tibet in Practice*, ed. Donald S. Lopez, Jr., 234–54. Princeton: Princeton University Press, 1997.

———. "Identifying the Unnamed Opponents of Tsong-kha-pa and Mkhas-grub-rje Concerning the Transformation of Ordinary Birth, Death and the Intermediate State into the Three Bodies." In *Tibetan Buddhist Literature and Praxis: Studies in Its Formative Period 900–1400*, ed. Ronald M. Davidson and Christian K. Wedemeyer, 185–200. Leiden: Brill, 2006.

Berzin, Alexander. "An Introduction to Tibetan Astonomy and Astrology." *Tibet Journal* 12/1 (1987): 17–28.

Beyer, Stephan. *The Cult of Tārā: Magic and Ritual in Tibet*. 1978. Reprint, Berkeley: University of California Press, 1978.

Bhattacharyya, Benoytosh, ed. *Guhyasamāja Tantra or Tathāgataguhyaka*. Baroda: Oriental Institute, 1931.

Bira, Shagdaryn. "The Worship of the *Suvarṇaprabhāsottama-sūtra* in Mongolia." In *Mongolyn tüükh, soyel, tüükh bichlegiin sudalgaa. Studies in Mongolian History, Culture, and Historiography: Selected Papers*, 3 vols, ed. Ts. Ishdorj and Kh. Purevtogtokh, 3: 322–31. Ulaanbaatar: International Association for Mongol Studies, Mongolian Academy of Sciences, Institute of History, International Institute for the Study of Nomadic Civilization, 2001.

Birtalan, Ágnes. "Typology of Stone Cairn Obos." In *Tibetan Mountain Deities, Their Cults and Representations*, ed. Anne-Marie Blondeau, 199–210. Vienna: Verlag der Österreichischen Akademie der Wissenschaften, 1998.

Bka' rgya karma bi ro gong khug rta mgrin lcags ral dpa' cig gi sgrub pa sangs rgyas gling pa'i gter ma yid 'od lung nas rnyed pa. Bon po brten 'gyur chen mo, vol. 209, sect. 35, chap. 1, 531–38. Lhasa: Sog ldan sprul sku Bstan pa'i nyi ma, 1998.

Blo bzang dpal ldan bstan pa'i nyi ma. *Pho lha dung skyong dkar po klu dang bcas ba'i bsangs mchod*. Dbu can mansucript acquired in Ulaanbaatar, 2004.

Blo bzang dpal mgon. *Sa bdag rgyal po rgan po dkar po la bsangs mchod gtor cho ga.* Dbu can manuscript acquired in Ulaanbaatar, 2004.

Blo bzang nor bu shes rab. *Bskal bzang sangs rgyas stong phrag gi phyag mchod smon lam dang bcas pa bsod nams kyi myu gu 'phel bar byed pa'i 'dud rtsi'i char chen*, 7 vols. Beijing: Yellow Pagoda, 1996–97.

———. 1996–97 (ed.). *Bzang po spyod pa'i sgo nas 'chi bslu ji ltar bya tshul gyi cho ga'i ngag 'don dus min 'chi 'joms.* In Blo bzang nor bu shes rab, *Bskal bzang sangs rgyas stong phrag gi phyag mchod smon lam dang bcas pa bsod nams kyi myu gu 'phel bar byed pa'i 'dud rtsi'i char chen*, 7 vols, vol. 2: 41–51. Beijing: Yellow Pagoda, 1996–97.

Blo bzang tshul khrims rgya mtsho. *Byang phyogs khal kha'i yul gyi 'od gsel ri bo gnas skyong rdo rje 'od ldan gyi gsol mchod bdud rgyal dung gi sdra dbyangs zhes bya ba.* Dbu can mansucript acquired in Ulaanbaatar, 2004.

Bloch, Maurice. *From Blessing to Violence: History and Ideology in the Circumcision Ritual of the Merina of Madagascar.* Cambridge: Cambridge University Press, 1986.

Blondeau, Anne-Marie. "Le Lha-'dre bKa'-thaṅ." In *Études tibétaines dédiées à la mémoire de Marcelle Lalou*, ed. Anne-Marie Blondeau, 29–126. Paris: Adrien-Maisonneuve, 1971.

———. "Mkhyen-bre'i dba-po: la biographie de Padmasambhava selon la tradition du bsgrags-pa bon, et ses sources." In *Orientalia Iosephi Tucci Memoriae Dicata, Istituto Italiano per il Medio ed Estremo Oriente*, 2 vols, ed. G. Gnoli and L. Lanciotti, vol. 1: 111–58. Rome: Istituto italiano per il Medio ed Estermo Oriente, 1988.

Bon po bka' 'gyur. Chengdu: Ha sa yon and Bon slob nam mkha' bstan 'dzin, 1991 (second printing).

Bon po brten 'gyur chen mo. Lhasa: Sog sde sprul sku Bstan pa'i nyi ma, 1998.

Boord, Martin. *The Cult of the Deity Vajrakīla according to the Texts of the Northern Treasures Tradition of Tibet (Byang-gter phur-ba).* Tring: The Institute of Buddhist Studies, 1993.

Bourdieu, Pierre. *The Logic of Practice*, tr. Richard Nice. Stanford: Stanford University Press, 1990.

Bowen, John R. "On Scriptural Essentialism and Ritual Variation: Muslim Sacrifice in Sumatra and Morocco." *American Ethnologist* 19/4 (1992): 656–71.

———. "The Forms Culture Takes: A State-of-the-Field Essay on the Anthropology of Southeast Asia." *The Journal of Asian Studies* 54/4 (1995): 1047–78.

Brauen, Martin. "A Bon-po Death Ceremony." In *Tibetan Studies: Presented at the Seminar of Young Tibetologists, Zürich, June 26–July 1, 1977*, ed. Martin Brauen and Per Kvaerne, 53–63. Zurich: Völkerkundemuseum der Universität Zürich, 1978.

Bskal bzang bstan pa'i rgyal mtshan. *Shar rdzas ba bkra shis rgyal mtshan gyi rnam thar.* Chengdu: Si khron mi rigs dpe skrun khang, 1998.

Bsod nams rgyal mtshan. *Rgyal rabs gsal ba'i me long.* Beijing: Mi rigs dpe skrun khang, 1981.

Bsod nams tshe ring. *Snga rabs bod kyi srid khrims.* Chengdu: Mi rigs dpe skrun khang, 2004.

Bu ston Rin chen grub. *Dpal gsang ba 'dus pa'i ṭīkkā sgron ma rab tu gsal ba (Sgron gsal bshad sbyar).* In *The Collected Works of Bu-ston*, 28 vols, vol. 9: 141–682. New Delhi: International Academy of Indian Culture, 1967.

———. *Dpal gsang ba 'dus pa'i sgrub thabs mdor byas kyi rgya cher bshad pa bskyed rim gsal byed (Mdor byas 'grel chen)*. In *The Collected Works of Bu-ston*, 28 vols, vol. 9: 683–878. New Delhi: International Academy of Indian Culture, 1967.

Buffetrille, Katia. *Pèlerinages tibétains aux montagnes sacrées*. Oslo: Norwegian University Press, The Institute for Comparative Research in Human Culture, forthcoming.

Bühnemann, Gudrun. "The Six Rites of Magic." In *Tantra in Practice*, ed. David G. White, 447–62. Princeton: Princeton University Press, 2000.

Bzang po spyod pa'i cho ga'i sgo nas 'chi bslu ba'i gdams pa gsal byed. In *Sgrub thabs kun btus: A Collection of Sādhanas and Related Texts of The Vajrayāna Traditions of Tibet*, 14 vols, compiled by 'Jam dbyangs mkhyen brtse'i dbang po and 'Jam dbyangs blo gter dbang po, vol. 1: 599–606. Dehradun: G.T.K. Lodoy, N. Gyaltsen & N. Lungtok, 1970.

Cabezón, José Ignacio. "Firm Feet and Long Lives: The *Zhabs brtan* Literature of Tibetan Buddhism." In *Tibetan Literature: Studies in Genre*, ed. José Ignacio Cabezón and Roger R. Jackson, 344–57. Ithaca: Snow Lion, 1996.

———. *The Hermitages of Sera*. Charlottesville: THDL Publications, 2006. Online. Available: http://www.thdl.org/collections/cultgeo/mons/sera/hermitages/pdfs/sera_hermitages.pdf. December 26, 2008.

———. "The Cult of Peaceful and Wrathful Avalokiteśvara at Sera Monastery." In *Bodhisattva Avalokiteśvara (Guanyin) and Modern Society: Proceedings of the Fifth Chung Hwa International Conference on Buddhism*, ed. William McGee and Yi-hsun Huang, 35–64. Taipei: Dharma Drum Publishing, 2007.

Candrakīrti (Zla ba grags pa). *Pradīpoddyotana-nāma-ṭīkā*. For an edition of the Sanskrit, see Chakravarti. Tibetan: *Sgron ma gsal bar byed pa zhes bya ba'i rgya cher bshad pa (Sgron gsal)*, Sde dge Bstan 'gyur, Toh. no. 1785, vol. 30 = Rgyud *ha*, ff. 1b-201b (pp. 2–402); Peking Bstan 'gyur, Ōtani no. 2650, vol. 60, 23.1.1–117.3.7; The Golden Tengyur, vol. 30, 1–151.

Cantwell, Cathy. "An Ethnographic Account of the Religious Practice in a Tibetan Buddhist Refugee Monastery in Northern India. Ph.D. diss., University of Kent, 1989.

———. "To Meditate upon Consciousness as *Vajra*: Ritual 'Killing and Liberation' in the Rnying-ma-pa Tradition." In *Tibetan Studies: Proceedings of the 7th Seminar of the International Association for Tibetan Studies, Graz 1995*, ed. Helmut Krasser, Michael Torsten Much, Ernst Steinkellner, and Helmut Tauscher, 107–18. Vienna: Verlag der Österreichischen Akademie der Wissenschaften, 1997.

Cantwell, Cathy and Robert Mayer. *The Kīlaya Nirvāṇa Tantra and the Vajra Wrath Tantra: Two Texts from the Ancient Tantra Collection*. Vienna: Verlag der Österreichischen Akademie der Wissenschaften, 2007.

———. "Why did the Phur pa Tradition Become So Prominent in Tibet?" In *Tibetan Literature: Proceedings of the Eleventh International Conference of Association of Tibetan Studies*, ed. Orna Olmogi. Halle (Saale): International Institute for Tibetan and Buddhist Studies, forthcoming.

Chakravarti, Chintaharan, ed. *Guhya-samāja-tantra-Pradīpoddyotana-ṭīkā-ṣaṭ-koṭī-vyākhyā*. Patna: Kashi Prasad Jayaswal Research Institute, 1984.

Chattopadhyaya, Alaka. *Catalogue of Kanjur and Tanjur: Vol. 1: Texts (Indian Titles) in Tanjur*. Calcutta: Indo-Tibetan Studies, 1972.

Che tshang sprul sku Bstan 'dzin padma'i rgyal mtshan. *Nges don bstan pa'i snying po 'bri gung pa chen po'i gdan rabs chos kyi byung tshul gser gyi phreng ba*, ed. Chab spel Tshe brtan phun tshogs. Gangs can rig mdzod 8. Lhasa: Bod ljongs bod yig dpe skrun khang, 1989.

'*Chi ba slu ba* (Skt. *Mṛtyuvañcana*). Peking Bstan 'gyur, no. 4864, Rgyud 'grel *zu*, ff. 173b.1–174a.7.

'*Chi ba slu ba'i gdams pa* (Skt. *Mṛtyuvañcanāmnāya*). Sde dge bstan 'gyur, Toh. no. 2839, Rgyud *nu*, ff. 180b.1–181a.4. TBRC Bstan 'gyur sde dge par ma, *vol.* 73, ff. 360.1–361.4.

'*Chi ba slu ba'i man ngag gi sgrol ma'i sgrub thabs* (Skt. *Mṛtyuvañcanopadeśatārāsādhana*). Sde dge bstan 'gyur, Toh. no. 3504, Rgyud 'grel, *mu*, ff. 154a.3–154b.5. TBRC Bstan 'gyur sde dge par ma, *vol.* 77, ff. 307.3–308.5.

'*Chi ba slu ba'i sgrol ma dkar mo'i sgrub thabs* (Skt. *Mṛtyuvañcanasitatārāsādhana*). Sde dge bstan 'gyur, Toh. no. 3496, Rgyud 'grel *mu*, ff. 150a.1–150b.3. TBRC Bstan 'gyur sde dge par ma, *vol.* 77, ff. 299.1–300.3. Attributed to a "chief disciple (*slob ma thu bo*) of Vāgīśvarakīrti."

'*Chi ba slu ba'i sgrol ma'i sgrub thabs* (Skt. *Mṛtyuvañcanatārāsādhana*). Sde dge bstan 'gyur, Toh. no. 3495, Rgyud 'grel *mu*, ff. 149b.4–150a.1. TBRC Bstan 'gyur sde dge par ma, *vol.* 77, ff. 298.4–299.1.

'*Chi blu'i bsdus don* (Skt. *Mṛtyuvañcanapiṇḍārtha*). Peking Bstan 'gyur, Rgyud 'grel *zhu*, ff. 147b.7–150b.8.

Childs, Geoff H. "How to Fund a Ritual: Notes on the Social Usage of the Kanjur (bKa' 'gyur) in a Tibetan Village." *Tibet Journal* 30/2 (2005): 41–48.

Choido, Elisabetta. *The Mongolian Manuscripts on Birch Bark from Xarbuxyn Balgas in the Collection of the Mongolian Academy of Sciences*, Part 1. Asiatische Forschungen: Monographienreihe zur Geschichte Kultur und Sprache der Völker Ost- Und Zentralasiens, vol. 137. Wiesbaden: Harrassowitz Verlag, 2000.

Chos kyi dbang phyug, Zhwa dmar. *Nyer mkho sna tshogs kyi dpe bum phan de rab ster.* Delhi: 1977.

Christian, William A., Jr. *Local Religion in Sixteenth-Century Spain.* Princeton: Princeton University, 1981.

Cohen, Richard S. "Nāga, Yakṣiṇī, Buddha: Local Deities and Local Buddhism at Ajanta." *History of Religions* 37/4 (1998): 360–400.

Coleman, Graham and Thupten Jinpa, eds., and Gyurme Dorje, tr. *The Tibetan Book of The Dead: The Great Liberation By Hearing In The Intermediate States.* New York, Viking, 2005.

Cornu, Philippe. *Tibetan Astrology.* Boston: Shambhala, 1997.

Cuevas, Bryan J. *Travels in the Netherworld: Buddhist Popular Narratives of Death and the Afterlife in Tibet.* Oxford: Oxford university Press, 2008.

Cutler, Joshua and Guy Newland eds., and The Lamrim Chenmo Translation Committee, tr. *The Great Treatise on the Stages of the Path to Enlightenment: Lam rim chen mo of Tsong kha pa*, 3 vols. Ithaca: Snow Lion, 2000–04.

Da jinse kongque wang zhou. Taishō no. 986, vol. 19: 477–78. Anonymous translation.

Da jinse kongque wang zhoujing. Taishō no. 987, vol. 19: 479–81. Anonymous translation.

Da kongque wang zhoujing. In Taishō no. 985, vol. 19: 459–77. Yijing, translator.

Dagyab, Loden Sherab. *Die Sadhanas der Sammlung Ba-ri Brgya-rtsa (Ikonographie und Symbolik des tibetischen Buddhismus)*. Wiesbaden: Otto Harrassowitz, 1983.

Dalai Lama, H. H. and Jeffrey Hopkins. *Kalachakra Tantra: Rite of Initiation*, 3rd ed. Boston: Wisdom Publications, 1999.

Dalton, Jacob. "The Early Development of the Padmasambhava Legend in Tibet: A Study of IOL Tib J 644 and Pelliot tibétain 307." *Journal of the American Oriental Society* 24/4 (2004): 759–72.

Dalton, Jacob and Sam van Schaik. *Catalogue of the Tibetan Tantric Manuscripts from Dunhuang in the Stein Collection*. Online, International Dunhuang Project, 2005. Online. Available: http://idp.bl.uk.

———. *Tibetan Tantric Manuscripts from Dunhuang: A Descriptive Catalogue of the Stein Collection at the British Library*. Leiden: Brill, 2006.

Dambii, Sukhiin. *Uul ovoo rashaan usny takhilgand oroltsoj baisan Mongol ulamjlal*. Ulaanbaatar, 2003. Pamphlet.

Damdinsüren, Tsendiin. "Two Mongolian Colophons to the Suvarnaprabhasottama-sutra." *Acta orientalia Academiae scientiarum Hungaricae* 33 (1979) fasc. 1.

———. *Mongolyn Uran Zokhiolyn Toim*, 2 vols. Ulaanbaatar: Bembi San, 1999.

———. *Mongol Uran Zokhiolyn Deej Zuun Bilig Orshiv*, 2 vols. Ulaanbaatar: Bembi San, 2001.

Das, Sarat Candra. *Tibetan-English Dictionary*. Kathmandu: Ratna Pustak Bhandar, 1985.

David-Neel, Alexandra. *The Superhuman Life of Gesar of Ling*. 1933. Reprint, Boston: Shambhala Publications, 1987.

Davidson, Ronald M. "Buddhist Systems of Transformation: Āśraya-parivṛtti/-parāvṛtti among the Yogācāra." Ph.D. diss., University of California, Berkeley, 1985.

———. *Tibetan Renaissance: Tantric Buddhism in the Rebirth of Tibetan Culture*. New York: Columbia University Press, 2005.

Dbang 'dus. *Gso ba rig pa'i tshig mdzod g.yu thog dgongs rgyan*. Beijing: Mi rigs dpe skrun khang, 1983.

Dbyangs can lha mo and Ko'o po'i kung. *Bod rgya nang don rig pa'i tshig mdzod*, 2 vols. Chengdu: Si khron mi rigs dpe skrun khang, 1993.

De bzhin gshegs pa thams cad kyi dgongs pa'i khro bo 'dus pa/ bde gshegs spyir dril rta mgrin rngog ma leb rgan gyi rgyud. Rnying ma rgyud 'bum, Gting skyes no. 303, vol. 24, *ya*, ff. 110.2–212.4.

"Deed bütsen khölgön altangerel nert sudryn khuraangui orshivoi." In *Khünii nasan zayaany amydral ajil üilsiig devjen ösgökh Burkhany surgaaliin khuraangui*, compiled by Getsel Tüvdenvaanchüg, 50–64. Ulaanbaatar: Uranbishrelt, 2004.

Dell'Angelo, Enrico, tr. from the Tibetan, and Robin Cooke, tr. from the Italian. *Namchö Mingyur Dorje: The Interpretation of Dreams in a 17th Century Tibetan Text*. Arcidosso Merigar: Shang Shung Edizioni, 1996.

Des Jardins, Marc. *Le Sūtra de la Mahāmāyūrī: rituel et politique dans la Chine des Tang (618–906)*. Québec: Les Presses de l'Université Laval, forthcoming.

Dge bshes Chos grags. *Dge bshes chos kyi grags pas brtsams pa'i brda dag ming tshig gsal ba*. Beijing: Mi rigs dpe skrun khang, 1995.

The Digital Sanskrit Buddhist Canon Site. Online. Available: http://www.uwest.edu/sanskritcanon/.

Dil mgo mkhyen brtse Bkra shis dpal 'byor. *Skyabs rje dil mgo mkhyen brtse rin po che'i bka' 'bum*. Delhi: Shechen Publications, 1994.

Doctor, Thomas. *Speech of Delight: Mipham's Commentary on Shantarakshita's Ornament of the Middle Way*. Ithaca: Snow Lion, 2004.

Dorje, Gyurme and Sangye Gyatso. *Tibetan Elemental Divination Paintings: Illuminated Manuscripts from the White Beryl of Sangs-rgyas rGya-mtsho with the Moonbeams Treatise of Lo-chen Dharmaśrī*. London: John Eskenazi in association with Sam Fogg, 2001.

Drang rje btsun pa Gser mig. *gZer mig*. Beijing: Krung go'i bod kyi shes rig dpe skrun khang, 1991.

Dreyfus, Georges. 1991. "The Shukden Affair: History and Nature of a Quarrel," *Journal of the International Association of Buddhist Studies* 21/2 (1991): 227–70.

———. *The Sound of Two Hands Clapping: The Education of a Tibetan Buddhist Monk*. Berkeley: University of California Press, 2003.

Dudjom Rinpoche, Jikdrel Yeshe Dorje. *The Nyingma School of Tibetan Buddhism: Its Fundamentals and History*, 2 vols, tr. Gyurme Dorje (with Matthew Kapstein). Boston: Wisdom Publications, 1991.

Dumont, Louis and David F. Pocock. "For a Sociology of India." *Contributions to Indian Sociology* 1 (1957): 7–22.

Dung dkar blo bzang 'phrin las. *Dung dkar tshig mdzod chen mo*. Beijing: Krung go'i bod rig pa dpe skrun khang, 2002.

Dunhuang Tibetan manuscripts cited in this volume.

- India Office Library (IOL) manuscripts held at the British Library, London: IOL Tib J 321; IOL Tib J 331; IOL Tib J 332; IOL Tib J 337; IOL Tib J 401; IOL Tib J 436; IOL Tib J 438; IOL Tib J 481, IOL Tib J 754. International Dunhuang Project (http://idp.bl.uk/) contains digital images of many items, and a catalogue (see under Dalton and van Schaik).
- Manuscripts held at the Bibliothèque nationale, Paris: Pelliot tibétain (PT) 42; PT 221; PT 307; PT 349; PT 849; PT 1051.

'Dus pa rin po che dri ma med pa gzi brjid rab tu 'bar ba'i mdo, 12 vols. In Bon po bka' 'gyur. Chengdu: Ha sa yon and Bon slob nam mkha' bstan 'dzin Publishers, 1991.

'Dus pa rin po che dri med gzi brjid las lha mthu chen dang lha ma yin sde lnga dbang du bsdus nas bon bstan pa'i mdo las rta mgrin rgyal po'i gzungs. In Bon po brten 'gyur chen mo, vol. 106, sect. 59, chap. 1, ff. 1489–1512. Lhasa: Sog sde sprul sku Bstan pa'i nyi ma, 1998.

Eastman, Kenneth W. "The Dun-huang Tibetan Manuscript of the Guhyasamājatantra." *Report of the Japanese Association for Tibetan Studies* 26, (March 1980): 8–12. [English language appended version of "Chibetto-go Guhyasamājatantra no tonkō shutsudo shahon."]

———. "Mahāyoga Texts at Tun-huang." Masters thesis, Stanford University, 1983.

Eckel, Malcolm David. *To See the Buddha*. San Francisco: HarperSanFrancisco, 1992.

Eimer, Helmut. "A Source for the First Narthang Kanjur: Two Early Sa skya pa Catalogues of the Tantras." In *Transmission of the Tibetan Canon: Papers Presented at a Panel of the 7th Seminar of the IATS*, ed. Helmut Eimer, 11–78. Vienna: Verlag der Österreichischen Akeademie der Wissenschaften, 1997.

Ekavīrākhyā śrīcaṇḍamahāroṣana tantrarāja nāma (*Dpal gtum po khro bo chen po'i rgyud kyi rgyal po dpa' bo gcig pa*). Sde dge Bka' 'gyur, Toh. no. 431, Rgyud *nga*, ff. 304b.1–343a.1.

Ekvall, Robert B. *Religious Observances in Tibet: Patterns and Functions*, 1964. Chicago: University of Chicago Press.

Elverskog, Johan. *The Jewel Translucent Sūtra: Altan Khan and the Mongols in the 16th Century*. Leiden: Brill, 2003.

Ferrari, Alfonsa. *mK'yen brtse's Guide to the Holy Places of Central Tibet*.

Serie Orientale Roma, vol. 14. Rome: Instituto Italiano Per il Medio ed Esremo Oriente, 1958.

Filippani-Ronconi, Pio. "La formulazione liturgica della dottrina del Bodhicitta nel 2 Capitolo de *Guhyasamājatantra*." *Annali* (Istituto Universitario Orientale di Napoli) 32/2 n.s. XXII (1972): 187–99.

Flood, Gavin. *An Introduction to Hinduism*. Cambridge: Cambridge University Press, 1996.

Fomu da kongque mingwang jing. In Taishō no. 982, vol. 19: 415–39. Amoghavajra (Pukong), translator.

Frazer, James G. *The Golden Bough: Abridged Edition*. 1922. Reprint, New York: Penguin, 1988.

Fremantle, Franceca. "A Critical Study of the Guhyasamāja-tantra." Ph.D. diss., School of Oriental and African Studies, London, 1971.

Fridman, Eva Jane Neumann. *Sacred Geography: Shamanism Among the Buddhist Peoples of Russia*. Budapest: Akadémiai Kiadó, 2004.

Fuller, Christopher J. *The Camphor Flame: Popular Hinduism and Society in India*. Princeton: Princeton University Press, 1992.

Gäng, Peter. *Das Tantra der Verborgenen Vereinigung: Guhyasamāja-Tantra*. München: Eugen Diederichs Verlag, 1988.

Geertz, Clifford. "Religion as a Cultural System." In *Anthropological approaches to the study of religion*, ed. M. Banton, 1–46. London: Tavistock Publications, 1966.

Gellner, David N. " 'The Perfection of Wisdom': A Text and its Uses in Kwā Bāhāh, Lalitpur." In *Change and Continuity: Studies in the Nepalese Culture of the Kathmandu Valley*, ed. Siegfried Lienhard, 223–40. Alessandrio: Edizioni dell'Orso, 1996.

———. "For Syncretism: The Position of Buddhism in Nepal and Japan Compared." *Social Anthropology: The Journal of the European Association of Social Anthropology* 5/3 (1997): 277–91.

Germano, David. "Dying, Death, and Other Opportunities." In *Religions of Tibet in Practice*, ed. Donald S. Lopez, Jr., 358–493. Princeton: Princeton University Press, 1997.

Getsel Tüvdenvaanchüg, compiler. *Khünii nasan zayaany amydral ajil üilsiig devjen ösgökh Burkhany surgaaliin khuraangui*. Ulaanbaatar: Uranbishrelt, 2004.

Gnoli, Raniero. "Guhyasamājatantra (chapters 1, 2, & 5)." *Testi Buddhisti*, 619–33. Turin: Unione Tipografico-editrice Torinese, 1983.

Gnubs chen Sangs rgyas ye shes and 'Jam dpal bshes gnyen. *Zla gsang be'u bum*. Dehra Dun: 1975.

Goldberg, Jay and Lobsang Dakpa, tr. *Mo: Tibetan Divination System [by] Jamgon Mipham*. Ithaca: Snow Lion, 1990.

Gonda, Jan. "Mudrā." *Studies in the History of Religions* 12 (1972): 21–31.

Goodman, Steven M. "Mi-Pham rgya-mtsho: An Account of His Life, the Printing of his Works, and the Structure of his Treatise Entitled *mKhas-pa'i tshul la 'jug-pa'i sgo*." In *Wind Horse: Proceedings of the North American Tibetological Society*, ed. Ronald M. Davidson, 58–78. Berkeley: Asian Humanities Press, 1981.

Goody, Jack. *The Logic of Writing and the Organization of Society*. Cambridge: Cambridge University Press, 1986.

Gorvine, William M. "The Life of a Bonpo Luminary: Sainthood, Partisanship and Literary Representation in 20th Century Tibetan Biography." Ph.D. diss., University of Virginia, Charlottesville, 2006.

Goudriaan, Teun. *Māyā Divine and Human: A Study of Magic and its Religious Foundations in Sanskrit Texts, with particular attention to a fragment on Viṣṇu's Māyā preserved in Bali*. Delhi: Motilal Banarsidass, 1978.

Graham, William A. *Beyond the Written Word: Oral Aspects of Scripture in the History of Religion*. Cambridge: Cambridge University Press, 1987.

Grimes, Ronald L., ed. *Readings in Ritual Studies*. Upper Saddle River, NJ: Prentice Hall, 1996.

———. *Rite out of Place: Ritual, Media, and the Arts*. Oxford: Oxford University Press, 2006.

'Gro 'dul bstan gnyis gsar gling pa'i skye gnas bar do'i rnam par thar pa brdzod pa sgyu ma'i 'khrul 'khor. Bon gyi brten 'gyur chen mo, vol. 149, no.4, ff. 443–798. Lhasa: Sog sde sprul sku Bstan pa'i nyi ma, 1998.

Gter slob mkhan ming 'dul 'dzin (Gter slob karma ratna). *Rgyal po'i thugs dam mdo bcu la sogs la bsten pa'i 'chi bslu 'chi bdag zhags gcod ye shes ral gri*. In *Brgya bzhi sdong brgyan kha 'bar ma rnams kyi mdos chog la nye bar mkho ba'i bdag mdun bskyed chog: Collected Rituals of the Rnying-ma-pa and Ris med Traditions for Use in Funerals, Death Ransoming, and Averting Ceremonies, etc.*, 1–20. Byllakuppe: Pema Norbu Rinpoche, 1985.

Gtsang pa sde srid dang ka.rma bstan skyong dbang po'i 'dus su gtan la phab pa khrims yig zhal lce bcu drug. In *Snga rabs bod kyi srid khrims*, ed. Bsod nams tshe ring, 164–219. Chengdu: Mi rigs dpe skrun khang, 2004.

Guhyasamāja Tantra (*Sarva-tathāgata-kāya-vāk-citta-rahasya-guhya-samāja-nāma-mahā-kalpa*-rāja). For editions of the Sanskrit see under Bagchi, Fremantle and Matsunaga. Tibetan: *De bzhin gshegs pa thams cad kyi sku gsung thugs kyi gsang chen gsang ba 'dus pa zhes bya ba brtag pa'i rgyal po chen po*, Dunhuang, IOL (India Office Library) Tib J 481 and IOL Tib. J 438; *The Rnying ma'i rgyud 'bum*, Thimbu: Dingo Khyentse Rimpoche, 1973, vol. 17, ff. 1b1–314a4; Sde dge Bka' 'gyur, Toh. no. 442, vol. 81 = Rgyud 'bum *ca*, ff. 90a-148a (pp. 181–295); Peking Bka' 'gyur, Ōtani 81, vol. 65,

174.3.5–203.2.1; Stog Palace, vol. 96, 2–190. Also in *Dpal gsang ba 'dus pa'i rtsa rgyud 'grel pa bzhi sbrags dang bcas pa*, Lhasa: Zhol Printing House, from blockprints carved in 1890.

Gu ru bkra shis ngag dbang blo gros. *Gu bkra'i chos 'byung*. Beijing: China's Tibetan Culture Publishing House, 1990.

Gyatso, Janet. *Apparitions of the Self: The Secret Biographies of a Tibetan Visionary*. Princeton: Princeton University Press, 1991.

———. "Autobiography in Tibetan Religious Literature: Reflections on its Modes of Self-Presentation." In *Tibetan Studies: Proceedings of the 5th International Association for Tibetan Studies, Narita 1989*, 2 vols, ed. Shōren Ihara and Zuihō Yamaguchi, 2: 465–78. Narita-shi, Chiba-Ken, Japan: Naritasan Shinshoji, 1992.

Hackin, J. *Formulaire Sanscrit-Tibétain du X^E Siècle*. Mission Pelliot en Asie Centrale, Série Petit in Octavo, vol. II. Paris: Librarie orientaliste Paul Geuthner, 1924.

Harding, Sarah. *The Life and Revelations of Pema Lingpa*. Ithaca: Snow Lion, 2003.

Heissig, Walther. "A Mongolian Text to the Lamaist Suppression of Shamanism in the 17th Century." *Anthropos* 48 (1953): 1–29, and 493–536.

———. *The Religions of Mongolia*, tr. Geoffrey Samuel. London: Routledge and Kegan Paul, 1980.

———. "Banishing of Illnesses into Effigies in Mongolia." *Asian Folklore Studies* 45 (1986): 33–43.

Heller, Amy. "Mongolian Mountain Deities and Local Gods: Examples of Rituals for Their Worship in Tibetan Language." In *Reflections of the Mountain: Essays on the History and Social Meaning of the Mountain Cult in Tibet and the Himalaya*, ed. Anne-Marie Blondeau and Ernst Steinkellner, 133–40. Vienna: Österreichische Akademie der Wissenschaften, 1996.

Herrmann-Pfandt, Adelheid. "Eine Quellenkunde des esoterischen (tantrischen) Buddhismus in Indien von den Anfängen bis zum 9. Jahrhundert." Unpublished Habilitationsschrift, Philipps-Universität Marburg/Lahn, 2000.

Horlemann, Bianca. "On the Origin of Jiaosiluo, the first ruler of the Tsong kha tribal confederation in the eleventh century A mdo." *Zentralasiatische Studien* 34 (2005): 127–54.

———. "The Relations of the Eleventh-Century Tsong kha Tribal Confederation to its Neighbour States on the Silk Road." In *Contributions to the Cultural History of Early Tibet*, ed. Matthew Kapstein and Brian Dotson, 79–101. Leiden: Brill, 2007.

Huber, Toni. "Putting the *gnas* back into *gnas-skor*: Rethinking Tibetan Budhist Pilgrimage Practice." In *Sacred Spaces and Powerful Places in Tibetan Religious Culture*, ed. Toni Huber, 77–104. Dharamsala: Library of Tibetan Works and Archives, 1999.

———. *The Cult of Pure Crystal Mountain: Popular Pilgrimage and Visionary Landscape in Southeast Tibet*. Oxford: Oxford University Press, 1999.

Humphrey, Caroline. "Chiefly and Shamanist Landscapes in Mongolia." In *The Anthropology of Landscape: Perspectives on Place and Space*, Eric Hirsch and Michael O'Hanlon, 135–62. Oxford: Clarendon Press, 1995.

———. *Marx Went Away—But Karl Stayed Behind*. Ann Arbor: University of Michigan Press, 1998.

Humphrey, Caroline and James Laidlaw. *The Archetypal Actions of Ritual: A Theory of Ritual Illustrated by the Jain Rite of Worship.* New York: Oxford University Press, 1994.

Humphrey, Caroline with Urgunge Onon. *Shamans and Elders: Experience, Knowledge, and Power Among the Daur Mongols.* Oxford: Oxford University Press, 1996.

Imaeda, Yoshiro, Karma Ura, Mynak Tulku, and Satoru Tabuchi, photographer. *Festival and Faith at Nyimalung.* Tokyo: Hirakawa, Shuppan Inc., 2002.

"The International Association of Tibetan Studies." [Online] Available at: http://www.thdl.org/collections/journal/jiats/index.php?m=iats [December 20, 2008].

Iwasaki, Tsutomu. "The Tibetan Tribes of Ho-hsi and Buddhism During the Northern Sung Period." *Acta Asiatica* 64 (1993): 17–37.

Jackson, David. *The Entrance Gate for the Wise [section III].* Vienna: Arbeitskreis für Tibetische und Buddhistische Studien, Universität Wien, 1987.

———. "The 'Bhutan Abbot' of Ngor." In *Lungta 14: "Aspects of Tibetan History,"* ed. Tashi Tsering, and guest ed. Roberto Vitali, 88–107. Dharamsala: Amnye Machen Institute, 2001.

Jacobson, David. *Reading Ethnography.* Albany: State University of New York Press, 1991.

'Jam dbyangs mkhyen brtse'i dbang po and 'Jam dbyangs blo gter dbang po, compilers. *Sgrub thabs kun btus: A Collection of Sādhanas and Related Texts of The Vajrayāna Traditions of Tibet,* 14 vols. Dehradun: G. T. K. Lodoy, N. Gyaltsen and N. Lungtok, 1970.

'Jam mgon Kong sprul blo gros mtha' yas. *Dpal rdo rje phur pa rtsa ba'i rgyud kyi dum bu'i 'grel pa snying po bsdud pa dpal chen dgyes pa'i zhal lung.* In Kong sprul, *Rgya chen bka' mdzod,* 20 vols, vol. *ga,* pp. 17–213. Paro: Ngodup, 1975–76.

———. *Rin chen gter mdzod chen mo.* 111 vols. Paro, Bhutan: Ngrodrup and Sherab Drimay, 1976–80.

Jinpa, Thupten. *Mind Training: The Great Collection.* Boston: Wisdom Publications, 2005.

Kaminishi, Ikumi. *Explaining Pictures: Buddhist Propaganda and Etoki Storytelling in Japan.* Honolulu: University of Hawai'i Press, 2006.

Kapstein, Matthew. "Mi-pham's Theory of Interpretation." In *Buddhist Hermeneutics,* ed. Donald S. Lopez, Jr., 149–74. Honolulu: University of Hawai'i Press, 1988.

———. *The Tibetan Assimilation of Buddhism: Conversion, Contestation, and Memory.* Oxford: Oxford University Press, 2000.

———. "A Dunhuang Tibetan Summary of the Transformation Text on Mulian Saving His Mother from Hell." In *Dunhuang wenxian lunji,* ed. Hao Chunwen, 235–47. Shenyang: Liaoning Renmin Chubanshe, 2001.

———. "New Light on an Old Friend: PT 849 Reconsidered." In *Tibetan Buddhist Literature and Praxis: Studies in its Formative period, 900–1400,* ed. Ronald M. Davidson and Christian K. Wedemeyer, 9–30. Leiden: Brill, 2006.

———. "Mulian in the Land of Snows and King Gesar in Hell: A Chinese Tale of Parental Death in Its Tibetan Tranformations." In *The Buddhist Dead: Practices, Discourses, Representations,* ed. Bryan J. Cuevas and Jacqueline I. Stone, 345–77. Honolulu: University of Hawai'i Press, 2007.

———. "The Tibetan *Yulanpen jing*." In *Contributions to the Cultural History of Early Tibet*, ed. Matthew Kapstein and Brandon Dotson, 219–46. Leiden: Brill, 2007.

Karmay, Samten G. *The Treasury of Good Sayings: A Tibetan History of Bon*. London Oriental Series, vol. 26. London: Oxford University Press, 1972.

———. *The Arrow and the Spindle, Studies in History, Myths, Rituals and Beliefs*. Kathmandu: Mandala Publications, vol. I, 1998; vol. II, 2005.

———. *The Great Perfection: A Philosophical and Meditative Teaching of Tibetan Buddhism*. Leiden: E. J. Brill, 1988.

———. "Dorje Lingpa and his Rediscovery of the 'Gold Needle' in Bhutan." *Journal of Bhutan Studies* 2/2 (Winter, 2000): 1–34. Also online. Available: http://www.digitalhimalaya.com/collections/journals/jbs/index.php?selection=3.

———. *Feast of the Morning Light: The Eighteenth Century Wood-engravings of Shenrab's Life-stories and the Bon Canon from Gyalrong*, Bon Studies 9, Senri Ethnological Reports 57. Osaka: National Museum of Ethnology, 2005.

Karmay, Samten G. and Yasuhiko Nagano, eds. *A Catalogue of the New Collection of Bonpo Katen Texts*, Bon Studies 4, Senri Ethnological Reports 24. Osaka: National Museum of Ethnology, 2001.

———. *A Survey of Bonpo Monasteries and Temples in Tibet and the Himalaya*, Bon Studies 7. Osaka: National Museum of Ethnology, 2003.

Kawamura, Leslie S. "An Analysis of Mi-pham's *mKhas-'jug*." In *Wind Horse: Proceedings of the North American Tibetological Society*, ed. Ronald M. Davidson, 112–26. Berkeley: Asian Humanities Press, 1981.

———. "An Outline of *Yāna-Kauśalya* in Mi-pham's *mKhas-'jug*." *Indogaku Bukkyōgaku Kenkyū* 29/1 (1981): 956–61.

———. "The *Akṣayamatinirdeśasūtra* and Mi-pham's *mKhas-'jug*." In *Contributions on Tibetan and Buddhist Philosophy*, ed. Ernst Steinkellner and Helmut Tauscher, 131–145. Vienna: Arbeitkreis für Tibetische und Buddhistische Studien Universität Wien, 1983.

Kelényi, Béla. "The Cult of Good Luck." In *Demons and Protectors: Folk Religion in Tibetan and Mongolian Buddhism*, ed. Béla Kelényi, 47–77. Budapest: Ferenc Hopp Museum of Eastern Asiatic Art, 2003.

Khal kha dam tshig rdo rje. *Rta mgrin yang gsang khros pa'i chos skor*, 3 vols. Bylakuppe, India: Sera Byes College, 1997.

Khri byang Blo bzang ye shes bstan' 'dzin rgya mtsho. *'Jam mgon bstan sruṅ Rgyal chen rdo rje Śugs ldan rtsal gyi be bum: The Collected Rituals for Performing All Tasks through the Propitiation of the Great Protective Deity of the Teachings of Tsoṅ kha pa Mañjuśrī reembodied, Rdo rje śugs ldan*. New Delhi: Mongolian Lama Guru Deva, 1984.

———. *'Jam mgon rgyal ba gnyis pa'i bstan srung rgyal chen rdo rje shugs ldan rtsal gyi chos skor be bum du bsgrigs pa*. Lhasa: Brag g.yab Blo bzang brston' 'grus, 1991.

Khro mchog 'dus pa sde brgyad 'byung po spyi 'dul gyi rgyud las che mchog rta mgrin gtum chen drag po'i sgrub gzhung chen mo. Bon po brten 'gyur chen mo, vol. 171, sect. 9, chap.1, ff. 91–136. Lhasa: Sog sde sprul sku Bstan pa'i nyi ma, 1998.

Khürelbaatar, Lkhamsürengiin. *Sudar Shastiryg Bilig*. Ulaanbaatar: Institute of Language and Literature, Academy of Sciences, 2002.

"Khutagt tseden-ish buyu tsend-ayush khemeekh sudryn khuraangui orshvoi." In *Khünii nasan zayany amydral ajil üilsiig devjeen ösgökh burkhany surgaaliin khuraangui*, compiled by Getsel Tüvdenvaanchüg, 207–40. Ulaanbaatar: Uranbishre, 2004.

Klong rdol Ngag dbang blo bzang. *Gsang sngags rig pa 'dzin pa'i sde snod las byung ba'i rgyud sde bzhi'i ming gi rnam grangs*. Lhasa: Bod ljongs bod yig dpe rnying dpe skrun khang, 1991.

Klu sgrub nag po (Kṛṣṇa Nāgārjuna). *Mgon po bya rog gdong gi gtor mdos* (Skt. *Nāthakāsyabaliyantra*). Peking Bstan 'gyur, no. 4962, Rgyud 'grel *'u*, ff. 48a.2–56a.6.

Ko shul grags pa 'byung gnas and Rgyal ba Blo bzang mkhas grub. *Gangs can mkhas grub rim byon ming mdzod* (*Ming mdzod*). Lanzhou: Kan su'u mi rigs dpe skrun Khang, 1992.

Kohn, Richard. *Lord of the Dance: The Mani Rimdu Festival in Tibet and Nepal*. Ithaca: State University of New York Press, 2001.

Kongque wang zhoujing. Taishō no. 984, vol. 19: 446–59. Tr. by Sengjiapoluo.

Kongque wang zhoujing. Taishō no. 988, vol. 19: 481–84. Tr. by Kumārajīva (344–413).

Krang dbyi sun et al. *Bod rgya tshig mdzod chen mo*. 1993. Reprint Chengdu: Mi rigs dpe skrun khang, 1998.

Kreinath, Jens, Jan Snoek and Michael Stausberg. *Theorizing Ritual: Annotated Bibliography of Ritual Theory, 1966–2005*. Leiden: Brill, 2007.

Kṛṣṇayamāri tantra (*Gshin rje gshed nag po'i rgyud*). Sde dge Bka' 'gyur, Toh. no. 467, Rgyud *ja*, ff. 134b.1–151b.4; Sde dge Bka' 'gyur, Toh. no. 469, Rgyud *ja*, ff. 164a.1–167b.5; and Sde dge Bka' 'gyur, Toh. no. 473, Rgyud *ja*, ff. 175a.1–185b.7.

Kun bzang nges don klong yangs. *Bod du byung ba'i gsang sngags snga 'gyur gyi bstan 'dzin skyes mchog rim byon gyi rnam thar nor bu'i do shal*. Dalhousie: Damchoe Sangpo, 1976.

Kun dga' blo gros. *Sa skya gdung rabs ngo mtshar bang mdzod kyi kha skong*. Chengdu: Mi rigs dpe skrun khang, 1991.

Kunsang, Erik Pema, tr. The *Light of Wisdom, Vol II*. Boudhanath: Rangjung Yeshe Publications, 1998.

Kunsang, Erik Pema and Marcia Binder Schmidt. *Blazing Splendor: The Memoirs of the Dzogchen Yogi Tulku Urgyen Rinpoche*. Boudnath: Rangjung Yeshe Publications, 2005.

Kuo li-ying. "La recitation des noms de BUDDHA en Chine et au Japon." *T'oung Pao* 81 (1995): 230–68.

la Vallée Poussin, Louis de, ed. *Études et textes tantriques: Pañcakrama*. Gand: H. Engelcke, 1896.

Lalou, Marcelle. "Fiefs, Poisons, Guérisseurs." *Journal Asiatique* 246/2 (1959): 1–45.

Lambek, Michael. "Certain Knowledge, Contestable Authority: Power and Practice on the Islamic Periphery." *American Ethnologist* 17/1 (1990): 23–40.

Lcang lung Paṇḍita Ngag dbang blo bzang bstan pa'i rgyal mtshan. *The Collected Works of Lcang lung Paṇḍita Ngag dbang blo bzang bstan pa'i rgyal mtshan*. Delhi: Mongolian Lama Gurudeva, 1975–85.

Lessing, Ferdinand. "The Topographical Identification of Peking with Yamāntaka." In *Ritual and Symbol: Collected Essays on Lamaism and Chinese Symbolism*, ed. Ferdinand Lessing, 89–90. Taipei: Orient Cultural Service, 1976.

Lévi-Strauss, Claude. *The Savage Mind*. London: Wiedenfield and Nicholson, 1976.

Lewis, Todd. *Popular Buddhist Texts from Nepal: Narratives and Rituals of Newar Buddhism*. Albany: State University of New York Press, 2000.

Lha btsun Rin chen rgya mtsho. *'Brong rtse be'u bum/ Man ngag bang mdzod*. Beijing: Mi rigs dpe skrun khang, 2005.

Lha mthu chen dang lha ma yin sde lnga dbang du bsdus nas bon bstan pa'i mdo las rta mgrin rgyal po'i gzungs. Bon po brten 'gyur chen mo, vol. 106, section 59, ff. 1489–1512. Lhasa: Sog sde sprul sku Bstan pa'i nyi ma, 1998.

Lham Dorji. "Religious Life and History of the Emanated Heart-son Thukse Dawa Gyeltshen." *Journal of Bhutan Studies* 13/2 (Winter, 2005): 74–104. Also Online. Available: http://www.digitalhimalaya.com/collections/journals/jbs/index.php?selection=13.

Lienhardt, Godfrey. *Divinity and Experience: The Religion of the Dinka*. Oxford: Clarendon Press, 1961.

Lin Shen-yu. "Tibetan Magic for Daily Life: Mi pham's Texts on *gTo*-rituals." *Cahiers d'Extrême-Asie* 15 (2005): 107–25.

Lindtner, Christian. "*Cittamātra* in Indian Mahāyāna until Kamalaśīla." *Wiener Zeitschrift für die Kunde Südasiens* 41 (1997): 159–206.

Lingbao wuliang durenpin miao jing. Daozang 1. In Ming Zheng tong dao zang, vol. 1: 1–417.

Lipman, Kennard. "A Controversial Topic from Mi-pham's Analysis of Śāntarakṣita's *Madhyamakālaṃkāra*." In *Wind Horse: Proceedings of the North American Tibetological Society*, ed. Ronald M. Davidson, 40–57. Berkeley: Asian Humanities Press, 1981.

Lo chen Dharmaśrī. *Mdo dbang gi spyi don*. In Rnying ma bka' ma rgyas pa, vol. *pha*: 5–345. Kalimpong: Dupjung Lama, 1982–87.

Longchen Rabjam. *A Treasure Trove of Scriptural Transmission: A Commentary on The Precious Treasury of the Basic Space of Phenomena*, tr. Richard Barron et al. Junction City, CA: Padma Publishing, 2001.

Lopez, Donald S. *Elaborations on Emptiness: Uses of the Heart Sūtra*. Princeton: Princeton University Press, 1996.

Loseries-Leick, Andrea. "The Use of Human Skulls in Tibetan Rituals." In *Tibetan Studies: Proceedings of the 5th International Association for Tibetan Studies, Narita 1989*, 2 vols, ed. Shōren Ihara and Zuihō Yamaguchi, 1: 159–73. Narita-shi, Chiba-Ken, Japan: Naritasan Shinshoji, 1992.

Luczanits, Christian. "Infinite Variety: Form and Appearance in Tibetan Buddhist Art, Part I," *Lotus Leaves* 7/2 (2005): 1–9; "Part II," *Lotus Leaves* 8/1 (2005): 7–14.

Macdonald, Alexander W., ed. *Mandala and Landscape*. New Delhi: DK Printworld. 1998.

Macdonald, Ariane and Yoshiro Imaeda. 1978–1990. *Choix de Documents tibétains conservé à la Bibliothèque nationale*, 3 vols. Paris: Bibliothèque national, 1978–90.

Mag gsar Kun bzang stobs ldan dbang po. *Phur pa'i rnam bshad he ru ka dpal bzhad pa'i zhal lung (Bcom ldan 'das dpal chen rdo rje gzhon nu'i 'phrin las kyi rnam par bshad pa he ru ka dpal bzhad pa'i zhal lung)*. Sngags mang zhib 'jug khang. Beijing: Mi rigs dpe skrun khang, 2003.

Mair, Victor. *Tun-huang Popular Narratives*. Cambridge: Cambridge University Press, 1983.

Mair, Victor. *Painting and Performance: Chinese Picture Recitation and Its Indian Genesis.* Honolulu: University of Hawai'i Press, 1988.

———. *T'ang Transformation Texts: A Study of the Buddhist Contribution to the Rise of Vernacular Fiction and Drama in China.* Cambridge: Harvard University Press, 1989.

Makransky, John. "Offering (mChod pa) in Tibetan Ritual Literature." In *Tibetan Literature: Studies in Genre*, ed. José Ignaio Cabezón and Roger R. Jackson, 312–30. Ithaca: Snow Lion, 1996.

Ma mo las thams cad kyi las rgyud lung. Rnying ma rgyud 'bum, Mtshams brag no. 713, vol. 39 (*ti*), text 6, ff. 638.5–677.5.

Martin, Dan, Per Kvaerne and Yasuhiko Nagano. *A Catalogue of the Bon Kanjur.* Bon Studies 8, Senri Ethnological Reports 40. Osaka: National Museum of Ethnology, 2003.

Mathes, Klaus-Dieter. *Unterscheidung der Gegebenheiten von ihrem wahren Wesen [Dharmadharmatāvibhāga].* Swisttal-Odendorf: Indica et Tibetica, 1996.

Matsunaga, Yukei, ed. *The Guhyasamāja Tantra: A New Critical Edition.* Osaka: Toho Shuppan, 1978.

Mayer, Robert. *A Scripture of the Ancient Tantra Collection: The Phur-pa bcu-gnyis*, 1996. Oxford: Kiscadale.

McKay, Alex, ed. *Pilgrimage in Tibet.* London: Routledge Curzon, 1998.

McKim, Marriott. "Little Communities in an Indigenous Civilization." In *Village India: Studies in the Little Community*, ed. McKim Marriott, 171–222. Chicago: University of Chicago Press, 1955.

Mdo mkhar zhabs drung Tshe ring dbang rgyal. *Dpal mi'i dbang po'i rtogs brjod 'jig rten kun tu dga' ba'i gtam.* Chengdu: Si khron mi rigs dpe skrun khang, 1981.

Messerschmidt, Donald A. "New Heights and New Insights in Himalayan Research." *Reviews in Anthropology* 6/2 (1979): 199–210.

Messick, Brinkley M. *Written Culture.* Comparative Study of Social Transformation (CSST) Working Paper #96, 1993.

Mgon po dbang rgyal. *Chos kyi rnam grangs shes bya'i nor gling 'jug pa'i gru gzings.* Delhi: 1993.

Mills, Martin A. *Identity, Ritual and State in Tibetan Buddhism: The Foundations of Authority in Gelukpa Monasticism.* Richmond: Curzon Press, 2003.

Mimaki, Katsumi. "The *Blo gsal grub mtha'* and the Mādhyamika Classification in Tibetan *Grub mtha'* Literature." In *Contributions on Tibetan and Buddhist Religion and Philosophy*, 2 vols, ed. Ernst Steinkellner, 2: 161–68. Vienna: Arbeitskreis für Tibetische und Buddhistische Studien Universität Wien, 1982.

———. "Le commentaire de Mipham sur le *Jñānasārasamuccaya.*" In *Indological and Buddhist Studies: Volume in Honour of Professor J.W. De Jong on his Sixtieth Birthday*, ed. Luise A. Hercus, 353–76. Canberra: Australian National University, 1982.

Mimaki, Katsumi and Samten Karmay. *Bon sgo gsal byed (Clarification of the Gates of Bon), A Fourteenth Century Bon po Doxographical Treatise.* Kyoto: Graduate School of Letters, Kyoto University, 2007.

Mimaki, Katsumi and Toru Tomabechi. *Pañcakrama: Sanskrit and Tibetan Texts Critically Edited with Verse Index and Facsimile Edition of the Sanskrit Manuscripts*, Bibliotheca

Codicum Asiaticorum 8. Tokyo: The Centre for East Asian Cultural Studies for UNESCO, 1994.

Mi pham rgya mtsho. *Las sna tshogs pa'i sngags kyi be'u bum dgos 'dod kun 'byung gter gyi bum pa bzang po*. New Delhi, 1972.

———. *Las sna tshogs pa'i sngags kyi be bum dgos 'dod kun 'byung gter gyi bum bzang*. New Delhi, 1974.

———. *Las sna tshogs pa'i sngags kyi be'u bum dgos 'dod kun 'byung gter gyi bum pa bzang po*. Hong Kong: Zhang kang then mā dpe skrun khang, 1999.

Mkha' khyab rdo rje. *Rgyal dbang mkha' khyab rdo rje'i bka' 'bum*, 10 vols. Paro: Lama Ngodrup, 1979–81.

———. *'Chi ba bslu ba'i cho ga mdor bsdus pa 'chi bdag g.yul 'joms*. In Mkha' khyab rdo rje, *Rgyal dbang mkha' khyab rdo rje'i bka' 'bum*, 10 vols, vol. 14: 117–28. Paro: Lama Ngodrup, 1979–81.

Mkhas grub Dge legs dpal bzang po. *Rgyud thams cad kyi rgyal po dpal gsang ba 'dus pa'i bskyed rim dngos grub rgya mtsho*. In Mkhas grub Dge legs dpal bzang, *The Collected Works (Gsung 'bum) of the Lord Mkhas-grub Rje Dge-legs-dpal-bzang-po*, 12 vols, vol. 7: 3–381. New Delhi: Gurudeva, 1982.

Monier-Williams, Monier. *Sanskrit-English Dictionary*. New Delhi: Munishram Manoharlal, 1988.

Mumford, Stan Royal. *Himalayan Dialogue: Tibetan Lamas and Gurung Shamans in Nepal*. Madison: University of Wisconsin Press, 1989.

Nāgabuddhi (Klu'i blo). *Samāja-sādhana-vyavasthālī ('Dus pa'i sgrub pa'i thabs rnam par gzhag pa'i rim pa)*. Sde dge Bstan 'gyur, Toh. no. 1809, Rgyud *ngi* (vol. 35), ff. 121a–131a; Peking Bstan 'gyur, Ōtani 2674, vol. 62, 7.3.7–12.1.4.

Nagao, Gadjin M. "What Remains in Śūnyatā: A Yogācāra Interpretation of Emptiness." In *Mahāyāna Buddhist Meditation: Theory and Practice*, ed., Minoru Kiyota, 66–82. Honolulu: University of Hawaii Press, 1978. Reprinted in Gadjin M. Nagao, *Mādhyamika and Yogācāra*, 51–60. Albany: State University of New York Press, 1991.

Nāgārjuna (Klu sgrub). *Piṇḍīkrama-sādhana = Piṇḍīkṛta-sādhana*. For editions of the Sanskrit, see La Vallée Poussin and Ram Shankar Tripathi. Tibetan: *Sgrub pa'i thabs mdor byas pa*, Sde dge Bstan 'gyur, Toh. no. 1796 (vol. 35), ff. 1b–11a; Peking Bstan 'gyur, Ōtani 2661, vol. 61, 268.1.1–273.1.6.

Namkhai Norbu. *Drung, Deu and Bön: Narrations, Symbolic Languages and the Bön Tradition in Ancient Tibet*. Dharamsala: Library of Tibetan Works and Archives, 1995.

Narantuya, Ch. *Mongol Bichmel Sudryn Tovch*. Ulaanbaatar: Admon, 2002.

Nayar, Kamala. *Hayagrīva in South India: Complexity and Selectivity of a Pan-Indian Hindu Deity*. Leiden: Brill, 2004.

Nebesky-Wojkowitz, René de. *Oracles and Demons of Tibet*. 1956. Reprint, Kathmandu, Nepal: Tiwari's Pilgrim's Book House, 1993; and Kathmandu, Nepal: Book Faith India, 1996.

Ngag dbang blo bzang rgya mtsho. *Rje thams cad mkhyen pa Bsod nams rgya mtsho'i rnam thar dngos grub rgya mtsho'i shing rta*. In Ngag dbang blo bzang rgya mtsho, *Collected Works of Vth Dalai Lama Ngag-dbang-blo-bzang-rgya-mtsho*, 25 vols, vol. 8: 31–246. Gangtok: Sikkim Research Institute of Tibetology, 1991–95.

Ngag dbang 'phrin las rgya mtsho. *Lha chen od hong theng ker sogs la bsangs mchod 'bul tshul bde legs 'dod dgu'i char 'bebs*. In *Mongolyn takhilgat uul usny sudar orshboi*, ed. Khatgin O. Sukhbaatar, 92–95. Ulaanbaatar: WWF Mongolia/ARC, 2001.

NGB. See Rnying ma rgyud 'bum.

Nicell, Joan, with Ven. Geshe Jampa Gyatso. "The Dharani of Glorious Vajra Claws." 1996. Reprint, Pomaia: Istituto Lama Tzong Khapa, 2000.

Obeyesekere, Gananath. "The Great Tradition and the Little in the Perspective of Sinhalese Buddhism," *Journal of Asian Studies* 22/2 (1963: 139–53.

Ochiroor Ogtlogch (*'Phags pa shes rab kyi pha rol tu phyin pa rdo rje gcod pa zhes bya ba bzhugs so*). Tr. from Tibetan and translit. from the classical Mongolian script into Cyrillic by G. Chantsal and L. Dulamsuren. Ulaanbaatar: New Mind Technology, 2000.

Ochiroor Ogtlogchiin Tus Erdem. Tr. from Tibetan and translit. from the classical Mongolian script into Cyrillic by G. Chantsal and L. Dulamsuren. Ulaanbaatar: New Mind Technology, 2000.

Okada, Hidehiro. "The Third Dalai Lama and Altan Khan of the Tümed." In *Tibetan Studies: Proceedings of the 5th International Association for Tibetan Studies, Narita 1989*, 2 vols, ed. Shōren Ihara and Zuihō Yamaguchi, vol. 2: 645–52. Narita-shi, Chiba-Ken, Japan: Naritasan Shinshoji, 1992.

Ortner, Sherry B. *Sherpas Through Their Rituals*. Cambridge: Cambridge University Press, 1978.

Owens, Bruce M. "The Politics of Divinity in the Kathmandu Valley: The Festival of Bungadya/Rato Matsyendranath." Ph.D. diss., Columbia University, 1989.

Padma gling pa. *Linga bri ba'i yig chung gsod byed gri gug rgya can*. In Padma gling pa, *Rig 'dzin Padma gling pa yi zab gter chos mdzod rin po che: The Rediscovered Teachings of the Great Padma-gliṅ-pa*, 21 vols, vol. 3: 365.1–367.3. Thimphu: Kunsang Tobgay, 1975.

———. *Kun gsal me long*. In Rig 'dzin padma gling pa, *Rig 'dzin Padma gling pa yi zab gter chos mdzod rin po che: The Rediscovered Teachings of the Great Padma-gliṅ-pa*, 21 vols, vol. 1: 19–138. Thimphu: Kunsang Tobgay, 1975.

Padma Tshe dbang, Slob dpon. *'Brug gi rgyal rabs slob dpon padma tshe dbang gis sbyar 'brug gsal ba'i sgron me*. Thimphu: National Library, 1994.

Pañcakrama. See "La Vallée Poussin, ed."

Parry, Jonathan P. "The Brahmanical Tradition and the Technology of the Intellect." In *Reason and Morality*, ed. Joanna Overing, 200–225. London: Tavistock Press, 1985.

Payne, Richard K. "Ritual." In *Encyclopedia of Buddhism*, ed. Robert E. Buswell, 723–26. New York: Macmillan Reference, 2004.

Peking Bka' 'gyur and Bstan 'gyur. *The Tibetan Tripitaka, Peking Edition, Kept in the Library of the Otani University, Kyoto*, 151 vols, ed. D. T. Suzuki. Tokyo and Kyoto: Suzuki Research Foundation, 1955–61.

Penjore, Dorji. "Oral Construction of Exile Life and Times of Künkhyen Longchen Rabjam in Bumthang." *Journal of Bhutan Studies* 13/2 (Winter, 2005): 60–73. Also online at http://www.digitalhimalaya.com/collections/journals/jbs/index.php?selection=13.

Petech, Luciano. *China and Tibet in the Early XVIIIth Century*. Leiden: Brill, 1972.

———. *Central Tibet and the Mongols: The Yüan-Sa skya Period of Tibetan History*, Serie Orientale Roma 65. Rome: Istituto Italiano Per il Medio ed Estremo Oriente, 1990.

Pettit, John Whitney. *Mipham's Beacon of Certainty: Illuminating the View of Dzogchen, the Great Perfection*. Boston: Wisdom Publications, 1990.

'Phrin las phun sum tshogs pa'i rgyud. Rnying ma rgyud 'bum, Sde dge edition, vol. *wa*, ff. 343a.–356a; Rnying ma rgyud 'bum, Mtshams brag edition., vol. *chi*, 1008–52.

Phuntsho, Karma. *Mipham's Dialectics and the Debates on Emptiness: To Be, Not to Be or Neither*. London: Routledge, 2005.

———. "'Ju Mi pham rNam rgyal rGya mtsho—His Position in the Tibetan Religious Hierarchy and a Synoptic Survey of His Contributions." In *The Pandita and the Siddha: Tibetan Studies in Honor of E. Gene Smith*, ed. Ramon N. Prats, 191–209. Dharamsala: Amnye Machen Institute, 2007.

Phur pa bcu gnyis kyi rgyud ces bya ba theg pa chen po'i mdo (*Phur pa bcu gnyis*). Rnying ma rgyud 'bum, Sde dge edition, vol. *pa*, ff. 176a–251a; Rnying ma rgyud 'bum, Mtshams brag edition, vol. *dza*, 785–1013.

Pommaret, Françoise. 2003. "Historical and Religious Relations between Lhodrak (Southern Tibet) and Bumthang (Bhutan) from the 18th to the early 20th Century: Preliminary Data." In *Tibet and Her Neighbours. Proceedings of the History of Tibet Conference St. Andrews University 2001*, ed. Alex McKay, 91–106. London: Ed. Hansjörg Mayer, 2003.

———. "The Fascinating Life of Lama Changchub Tsöngru (1817–1856) According to his Biography." In *The Spider and the Piglet: Proceedings of the 1st International Seminar on Bhutanese Studies 2003*, ed. Karma Ura and Sonam Kinga, 73–89. Thimphu: Centre for Bhutan Studies, 2004. Also online at: http://www.bhutan-studies.org.bt/main/pub_detail.php?pubid = 58.

———. "Protectors of Bhutan: The Role of Guru Rinpoche and the Eight Categories of Gods and Demons (*lHa srin sde brgyad*)." In *Written Treasures, Hidden Texts*. Thimphu: National Library, forthcoming.

———. "Bon and Chos: Local Community Rituals in Bhutan." In *Buddhism Beyond Monasticism*, ed. Antonio Terrone. Leiden: Brill, forthcoming.

Ramble, Charles. "Recent Books on Tibet and the Buddhist Himalaya II." *Journal of the Anthropological Society of Oxford* 1/2 (1980): 107–17.

———. "The Founding of a Tibetan Village: The Popular Transformation of History." *Kailash, a Journal of Himalayan Studies* 10/3–4 (1983): 267–90.

Rappaport, Roy A. "The Obvious Aspects of Ritual." In Roy A. Rappaport, *Ecology, Meaning and Religion*, 173–221. Richmond, CA: North Atlantic Books, 1979.

Rdo rje phur bu chos thams cad mya ngan las 'das pa'i rgyud chen po (*Myang 'das*). Rnying ma rgyud 'bum, Sde dge edition, vol. *zha*, ff. 46a–82a; Rnying ma rgyud 'bum, Mtshams brag edition, vol. *chi*, 229–339.

Rdo rje sems dpa'i sgyu 'phrul dra ba gsang ba thams cad kyi me long zhes bya ba'i rgyud. Rnying ma rgyud 'bum, Mtshams brag no. 441, vol. 22 (*za*), text 5, ff. 480.6–692.6.

Redfield, Robert. "The Social Organization of Tradition." *Far Eastern Quarterly* 15/1 (1955): 13–21.

Revue d'Etudes Tibétains 2 (April 2003), Numéro special Lha srin sde brgyad.

Richardson, Hugh. *Ceremonies of the Lhasa Year*, ed. by Michael Aris. London: Serindia Publications, 1993.

Ricœur, Paul. "Speaking and Writing," In Paul Ricœur, *Interpretation Theory: Discourse and the Surplus of Meaning*, 25–44. Fort Worth: Texas Christian University Press, 1976.

Rig 'dzin Padma gling pa. *Kun gsal me long*. In Padma gling pa, *Rig 'dzin Padma gling pa yi zab gter chos mdzod rin po che*, 21 vols, vol. 1, 19–138. Thimphu: Kunsang Tobgay, 1975–76.

Rig sngags kyi rgyal mo rma bya chen mo. Peking Bka' 'gyur, no. 178, Rgyud XV (vol. 7): 111–25.

Rje btsun sgrol ma dkar mo la brten pa'i 'chi [b]slu'i cho ga ring 'tsho'i dpal ster. In *Sgrub thabs kun btus: A Collection of Sādhanas and Related Texts of The Vajrayāna Traditions of Tibet*, 14 vols, compiled by 'Jam dbyangs mkhyen brtse'i dbang po and 'Jam dbyangs blo gter dbang po, vol. 1: 636–48. Dehradun: G.T.K. Lodoy, N. Gyaltsen and N. Lungtok, 1970.

Rngog Blo dlan shes rab. *Kha 'bar ma nag mo'i 'chi bslu bsdus pa*. Sukhia Pokhari, 1996.

Rnying ma [ma'i] rgyud 'bum [NGB].

- Mtshams brag edition: *The Mtshams brag manuscript of the Rñiṅ ma rgyud 'bum (rgyud 'bum/ mtshams brag dgon pa)*, 46 vols. Thimpu: National Library, Royal Government of Bhutan, 1982. Microfiche, The Institute for Advanced Studies of World Religions, LMpj 014,862–014, 907. Also available online, at http://www.thdl.org/xml/ngb/showNgb.php?doc=Tb.ed.xml).
- Sde dge edition: *rNying ma rgyud 'bum*, 26 vols + catalogue (*Dkar chags*). Khams: Sde dge par khang, 200?
- Sting skyes edition: *Rnying ma rgyud 'bum: A Collection of Treasure Tantras Translated During the Period of the First Propagation of Buddhism in Tibet*, 36 vols. Thimbu: Dingo Khyentse Rinpoche, 1975.

Roesler, Ulrike. "Not a Mere Imitation: Indian Narratives in a Tibetan Context." In *Facets of Tibetan Religious Tradition and Contacts with Neighbouring Cultural Areas*, ed. Alfredo Cadonna and Ester Bianchi, 153–77. Firenze: Leo S. Olschki Editore, 2002.

Rta mgrin padma yang gsang khros pa'i chos skor. Photoreproduction of a blockprint, no bibliographical information.

Ruch, Barbara. "Medieval Jongleurs and the Making of a National Literature." In *Japan in the Muromachi Age*, ed. John W. Hall and Toyoda Takeshi, 279–309. Berkeley: University of California Press, 1977.

Sambotha Dictionary. CD ROM. Seattle: Nithartha International, 2008.

Samuel, Geoffrey. *Civilized Shamans: Buddhism in Tibetan Societies*. Washington D. C.: Smithsonian Institution Press, 1993.

Sangren, P. Steven. "Great Tradition and Little Traditions Reconsidered: The Question of Cultural Integration in China." *Journal of Chinese Studies* 1 (1984): 1–24.

Śāntipa (Ratnākaraśānti). *Piṇḍī-kṛta-sādhana-vṛtti-ratnāvalī* (*Mdor bsdus pa'i sgrub thabs kyi 'grel pa rin chen phreng ba* = *Rin chen phreng ba*). Sde dge Bstan 'gyur, Toh. no. 1826, Rgyud *ci*, ff. 1b–95a.

———. *Kusumāñjali-guhyasamāja-nibandha* (*Gsang ba 'dus pa'i bshad sbyar snyim pa'i me tog*). Sde dge Bstan 'gyur, Toh. no. 1851, Rgyud *ti*, ff. 202b–325a, and Rgyud *thi*, ff. 1b–120a; Peking Bstan 'gyur, Ōtani no. 2714, vol. 64, 95–217, Rgyud *ji*, f. 233b.8 to Rgyud *nyi*, f. 147a.6.

Sárközi, Alice. "A Mongolian Text of Exorcism." In *Shamanism in Eurasia*, ed. Mihály Hoppál, 325–43. Gottigen: Edition Herodot, 1984.

———. "A Text of Popular Religious Belief: Cutting off the Lasso." *Acta Orientalia* 39/1 (1985): 39–44.

———. "A Bon Funeral Rite in Lamaist Mongolia." In *Synkretismus in den Religionen Zentralasiens*, ed. Walther Heissig and Hans-Joachim Klimkeit, 119–35. Wiesbaden: Otto Harrassowitz, 1987.

———. *Political Prophecies in Mongolia in the 17–20th Centuries.* Asiatische Forschungen: Monographienreihe zur Geschichte Kultur und Sprache der Völker Ost- und Zentralasiens 116. Wiesbaden: Otto Harrassowitz, 1992.

Sa skya Phur chen: Dpal rdo rje gzhon nu sgrub pa'i thabs bklags pas don grub. Rajpur, India: Dpal sa skya'i chos tshogs, nd.

Sazykin, A. G. *Katalog mongolskih rukopisei i ksilografov instituta vostokovodeniya akademii nauk SSSR*. Moskva: Nauka, 1988.

Schaik, Sam van and Jacob Dalton. "Where Chan and Tantra Meet: Tibetan Syncretism in Dunhuang." In *The Silk Road: Trade, Travel, War and Faith*, ed. Susan Whitfield and Ursula Sims-Williams, 63–71. London: The British Library, 2004.

Schiefner, Anton. "Über das Bonpo-Sutra: 'Das weisse Nâga-Hunderttausend.'" *Mémoires de l'Académie impériale des Sciences de St. Pétersbourg (MAIS)*, VIIe Sér., XXVIII/1 (1880): 1–86.

Schipper, Kristofer and Franciscus Verellen, eds. *The Taoist Canon: A Historical Companion to the Daozang* (Daozang tongkao). Chicago: University of Chicago Press, 2004–05.

Schøyen Collection of Manuscripts. Online. Available: http://www.schoyencollection.com/china.htm.

Schwarz, Ronald D. *Circle of Protest: Political Ritual in the Tibetan Uprising*. London: Hurst and Company, 1994.

Schwieger, Peter. "Schwarze Magie im tibetischen Buddhismus." *Studies in Central and East Asian Religion* 9 (1988): 18–36.

Sde dge Bka' 'gyur. *The Sde-dge mtshal-par bka'-'gyur: A Facsimile Edition of the 18th Century Redaction of Si-tu chos-kyi-'byun-gnas Prepared Under the Direction of H.H. the 16th Rgyal-dbang karma-pa*, 103 vols. Delhi: Karmapae Chodhey, Gyalwae Sungrab Partun Khang, 1976–79. Also available online, TBRC W22084, Bstan 'gyur sde dge par ma, at: http://tbrc.org/kb/tbrc-detail-outline.xq;jsessionid=7D067B1D0EDC6D96655E467D8ACE4CD6?RID=O1GS12980&wylie=n.

Sengge sprul sku Rig 'dzin nyi ma. *Bla ma a g.yung gi rnam thar dang mchog rgyal gyi rnam thar*. Chengdu: Si khrun lho nub mi rig slob grwa'i par khang, 2003.

———. *Nyag rong ye shes dgon pa'i lo rgyus*. Chengdu: Sengge sprul sku Rig 'dzin nyi ma, 2004.

Serruys, Henry. "Early Lamaism in Mongolia." *Oriens Extremus* 10 (1963): 181–216.

Shahar, Meir and Robert P. Weller. "Introduction: Gods and Society in China." In *Unruly Gods: Divinity and Society in China*, ed. Meir Shahar and Robert P. Weller, 1–36. Honolulu: University of Hawai'i Press, 1996.

Sharf, Robert H. "Ritual." In *Critical Terms for the Study of Buddhism*, ed. Donald S. Lopez, Jr., 245–69. Chicago: University of Chicago Press, 2005.

Sharot, Stephen. *A Comparative Sociology of World Religions: Virtuosos, Priests, and Popular Religion*. New York: New York University Press, 2001.

Si tu paṇ chen Chos kyi 'byung gnas. *Sgrub brgyud karma kaṁ tshang brgyud pa rin po che'i rnam par thar pa rab 'byams nor bu zla ba chu shel gyi phreng ba*. New Delhi: D. Gyaltsan and Kesang Legshay, 1971.

———. *Ta'i si tu pa kun mkhyen chos kyi 'byung gnas bstan pa'i nyin byed kyi bka' 'bum: Collected Works of the Great Ta'i Si tu pa kun mkhyen chos kyi 'byung gnas bstan pa'i nyin byed*. Sansal: Palpung Sungrab Nyamso Khang, 1990.

Sierksma, F. "Sacred Cairns in Pastoral Cultures." *History of Religions* 2/2 (1963): 227–41.

Sihlé, Nicolas. "Les tantristes tibétains (ngakpa), religieux dans le monde, religieux du rituel terrible: Etude de Ch'ongkor, communauté villageoise de tantristes du Baragaon (nord du Népal)." Ph.D. diss., Université de Paris-X Nanterre, 2001.

———. "Lhachö [Lha mchod] and Hrinän [Sri gnon]: The Structure and Diachrony of a Pair of Rituals (Baragaon, Northern Nepal)." In *Religion and Secular Culture in Tibet: Tibetan Studies II*, ed. Henk Blezer, 185–206. Leiden: Brill, 2002.

———. "Buddhism in Tibet and Nepal: Vicissitudes of Traditions of Power and Merit." In *Buddhism in World Cultures: Comparative Perspectives*, ed. Stephen C. Berkwitz, 245–84. Santa Barbara: ABC-CLIO, 2006.

———. *Rituels de pouvoir et de violence: Bouddhisme tantrique dans l'Himalaya tibétain*, forthcoming.

Skorupski, Tadeusz. *A Catalogue of the Stog Palace Kanjur*. Tokyo: The International Institute for Buddhist Studies, 1985.

———. *Kriyāsaṃgraha: Compendium of Buddhist Rituals, An Abridged Version*, Bibliotheca Britannica, Series Continua X. Tring, United Kingdom: The Institute of Buddhist Studies, 2002.

Sku gsum khro rgyal gyis ngo g.yo dri ma 'jig skyobs g.yung drung go cha = Rta mgrin skor, 216 ff. blockprint of a handwritten manuscript edition. No bibliographical information.

Sle lung rje drung Bzhad pa'i rdor rje. *Dam can bstan srung rgya mtsho rnam par thar pa cha shas tsam brjod pa sngon med legs bshad*, 2 vols. Leh, Ladakh: T. S. Tashigang, 1979.

Smith, E. Gene. *Among Tibetan Texts: History and Literature of the Himalayan Plateau*. Boston: Wisdom Publications, 2001.

Smith, Jonathan Z. *Imagining Religion: From Babylon to Jonestown*. Chicago: University of Chicago Press, 1982.

———. *To Take Place: Toward Theory in Ritual*. Chicago: University of Chicago Press, 1987.

Smith, Paul J. *Taxing Heaven's Storehouse: Horses, Bureacrats, and the Destruction of the Sichuan Tea Industry 1074–1224*. Harvard-Yenching Institute Monograph Series no. 32. Cambridge, MA: Harvard University, 1991.

Snellgrove, David L. *Hevajra Tantra: A Critical Study*. London: Oxford University Press, 1959.

———. "For a Sociology of Tibetan Speaking Regions," *Central Asiatic Journal* 11/3 (1966): 199–219.

———. *The Nine Ways of Bon*. London: Oxford University Press, 1967.

Sog bzlog pa Blo gros rgyal mtshan. *Gsang ngags snga 'gyur la bod du rtsod pa snga phyir byung ba rnams kyi lan du brjod pa nges pa don gyi 'brug sgra*. In *Collected Works of Sog bzlog pa blo gros rgyal mtshan*, 2 vols, vol. 1, 261–601. New Delhi: Sanje Dorji, 1975.

———. *Ma sgom sangs rgyas kyi rtsod spong bla ma go 'jo'i dris lan*. In *Collected Works of Sog bzlog pa blo gros rgyal mtshan*, 2 vols, vol. 2, 191–212. New Delhi: Sanje Dorji, 1975.

———. *Rdzogs chen pa sprul sku zhig po gling pa gar gyi dbang phyug rtsal gyi skyes rabs rags bsdus dang rnam thar*. In *Collected Works of Sog bzlog pa blo gros rgyal mtshan*, 2 vols, vol. 1, 9–109. New Delhi: Sanje Dorji, 1975.

———. *Rig 'dzin kyi rnam dbye*. In *Collected Works of Sog bzlog pa blo gros rgyal mtshan*, 2 vols, vol. 1, 307–10. New Delhi: Sanje Dorji, 1975.

———. *Sog bzlog bgyis tshul gyi lo rgyus*. In *Collected Works of Sog bzlog pa blo gros rgyal mtshan*, 2 vols, vol. 1, 203–59. New Delhi: Sanje Dorji, 1975.

———. *Slob dpon sangs rgyas gnyis pa padma 'byung gnas kyi rnam par thar pa yid kyi mun sel*. In *Dpal o rgyan gyi gu ru padma sam bha ba'i rnam thar gyi skor*, 475–792. Berkeley: Dharma Publications, 2004.

Sog ldan Bstan pa'i nyi ma, ed. Bon po brten 'gyur chen mo. Lhasa: Sog sde sprul sku Bstan pa'i nyi ma, 1998.

Sørensen, Per. *Tibetan Buddhist Historiography—The Mirror Illuminating the Royal Genealogies: An Annotated Translation of the XIVth Century Tibetan Chronicle: rGyal-rabs gsal-ba'i me-long*. Wiesbaden: Harrassowitz Verlag, 1994.

Śrī mahākāla tantra (*'Phags pa nag po chen po'i rgyud*). Sde dge Bka' 'gyur, Toh. no. 667, Rgyud *ba*, ff. 199a.6–201b.3.

Stein, Rolf A. "Le *Liṅga* des danses masquées lamaïques et la théorie des âmes." *Sino-Indian Studies* (*Liebenthal Festschrift*) 5/3–4 (1957): 200–34.

———. *Recherches sur l'Épopée et le Barde au Tibet*. Paris: Presses Universitaires, 1959.

———. *L'annuaire de Collège de France, Résumé des Cours de 1966–1970*.

———. "Du récit au rituel dans les manuscrits tibétains de Touen-houang." In *Études tibétaines dédiées à la mémoire de Marcelle Lalou*, ed. Ariane Macdonald, 479–547. Paris: A. Maisonneuve, 1971.

———. *Tibetan Civilization*. Stanford: Stanford University Press, 1972.

Strickmann, Michel. "History, Anthropology, and Chinese Religion." *Harvard Journal of Asiatic Studies* 40/1 (1980): 201–48.

———. "Homa in East Asia." In *Agni: The Vedic Ritual of the Fire Altar*, 2 vols, ed. Fritz Staal, 2: 418–55. Delhi: Motilal Banarsidass, 1983.

———. *Mantras et mandarins: le Bouddhisme tantrique en Chine*. Bibliothèque des sciences humaines. Paris: Gallimard, 1996.

Sukhbaatar, Khatgin O. *Mongolyn gazar usny neryn domog*. Ulaanbaatar: Alliance of Religions and Conservation, 2001.

Sukhbaatar, Khatgin O. *Mongolyn takhilgat uul usny sudar orshboi.* Ulaanbaatar: WWF Mongolia/Alliance of Religions and Conservation, 2001.

Sum pa mkhan po Ye shes dpal 'byor. *Chos 'byung dpag bsam ljon bzang*, Lanzhou, PRC: Gansu Nationalities Publishing House, 1992.

Suzuki, Daisetz T., ed. *The Tibetan Tripitaka.* See under "Peking."

———. *Catalogue and Index to The Tibetan Tripitaka.* In *The Tibetan Tripitaka, Peking Edition*, vol. 165–68. Tokyo: Suzuki Research Foundation, 1960.

Taishō Shinshū Daizōkyō. Tokyo: Taishō Shinshū Daizōkyō Kankōkai, 1924–34.

Tambiah, Stanley J. "The Magical Power of Words." *Man*, N. S., 3/2 (1968): 175–208.

———. *Buddhism and the Spirit Cults in North-East Thailand.* Cambridge: Cambridge University Press, 1970.

———. "Form and Meaning of Magical Acts." In *Culture, Thought, and Social Action: An Anthropological Perspective*, ed. Stanley J. Tambiah, 60–86. Cambridge, MA: Harvard University Press, 1985.

———. *Magic, Science, Religion, and the Scope of Rationality.* Cambridge: Cambridge University Press, 1990.

Tāranātha. *Yi dam rgya mtsho'i sgrub thabs rin chen 'byung gnas*, 2 vols. New Delhi: Chophel Legdan, 1974–75.

Tatár, Magdalena. "Two Mongol Texts Concerning the Cult of the Mountains." *Acta Orientalia* 30/1 (1976): 1–58.

Tathāgatarakṣita. *'Chi ba bslu ba (Mṛtyuṣṭhāpaka).* Sde dge Bstan 'gyur, Toh. no. 1702, Rgyud 'grel *sha*, ff. 57b.5–58a6. TBRC Bstan 'gyur sde dge par ma, vol. 28, ff. 114.5–115.6.

Taussig, Michael. *Shamanism, Colonialism and the Wild Man: A Study in Terror and Healing*, Chicago: University of Chicago Press, 1986.

TBRC. Tibetan Buddhist Resource Center. An online database and library of digital texts. Available: www.tbrc.org.

Thabs kyi zhags pa padmo'i phreng (Thabs zhags). In Rnying ma rgyud 'bum, Sde dge edition, vol. *pa*, ff. 286a–298b; Rnying ma rgyud 'bum, Mtshams brag edition, vol. *wa*, pp. 123–52. Also IOL Tib J 321; see under "Dunhuang."

Theg chen g.yung drung bon gyi bka' 'gyur. Lhasa: Kun grol lha sras mi pham rnam rgyal, 1996.

Thomas, Frederic William. "The Nam language." *Journal of the Royal Asiatic Society, London* (1938): 281–82.

———. *Nam, An Ancient Language of the Sino-Tibetan Borderland. Text, with introduction, vocabulary and linguistic studies.* Publications of the Philological Society XIV. London: Oxford University Press, 1948.

———. *Ancient Folk-literature from North-Eastern Tibet.* Berlin: Akademie-Verlag, 1957.

Thu'u bkwan Blo bzang chos kyi nyi ma. *Grub mtha' shel gyi me long.* Lanzhou: Kan su'u mi rigs dpe skrun khang, 1984.

Tripathi, Ram Shankar. *Piṇḍīkrama and Pañcakrama of Ācārya Nāgārjuna.* Sarnath: Central Institute of Higher Tibetan Studies, 2001.

Tseredsodnom, D. *Mongolyn Burkhany Shashny Uran Zokhiol*, 2 vols. Ulaanbaatar: Shinjlekh Ukhaany Akademiin Khel Zokhiolyn Khureelen, 1997.

Tseten Dorjee. "Tibetan art of divination." Online. Available: www.tibet.com/Buddhism/divination.html.

Tshe dbang pad ma rab khrod yang zab ga'u dmar nag mkhrin bzlog pa'i gzhi 'dzugs. In Bon po brten 'gyur chen mo, vol. 8, sect. 35, chap.1: 515–21. Lhasa: Sog sde sprul sku Bstan pa'i nyi ma, 1998.

Tshe dbang pad ma rab khrod yang zab ga'u dmar nag rta mgrin bzlog pa'i bskyed rim. In Bon po brten 'gyur chen mo, vol. 8, sect. 35, chap. 1, ff. 523–28. Lhasa: Sog sde sprul sku Bstan pa'i nyi ma, 1998.

Tshogs chen 'dus pa'i sgrub thabs dngogs grub char 'bebs. In Bdud-'Joms 'Jigs-bral-ye-śes-rdo-rje, *Bdud 'joms Bka' ma: Rñin ma Bka' ma rgyas pa*, 25 vols, vol. *pha*, pp. 349–443. Kalimpong: Dupjung Lama, 1982–87.

Tshul khrims. 2004. "The Chapel of the Protector Deity Taok at the Mé College of Sera Monastery." Online video in Tibetan with tr. by José I. Cabezón. Available: http://www.thdl.org/avarch/mediaflowcat/titles_browse.php?searchTerms=1044&searchType=id

Tsong kha pa Blo bzang grags pa. *Rgyud kyi rgyal po dpal gsang ba 'dus pa'i rgya cher bshad pa sgron ma gsal ba'i dka' gnas kyi mtha' gcod rin chen myu gu (Mtha' gcod).* In *The Collected Works (Gsung 'bum) of Rje Tsong-kha-pa Blo-bzang-grags-pa*, 27 vols, vol. 8: 64–349. New Delhi: Ngawang Gelek Demo, 1977.

———. *Rnam gzhag rim pa'i rnam bshad dpal gsang ba 'dus pa'i gnad kyi don gsal ba (Don gsal).* In *The Collected Works (Gsung 'bum) of Rje Tsong-kha-pa Blo-bzang-grags-pa*, 27 vols, vol. 9, 280–459. New Delhi: Ngawang Gelek Demo, 1977.

———. *Rgyud thams cad kyi rgyal po dpal gsang ba 'dus pa'i rgya cher bshad pa sgron me gsal ba'i tshig don ji bzhin 'byed pa'i mchan gyi yang 'grel (Sgron gsal mchan).* In *The Collected Works (Gsung 'bum) of Rje Tsong-kha-pa Blo-bzang-grags-pa*, 27 vols, vols. 6–7 complete. New Delhi: Ngawang Gelek Demo, 1978. Also in *Dpal gsang ba 'dus pa'i rtsa rgyud 'grel pa bzhi sbrags dang bcas pa.* Lhasa: Zhol Printing House, from the block-prints carved in 1890.

———. *Lam rim chen mo.* Joshua Cutler and Guy Newland eds. and The Lamrim Chenmo Translation Committee, tr. *The Great Treatise on the Stages of the Path to Enlightenment: Lam rim chen mo of Tsong kha pa*, 3 vols, Ithaca: Snow Lion, 2000–04.

Tucci, Giuseppe. "Some Glosses upon the Guhyasamāja." *Mélanges Chinois et Bouddhiques* 3 (1934–35): 339–53. Reprinted in Giuseppe Tucci, *Opera Minora* (Roma: G. Bardi, 1971), 337–48.

———. *Tibetan Painted Scrolls*, 2 vols. Rome: Libreria dello Stato, 1949.

Türstig, H. G. "The Indian Sorcery Called *Abhicāra*." *Wiener Zeitschrift fur die Kunde Südasiens* 29 (1985): 69–117.

Uebach, Helga. "On Dharma Colleges and Their Teachers in the Ninth Century Tibetan Empire." In *Indo-sino-tibetica: studi in onore di Luciano Petech*, ed. Paolo Daffinà, 393–417. Rome: Universita di Roma, 1990.

Unenbiligt, Dashravdan. *Pho lha dung skyong dkar po'i gsol mchod.* In *Mongolyn takhilgat uul usny sudar orshboi*, ed. Khatgin O. Sukhbaatar, 84–88. Ulaanbaatar: WWF Mongolia/ARC, 2001.

UNESCO and the Mongolian Ministry of Enlightenment. "Mongolia's Tentative List: Cultural and Natural Heritage." Paris: UNESCO/WHC, 1996. Pamphlet.

Uray, Geza. "The Four Horns of Tibet According to the Royal Annals." *Acta Orientalia: Academiae Scientiarum Hungaricae* 10/1 (1960): 31–57.

Vāgīśvarakīrti (Ngag gi dbang phyug grags pa). *'Chi ba blu ba'i man ngag* (*Mṛtyuvañcanopadeśa*). Sde dge Bstan 'gyur, Toh. no. 1748, Rgyud 'grel *sha*, ff. 118b.7–133b.3. Revised tr. by Si tu paṇ chen in Si tu paṇ chen, *Collected Works, vol.* 7, 1–61. TBRC Bstan 'gyur sde dge par ma, *vol.* 28, ff. 236.5–266.3.

———. *'Chi ba blu ba'i bsdus don* (*Mṛtyuvañcanapiṇḍārtha*). Peking Bstan 'gyur, no. 4806, Rgyud 'grel *zhu*, ff. 146a2–147b7.

———. *Rnal 'byor ma kun tu spyod pa'i bshad sbyar* (*Yoginīsaṃcāryanibandha*). Peking Bstan 'gyur, no. 2139, Rgyud 'grel *na*, ff. 139b5–160a7; Sde dge Bstan 'gyur, Toh. no. 1422, Rgyud 'grel *wa*, ff. 120a5–139a3.

Wallace, Vesna. "Buddist Tantric Medicine in the *Kālacakratantra*." *Pacific World* (New Series) 11 (1995): 155–73.

Wilson, Martin and Martin Brauen. *Deities of Tibetan Buddhism: The Zürich Paintings of the* Icons Worthwhile to See (Bris sku mthoṅ ba don ldan). Boston: Wisdom Publications, 2000.

Wolf, Eric R. *Europe and the People without History*. Berkeley: University of California Press, 1982.

Wu, Chaolu and Kevin Stuart. "Rethinking the Mongol *Oboo*." *Anthropos* 90 (1995): 544–54.

Wylie, Turell. *A Place Name Index to George N. Roerich's Translation of 'The Blue Annals.'* Serie Orientale Roma, vol. 15. Rome: Istituto Italiano Per il Medio ed Estremo Oriente, 1957.

———. *The Geography of Tibet According to the 'Dzam gling rgyas bshad*, Serie Orientale Roma, vol. 25. Rome: Istituto Italiano Per il Medio ed Esremo Oriente, 1962.

———. "The First Mongol Conquest of Tibet Reinterpreted." *Harvard Journal of Asiatic Studies* 37/1 (1977): 103–33.

Yeshe Tsogyal. *The Lotus Born: The Life Story of Padmasambhava*. Nyang Ral Nyima Öser, revealer. Eric Pema Kunsang, tr. Boudnath: Rangjung Yeshe Publications, 2004.

Yonten Dargye and Per K. Sørensen, with Gyönpo Tshering. *Play of the Omniscient: Life and works of Jamgön Ngawang Gyaltshen, an eminent 17–18th century Drukpa master*. Thimphu: National Library and the Archives of Bhutan, 2008.

Yoshimizu Chizuko. "The Theoretical Basis of the *bskyed rim* as Reflected in the *bskyed rim* Practice of the Ārya School." *Report of the Japanese Association for Tibetan Studies* 33 (1987): 21–33.

Zava Damdin (Blo bzang rta mgrim = Blo bzang rta dbyangs). *Kun tu bzang po zhes grags pa'i sa 'dzin dbang po'i lha klu gzhi bdag rnams la bsangs mchod 'bul tshul kun bzang dga' ston zhes bya ba*. In *Mongolyn takhilgat uul usny sudar orshboi*, ed. Khatgin O. Sukhbaatar, 96–100. Ulaanbaatar: WWF Mongolia/ARC, 2001.

Zhig po gling pa. *Dmag zlog nyi shu rtsa lnga las spyi ru zlog thabs kyi rim pa sde tshan du byas pa*. In *Rin chen gter mdzod*, 111 vols, compiled by 'Jam mgon Kong sprul, vol. 44 (*phi*), 57–72. Paro, Bhutan: Ngrodrup and Sherab Drimay, 1978.

Zhu chen Tshul khrims rin chen. *Gsung 'bum, reproduced from Luding Rinpoche's example.* New Delhi: B. Jamyang Norbu, 1972.

———. *Kha 'bar ma dkar mo la brten nas 'chi ba bslu zhing bar bcod bzlog pa'i thabs 'chi med bde ster.* In Zhu chen Tshul khrims rin chen, *Gsung 'bum*, vol. 6, 339–345. New Delhi: B. Jamyang Norbu, 1972.

———. *Byung ba lnga'i tsha tsha bskrun pa'i mchod sbyin la brten pa'i 'chi bslu'i cho ga grub pa'i zhal lung 'dab brgya 'grol byed.* In Zhu chen Tshul khrims rin chen, *Gsung 'bum*, vol. 6, pp. 319–37. New Delhi: B. Jamyang Norbu, 1972.

Index

www.ingramcontent.com/pod-product-compliance
Lightning Source LLC
Chambersburg PA
CBHW030117290426
44082CB00036B/405
* 9 7 8 0 1 9 5 3 9 2 8 2 1 *